The Intifada

The Intifada

Its Impact on Israel, the Arab World, and the Superpowers

Edited by Robert O. Freedman

Florida International University Press
Miami

Copyright 1991 by the Board of Regents of the State of Florida
Printed in the U.S.A. on acid-free paper ∞

Library of Congress Cataloging-in-Publication Data

The Intifada and its impact on Israel, the Arab World, and
  the superpowers/ edited by Robert O. Freedman.
    p.   cm.
  Includes bibliographical references and index.
  ISBN 0-8130-1040-3 (cloth). —
  ISBN 0-8130-1059-4 (paper)
    1. West Bank—History—Palestinian Uprising, 1987-
  —Influence.   2. Gaza Strip—History—Palestinian
  Uprising, 1987- —Influence.   3. Israel—Politics and
  government.   I. Freedman, Robert Owen.
  DS110.W47I555   1991
  956.9405'4—dc20   90-48019
                        CIP

The Florida International University Press is a member of
University Presses of Florida, the scholarly publishing
agency of the State University System of Florida. Books are
selected for publication by faculty editorial committees at
each of Florida's nine public universities: Florida A&M University (Tallahassee), Florida Atlantic University (Boca
Raton), Florida International University (Miami), Florida
State University (Tallahassee), University of Central Florida (Orlando), University of Florida (Gainesville), University of North Florida (Jacksonville), University of South
Florida (Tampa), University of West Florida (Pensacola).

Orders of books published by all member presses should be
addressed to University Presses of Florida, 15 NW 15th St.,
Gainesville, FL 32611.

Chapter 12, "The Economic Consequences of the Intifada on
Israel and the Administered Territories," by Howard Rosen,
reprinted with permission of the Institute for International
Economics, Washington, DC.

This book is dedicated to my wonderful children,
Debbie and David.

May it be their good fortune to see a just and lasting peace between Israelis and Palestinians.

Contents

Preface ix
Introduction xi

ONE: THE NATURE OF THE INTIFADA

1. **The Intifada and the Uprising of 1936–1939: A Comparison of the Palestinian Arab Communities** 3
   Kenneth W. Stein
2. **The Intifada in the Context of Armed Struggle** 37
   Bard E. O'Neill
3. **The PLO and the Intifada** 70
   Helena Cobban

TWO: THE RESPONSE OF EXTERNAL PLAYERS TO THE INTIFADA

4. **The American Response to the Intifada** 109
   David Pollock
5. **The Soviet Union and the Arab-Israeli Conflict since the Intifada** 136
   Robert O. Freedman
6. **The Arab World and the Intifada** 191
   F. Gregory Gause III
7. **Impact of the Intifada on American Jews and the Reaction of the American Public and of Israeli Jews** 220
   George E. Gruen

THREE: THE IMPACT OF THE INTIFADA ON ISRAELI POLITICS AND SOCIETY

8. **Israeli Public Opinion and the Intifada** 269
   Asher Arian
9. **The Impact of the Intifada on the Likud Party in the Framework of Israeli Politics, 1987–1990** 293
   Nathan Yanai
10. **The Labor Party and the Intifada** 325
    Myron J. Aronoff
11. **The Arabs in Israel and the Intifada** 343
    Elie Rekhess
12. **Economic Consequences of the Intifada in Israel and the Administered Territories** 370
    Howard Rosen

About the Authors 397
Index 401

Preface

At key junctures in Middle Eastern politics, the Institute for Israel and the Contemporary Middle East of Baltimore Hebrew University has sponsored conferences of specialists on the Middle East to assess critical changes in the region. The papers presented at each conference have been published as a separate volume, and I, as director of the institute, have been volume editor since the inception of the series. Thus in 1982, a conference was held that dealt with Middle Eastern developments since Camp David. The papers of the conference were published as *The Middle East since Camp David* (Boulder, Colo.: Westview Press, 1984). In 1985, a conference was held to evaluate the impact of the Israeli invasion of Lebanon. The papers presented at that conference were published as *The Middle East after the Israeli Invasion of Lebanon* (Syracuse: Syracuse University Press, 1986). In 1988, following the Iran-Contra affair, a conference was held to assess its impact on the Middle East. The papers of the conference were published as *The Middle East from the Iran-Contra Affair to the Intifada* (Syracuse: Syracuse University Press, 1990).

In December 1989, with the Intifada (Palestinian uprising) raging into its third year, a conference was held to analyze its impact on Israel, the Arab world, and the superpowers. This book is an outgrowth of the December 1989 conference.

Many individuals and institutions should be thanked for their help in making this conference possible. First and foremost, generous grants from Baltimore Hebrew University and the Jack Pearlstone Institute for Living Judaism provided the bulk of the financial support for the conference. The president of Baltimore Hebrew University, Leivy Smolar, has been a strong supporter of the Institute for Israel and the Contemporary Middle East, and I would like to offer him special thanks. Second, additional assistance was provided by the Baltimore Jewish Council, which cosponsored the conference. Third, the director of Baltimore Hebrew University's library, Arthur Lesley, and his staff assistant, Jeanette Katcoff, provided special assistance in expediting publication of the book, as did Rosa Zumer, my administrative assistant, who has helped to maintain the institute's research files on the Middle East. Finally, special thanks are also due to my secretary, Elise Baron, who typed the manuscript while also maintaining the Graduate Office of Baltimore Hebrew University in an exemplary manner.

Robert O. Freedman
May 1990

Introduction

The Palestinian uprising, or Intifada, which erupted in December 1987, has now been going on for more than two and one-half years. During this period successive Israeli National Unity governments have sought to deal with the Intifada in a number of different ways, ranging from military repression to the offer of elections for Palestinians living on the occupied West Bank and Gaza Strip. For its part, the Palestine Liberation Organization (PLO), seeking to exploit the diplomatic momentum created by the Intifada, and under heavy pressure from the Palestinians in the occupied territories, came out for a two-state solution to the Israeli-Palestinian conflict, and PLO leader Yasser Arafat renounced terrorism—although many Israelis (and others) did not believe that the PLO had really changed. The United States, under both the Reagan and Bush administrations, sought to cope with the Intifada but was criticized by both Arabs and Israelis for not playing a sufficiently active role in Middle East diplomacy. The Soviet Union, the PLO's superpower champion, actually improved relations with Israel despite the Intifada, although Soviet leader Mikhail Gorbachev echoed the PLO call for a two-state solution to the Palestinian-Israeli conflict and called for an international conference to implement it. Some American Jews grew increasingly uncomfortable with Israeli policy during the Intifada and openly criticized the way Israel was handling it, while the Arab world, preoccupied first with the Iran-Iraq conflict and then with the fighting in Lebanon and internal Arab disputes, tended to give rhetorical rather than material support to the Palestinians.

Meanwhile, the Intifada was having a significant impact on Israeli politics and society. As Israeli public opinion turned rightward because of the Intifada, the Likud party was aided, winning a narrow election victory over the rival Labor party in the November 1988 elections and assuming the dominant role in the National Unity government formed after the election. Conflict within the Likud party over how to react to the Intifada, however, helped lead to the collapse of the National Unity government in March 1990. At the same time Israel's Arab citizens became more Palestinized as a result of the Intifada, while the agricultural, construction and tourist sectors of Israel's economy suffered losses because of the Palestinian uprising.

Given the dramatic events precipitated by the Intifada, it was decided to hold a conference at Baltimore Hebrew University to assess the Intifada and its consequences, and this book is an outgrowth of that conference. The book is organized in three major parts. First, an analysis is made of the nature of the Intifada itself. The second part of the book examines the impact of the Intifada on key outside actors—the United States, the Soviet Union, the Arab world, and American Jewry. The final section of the book deals with the impact of the Intifada on Israel itself: its public opinion; its two major parties, Likud and Labor; its Arab minority; and its economy.

A major effort has been made to ensure that a wide spectrum of viewpoints is reflected in this book. Thus, in the section dealing with the nature of the Intifada, Helena Cobban, of George Mason University, who is a specialist on the PLO and has frequent contacts with its top leadership, was assigned the task of writing the chapter on the PLO's relationship with the Intifada. Similarly, Bard O'Neill, of the National Defense University of the United States, an expert in guerrilla warfare, was selected to analyze the Intifada as it related to the Palestinian concept of "armed struggle." Finally, Kenneth Stein of Emory University, a historian who has specialized in the period of the British Mandate over Palestine, was chosen to compare the Intifada to the 1936-39 Palestinian uprising.

A similar effort to obtain a wide spectrum of viewpoints is reflected in the second section of the book, which deals with the impact of the Intifada on external actors. Thus David Pollock, a Middle East specialist in the United States Information Agency, has written the chapter on U.S. policy toward the Intifada. Robert O. Freedman, of Baltimore Hebrew University, a longtime analyst of Soviet policy toward the Middle East who has twice participated in exchange programs with Soviet Middle East scholars, has written about the Soviet reaction to the Intifada. Gregory Gause, a specialist in the Arab world at Columbia University, was selected to write the chapter on the reaction of the Arab states to the Intifada, while George Gruen, director of Israel and Middle East affairs at the American Jewish Committee, was selected to write about the American Jewish reaction to the Intifada.

In the section of the book dealing with the impact of the Intifada on Israel, five scholars were selected who have had extensive experience living in Israel. Asher Arian, now of City University of New York, a specialist on Israeli public opinion, was for a long period associated with Tel Aviv University, as was Myron Aronoff, a specialist on Israel's Labor party who is now at Rutgers University. Howard Rosen, who has written the chapter on the impact of the Intifada on Israel's economy, was, until recently, a research economist at the Bank of Israel and is now with the Institute for International Economics. Elie Rekhess, long a specialist on the Israeli Arabs, in an associate of the Dayan Center of Tel Aviv University, while Nathan Yanai, a specialist on Israel's political parties who has written the chapter for this book on the Likud party, is a professor at Haifa University.

All in all, this collection of authors brings a high degree of expertise and a broad spectrum of viewpoints to the challenging task of understanding the Intifada and its impact.

One of the most interesting questions about the Intifada is its degree of similarity to the Palestinian uprising of 1936-39. In the first chapter of this volume, Kenneth Stein presents a detailed comparison of the two events. While Stein notes a number of very important similarities, including underlying Palestinian unemployment and underemployment, a militant Islamic movement, opposition to Jewish settlement, and frustrated Palestinian political aspirations, he also describes a number of significant differences. Thus while the 1936-39 uprising was fought primarily by uneducated peasants, the Intifada was carried out by wide segments of a highly educated population in a coordinated fashion. In addition, unlike the 1936-39 uprising, during the Intifada, political leadership outside of Palestine worked more harmoniously with the leadership and rank-and-file protestors in the West Bank and Gaza Strip. Stein also notes that while in 1936-39 the organizational centers of the uprising were the family and the village, the Intifada has tended to galvanize an already existing Palestinian national consciousness across class, clan, and geographic lines. As far as the peace process is concerned, Stein concludes his comparative analysis on an optimistic note: "Unlike its equivalent in the 1936-39 uprising, the group of participants in this Palestinian national assertion [the Intifada] is broadly based, pluralistic, [and] interested in political compromise."

While both the 1936-39 Palestinian uprising against the British and Palestinian resistance against the Israelis had political goals, they also were characterized by what Palestinians have called "armed struggle." Bard O'Neill next assesses the military significance of the Intifada as a means of resistance against Israel. Like Stein, O'Neill compares the Intifada to an earlier period of Palestinian resistance, but he deals with the "armed struggle" of the 1968-73 period, which O'Neill contends was a failure due to poor Palestinian organization, Israel's relatively successful efforts to improve economic and social services (particularly in the West Bank), and Israeli reprisal strategies against Jordan and Lebanon. By contrast, exacerbated by the Likud party's settlement policy on the West Bank, and limits on Palestinian access to land and water, and spurred by the growth of a younger Palestinian generation that is more militant, better educated, and less compliant than the older generation, Arab resentment grew by 1987 and set the stage for the Intifada. In assessing the Intifada, O'Neill notes that although it has won widespread local support among the Palestinians in the occupied territories, and extensive international support as well, due to Israel's heavy-handed tactics in seeking to control it, the Intifada could lose its gains if it escalates the level of violence from stone and Molotov cocktail throwing to the use of rifles, grenades, and bombs. Similarly, should the current disputes between the secular PLO and Islamic groups such as HAMAS and Islamic Jihad grow in intensity, the Intifada could also be endangered, particularly if it were to lead to a self-defeating escalation of the conflict with Israel. O'Neill concludes that "in terms of criteria for successful protracted popular war, the changes [that have occurred in the West Bank and Gaza] are conducive to civil disobedience but not to a rejuvenation of armed struggle. This does not mean that frustrated PLO leaders under pressure from rivals will not decide to intensify the armed struggle; they may very well do so. But if the past is prologue, they will again fail."

One of the most intriguing questions about the Intifada has been its relationship to the PLO leadership in Tunis. Helena Cobban analyzes this highly complex relationship in her contribution to this volume. After describing the four major secular nationalist organizations active within the West Bank that joined together to form the Unified National Leadership of the Uprising (UNLU)—Fatah; the Popular Front for the Liberation of Palestine; the Democratic Front for the Liberation of Palestine; and the Palestine Communist party—Cobban describes their close contacts with the PLO leadership in Tunis. She also describes the sometimes strained relationship between the secular nationalist forces in the UNLU and the two main Moslem movements, the Moslem Brotherhood, whose leader, Sheikh Yasin, created HAMAS in August 1988, and the Islamic Jihad, which had broken away from the Moslem Brotherhood in the mid-1960s and had been active in the Intifada from its beginning. While Cobban notes the differences in goals between the secular and Moslem resistance organizations—the Moslem groups are clear in desiring a Palestinian state based on Islamic law in all of historic Palestine—she notes that at the tactical level, both secular and Moslem groups have been able to cooperate against Israel. Cobban also demonstrates how Palestinian intellectuals, like Faisal Husseini and Hanna Siniora, far from being the substitute Palestinian leadership whom some Israelis hoped would take the place of the PLO, were in fact spokesmen for the PLO, and she contends that their behavior and concerns suggested those of leaders of a branch of a Palestinian "State Department," far more than those of leaders of a mass-based movement. Cobban further notes that the fact that the resident Palestinian communities of the occupied territories have proven incapable of generating a nationwide leadership independent of the exile-based PLO was primarily due to Israel's policy of expelling some nationalist leaders while giving other Palestinians little political incentive for cooperation. She concludes that while the PLO "had been unable to impose meaningful negotiations on an unwilling Shamir," he, in turn, "had been unable to find any group or even individual among the resident Palestinians who was willing to challenge the PLO's national leadership, and given the huge disparity between the two sides in all the measurable attributes of power, the PLO leaders' ability to sustain even this situation spoke highly of the resolution, political acumen, and internal discipline of their movement."

The second section of the book deals with the impact of the Intifada on key external actors: the United States, the Soviet Union, the Arab world, and American Jewry. David Pollock asserts that the Intifada has caused some important tactical shifts in U.S. policy, although there remains a great deal of continuity in the long-term U.S. strategy for a Palestinian-Israeli peace settlement. Thus Pollock notes that on the tactical level, the United States no longer either advocates the "Jordanian option" or boycotts the PLO, and he demonstrates how the Intifada raised the salience of the Palestinian-Israeli conflict for U.S. policymakers both in the last year of the Reagan administration and the first years of the Bush administration. This, in turn, caused the United States to step up its diplomatic efforts—albeit so far with limited success—to create the conditions that would facilitate a peace settlement. In the last year of the Reagan administration, Secretary of State George Shultz made repeated trips to the Middle East to try to spur a settlement, while for its part the Bush administration first warmly endorsed Israeli Prime Minister Yitzhak Shamir's election plan, and then sought to keep it on track, despite backsliding by Shamir himself. Pollock concludes his analysis by stating that continued U.S. diplomatic efforts—necessarily deliberate and cautiously persistent—are needed if a Palestinian-Israeli settlement is to be achieved, but so too is "creative local input" from the Palestinians and Israelis themselves unless the two peoples "would willingly turn their shared patrimony into another Lebanon."

Of the two superpowers, the Soviet Union's policy changed the most toward the Arab-Israeli conflict during the Intifada, but not in a way that might have been predicted, given the anti-Israeli policy of Soviet leaders since 1955. Indeed, despite the Intifada, under Gorbachev in the period 1987–1990, Soviet-Israeli relations improved markedly, both in state-to-state relations (consular delegations were exchanged; trade agreements were signed; and Israeli cabinet members made repeated trips to Moscow), as well as on the level of people-to-people diplomacy (numerous cultural groups made exchange visits; Jewish emigration from the USSR, increasingly to Israel, skyrocketed—much to the consternation of the Arabs; Soviet tourism to Israel began; and Israeli teachers and other professionals went to the USSR to teach courses in Hebrew and Judaism). Robert O. Freedman analyzes these developments and concludes they were due to three main factors: (1) Gorbachev's desire to improve his image in the United States for strategic arms agreement and trade purposes; (2) the Soviet desire to play a role in a Middle East settlement; and (3) the growing importance of Soviet public opinion that, because of Israeli aid to the USSR during the Armenian earthquake and an airplane hijacking, was becoming increasingly pro-Israel. Freedman also notes how Gorbachev urged Arafat to reach a political settlement with Israel, and how Moscow warmly endorsed the PLO's November 1988 decision for a two-state solution for the Palestinian-Israeli conflict, since it coincided with the USSR's own peace plan although initially Moscow seemed concerned that because of its dialogue with the PLO, the United States might be able to work out the parameters of a settlement without the participation of the Soviet Union.

While the superpowers sought both to adjust to the Intifada and use it to achieve their own policy goals in the Middle East, the states of the Arab world had a more difficult time. Gregory Gause shows how the Intifada posed a particularly challenging problem as it sharply set off the conflict between the Arab countries' regime and state interests on the one hand, and their pan-Arab obligations on the other. After discussing how the Arab world has been long on rhetorical support for the Intifada, but short on financial aid, Gause then turns to a detailed analysis of the policies of Jordan, Syria, and Egypt. He attributes King Hussein's July 1988 decision to sever ties with the West Bank—a decision Gause considers strategic, not tactical—to the king's realization that it was counterproductive both from the perspective of internal Jordanian politics and for Jordan's position in the Arab world for it to try to maintain a political presence on the West Bank, and he notes that Jordanian-PLO relations have sharply improved as a result of the king's decision.

In the case of Syria, Gause notes that while Hafiz al-Assad remains highly suspicious of Arafat, the Syrian leader was forced both by the Arab consensus and by his weakened internal and intra-Arab position to accept publicly the November 1988 PLO declaration of independence and the decision of the Casablanca Arab summit in May 1989 supporting Arafat's position, although Palestinian groups controlled by Syria continued to criticize Arafat sharply. By contrast, Egyptian leader Hosni Mubarak, while anxious to preserve both the Egyptian peace agreement with Israel and Egypt's ties to the United States, strongly supported both the Intifada and Arafat's decision to recognize Israel and accept a two-state solution to the Israeli-Palestinian conflict. As Gause notes, the Egyptian leader sought to use the diplomacy attendant to the Intifada to speed up the peace process, with Egypt playing a leading role in supporting the Palestinians, something that also strengthened Mubarak's domestic position. Gause concludes that the Intifada has shown that state interests continue to dominate Pan-Arab obligations, but these obligations cannot be completely ignored, and he warns that the rising challenge of Islamic movements may shift this balance, particularly if no settlement of the Palestinian-Israeli conflict is achieved.

While the states of the Arab world professed solidarity with the Intifada, although *raison d'état* continued to dominate their reactions to it, the American Jewish community, already uncomfortable with a number of recent Israeli actions, such as the Pollard affair and the Israeli invasion and occupation of Lebanon, became even more uncomfortable with Israeli efforts to control the Intifada. George Gruen, in his assessment of American Jewry's reaction to the Intifada, analyzes numerous polls of American Jews and also the actions of prominent Jews, from U.S. senators to Jewish communal leaders, and concludes that most American Jews favor active American diplomatic efforts to solve the Arab-Israeli conflict, even when the stated American position may be at some variance from the official Israeli position as in the case when, despite heavy pressure from Israel, American Jews did not oppose the beginning of the U.S.-PLO dialogue. Then, citing such actions as the letter drafted by two Jewish senators (Carl Levin, Democrat of Michigan, and Rudy Boschowitz, Republican of Minnesota) to Israeli Prime Minister Shamir, urging him not to abandon territorial compromise, and the letter of forty-one prominent Jewish leaders to Shamir, making the same point, Gruen asserts that in the past few years, and especially because of the Intifada, even prominent American Jews have been more and more willing to criticize Israeli actions publicly. He asserts, however, "Despite whatever misgivings many individual [American] Jews may have concerning specific Israeli governmental policies or actions, the overwhelming majority of American Jews remain firm in their support for the State of Israel and are deeply committed to the security and survival of their brethren in the Jewish State."

The third section of the book deals with the impact of the Intifada on Israel itself. The areas covered include Israeli public opinion; the reactions of the two largest Israeli political parties, Likud and Labor; its impact on Israeli Arabs; and the effect of the Intifada on the Israeli economy.

Asher Arian discusses the impact of the Intifada on Israeli Jews in his study of Israeli public opinion. Referring to two major public opinion polls, one taken (by chance) the day the Intifada started and the other almost one year later, he concludes that there were three simultaneous processes operating on Israeli public opinion: (1) a generalized, short-term hardening of positions since the beginning of the Intifada, a development that aided Likud and the parties to its right in the November 1988 elections; (2) a steady and increasing moderation of Israeli public opinion on such issues as Israeli willingness to accept the principle of exchanging land for peace, and ultimately, a Palestinian state; and (3) a growing polarization of attitudes and political power between the more conciliatory left and the more hard-line right. Arian also notes that Israeli public opinion is malleable and that because Israelis have low levels of perceived influence on security issues, the Israeli political leadership has "enormous leverage" to change policy, "secure in the knowledge that they will be able to swing public opinion to their position if they properly present it; in short, if they lead."

From a political standpoint, the Likud was strengthened in two ways by the Intifada. First, as the country shifted to the right politically, Likud's fortunes in both the pre-election polls and the November 1988 election itself were enhanced. Second, King Hussein's decision to end Jordan's political responsibility for the West Bank undercut the Labor party's long hoped for "Jordanian option." The end result of the election was a narrow Likud victory, and a new National Unity government, this time one dominated by Likud, which had full control of the post of prime minister and foreign minister for the duration of the National Unity government, which lasted until March 1990. Nathan Yanai analyzes Likud policies during this period and argues that Likud leader Shamir, much like his predecessor Menachem Begin, acted as prime minister primarily in a consensual manner and undertook policies with mainstream support from both Labor and Likud, although both the "hawks" in Likud and the "doves" in Labor strongly criticized him, as did parties on the far left and right. Yanai also analyzes the debate within Israel on the future of the West Bank and Gaza in light of the Intifada, noting that there are no fewer than five different political positions held by Israelis on this issue, ranging from what Yanai calls the "radical anti-Zionist or a-Zionist left" to the "radical political right," with intermediary positions held by what he terms the "radical Zionist left (Ratz, Mapam, Shinui, and one-third of Labor)"; the majority position within Labor; and the Likud mainstream. Yanai also examines internal Likud policies in detail, particularly the leadership conflict between Shamir and his ally, Moshe Arens, on the one hand, and Ariel Sharon, David Levy, and Yitzhak Moda'i on the other. Yanai concludes that "Shamir's conservative and largely passive style of leadership helped him to survive many crises; by the same token, it also prevented him from preempting crises or conclusively resolving them," and this ultimately led to the fall of the National Unity government in March 1990, as the patience of the leadership of the Labor party ran out because of Shamir's stalling on the peace process.

While Yanai's evaluation of Shamir was basically a positive one, the same cannot be said for the evaluation of Shamir's counterpart in the Labor party, Shimon Peres, who is strongly criticized by Myron Aronoff in his analysis of the impact of the Intifada on Israel's Labor party. Aronoff discusses both Peres's weaknesses and the conflicts within the Labor party between Peres and Yitzhak Rabin at the top of the party and between Labor's hawks and doves in the Knesset. Aronoff concludes that for Labor to have a future in Israeli politics it has to offer a genuine alternative to Likud for the Israeli electorate by articulating policies that realistically relate to the new Middle East realities, such as the end of the "Jordanian option" and the PLO's acceptance of a two-state solution to the Israeli-Palestinian conflict, even if this means that the Labor party should advocate negotiations with the PLO.

Although the Intifada had a major affect on the attitudes of Israeli Jews, it also had a profound affect on Israel's Arab population. Elie Rekhess examines the reactions of various Israeli Arab political organizations from the radical "Sons of the Village" to the more establishment Israeli Communist party and Progressive List for Peace party. Rekhess also analyzes the increased role of Islamic forces which, at least partially because of the Intifada, sharply increased their vote in Israeli Arab communities in the February 1989 local Israeli elections, winning the mayoralty of four Arab villages and one Arab town (Umm al-Fahm). Rekhess concludes that Israeli Arabs have become far more Palestinized as a result of the Intifada, but that their Palestinization has, so far at least, remained primarily rhetorical, although there was a tripling of the number of terror-related acts of sabotage in Israel between 1987 and 1989 (60 to 208), with Israeli officials estimating that the vast majority of these acts were attributable to Israeli Arabs.

While the impact of the Intifada has been primarily political, one should not overlook its economic effects. Howard Rosen studies the Intifada's economic impact and concludes that the cost has been relatively substantial both for Israel and the occupied territories, but as the Intifada goes on, it appears to have increasingly less effect on Israel but more effect on the West Bank and Gaza. For Israel, the economic burden has been concentrated in agriculture, construction, tourism, and military expenditures and has exacerbated the problems of an economy already hurt by the effects of the nation's 1985 economic stabilization program. Nonetheless, Rosen feels that the costs of the Intifada have been declining as the affected sectors of the Israeli economy have adjusted and made the necessary substitutions.

By contrast, the Intifada, with its frequent strikes and boycotts of Israeli employers and Israeli goods, has led to a downturn in the economies of the West Bank and Gaza. While Rosen notes the difficulty of acquiring economic data on Palestinian activities since the start of the Intifada in December 1987, he expresses concern that damage to the economic base of the occupied areas may inhibit their future political independence.

In sum, the contributors to this volume have analyzed the Intifada and its impact on Israelis, Palestinians, the Arab world, and the superpowers. It is hoped that this book will help in the understanding of what is both a highly complex and an extremely important development in Middle East politics.

Part One

The Nature of the Intifida

The Intifada and the Uprising of 1936-1939: A Comparison of the Palestinian Arab Communities

Kenneth W. Stein

When comparing the 1936-39 Palestinian uprising in various parts of western Palestine to the present Intifada,[1] taking place in the West Bank, the Gaza Strip, and East Jerusalem, the most striking conclusion is the large number of general similarities between these two manifestations of Palestinian national consciousness.[2] The two most significant differences between the uprisings, however, are that the Intifada generated a deeper and prolonged Palestinian national coherence across all classes than did its predecessor. And second, it clarified and crystallized Palestinian opinion which, in conjunction with other events, helped to create a historic compromise in Palestinian public policy. Other major differences between the two uprisings are self-evident. Many pertain to the political environments in which both uprisings unfolded. During the 1936-39 uprising there were no existing U.N. resolutions about Palestine, no Israel, no Israeli Arab population, no Palestinian political organization of the stature and strength of the Palestine Liberation Organization (PLO), no decade-old Egyptian-Israeli peace treaty as a backdrop to an ongoing larger negotiating process, no decision made by the Hashemites in the midst of the uprising to place the responsibility of diplomatic progress on the shoulders of the Palestinian leadership, no willingness by a significant number of leading Palestinian Arab politicians to accept a Jewish state in a portion of Palestine, and no corresponding willingness on the part of an equally important number of Zionist/Israel leaders to assent to the legitimacy of Palestinian national aspirations. Of course, fifty years ago Britain, not Israel, controlled all of mandatory Palestine. And whereas the Palestinian Arab community was then almost totally resident in Palestine, during the Intifada, the community was geographically divided and dispersed, with major population segments living in Jordan, Israel, and elsewhere.

This chapter focuses primarily on just one variable present in both uprisings, the Palestinian Arab community. In a comparative fashion, participant composition, organizational structures, and the political reactions of the Palestinian Arab community are analyzed. By way of introduction, the first part is a composite, which stresses the general similarities between the two uprisings. It should be read as if it could describe either uprising. The second part discusses the Palestinian Arab community. An obvious analytical and methodological constraint is that neither the period during nor the period after the present uprising is complete. At the writing of this chapter in early 1990, the duration and political outcome of the Intifada are still unknown. Therefore, making fully accurate and judicious juxtapositions between the two Palestinian uprisings is at best problematic. Comparisons made herein are therefore presented with considerable caution and with the severe limitations imposed upon them by the historical analysis of a current event.

Similarities

Which of the two uprisings is described below?

Over the last several years, Palestinian Arabs engaged in civil disobedience and political violence in different parts of the Holy Land.[3] Palestinians were frustrated politically and economically. In general, they possessed a sense of despair and of being overwhelmed by forces beyond their control.

Several general factors can be identified as direct or ancillary causes of the recent uprising against the occupying administration.

Among Palestinians, these factors collectively generated a sense of despondency about the future. A political stalemate was impending, while Jewish presence continued to envelop Palestinians. None of the world powers, and especially not the world power with the dominant influence in the Zionist–Palestinian Arab struggle, seemed prepared to change unilaterally the Palestinians' discomforting status quo. Economically, the underemployment and unemployment among Palestinians was caused by local factors and regional insecurity. Religiously, the shared disillusionment among many Palestinian Moslems infused an Islamic component into the ardor, which they directed against the Zionists and the West in general. In addition, political leaders in neighboring Arab states, while showing sincere interest in the Palestinian cause, were truly more interested in items on their own domestic agendas.

For several decades now, Palestinian national identity had developed in response to Zionist presence, growth, and development. Palestinians were seeking self-government and self-determination in areas where they were clearly the demographic majority and where they had resided for generations. But Palestinian demands went unheeded. Since Palestinians lacked a viable military option, they used pressure, boycott, demonstrations, and physical attacks against the administration that had denied them fulfillment of their political aspirations. Palestinians thoroughly disliked the occupation of their land by what was from their perspective a foreign force. Palestinian Arabs openly feared that continued Jewish immigration, as well as the establishment and expansion of Jewish settlements, would eventually push them from what they considered to be their homeland. Spatially and demographically, Palestinians feared that unrestrained Jewish growth would ultimately leave them landless and totally disconnected from their patrimony. There was an existing fear among Palestinians that they would be steadily pushed eastward, perhaps even across the Jordan River, and totally expelled from western Palestine.

Prior to the outbreak of the unrest, the most important great power in the region resolved to support Zionist growth and development. These objectives basically entailed the protection of Jewish security and presence in Palestine. Not unexpectedly, Palestinians developed an extremely skeptical, if not hostile, attitude toward the great power because of its willingness to assist the Jews, particularly since previous great power promises about limiting Jewish settlement in parts of Palestine had not been enforced. It seemed that the sympathizers of Zionism were extraordinarily adept at lobbying politicians and Gentile advocates to support continued Jewish security and growth in the Holy Land. Whenever the great power tilted slightly toward the Palestinian view, the Zionists were able to neutralize policy options that might have damaged either Jewish political prerogatives, demographic expansion, or physical safety. For some of the great powers' decision-makers, the Jews in Palestine were seen as a strategic asset, which enhanced the great power presence in the larger Middle Eastern theater.

The uprising occurred in an economic setting in which many middle- and lower-class Palestinians found themselves suffering from several years of severe financial hardship. Dramatic price drops, particularly in agriculture and amputated international markets, caused enormous strain on the local economy. Although present in previous years, traditional sources of capital import into Palestine were stringently reduced by changes in regional and international conditions. There were intense discussions, plans outlined, and promises made about development assistance for portions of the Palestinian Arab economy. But after Palestinian Arab expectations had been raised repeatedly, these externally promised funds were not made available. In response, Palestinians, already sullen from years of promises made and not kept, became despairingly distraught about their present economic condition.

In the half decade before the uprising, the mosque and Islamic symbols became focuses and platforms for political action. The immediate presence and influence of forceful Islamic religious leaders catalyzed the Palestinians' resistance against Jewish presence, the occupation of their lands, and the unwanted administration of their lives by foreigners. Among other central themes, the religious philosophy that was posited included the promotion of fundamentalist Islam, a pronounced rejection of the West, the adoption of a militant course of political action through armed struggle, and a keen desire to expel the influence and presence of the great power and the Jewish invaders. In addition, before the outbreak of the uprising itself, philosophies associated with the Moslem Brotherhood in Egypt emerged with some degree of prominence in a few urban areas.

Surrounding Arab states, which were attentive to the Palestinian quest for self-determination, were consumed by their own parochial national aspirations. Indeed, some political leaders in these states made public statements in support of the Palestinians. Others supplied monies and logistical support for the Palestinian resistance against occupation, but most of the support was rhetorical and self-serving.

Leaders of neighboring Arab states, while sympathetic to the Palestinian demand for majority self-rule and supportive of Arab cooperation in general, were primarily concerned with their bilateral relationships with countries outside the region. After the uprising began, concerted efforts by the Palestinian political leadership caused Arab politicians throughout the Middle East to convene a meeting as a demonstrative sign of their solidarity with the Palestinian demand for self-government and their collective opposition to Jewish development in Palestine. Before the uprising began, the Hashemite rulers, residing east of the Jordan River, sought ways to influence both the outcome of the Palestinian quest for self-determination and the future territorial disposition of portions of Palestine. In the past, the Hashemite leadership had not hidden its disdain for the domineering style of the current Palestinian Arab political leader. In the years before the uprising, the Hashemites maintained less-than-secret contacts with the Zionists. Certainly, the Hashemite preference was to contain the spread of the Palestinian uprising, in part because its ongoing nature enhanced the status of the Palestinian leader they found objectionable; and, the Hashemites sought to maintain their territorial hopes for Palestine's future disposition.

One loosely defined umbrella organization represented Palestinian Arab national aspirations. In the years leading up to the unrest in Palestine, Palestinian political organizations were traumatized by deep philosophical divisions and by geographic constraints and fragmented by personal animosities. Disagreements within the current Palestinian leadership existed over differences in strategies and tactics and over the right mix of political and military options to be applied in stopping Jewish growth. Sometimes those animosities were directed solely at the leader of the Palestinian community, a man who came to symbolize Palestinian resistance against Zionism, a charismatic leader who insisted on the combined use of armed struggle and a political course to liberate Palestine from Zionist presence. Some members of the Palestinian political elite opposed this leader's arrogant style and, particularly, his enduring personal dominance over the Palestinian cause. His presence became a focal point of anti-Palestinian feeling among Zionists who saw him as a demon.

Most Palestinians were staunch and steadfast nationalists, while a distinct minority eagerly collaborated with the Zionists. Various forms of intimidation, including death threats and assassinations, were used by Palestinians against each other because of perceived inconsistency in one's anti-Zionist actions. Some of these intra-Palestinian conflicts were strictly personal vendettas; others were aimed exclusively at people who collaborated with the Zionists for what were considered repeated violations of the national cause. Among the most strident Palestinian nationalists there was a concern that more moderate Palestinian leaders might accept a settlement that was sponsored by the great power. Moreover, the primary Palestinian political leader was worried that there could be future discussions with the Zionists from which he (or his appointed representatives) would be excluded and in which the political conclusion would be something less than national independence.

As the uprising unfolded, many Palestinians found themselves despising Jewish presence but earning a living in predominantly Jewish neighborhoods, urban areas, and rural settlements. A mutually beneficial vocational relationship developed between Palestinian Arab workers and Jewish employers. Nonetheless, the uprising itself hurt the Jewish and Arab economies to varying degrees.

In a spontaneous fashion, without the knowledge of either the organized Palestinian or Zionist leadership, Palestinian Arab youths physically rebelled against the occupying administration. More radical in their orientation, these younger Palestinians felt frustrated that their established leaders, though fully committed to Palestinian self-government, had succeeded neither in obtaining basic Palestinian rights nor in liberating Palestine from its unwanted control by the Zionists. As the general strike unfolded, local and national committees were established in the areas of the largest concentrations of Arab population. Quickly, the traditional national leadership sought to organize and direct the uprising. After the uprising began, more than several dozen nationalist leaders were deported from Palestine by the occupying administration for what were considered insidious and dangerous political actions. Elements of their external leadership remained deeply committed to Palestine's liberation.

Within the circles of Jewish leadership, there were distinct political divisions about the substance of the Zionists' future relationship with the Palestinian Arabs in Eretz Yisrael and the relationship of both Zionists and Palestinians with the Hashemite neighbor east of the Jordan. In Palestine, a vast majority of Zionists possessed one of two general ideological philosophies: one group saw all of Palestine and even the lands east of the Jordan River as historically part of Eretz Yisrael, and the other group was willing to make a territorial compromise about sharing Palestine with the Arab population.

Because of previous Zionist and Jewish experience in Europe, the Jewish leadership emphasized its relationship with the dominant great power in determining the nature of the Zionist relationship with the Palestinian Arabs. Zionists clearly wanted the great power to assist them in their physical protection. Regardless of other philosophical differences, Zionists always seemed able to coalesce when their security was threatened. Those Jews who followed "Revisionist" Zionist philosophy wanted to arm Jewish settlers, believing that Palestinian Arab violence against Jewish presence was inevitable. Among some Zionists, there was talk of transferring the Arab population to areas distant from Jewish demographic settlements. Many Jews in the Diaspora felt akin to the Jewish community of Eretz Yisrael; many were equally disturbed by the current unrest and loss of life. Beyond their philosophical differences, however, the Jewish communities in the Diaspora and in Eretz Yisrael were equally committed to the uncompromising preservation of the Jewish community's identity, presence, and security in Eretz Yisrael.

Within the world community, many documents, policy statements, and reports were published in the several preceding years, suggesting that a measure of self-determination should be granted to the Palestinians. There was an increasing awareness by the great power that the dual obligation to Zionist and Arab should be equalized and that some geographic division of western Palestine should be undertaken. Dividing Palestine into Jewish and Arab states had been suggested, but it seemed that neither the Zionists nor the great power was fully convinced that the time was right for partition. It was abundantly clear that the Palestinians did not want to participate in any political solution in which they attained less than the right to govern themselves and to determine their own future. Those in physical occupation of Palestine wanted to provide only limited self-rule: full autonomy for the Palestinians through governance by a council, with circumscribed legislative authority and the occupying power maintaining control over security matters and foreign affairs. At that time, the occupying power wanted to retain for itself the ultimate source of power over all of western Palestine, which negated the prospects of full independence for the Palestinian Arabs and preserved the occupying power's security interests.

Clearly those in control of Palestine had no interest in sharing power with the Palestinian Arabs. A perception existed that the Palestinian Arabs could not be trusted as equals in the future administration of Palestine or portions of it. Many Palestinians were seen only as thugs, terrorists, or insincere nationalists. Yet at all costs, the great power wanted to preserve its strategic presence in the region, protect the security of Jewish presence, and maintain access to Middle Eastern oil. The occupying administration refused to adopt a policy of accommodation under the pressures of duress created by the contemporaneous violence. Since the occupying administration did not want to appease or condone violence, it required that the uprising end before serious political discussions and negotiations could commence. Then the occupying administration used force to gain control of the uprising.

Meanwhile, in European capitals, there was notice of the Palestinian quest for self-determination. After the uprising entered its third year, genuine European concern expressed for the Palestinians was overshadowed by dramatic changes in Eastern Europe, the strategic military balance between the powers, a resurgent Japan, and the continued consolidation of authority by the leader of the Soviet Union.

Concerning the status of political discussions about Palestine's future, there was serious and constant debate among Palestinians about who was eligible to be present as Palestinian representatives at any future negotiations and about the proposed international conference. Palestinians wanted the great power to coerce the Jewish community in Palestine into making political concessions. Zionists wanted direct negotiations and shunned outside pressure aimed at changing their political positions. There was already public discussion about several key issues: the nature and duration of a transitional period before a state or states would be created, the future special status of Jerusalem, and the continuing interests and guarantees to be provided by the great power during the transitional process. Prominent Palestinians from the Husseini family in Jerusalem had cautioned that a transitional period would never come as long as the Jews felt they could delay Palestinian independence or the establishment of a Palestinian national authority.[4] Meanwhile, prominent Zionist officials warned that if the great powers forced the Zionists to make political concessions, the Arab world would later support the Palestinian Arab demands for further concessions from the Zionists.[5]

Is this not a description of both uprisings?

Comparisons: Palestinian Leadership

Prior to the outbreak of both uprisings,[6] the self-anointed Palestinian political elites focused on high politics, maintenance, and control of their political communities; fractious organizational issues; and the increasing role that Islam was playing in influencing Palestinian national awareness. As a consequence, both elites were somewhat surprised by the uprisings' outbreak. Both dominant Palestinian leaders were keen to retain their respective control over the direction of the national movement. Both were eager to enhance regional and international support for the Palestinian problem. They directed their attention toward political proposals made previously by dominant great power(s), were very keen to maintain their own status as (un)official representatives of the Palestinian national movement, and were greatly concerned about other emerging contenders for leadership. They were aware of a growing Islamic dimension in Palestinian self-consciousness, which in turn necessitated the formation and implementation of a response that would co-opt, if not control, politically molding Islamic sentiments. Both Palestinian leaders and their associates consistently preached absolute opposition to the foreign occupation.

Neither the political leadership led by Hajj Amin al-Husseini, the titular head of the Arab community in Palestine, nor his contemporaneous political opponents; neither the Palestinian leadership headed by Yasser Arafat, the PLO chairman, nor his detractors within the Palestinian community were completely concentrating on the degree of despair and despondency that the lower-class Palestinians had endured under foreign occupation and administration. Both vehemently opposed Jewish land settlement and Jewish immigration. Although neither political elite was disinterested in its most cherished constituencies, both failed to understand how the duration of duress and the level of regular personal suffering were steadily eroding the patience of Palestinians under the occupation's governance.[7] The absence of a fully accurate assessment by the leadership of the depth of disillusionment among *fellaheen* in the 1930s, and the lack of a true understanding by the contemporary leadership of the anger and frustration two decades of Israeli occupation had caused among the Palestinian population, explain to some degree why both political elites were considerably surprised when local violence turned into a prolonged general uprising. Perhaps more startling to the current Palestinian leadership on the eve of the Intifada was the "external" leadership's surprise that a sustained confrontation against Israeli presence could be mounted and maintained by what seemed to be a disjointed network of women and student groups, trade unions, local charitable organizations, and other loosely knit professional associations. Mass mobilization in the Intifada was not organizationally akin to the formal organization and patrimonial leadership that had traditionally characterized the PLO.

In the years prior to the uprisings, both leadership elites were interested in "internationalizing" the Palestinian question, in gaining recognition for the Palestinian position as it opposed Zionism and Israel. The mufti hosted the Islamic Conference in 1931 in an effort to focus international attention on the Palestinian issue. But this conference did nothing to alleviate immediate daily problems of the lower classes.[8] During the early stages of both uprisings, the political elites sought to advance Palestinian political demands through inter-Arab action. For his part, prior to and during the Intifada, Arafat was traveling extensively, engaging in the highest levels of diplomacy with heads of state, using sympathy for the PLO at the United Nations, constantly seeking international legitimacy, and pursuing recognition and reaffirmation of the PLO as the sole legitimate representative of the Palestinian people.

At the outset of the uprisings (1936 and 1987), the two key Palestinian leaders were very concerned with fending off challenges to their leadership from the Palestinian Arab national movement. In the years immediately prior to the outbreak of the uprisings, both political elites had undergone severe political fragmentation. In December 1934, the Palestinian Arab Executive virtually came to an end as an unofficially recognized organization representing Palestinian political interests vis-à-vis the British. The death of Musa Kazem Pasha al-Husseini, the head of the Arab Executive, generated an immediate splintering of the political leadership into a half-dozen separate political parties, reflecting deep personal animosities and representing local geographical interests in Palestine. Hajj Amin al-Husseini was an immediate beneficiary of Musa Kazim's death, since it ended an unpleasant competition with his uncle for ascendancy in Palestinian Arab politics. The presence of the more radical *Istiqlal* party and the so-called moderates had already posed a challenge to the mufti prior to Musa Kazim's death.[9] At the outbreak of the 1936 uprising and general strike, the mufti extrapolated from the unrest an opportunity to concentrate authority in his hands and deny it to adversaries.

More recently, particularly after the Israeli invasion of Lebanon in 1982, Arafat's leadership was personally challenged by a variety of groups and individuals, especially between 1983 and 1986, including direct challenges from Arab heads of state and other Palestinian leaders. Among Palestinians, Abu Nidal, an Arafat antagonist; Abu Musa, head of a dissident faction of al-Fatah, allied to Syria; Ahmed Jibril, head of the Popular Front for the Liberation of Palestine-General Command, also allied to Syria; and the Palestine National Salvation front (an umbrella organization opposing Arafat's policies and leadership) forced the PLO leader to focus considerable attention on his political flanks. The outbreak of the Intifada gave Arafat an opportunity to tighten his control over the "external" leadership of the Palestinian Arab community, a process that had begun in 1987 in formal and practical reconciliation between the major PLO factions. Arafat used the Intifada as a vehicle to fend off rivals and to prevent further organizational splintering, while seeking to reaffirm the PLO's status among Palestinians and in the world community.

In terms of policy focus, both political elites were in the midst of reacting to or negating political ideas and proposals put forth previously by Britain, the United States, and others. When the uprisings occurred in April 1936 and December 1987, neither Hajj Amin al-Husseini nor Yasser Arafat enjoyed a formal, working relationship with either Britain or the United States, respectively; yet both men had opened unofficial channels of communication to the great powers in the years prior to the uprisings. In contrast rather than comparison, the leadership under Hajj Amin had developed a longer working relationship with the British than the very sporadic and distant contacts that the PLO and Arafat had established with the United States.

In early 1936, the mufti and other Palestinian Arab leaders were debating the merits involved in acceptance of a British proposal for a Legislative Council in Palestine; between 1978 and 1987, there were internal Palestinian political debates about the contents of the Camp David Accords, the Venice Declaration, the Reagan Plan, the Fez Plan, the Brezhnev Plan, the Jordanian-PLO Accord, and a variety of United Nations resolutions on Palestine. Naturally, in the latter period the length and complexity of the debate were greater than the request for a halt to Jewish immigration or land purchases, which had accompanied the call in November 1935 for the establishment of a legislative council. But at both times, the Palestinian political leadership was focused on proposals, ideas, and resolutions offered primarily by others in response to the Palestinian quest for self-determination. Both political elites were reacting to events at the time of the outbreak of the uprisings. Equally important, while seeking to engage the great power in political discussions and somehow to capture the political initiative unleashed by the physical nature of the unrest, the Palestinian leadership at the outset of each uprising remained initially on the defensive politically. In 1937, the leadership replied negatively to the Peel Commission partition plan. In 1988, the PLO leadership replied negatively to the "Shultz initiative," which aimed at telescoping in time the previously proposed Camp David Accords, and initially to an idea for the election of Palestinian representatives for the formation of a delegation for negotiations.[10] But by the end of 1988, the PLO sought to take the diplomatic offensive, as it recognized the legitimacy of a two-state political solution, renounced terrorism, and conditionally accepted Israel's existence linked to the establishment of an independent Palestinian state. No such political solution was offered by the mufti in the midst of the 1936-39 uprising. The mufti and the Arab Higher Committee accepted the adoption of the May 1939 White Paper, which truncated Jewish development and promised a unitary state in Palestine in ten years. In 1936-39, the political leadership sought to contain Zionist growth, while on the second occasion the political leadership accepted the Zionist presence and created a diplomatic initiative out of the Intifada.

From all available sources, there seems to be a uniform understanding that both Palestinian Arab political elites were caught off-guard by the outbreak, its spontaneity, and the duration of the uprisings.[11] At the beginning of the Intifada, the Gaza Strip's political leadership was apparently more aware than the West Bank leadership elite of the deep despair of local Palestinians, in part because the level of economic deprivation was greater in the Gaza Strip. Prior to the outbreak of both uprisings, there were increasing incidents of violence and deepening tensions between Jewish and Arab populations. In the 1930s, there were land disputes, one-day strikes, Palestinian evictions from land, and sporadic attacks against Jewish settlers.[12] Particularly in the two years prior to the outbreak of the Intifada in December 1987, communal violence manifested itself in land disputes, in attacks against Jewish settlers, in requisitioning of land, and in one-day strikes.[13]

After the outbreak of each uprising, the Palestinian leadership sought to strengthen, reassert, and reaffirm control over its community; it sought to enhance its status organizationally, and, at least initially, gain international publicity for its cause. The Arab Higher Committee was physically and socially much more distant from the peasant bands that dominated the 1936–39 uprising than was the PLO, which was the consensus nationalist symbol for virtually every nonreligious organization in the West Bank and Gaza Strip prior to and during the Intifada. Moreover, each uprising gave the political elite renewed bargaining power with the occupying administration.[14] But while he personally asserted himself, the mufti found it difficult throughout the different phases of the 1936–39 uprising to control the rebel bands that were the backbone of the revolt. The mufti and the Arab Higher Committee wanted "the bands to continue their activities against the British and Zionists, but they did not wish to see them grow sufficiently strong and cohesive to challenge their [Arab Higher Committee's] authority and possibly disregard future instructions to halt their actions."[15] By comparison, it seems that while the PLO came into a fully influential position in copiloting the Intifada with the various local elites in the West Bank and Gaza only by the second or third month of the uprising, the PLO was able to establish a significant degree of control over political and street action within the West Bank and Gaza as the Intifada unfolded. Even after the mufti's departure from Palestine in October 1937, the British turned to his designates when they sought to create a dialogue with the Palestinian Arab community during and after the conclusion of the 1936–39 uprising. With striking similarity to this British action in the earlier uprising, the United States turned to the PLO, albeit with conditions, as a legitimate interlocutor representing the interests of the Palestinian Arab community. But unlike the 1936–39 uprising, during the Intifada, political leadership outside of Palestine worked more harmoniously with the leadership and rank-and-file protestors in the West Bank and Gaza Strip.

Comparison: Character and Participation

Close comparison of the two uprisings reveals that, at the time of eruption, there were critical differences in the character and composition of Palestinian society. These differences obviously affected recruitment into the uprising. By the time the Intifada had broken out, the traditional strength of the Palestinian landowner, urban merchant, and village leader in the West Bank and Gaza Strip had been replaced or was being supplanted by leadership elites based not only on wealth but also on educational achievement, professional attainment, and an accumulated personal résumé of confronting Israeli presence. In the period before each uprising, a better-educated and more radical younger generation emerged to confront traditional leaders. But in the earlier event, the number of these younger leaders was relatively small in comparison to the majority *fellaheen* class and was certainly less influential than the landowning elites. In December 1987, Palestinians of all classes were more politicized and more clarified in their general goals than were the Palestinians in April 1936. Like the 1936–39 uprising, the Intifada, as far as the area of the "West Bank" was concerned, broke out in the towns and spread to the countryside. But unlike the 1936–39 uprising, the Intifada did not have the townsmen dropping out and abrogating their engagement against the occupying force to the *fellaheen* as the predominant, if not the sole, social component of public protest.[16] Although the 1936–1939 uprising was fought primarily by uneducated peasants, the Intifada was carried out by wide segments of a highly educated population in a coordinated fashion. A great difference in participatory commitment in the Intifada was the new role that Palestinian women and students played in street demonstrations and in engaging the Israeli authorities, particularly in the West Bank. It was estimated that children were responsible for 85 percent of all incidents during the first two years of the Intifada.[17]

There is little doubt that the 1936–39 uprising was largely a marked challenge against Great Britain's presence in governing Palestine, against the League of Nations' ratified Palestine Mandate, which gave legitimacy to the Balfour Declaration, and against the twin "evils" of Zionism and Jewish immigration and land purchases. But the 1936–39 uprising also developed as an angry opposition and as a rebellion against the urban social caste from which the political and social elite had sprung. Then, there were very sharp social distinctions drawn between the upper-class urban elite with landowning interests and the impoverished lower-class *fellaheen* population.[18] During the Intifada's unfolding, many social and class distinctions among rural, urban, refugee, and non-refugee Palestinian communities were further blurred in the West Bank and Gaza; whether those distinctions were to change in some rearranged fashion remained to be determined during the period after the Intifada's conclusion. In neither uprising was there evidence to suggest that a distinct social class consciousness developed as a result of the unrest. Certainly in the 1936–39 uprising there were a greater number of intertwining issues motivating a person's participation. These included racial, religious, anticolonial, and familial motivations, as well as simply brigandage. What appeared as an outburst against Great Britain and Zionism in the 1936–39 uprising degenerated into a pronounced internecine communal conflict, if not a civil war.[19]

Well before the outbreak of the 1936–39 uprising, social bonds had begun to fray within the Palestinian Arab community, partially because of the intrusive changes brought about by Zionist growth and by British administration. In the 1930s the existence of the majority of Palestinian Arabs was significantly bounded and geographically limited to its *hamula*, or village, and by its social and financial dependence upon urban notables and moneylenders. The effect of the 1936–39 uprising stimulated a further weakening in the social moorings that had traditionally sustained and connected rural dependence upon the urban elite. In the aftermath of the 1936–39 uprising, Palestinian Arab social bonds were weakened by the emergence of a nascent bourgeoisie and merchant class, located primarily on Palestine's coast, which challenged traditional leaders. The badly decimated traditional urban elite which had guided the Palestinian political community in the late Ottoman and Mandatory period retained minimal influence over a severely disjointed Palestinian Arab community.[20] Palestinian social upheaval and political fragmentation easily enabled surrounding Arab capitals to intervene in Palestinian affairs during the 1936-39 uprising. In the absence of an emerging and coherent Palestinian leadership, Egypt, Syria, Iraq, Saudi Arabia, and Transjordan had an unchallenged opportunity to speak on behalf of the Palestinian cause in the late 1930s, during, and after World War II. By comparison, a distinct motivation for the development of a collective Palestinian anger that emerged prior to the outbreak of the Intifada was the Palestinian sense of abandonment by the Arab world. Unlike the period prior to the 1936-39 uprising, West Bank and Gaza Strip Palestinians had already disengaged from a Jordanian option prior to the Intifada. Palestinian Arab alienation was amply evidenced at the Amman Summit in November 1987 when attention was concentrated on the Gulf war and not on the Palestinian issue.

A major difference between the Intifada and the 1936-39 uprising was the level of individual commitment to a collectively defined Palestinian nationalist feeling, which had begun to develop during the twenty years of Israeli administration of the West Bank, Gaza Strip, and East Jerusalem. The intrusive legal changes and financial demands imposed upon the Palestinian Arab community by the Israeli administration, rather than fraying social bonds, generated a localized social cement. Palestinians were deeply entangled in the tentacles of Israeli economic and personal control over their lives. Struggle by Palestinians prior to the Intifada was not against their political leaders or against a social caste, but against a collective subordination to Israeli rule.[21] Israeli military presence and administrative dominance stimulated a collective Palestinian Arab response of steadfastness, or *sumud*. Prior to the outbreak of the Intifada, *sumud* focused on the communal struggle to stay on the land and maintain Palestinian social, economic, and educational institutions.[22] The Intifada was unlike its predecessor in that it became a participatory undertaking for most segments of Palestinian society, with organizational mechanisms established to articulate people's demands and to answer in some measure their needs. During the Intifada an atmosphere of self-reliance, self-sufficiency, and mutual interest developed across class lines,[23] a natural extension of what had occurred within Palestinian society in the years immediately prior to the Intifada.

The 1936-39 uprising was an admixture: a peasant revolt, driven by distinctively personal frustrations and motivations and overlaid by a nationalist veneer. While both uprisings were a negative reaction to Zionism and foreign presence, the Intifada contained a positive assertion of a more mature, broadly based, and clearly articulated national consciousness. The Intifada emitted self-esteem, a sense of confidence in, and significant international sympathy for the Palestinian quest for self-determination and for removal of Israeli rule. In the earlier uprising, the individual rather than the collectivity expressed itself against Zionism. Both uprisings were sparked by a fear of lost destiny; in the 1936–39 uprising the emphasis was on a sense of sporadic individual encroachment, displacement, and economic deprivation rather than a developed collective sense of a peoplehood being systematically denied or wronged. In 1936–39 the organizational centers of the uprising were the family and the village. Rebel bands were organized along family, clan, and village lines. Some Palestinians who recalled the 1936–39 uprising associated their "national" identity with a need to restore their personal honor because their village lands were lost.[24] Significantly, Palestinians during the Intifada possessed a more distinct view of their territorial affinity, geographically defined as at least the West Bank, the Gaza Strip, and East Jerusalem. Unlike the 1936–39 uprising, the Intifada tended to galvanize an already existing Palestinian national consciousness across class, clan, and geographic lines.

Organizational aspects of the two uprisings were noticeably different. Through its various phases, the 1936–39 uprising was more spontaneous and less organized. It was an unsystematic, undisciplined, and unstable insurgency, often prone to anarchic lapses.[25] Both the rebel bands and the individuals within them were virtually independent actors, with little coordination between them and little ideological distinction to differentiate among them. In the Intifada, however, participants and leadership represented essentially four political ideologies within the Palestinian community. They collectively made decisions through constructive dialogue. Potentially divisive issues involved in carrying out tactical aspects of planning and coordination were intentionally postponed, lest they detract from the communal coherence generated by the Intifada.[26] In the years before the outbreak of the Intifada, a wide variety of professional groups, women and student organizations, trade unions, and religious associations had formed, comparable on a smaller scale to the Young Men's Muslim Associations, which had developed prior to the 1936–39 uprising. But in the latter uprising, the degree of organization and the extensiveness of participation made these communal groups an interwoven network that formed the basis for maintaining the uprising.

By comparison, the Intifada was more than civil disobedience but less than an armed revolt, which characterized portions of the 1936–39 uprising. In the earlier uprising, the urban leadership had little success in imposing itself on individual band leaders. Those local leaders refused to assimilate into a larger structure in order not to forfeit their independence. In the name of the uprising, band leaders and *fellaheen* participated in the 1936–39 uprising by engaging in acts of violence, sabotage, and attacks on life and property.[27] By comparison the Intifada was more controlled and more organized in a decentralized fashion. Palestinian Intifada participants aimed at the Israeli occupation, which was their central target of confrontation, rather than attacking Israelis or physical symbols of the occupation, such as Jewish settlements and British strategic objectives, as was the case in the 1936–39 uprising. At the end of the second year of the Intifada, while more radical elements of the PLO leadership repeatedly threatened to "upgrade" the Intifada with the use of guns and weapons against the Israelis, the clearly prevailing view was not to use such weapons.[28]

Distinctive and characteristic of the Intifada were the varying layers and frequency of consultation between the uprising's leadership and its participants. There were pamphlets and brochures published during the 1936–39 rebellion, but there was none of the detail, complexity, timeliness, regularity, and care that characterized the composition of calls or communiqués regularly issued during the Intifada by the Unified National Leadership of the Uprising.[29] By comparison, the Unified National Leadership of the Uprising was more responsive to the population's needs and requests than was the Arab Higher Committee, in part because the Intifada's protests against the Israelis were finely tuned to each locality and to an understanding of just what might be the population's limits of personal and economic sacrifice. Unlike the 1936–39 uprising, organization of the Intifada was enhanced by the attributes and benefits of mass communication—copy and facsimile (fax) machines, radio broadcasts, telephone communication, easy vehicle access to all parts of the West Bank and Gaza, and an attendant international media. All were gainfully used to advance communal interaction and cooperation.

Comparison: The Islamic Dimension

In addition to the personal grievances that pained Palestinians before the outbreak of both uprisings, the looming resurgence of Islamic values and sensibilities helped to catalyze and radicalize individual Palestinian motivation to action against both Great Britain/Zionism and Israel. In the several years before both uprisings, a definite Islamic dimension played a role in mobilizing antipathy against the "foreign invaders" of Palestine. On both occasions, a distinctly Islamic component was interlaced with the more secular and politically moderate mainstream of Palestinian leadership. Although organized into relatively small cells that preserved their autonomy, Islamic groups maintained contacts with the more dominant Palestinian elites that were leading the national movement. In each uprising, Islamic groups contributed in some measure to the general radicalization of the Palestinian political community. In the case of the 1936-39 uprising, the Islamic component dissipated; but during the Intifada, the Islamic elements, at least after the second year, played a formidable role.

In the late 1920s and early 1930s, Syrian-born Sheikh Izz al-Din al-Qassam took up residence in Haifa, organized an armed resistance based upon small cells, preached holy war against the Jews, and sought a purified Islam similar to that championed by Rashid Rida in Cairo. He was not controlled by either the most uncompromising anti-Zionist interests or the mufti, but he most certainly worked against the interests of the secular landowning elite that dominated the national movement at the time.[30] Perhaps to preempt the quickly rising popular peasant support for Sheikh Izz al-Din al-Qassam, the mufti issued *fatwas*, religious legal injunctions against Zionism, summoned a conference of Moslem villagers in December 1934, convened two *ulama* conferences, and preached the protection of Palestine against the Jews. At an ulama conference held in January 1935, a fatwa was issued, signed by 248 religious figures. The significance of the fatwa was not in the numbers who signed it collectively, but rather in its contents, which were clearly more anti-Jewish than anti-Zionist.[31]

In contrast to al-Qassam, the mufti did not invoke the cry for a *jihad* against Jews, as he could have done after the outbreak of the 1936 uprising, and especially after al-Qassam's death, at the hands of the British in October 1935. Al-Qassam's death then, unlike any one incident prior to the outbreak of the Intifada, personalized the feelings of penetrating frustration and deep despair felt by the peasant and working classes. One author suggests that Qassam's death showed that militant activity was an appropriate mechanism of rebellion by the lower classes against the landowning establishment and against the Zionists and British.[32] Qassam's death was an exhortation to action for many peasants, particularly in northern Palestine where he died. In the decades prior to the outbreak of the Intifada, Islamic religious leaders in Gaza organized several different Islamic groups, mostly in the very poor areas of the Gaza refugee camps.[33] Some groups, such as HAMAS, were organized after the Intifada began. Palestinian Islamic groups derived their historical origins from local precursors, like the presence of the Moslem Brotherhood in Egypt and Palestine in the post–World War II period. The effects of Israeli occupation reaffirmed the historically based, uncompromising attitudes toward Zionism and toward Jews that had been traditionally held by the Moslem Brotherhood.

Major differences are evident in the degree of Islamic texture in the fiber of the two uprisings. In the 1936–39 period, the Islamic tendencies were successfully absorbed by the mufti before the outbreak of the uprising; alternative Islamic leaders were only minor figures compared to Hajj Amin's persona during and after the beginning of the uprising. Although used in the earlier period, the mosque network was not organizationally or effectively developed for providing educational, charitable, and religious services to the underclass populations, particularly as compared to the Gaza Strip during the Intifada. Moreover, before the Intifada, the PLO and some Islamic groups, such as Islamic Jihad, converged their activities in the West Bank and Gaza. Islamic Jihad had an emotive influence that impelled people into the streets prior to the Intifada.[34] Additional general support for an Islamic underpinning during the Intifada came from the contemporaneous Middle Eastern environment, which before and during the Intifada sustained many significant and highly committed Islamic groups that were organizing to provide Islam as the primary and guiding alternative to parochial, secular, and nationalist regimes. For the purpose of maintaining a solid political position and organizational unity, the "external" PLO political leadership sought to engage and co-opt coordination from the increasingly popular Palestinian Islamic groups, but sometimes with less than uniform success. Elements within HAMAS, for example, wanted to liberate all of Palestine and were opposed to the PLO's compromise of a two-state political solution.[35]

Comparisons: Duration and Effects

Unlike its precursor, the Intifada did not have a major interruption in its continuum. The 1936–39 uprising was a captive of Palestine's agricultural calendar and of intervention by Palestinian and Arab political leaders. The first phase of the general strike started at the end of the citrus picking season of 1935–36 and was completed prior to the citrus harvest of 1936–37. The second phase did not begin until the summer of 1938 when the regular harvest season was over. Unlike the 1936–39 uprising, the Intifada's duration demonstrated stamina and a low but continuous level of intensity.

Both uprisings show ample evidence that some local leaders were assassinated for collaborating with the Zionists/Israelis. In both instances, intimidation and assassination of those not fully imbued with sympathy for the cause occurred later on in the uprisings. There is evidence that suggests that the mufti carried out such personal vendettas indirectly through intermediaries in hopes of settling scores against those who opposed his leadership and against those who supported the suggested partition of Palestine in 1937.[36] In 1938, for example, there were campaigns of physical violence waged directly against village *mukhtars* and against landowners who had previously sold land to the Zionists; there was also regular intimidation by rebel bands against villagers who were forced to provide supplies, weapons, and food necessary to keep the bands active. It is not known in each case why an accused collaborationist was killed, nor is it known if the external or internal Palestinian leadership had any influence about that person's "commitment" to the Intifada. But there is ample evidence to indicate that the PLO and the unified leadership of the Intifada publicly condemned the uncontrolled violence against people accused of collaboration. In the 1936–39 period, 494 Arabs were killed by Arabs, which was approximately 16 percent of the total number of Arabs killed during the uprising. By the end of the second year of the Intifada, about one-fifth of the Palestinians killed were victims of other Palestinians,[37] and the level of intra-Palestinian skirmishing was clearly escalating during the latter half of the Intifada's second year. In both cases, it seems that collaborationist killings were carried out for a variety of reasons, which included personal and political animosities, disputes over local issues, perceived laxity in commitment to the national cause, and even general brigandage and banditry. However, motivations for the Intifada collaborationist assassinations were generally not based upon family identity or social class, which were evident causes for Palestinian against Palestinian killings in the 1936–39 uprising.

A comparison of the political actions taken by the respective main Palestinian political leaders during the uprisings provides a distinguishable contrast. When both uprisings began, the mufti and Arafat were in the amorphous center of the Palestinian Arab political spectrum. In the 1936–39 period, the mufti, in failing to control the pace or direction of the undisciplined violence, became more resistant to political compromise. When he could not control the bands in the summer of 1936, he invited the intervention of Ibn Saud, Emir Abdallah, and Nuri al-Said. The mufti assumed an increasingly radicalized view of Britain and Zionism, reaching a point that made any possible accommodation with the British or the Zionists virtually impossible. His radicalization occurred in part because he needed to reassert his political authority over a highly fragmented Palestinian community, especially after he was exiled from Palestine in October 1937. Any signs of accommodation would have put him closer politically to both the Palestinian Arab moderates and the Hashemites, which would in turn have forced a sharing of the political community's decisionmaking prerogatives. Also in the mufti's case, any complete embrace of Emir Abdallah, besides merely seeking his intervention to stop the uprising, would by necessity have given additional credibility to his Palestinian rivals who were openly supported by the Transjordan leader.

By comparison, when the Intifada broke out, Arafat and his dominant wing of the PLO were already considered centrist within the Palestinian Arab political community. Since 1974, the PLO had accepted the notion of a state in any area liberated from Israel.[38] Only after July 1988, when the Hashemites significantly withdrew their interest in controlling Palestinian territory west of the Jordan, did Arafat begin to intimate more precisely a willingness to accept a two-state solution. Thereafter, the Intifada became the PLO's prime engine for political action for clearly articulating the possibility of a two-state solution. Unlike the mufti, Arafat could assert a political accommodation without being forced to adopt some form of Hashemite hegemony over Palestinian decision making. At that point, as one PLO Executive Committee member commented, the Intifada became "an incentive to take action in the region, . . . [as] an activator, a catalyst, to attain peace."[39]

Consequently, the Palestinians made their most conciliatory public gestures toward Zionism ever, including: the PNC's November 1988 resolution to accept a two-state solution based upon the November 1947 partition resolution, Yasser Arafat's public recognition of Israel in December 1988, and the subsequent opening of a diplomatic dialogue between the PLO and the United States. The PLO labeled the combination of these events as its "peace initiative," a term that certainly had been unthinkable among the Palestinian leadership half a century before. In February 1939, the St. James Palace conference followed the earlier uprising, and diplomatic efforts were undertaken by Great Britain to bring Zionists and Palestinian Arabs together. However, the publication and implementation of the 1939 White Paper, which severely limited Jewish immigration and land acquisition in the early 1940s, were viewed by Palestinian Arabs as a major political victory against Zionism. While certainly not satisfying Palestinian aspirations for Arab majority self-rule, the application of the white paper and the intervention of World War II considerably neutralized additional

Palestinian Arab political demands to the British and against the Zionists. By comparison, the limited continuation of the Intifada after two years remains a carefully husbanded political currency, savored and nurtured by the Palestinian political leadership. With the focus of the international media diverted elsewhere at the end of the Intifada's second year, with some frustration among Palestinians that the Intifada had not yet created progress either in political advancement toward statehood or in persuading the United States to pressure Israel into political and territorial concessions, there is evidence to suggest that the Intifada and its maintenance has become more precious to the political leadership in 1989 than perhaps it was in December 1987. The former Palestine National Council speaker and current chairman of the Palestine National Salvation Front, which opposes Arafat's leadership, remarked in August 1989, that "if the Intifada were terminated, we [the Palestinians] would not have bargaining power."[40] Several months later, Salah Khalaf, a leading member of *Fatah* and considered the number two man in the PLO, noted, "We Arabs have nothing other than this Intifada in our hands. Through it we reactivate political action. So if God forbid, the Intifada suffers a setback, I do not know what our position as Arabs will be."[41] In 1939, the Palestinian leadership settled for the white paper and the promise of a unitary state within ten years. Whether the present Palestinian leadership will accept a similar promise remains, of course, to be seen; but there persists some worry that a political process, such as elections in the West Bank and Gaza Strip, could be used both to end slowly the Intifada and to uncouple it from the achievement of the articulated goal of an independent Palestinian state.[42]

A major reason why the PLO leadership had the option to use the Intifada as a force for diplomatic action was the relative freedom of political autonomy within the Arab world that the Palestinian leadership enjoyed prior to and during the Intifada. The independence of political decision making is a lesson that the present Palestinian leadership has learned from the earlier uprising. While the present leadership is eager to have President Mubarak of Egypt act as a diplomatic lubricant in the negotiating process with the United States, it is concerned that Egypt might begin to usurp the Palestinian prerogative of independent decision making. PLO leaders want "to differentiate between the Egyptian [diplomatic] role which [was] welcomed and an attempt to represent the Palestinians and speaking on their behalf."[43] In the 1936–39 period, the Arab Higher Committee sought the intervention of Arab states to end the uprising in order to protect its own image and to preserve its own status as leader of the Palestinian Arab community. In the midst of the uprisings, Arab leaders met in Bludan in September 1937, at Algiers in June 1988, and in Casablanca in May 1989. During the conferences, greater venom was directed at Zionism and Israel than at the important powers, Britain and the United States. Most historians recognize the Bludan Congress as a benchmark for the Arab world's initial intervention in the Palestine problem.[44] The Algiers and Casablanca Arab summits, however, affirmed or ratified Arab League political support for an independent political course set by the PLO. By adopting a conciliatory political option in the midst of the Intifada, the PLO leadership demonstrated its desire to retain firm control of the diplomatic and political direction of the national movement, to retain full control undivided with any emerging pretenders for leadership in the West Bank and Gaza, and certainly to retain the prerogative of independent decision making free from the control of Arab capitals such as Damascus, which wished to contain the Palestinian diplomatic initiative with Israel. But it must be stressed that the Arab world during the period prior to and after the Intifada was, in comparison to fifty years before, much less inclined to be concerned with the control of the Palestinian issue. In the earlier uprising, Arab leaders in states surrounding Palestine primarily intervened to help end the various phases of the 1936–39 uprising in order to promote their own political purposes.[45]

While the 1936–39 uprising set the precedent for Arab state meddling in Palestinian affairs, the willingness during the Intifada of some Arab capitals, most particularly Amman, to dissociate themselves from a territorial competition for the West Bank provided the Palestinian leadership with a political option it had not enjoyed during the 1936–39 uprising. But Arab world distance from the Palestinian question, especially the restrained form of merely verbal political and meager financial support given during the Intifada, has been, to date, bittersweet. The November 1987 Arab

Summit Conference in Amman, meeting just a month before the outbreak of the Intifada, displayed, if not abandonment or indifference to the Palestinian question, then certainly a lack of substantive commitment. While the PLO leadership enjoyed broader political options during the Intifada, it also lamented the disinterest that the Arab world demonstrated toward tangible support for the uprising. Particularly during its second year, most of the Arab world, except for Saudi Arabia, failed to meet the financial obligations toward the Intifada as promised at the Casablanca summit in May 1989.[46] Khalid al-Hasan, a Fatah Central Committee member, remarked after that summit that "the Arab stand no longer exists. It is no use saying that the Arab stand is disunited, fragmented, or tentative—it is now less than zero. As far as the Palestine question and the Intifada are concerned, there is no Arab stand."[47] As compared to fifty years before, the Arab world no longer coveted protection and control over the Palestinian issue; not only was it being left to PLO policies almost exclusively, but there was also a profound absence of intense political commitment to the Palestinian issue, which distressed the Palestinian leadership.

Finally, it should be noted that on the occasion of each uprising, substantial international exposure was given to the Palestinian issue. But in 1938–39 and again in 1988–89, other and more pressing international issue considerably reduced the initial publicity that the Palestinian uprisings received. In 1938 and 1939, Britain turned its attention almost exclusively to Europe and the changes being wrought by fascism's emergence. In 1988–89, within the Middle East, the Intifada became a secondary issue to events in Lebanon; it became an international issue of marginal interest as historic challenges to socialism and communism occurred in China and Eastern Europe. In the 1936–39 period, Britain postponed any decision to leave Palestine that might have ensued had the partition notion been adopted. It changed its plans not because of the uprising, but because of global considerations. During the Intifada, while the United States put forth the 1988 Shultz initiative as an ambiguous way to start negotiations, Washington withdrew active support of the initiative and therefore some of its attention to the Palestinian issue, not for considerations of global politics, but because the United States was not yet convinced that either side was willing to overcome its respective ideological constraints and political paralysis and to engage in direct and substantive negotiations. But like Great Britain, the United States realized the importance of engaging in a dialogue with all sides. As a cumulative result of the Intifada, the Hashemite disengagement from the West Bank, and Arafat's willingness to renounce terrorism and recognize Israel, Washington opened that dialogue. Like Great Britain in 1939, Washington was, at least by the Intifada's second anniversary, not able to start direct Palestinian-Zionist/Israel talks. Fifty years ago it was the Palestinian leadership who refused to sit with the Zionists; now it is the Israelis who refuse to sit with the PLO leadership.

Conclusions

Because this essay is inherently limited by the ongoing nature of one of the variables under review, any substantive conclusions are speculative. The most prominent prognosis, of course, is that the chances for negotiations to ensue between the parties after this current uprising are greater than they were in 1939. Both Palestinians and Israelis are more mature about accepting, albeit with reservations, the other's legitimacy. Both communities are more intertwined with one another physically and economically than fifty years ago; the Intifada has catalyzed the interaction through confrontation. Both communities look to an outside arbiter to broker mutually acceptable procedures. Both sides remain partially bound by fossilized ideologies, but they each have developed some pragmatic resiliency as a result of the Intifada and events that preceded and accompanied it. For the Palestinian community, the main danger is that further disharmony may evolve if no satisfactory political process unfolds. Such disunity could be augmented by several factors: the Intifada's losing its discipline; continued Israeli deportations of political leaders; a reinvigorated Palestinian-Islamic movement inspired by the November 1989 parliamentary election results in Jordan; and the results of local Palestinian elections which, if held and not properly managed, could be more divisive than harmonizing in their end result. In addition, the PLO could be organizationally threatened by a political process which, though headed toward a negotiated settlement, might simultaneously contribute to an erosion of PLO "external" leadership dominance over the Palestinian political community.

The aftermath of the 1936–39 uprising saw an almost total disintegration of the local Palestinian political leadership in the following decade. For the current external leadership and the Unified National Leadership of the Uprising in the West Bank and Gaza Strip, how and when the Intifada ends are of utmost importance to the future nature and composition of the Palestinian leadership. It is ironic that although Palestinian leadership enjoys almost total political autonomy in the inter-Arab political system today, something it did not enjoy fifty years ago, its West Bank and Gaza constituents have greater dependency upon the Jewish economy than their predecessors of the 1936–39 uprising. For it to survive, the present PLO leadership will not only have to make some accommodation with Israel, but it will also have to find ways to extend formal coordination with the amorphously defined Palestinian leaders in the occupied territories, who have become the center of gravity for Palestinian nationalism. The emergence of these leaders has been one of the most significant political results of this uprising.[48] Unlike its equivalent in the 1936–39 uprising, the group of participants in this Palestinian national assertion is broadly based, pluralistic, interested in political compromise, acceptable to Israeli political leaders, and apparently a durable component of the Palestinian community.

Author's Note

In preparing the final draft of this chapter I would like to acknowledge the useful and thoughtful suggestions made by my colleagues Rex Brynen, Neil Caplan, Emile Nakhleh, and Bruce Maddy-Weitzman. I am grateful to all of them for making the manuscript more comprehensive and concise. While I thank them for their efforts, I alone am responsible for the contents.

Notes

1. For a recent comparative examination of the Intifada with the 1936–39 uprising, see M. Khalid al-Azhari, "Thawrah 1936 wa Intifadah

1987" (The 1936 Revolt and the 1987 Intifadah), *Shu'un Filastiniyah* (Beirut) (October 1989): 3–26.

2. For convenience' sake, the term *uprising* is used to describe the events during both chronological periods. The 1936–39 uprising has been variously described by historians as a "revolt" and "rebellion." The term *intifada*, meaning shudder or tremor, comes from the Arabic verb meaning "to be shaken off."

3. Adapted, revised, and expanded from Kenneth W. Stein, "1938, 50 Years On," *Jerusalem Post*, January 27, 1988, p. 5.

4. Remarks by Jemal Husseini, member of the Palestinian Arab delegation, third meeting of the St. James Palace (London) Conference, March 6, 1939, Central Zionist Archives (hereafter CZA), Jerusalem, Record Group S25/File 7638, and remarks by Feisal Husseini, *al-Fajr* (Jerusalem), April 20, 1989.

5. Remarks by Chaim Weizmann, later Israel's first president, in note of an interview with British prime minister Neville Chamberlain, February 16, 1939, CZA, S25/7642.

6. For excellent general descriptions of the 1936–39 uprising, see W. F. Abboushi, "The Road to Rebellion: Arab Palestine in the 1930s," *Journal of Palestine Studies* (Spring 1977): 23–46; Yehuda Bauer, "The Arab Revolt of 1936," Part I, *New Outlook* (July/August 1966): 49–57, and Part II, *New Outlook* (September 1966): 21–28; Tom Bowden, "The Politics of the Arab Rebellion in Palestine 1936–39," *Middle Eastern Studies* (May 1975): 147–74; Ghasan Kanafani, "Thawrah 1936–39 fi Filastin" (The 1936–39 Revolt in Palestine), *Shu'un Filastiniyah* (1972): 45–77; Zvi El-Peleg "The 1936–1939 Disturbances: Riot or Rebellion," *Wiener Library Bulletin* (1978): 40–51; Yehoshua Porath, *The Palestine Arab National Movement, 1929–1939* (London: Cass, 1972), 109–273; Subhi Yasin, *Al-Thawrah al'Arabiyah al-Kubra fi Filastin* (The Great Arab Revolt in Palestine) (Cairo: Dar al-Kitab al-'Arabi, 1967), passim.

7. For an assessment of the personal rather than "nationalistic" opposition to Israel present in the minds of many Palestinians prior to the outbreak of the Intifada, see Emile A. Nakhleh, "The West Bank and Gaza: Twenty Years Later," *Middle East Journal* (Spring 1988): 209–26. For an assessment of the Palestinian *fellaheen*'s declining economic condition and its relationship to the 1936–39 Palestinian uprising, see Kenneth W. Stein, "Peasant Destitution and Rural Change: Contributing Causes to the 1936–39 Arab Disturbances in Palestine," in *Peasants and Politics in the Modern Middle East*, ed. John Waterbury and Farhad Kazemi (Miami: Florida International University Press, 1991).

8. Nels Johnson, *Islam and the Politics of Meaning in Palestinian Nationalism* (London: Kegan Paul International, 1982), pp. 35–36.

9. Philip Mattar, "The Mufti of Jerusalem and the Politics of Palestine," *Middle East Journal* (Summer 1988): 234.

10. Remarks by Khalid al-Hasan, Fatah Central Committee member, *al-Watan* (Kuwait), October 13, 1989, p. 20.

11. See the citations in note 6. See also Issa Khalaf, "Palestine Arab Factionalist Politics and Social Disintegration, 1939–1948," unpublished doctoral thesis, Oxford University, 1985; Salim Tamari, "What the Uprising Means," in *Intifadah: The Palestinian Uprising Against Israeli Occupation*, ed. Zachary Lockman and Joel Beinin (Middle East Research and Information Project [MERIP] 1989), pp. 132, 135.

12. Pamela Ann Smith, *Palestine and the Palestinians, 1876–1983* (New York: St. Martin's Press, 1984), pp. 62–63.

13. For examples of the frequency and growing intensity of Israeli and Palestinian Arab intercommunal unrest in the West Bank, Gaza Strip, and East Jerusalem area, see the chronology section, "Arab-Israeli Conflict," *Middle East Journal* 41–42 (1987–88).

14. John Marlowe, *Rebellion in Palestine* (London, 1946) p. 169; Bowden, "The Politics of the Arab Rebellion in Palestine, 1936–39," pp. 173–74; Zvi El-Peleg, *Hamufti Hagadol* (The Grand Mufti) (Israel, 1989), pp. 46–58; El-Peleg, "The 1936–39 Disturbances: Riot or Rebellion," p. 43; Philip Mattar, *The Mufti of Jerusalem: Al Hajj Amin Al-Husayni and the Palestinian National Movement*, (New York: Columbia University Press, 1988), pp. 65–85.

15. Yuval Arnon-Ohanna, "The Bands in the Palestinian Arab Revolt, 1936–39: Structure and Organization," *Asian and African Studies* (1981): 234.

16. Ibid., 229–30.

17. Interview with Israeli Defense Minister Yitzhak Rabin, *Wochenpresse* (Vienna), December 15, 1989.

18. See George Antonius, *The Arab Awakening* (New York, 1963), p. 405.

19. Bowden, "The Politics of the Arab Rebellion," p. 147.

20. See Khalaf, "Palestine Arab Factionalist Politics," chaps. 4, 5, 6.

21. See for example, *The Palestinian Economy: Studies in Development Under Prolonged Occupation*, ed. George Abed (London: Institute for Palestine Studies, 1991).

22. See Nakhleh, "The West Bank and Gaza: Twenty Years Later," p. 213.

23. Yezid Sayigh, "The Intifada Continues: Legacy, Dynamics, and Challenges," *Third World Quarterly* 3 (July 1989): 20–49; interview with Mona Rishmawi and Fateh Azzam, executive and administrative directors, respectively, of *al-Haq*, Atlanta, Georgia, December 7, 1989.

24. See Theodore Swedenburg, "Memories of Revolt: The 1936–39 Rebellion and the Struggle for a Palestinian National Past," doctoral thesis, University of Texas at Austin, August 1988.

25. See Bowden, "The Politics of the Arab Rebellion," p. 169; see also High Commissioner Sir Harold MacMichael to Malcolm MacDonald, Colonial Secretary, January 2, 1939, CO 733/398/75156.

26. Interview with Mona Rishmawi and Fateh Azzam.

27. Excellent descriptions of the peasant bands in the 1936–39 uprising are provided in Arnon-Ohanna, "The Bands in the Palestinian Arab Revolt, 1936–39," pp. 229–47; and Bowden, "The Politics of the Arab Rebellion," pp. 147–74.

28. See remarks by Salah Khalaf, Fatah Central Committee member, December 8, 1989, Radio Monte Carlo, as quoted in *Foreign Broadcast Information Service Daily Report: Near East and South Asia* (hereafter *FBIS:NESA*), December 11, 1989, p. 5.

29. For examples of the notices posted during the 1936–39 uprising, see Yuval Arnon, *Fellaheem Bamered Ha'aravi Beeretz Yisrael 1936–39* (Peasants in the Arab Revolt in Eretz Yisrael 1936–39) (Tel Aviv University, 1978), pp. 176–79. For rebel band commanders' documents and their detailed analyses, see Ezra Danin and Ya'acov Shimoni, *Te'udot Vedemuyot Meginzay Haknufiyot Ha'araviyot BeMeora'ot 1936–39* (Documents and Portraits from the Records of the Arab Bands in the Revolt of 1936–39) (Jerusalem: Magnes Press, 1981). For an analytical summary of the calls issued during the first year of the Intifada by the Unified National Leadership of the Uprising, see Karen Schneiderman, "The Calls of the Palestinian Uprising," *Emory Journal of International Affairs* (Spring 1989): 31–38; and Shaul Mishal, "Paper War-Words Behind Stones: The Intifada Leaflets," *Jerusalem Quarterly* (Summer 1989): 71–94. The first twenty-nine calls were republished in Lockman and Beinin, *Intifadah*, pp. 327–99.

30. See Johnson, *Islam and Palestinian Nationalism*, pp. 42–44; see also Shai Lachman, "Arab Rebellion and Terrorism in Palestine, 1929–39, The Case of Sheikh Izz al-Din al-Qassam and his Movement," in *Zionism and Arabism in Palestine and Israel*, ed. Elie Kedourie and Sylvia Haim (London: Cass, 1982), pp. 52–99.

31. Uri M. Kupferschmidt, *The Supreme Muslim Council: Islam Under the British Mandate for Palestine* (Leiden: E. J. Brill, 1987), pp. 240–54.

32. Johnson, *Islam and Palestinian Nationalism*, p. 45.

33. For a sampling of the numerous articles focusing on the Islamic components present and developing during the Intifada, see Elie Rekhess, "The Arabs in Israel and the Intifada," in this volume and his article, "The Rise of the Palestinian Islamic Jihad," *Jerusalem Post*, October 21, 1987; see also Robert Satloff, "Islam in the Palestinian Uprising," *Orbis* (Summer 1989): 389–401; interview with Sheikh Khalil Quqa, Gazan lead-

er of the Islamic Resistance Movement (HAMAS), in *an-Anba'* (Kuwait), October 8, 1988; and Oren Cohen, "This Is Hamas," *Hadashot*, October 7, 1988, pp. 24–25.

34. Satloff, "Islam in the Palestinian Uprising," pp. 394–96.

35. See remarks by Salah Khalaf, *al-Anba'* (Kuwait), December 4, 1989.

36. See Swedenburg, "Memories of Revolt," pp. 160–72.

37. *Ha'olam Hazeh*, October 25, 1989.

38. See Salim Tamari, "The Palestinian Movement in Transition," in *Intifada: Regional Implications and Repercussions of the Palestinian Uprising*, ed. Rex Brynen (Washington, D.C.: Institute for Palestine Studies, 1991).

39. Remarks by PLO Executive Committee member Mahmud 'Abbas, *Al-Quds al-'Arabi* (London), October 14–15, 1989. For an excellent analysis of what changes the Intifada and associated events brought to the PLO, see Adam Garfinkle, "Plus Ca Change . . . in the Middle East," *World Affairs* (Summer 1988): 3–15.

40. Remarks by Khalid al-Fahum, *al-Anba* (Kuwait), August 10, 1989.

41. Remarks by Salah Khalaf, *Ukaz* (Jeddah), November 16, 1989, as quoted in *FBIS:NESA*, November 27, 1989, p. 5.

42. See Palestinian document on elections of May 1, 1989, in *al-Fajr* (Jerusalem), May 1, 1989.

43. See remarks by Salah Khalaf, *al-Watan* (Kuwait), December 15, 1989; see also *Voice of the Mountain* (Lebanon), June 9, 1989, as quoted in *FBIS:NES*, June 13, 1989, p. 4. It reported that "several factors can be adduced why the revolution of 1936 was aborted, but the most important of these was the fact that the Palestinian leaders of the time accepted the advice of the Arab regimes."

44. Elie Kedourie, "The Bludan Congress on Palestine," *Middle Eastern Studies* (January 1981): 107–25; Philip Khoury, *Syria and the French Mandate: The Politics of Arab Nationalism* (Princeton: Princeton University Press, 1987), p. 555; and Yehoshua Porath, *In Search of Arab Unity 1930–45* (London: Cass, 1986), pp. 168–70.

45. See Khoury, *Syria and the French Mandate*, pp. 535–62; see also Gabriel Sheffer, "The Involvement of Arab States in the Palestine Conflict and British-Arab Relationship before World War II," *Asian and African Studies* 10 (1974): 59–78; and Gabriel Sheffer, " 'Arav Hasa'udit Vebe'ayot Eretz Yisrael Bitekufat Hamered Ha'aravi, 1936–1939" (Saudi Arabia and the Palestine Problem, 1936–1939), *Hamizrah Hehadash* 22 (1972): 137–51.

46. See remarks by Yasser Arafat, *Al-Hawadith* (London), November 24, 1989, pp. 20–22.

47. Remarks by Khalid al-Hasan, Fatah Central Committee member, *al-Watan* (Kuwait), October 13, 1989, p. 20.

48. On the difference between the PLO leadership and the leadership/participants of the Intifada, Salah Khalaf said, "I admit that the generation of Intifada is entirely different from the generation of the PLO leadership. In other words, it is different from my generation. It is even better and more efficient than we are. Yet, this Intifada is our child. I am very proud of this child because it is better than its parents." *Der Spiegel*, August 29, 1988, pp. 131–36.

The Intifada in the Context of Armed Struggle

2

Bard E. O'Neill

The Intifada (uprising) that began in the Gaza Strip and West Bank in December 1987 ushered in a new—and perhaps the most important—phase in the Palestinian resistance.[1] It came at a time when the Palestine Liberation Organization's (PLO) armed struggle had reached its lowest point and its political image and influence were in decline both regionally and internationally. Whether the Intifada will prove to be a historic turning point in the Israeli-PLO conflict, or eventually subside and become another sad chapter in the history of the Palestinian resistance, remains to be seen.

While few believe that the Intifada alone can compel Israel to accept Palestinian self-determination and an independent state, some, like Ziad Abu Amr of Bir Zeit University in the West Bank, think that the Intifada may have created conditions that will make renewed armed struggle a feasible option if material means and clear political leadership can be provided.[2] These, of course, are two big "ifs" that raise the central issue I will address in this chapter, namely the requirements for a successful armed struggle in the Palestinian case and the Intifada's contributions to a satisfaction of those requirements.

I will use the following generally accepted criteria for analyzing insurgencies for my summary analysis of the Palestinian resistance from 1964 to 1987: the environment, popular support, organization, unity, external support, and government response.[3] The factors are interrelated and their varying importance in particular cases is closely tied to the goals and strategy adopted by insurgent leaders.

By looking at the Palestinian resistance with explicit criteria in mind, we can be more specific about the strengths and deficiencies of the Palestinian armed struggle prior to the Intifada. The deficiencies are crucial because they suggest what was not done in the past and thus needs to be done in the future if armed struggle is to be a viable option for the PLO.

Armed Struggle, 1964–1973

From the creation of Israel until the mid-1960s the Palestinian situation was marked by despair and the absence of effective leadership. In the 1960s two major organizations emerged—the PLO and Fatah—that sought to rectify this situation by liberating all of Palestine through a war of liberation. The PLO was established at an Arab summit conference in 1964 as the official voice of the Palestinian people and shortly thereafter organized a conventional military component, the Palestine Liberation Army (PLA). Both the PLO and the PLA were centered in the Egyptian-controlled Gaza Strip and kept on a tight leash by Cairo. Fatah, which was formed in the late 1950s, was committed to guerrilla warfare. While Fatah's small size and lack of support from the Arab states (except Syria, which carefully controlled its activities inside Syrian borders) limited its operations, some of its attacks did exacerbate tensions between the Arab states and Israel. In a larger sense, however, neither Fatah nor the PLO was a serious part of the regional strategic equation prior to the 1967 war. The war, of course, changed all of this. It was a catastrophe for Egypt, Syria, and Jordan, whose armies were left in defeat and disarray.

The magnitude of the defeat suffered by the Arab armies led Palestinian leaders to question the feasibility of conventional combat against Israeli forces. The thought of a regular armed confrontation with an enemy whose relative military strength had increased substantially as a result of the war seemed ludicrous. Minimally, such a course of action would require many years of preparation, years that the new, more militant *fedayeen* leaders* believed they could ill afford to lose. Moreover, the Palestinians, along with many Arabs outside the resistance movement, felt a strong psychological compulsion to redeem their wounded honor and dignity. In a military-psychological setting such as this, the call for an active and immediate armed struggle relying on popular support and using unconventional techniques (a so-called people's war) became an increasingly attractive strategic approach to many Arabs.

The attractiveness of a people's war was further increased by the spatial and demographic changes affecting the area controlled by Israel. Before the war, the idea of conducting a people's war in Israel, relying on some 300,000 Arabs living amid 2.5 million Jews, seemed absurd. When the war ended, however, some 1 million Arabs found themselves under Israeli control; the potential area of operations had expanded to include the occupied territories as well as Israel. Consequently, a number of Arabs concluded that armed struggle, in the form of guerrilla warfare and terrorism, had become a more plausible course of action.†

The Strategic Goal of the Palestinian Resistance

Taking advantage of the new developments, the *fedayeen* quickly began to carry out guerrilla and terrorist attacks and to organize for a protracted struggle against Israel. As part of this effort, the Palestine National Council (PNC) adopted a Palestinian National Charter in July 1968, which formally codified the ultimate aim of the movement as the total liberation of Palestine from Zionist con-

---

*The term *fedayeen*, derived from the Arabic word *feda* or sacrifice, means "men of sacrifice." It is used to refer to all Palestinian insurgents, regardless of their organizational affiliation.

†The Arabs, of course, did not designate any of their actions as "terrorism." Instead they preferred terms like "armed struggle," "military actions," and so on. Since such terms do not discriminate among forms of violence, they have limited utility for analysis. For my purposes, guerrilla warfare involves hit-and-run attacks against the military and police, usually in rural areas. Terrorism refers to small-scale violence against noncombatants, primarily civilians.

trol.⁴ It was clear that the Palestinian aim was tantamount to the destruction of the existing political-social-economic system of the Jewish state. As a Fatah pamphlet put it:

> The liberation action is not only the removal of an armed imperialist base, but, more important—it is the destruction of a society. [Our] armed violence will be expressed in many ways. In addition to the destruction of the military force of the Zionist occupying state, it will also be turned towards the destruction of the means of life of Zionist society in all their forms—industrial, agricultural and financial. The armed violence must seek to destroy the military, political, economic, financial and ideological institutions of the Zionist occupying State, so as to prevent all possibility of the growth of a new Zionist society. The aim of the Palestine liberation war is not only to inflict a military defeat but also to destroy the Zionist character of the occupied land, whether it is human or social.⁵

Since the *fedayeen* considered the attitude of the international community to be important in the liberation struggle against Israel, they made a concentrated attempt to transform their pre-1967 public image as a group that merely wished to "throw the Jews into the sea" into one that wished to establish a "secular, democratic, non-sectarian" state in Palestine.

The Strategy of Protracted Popular War

The new phraseology of the Palestinians was viewed by Israel as nothing more than a public-relations gimmick. Aware that the Israelis were more determined than ever to confront them, Palestinian leaders needed a strategy that would overcome Israel's enhanced military superiority. Consistent with prewar thinking, they concluded that the struggle would have to be a protracted one that relied on guerrilla warfare, terrorism, and the mobilization of popular support through political activities.⁶ Inspiration was provided by the Chinese, Algerian, Vietnamese, and Cuban successes (which were studied carefully).

The assumption that the conflict would be a long one in which popular support would be essential inclined most Palestinian leaders toward the protracted popular war strategy set forth by Mao Tse-tung and modified by others, such as the Algerians and Vietnamese.[7] Basically, this approach calls for gradually escalating violence, principally guerrilla warfare, to wear down the enemy. Such violence must be *preceded* by the careful organization of popular support. The eventual introduction of violent acts does not mean an end to political activities. To the contrary, they must be accompanied by the extension of organizational efforts into new areas to gain new supporters. Tight control by a highly centralized elite is necessary to provide cohesion and coordination. Secure bases in well-concealed areas are also crucial throughout the struggle.

The protracted popular war strategy is very demanding. It involves the performance and coordination of myriad political and military actions and thus places a premium on patient political organization, particularly early in the struggle. Since patience does not come easily to men who feel they must act, quiet political activity was difficult for the Palestinian leaders to accept in the wake of the 1967 war. Accordingly, a number of groups, such as Fatah, initiated violence without solid organizational preparation, even though their rhetoric suggested a commitment to the protracted popular war approach.

Fatah's emphasis on violent resistance was, in part, due to the attractiveness of the alternative guerrilla focus strategy popularized by the Cuban revolution. The guerrilla focus strategy differed sharply from the popular war strategy in that it downplayed the need for substantial political organization prior to hostilities.[8] Instead, it was assumed that repression and poor socioeconomic conditions provided sufficient conditions for guerrilla warfare. As guerrilla warfare increased, the guerrillas would create a political organization. Besides being action oriented, this approach was also attractive to Fatah because it might avoid political conflicts and machinations among various Palestinian political factions. The Popular Front for the Liberation of Palestine-General Command (PFLP-GC), which came on the scene in 1969, was even more committed than Fatah to the guerrilla focus strategy. Conversely, the

Popular Front for the Liberation of Palestine (PFLP) and the Popular Democratic Front for the Liberation of Palestine (PDFLP) subscribed to the popular war strategy.

The strategic assessment of the PFLP and PDFLP was more realistic in light of conditions in the area, mainly because a critical element in the Cuban strategic calculus was missing, namely, a weak opponent that was likely to capitulate rather quickly. Since Israel was just the opposite, events soon reinforced the original assumptions that the conflict would be a long one and that success would depend on popular mobilization. As circumstances moved Fatah back toward the popular war strategy, the requisites for successful implementation of that strategy became important. To understand Palestinian successes and problems within the context of the popular war strategy, we must now return to the evaluative criteria introduced earlier, starting with the environment.

The Environment

The environment has two dimensions, human and physical. When assessing the human environment, we must look at social groups and their relationships, the political system, economic trends and distribution, and societal values and structures, and then ask ourselves what impact they have on the insurgency.

In the period after the 1967 war, the human environment was moderately conducive to armed struggle. The majority of people in the West Bank and Gaza Strip were Arabs (mostly Moslem), who resented subjugation to Jewish military rule under which they were expected to be quiescent subjects. Moreover, tens of thousands who had fled Israel in 1948 were in refugee camps, where living conditions were marginal at best. While these political and economic conditions contained the seeds of potential popular support, there were limitations inherent in other elements of the human milieu. The fractious nature of Palestinian society, with its segmentary structure of competing families and clans, plus residual political loyalties to the Hashemite regime in Jordan on the part of some local elites (rooted in patron-client relationships), impeded insurgent efforts to mobilize the people behind their cause. Moreover, Jordanian political and economic discrimination against West

Bank Palestinians prior to the war provided an opportunity for Israel to make *relative* improvements, especially in the economic area, which might contribute to stability in the short term. In short, while the human environment contained some aspects generally favorable to an insurrection, it was not ideal.

The physical environment was far worse. Previously successful protracted popular wars elsewhere had been waged in large countries where there was rough topography with adequate vegetation, and where the road, transportation, and communications systems were marginal to poor. This meant that insurgents could set up bases in secure hinterland areas that were difficult to penetrate. Moreover, the absence of good roads and communications hampered the mobility of government forces, which was essential for denying the insurgents the initiative. In sharp contrast to these conditions, the physical environment in Palestine was highly unsuitable for protracted popular war since the area was small and open, and the road and communications systems were excellent in Israel and good in the territories. Where deficiencies existed, Israel quickly rectified them by building roads. The major effect of this situation was that the *fedayeen* could not set up bases in the rural areas of the West Bank. Even moderate concentrations of fighters or supplies were easy to spot and destroy.[9] The Gaza Strip, with its heavily concentrated and urbanized population, was out of the question as far as guerrilla bases were concerned. Under these circumstances, the key form of violence in the protracted popular warfare strategy, guerrilla warfare, could never amount to anything more than minute, intermittent hit-and-run attacks. In the final analysis, the poor physical environment was a major impediment to the protracted popular war waged by the *fedayeen*.

Organization

While there was nothing the Palestinians could do about the physical environment, they did have an opportunity to take advantage of the potential for support among Palestinians in Israel, the territories, and adjacent Arab states. To do so it was necessary to gradually establish and expand organizational structures, in effect creating a shadow government. As things turned out, their efforts mixed success and failure. Success came in the form of a centralized PLO apparatus that by 1969 contained most insurgent groups, with Fatah as the largest and its leader, Yasser Arafat, as chairman. Despite its divisiveness, the PLO created a quasi-government structure, which performed familiar tasks in the areas of internal security, military operations, information, finance, foreign relations, and so on. This achievement was an important ingredient in the PLO's success in acquiring international support over the years. It also made it easier to establish control in refugee camps in Jordan and Lebanon. But although this meant more recruits and base areas in the short term, it led to conflicts with host governments over the longer term. In Jordan, the state within a state created by the shadow governments of the camps was an intolerable affront to Jordanian sovereignty and contributed to a civil war and expulsion of the fedayeen in 1970–71. The subsequent consolidation of the PLO in Lebanon, especially in the south (which the PLO controlled), resulted in renewed hostilities with the Lebanese, principally the Maronites and the Shiites. The problems in Lebanon and Jordan were directly related to the PLO's failure to establish a shadow government in the West Bank and Gaza (to say nothing of Arab communities inside Israel). To understand the significance of this departure from the protracted popular war strategy, one need only imagine what the fate of Mao or Ho Chi Minh would have been without the extensive shadow governments they set up *inside* China and Vietnam.

Whether the PLO could ever have established an internal shadow government is, of course, open to question, given the impressive capability of Israel's intelligence and security services. What we do know is that early organizational efforts in 1968 were as much, if not more, oriented toward violence, rather than political control and that by 1971 Israel had reduced the organizational threat to one of small terrorist cells in the West Bank and Gaza Strip. Subsequent Palestinian attempts to create larger political structures inside the territories, such as the National Guidance Council (which the Israelis banned in 1982), did not amount to much and bore little resemblance to the sophisticated organization called for by the popular war strategy.[10]

Unity

The chronic disunity of the Palestinian resistance, which was caused by personal rivalries and clashes over ideology, strategy, and policies, was another sharp departure from the popular war strategy. Moreover, it was worsened by the injection of conflicts among Arab states into the resistance. Among the many negative effects of disunity were the loss of men and resources because of internecine fighting, contradictory actions (such as violent acts by one group designed to undercut another's diplomatic moves), the provocation of Arab governments (e.g., the challenge to Arab regimes such as Jordan's by the PFLP and PDFLP), and lax security rooted in competition for recruits (which facilitated penetration by Israeli agents). Looking back, the adverse impact of disunity on the ability to organize popular support and acquire strong external support was one of the biggest problems the resistance encountered.[11]

Popular Support

Active support from the people is absolutely crucial if protracted popular war strategy is to succeed. Basically, active support involves a willingness to sacrifice life and limb by aiding insurgents (e.g., providing concealment, food, information, and so on). Palestinian insurgents did in fact receive active support; but it essentially came from the refugee camps in Jordan and Lebanon. The modicum of active backing they enjoyed in the territories after the June war dissipated, first in the West Bank and then in Gaza. The population's apathy and retreat into sullen resentment of the military government in the early 1970s resulted from several interrelated factors—relative socioeconomic improvements, a drop in the popularity of Palestinian leaders, the efficiency of Israeli security services, and the allegiance of a number of notables and their followers to King Hussein rather than to PLO leaders.

Although there was a lack of active support for violence, the PLO did retain and eventually increase passive support as shown by the 1976 victories of known PLO candidates in municipal elections. While such support was of little help with respect to armed struggle, it would prove to be significant by the time the Intifada started.[12]

External Support

The grave weaknesses of the PLO in the areas of popular support, organization, and cohesion, as well as the strength of the Israeli security establishment, made external support more important than it normally is in the popular war strategic scheme. Unhappily for the Palestinians, the situation here was also rather gloomy. Although *moral* (verbal) support was generously given by the Arab states, China, and the Soviet Union, several Arab states and the Soviet Union were either ambivalent or refused active support of the *political* goal of the Palestinians (i.e., eliminating the state of Israel). Although there were various reasons for the lack of support from the Arab states, undoubtedly the most important was incompatible political aims. For example, since both Syria and Jordan wished to exercise hegemony, if not control, over all or part of Palestine, they hardly welcomed the idea of a Palestinian state ruled by an independent PLO. Egypt's president, Gamal Abdel Nasser, was no more enthusiastic than his Syrian and Jordanian counterparts, albeit for somewhat different reasons. With his carefully nurtured image as the preeminent Arab leader tarnished by the 1967 debacle, he saw the rise of Arafat as a new Arab hero as a clear threat. The Egyptians and Jordanians also saw little hope that the PLO's strategy would succeed.

Since the PLO did not have the capability to generate adequate *material* supplies—particularly weapons and ammunition—from within and could not rely on capturing appreciable amounts from the Israeli military forces, it turned to outside donors. In this search there was some initial success, with assistance in the form of finances, arms, and munitions coming directly from several Arab states, indirectly from the USSR, and directly but clandestinely from China. Yet, in spite of these external contributions, Arafat complained in 1970 that the PLO lacked adequate weapons stocks, and in 1971 the supplies that the fedayeen did have were depleted by confiscations by Jordan. At the same time, the financial contributions to the PLO began to lag. With conflicts between several donor states and the fedayeen as a backdrop, the impotence and confusion that marked the movement after September 1971 may have led some donors to decide that investment in a lost cause would not yield many political dividends. In any event, the material support that had been fairly solid in 1968–69 had weakened seriously by 1971.

In light of the inability of the insurgents to establish a popular base in the target area (i.e., Israel and the territories), the need for *sanctuary* and freedom of movement in the states contiguous to the target area became essential. Unfortunately for the Palestinians, a number of factors prompted these states to restrict or, as in the case of Jordan, to terminate fedayeen activity within their boundaries. Syrian and Jordanian success in severely restricting or eliminating PLO influence within their borders was not matched by the Lebanese because the latter's government lacked sufficient capability and because various Lebanese groups, such as the Druze, became allies of the PLO. The positive result for the PLO was a sanctuary in Lebanon, especially the south. The negative result was entanglement in Lebanon's civil strife. Israel, of course, was hardly a willing bystander. It carried out air, ground, and commando attacks against Palestinian bases across the border.[13] These actions were part of its larger counterinsurgency policy.

The Government Response

The Israeli response to the threats posed by the PLO, particularly during the height of its armed struggle in the 1968–71 period, was based on a combination of administrative, economic, and military actions. I will address these in more detail than the previous factors because of important changes that took place prior to and during the Intifada.

As soon as the military government had been set up in the territories, it faced a campaign of civil disobedience and terrorist incidents. In response, the Israelis moved to eliminate the nascent insurgent organization through effective security and intelligence operations and to counterorganize the population. The counterorganization efforts sought not to encourage the people to identify with the State of Israel but to restore normal life patterns and increase the people's stake in tranquility by improving their material well-being.

Although the military government was in charge of administration of the occupied territories, provision was made at both central and local levels for civil-military coordination. To restore essential services and, at the same time, to avoid both unnecessary friction with the local population and imposition of a manpower burden on Israel, administration was left largely to the Arab population, a decision that proved to be very successful, particularly on the West Bank.

On the security level, the treatment of the Arab populace was a blend of liberalism toward those who wished to pursue life as normal and firmness toward those who joined or supported the *fedayeen*. Within the occupied areas the Israelis used a number of punitive measures to establish order and security and to isolate the insurgents from the people. Those found guilty of security offenses were given stiff sentences, and there was no tendency to release prisoners on pardons, even in the face of blackmail (e.g., the September 1970 hijacking to Jordan). There were few experienced observers in the Middle East who denied that, with the partial exception of Gaza, Israel had been able to thwart insurgent attempts to galvanize active popular support for resistance within Palestine. Few, also, denied that the effectiveness of the Israeli intelligence and security apparatus, economic policy, and liberal administration policy were major factors in Israel's success.

Israel's response to internal terrorism was not without problems, however. One was spontaneous violence by irate Jewish civilians against innocent Arabs in reaction to Palestinian acts of terror. Typifying such violence was a response by Jewish citizens after an explosion in a Tel Aviv bus station on September 4, 1968, which killed one and wounded fifty-one. In retaliation, a Jewish mob attacked Arabs in the terminal, beating eight severely, and turned on Arabs arriving in buses, none of whom was among the suspects in the incident. The following day, one of Israel's most respected newspapers, *Ha'aretz*, called attention to the counterproductive nature of such behavior when it said that the perpetrators "must be considered active, unwilling allies of the Arab terrorists." Recognizing the validity of this point and concerned that such violence could lead victims to support the Palestinian resistance, the Israeli government undertook an intensive education drive to prevent recurrences. In addition, government leaders visited Arab representatives in an effort to convince them that such actions did not reflect official policy or attitudes. The crackdown on illegal reprisals extended to the security establishment. In November, two frontier policemen were sentenced to life imprisonment for murdering two local Arabs, and three months later it was announced that an Israeli captain would be tried for killing an Arab woman and wounding several others. As a consequence of the attention and effort devoted to the violent reprisals, such behavior decreased and became an exceptional rather than a normal phenomenon, until the hardline Likud came to power in 1977 and ushered in an era of regressive counterinsurgency policies. These, among other things, involved a less discriminant use of force and more collective punishments which, in turn, increased Palestinian resentment and thus contributed to the Intifada in 1987.

While the Israelis were taking action against terrorism within Israel and occupied areas, they were also faced with guerrilla-type raids from across their borders. Although the infiltrators were at a disadvantage because they had no popular bases in the occupied areas, the casualties they inflicted and their eventual objective of getting a foothold on the West Bank could not be ignored. Israel responded with a blend of constant patrolling, security barriers, good intelligence, air strikes, and search-and-destroy operations to increase guerrilla losses and to reduce successfully the infiltration problem to a negligible threat by 1971.

Aside from the direct material and human losses inflicted on the fedayeen, Israeli cross-border attacks also had the long-term effect of contributing to Lebanese and Jordanian efforts to control the Palestinian guerrillas. If the damage inflicted by Israeli reprisals was to be avoided, insurgent attacks along the borders had to be restricted.

In the final analysis, Israel was able to fashion and implement a sound response to the Palestinian armed struggle in the late 1960s and early 1970s. Economic conditions and social services, particularly in the West Bank, were better than under Jordanian rule, guerrilla attacks were all but eliminated, and internal terrorism became episodic. Sensational actions of terrorism abroad (transnational terrorism) bore witness to the serious regression of the armed struggle in Israel and the occupied territories.[14]

From Armed Struggle to the Intifada, 1974–1987

The regression of the armed struggle led to a strategic reassessment inside the PLO that resulted in a 1974 decision to concentrate on the establishment of a Palestinian state in the West Bank and Gaza Strip, while leaving the question of Israel's ultimate status somewhat ambiguous. Moreover, greater emphasis was to be be placed on diplomacy as a means to accomplish this aim. Although armed struggle was not disavowed, its decreasing effectiveness reduced its importance, periodic terrorist attacks inside Israel and outside the Middle East notwithstanding.

Many of the transnational acts of terrorism were carried out by maverick groups that violently rejected the new PLO pragmatism, like Abu Nidal's Fatah–the Revolution Council (FRC) and the PFLP–GC. Frequently, the targets were pragmatic Palestinians (e.g., Issam Sartawi) who were Fatah representatives or officials. Arafat himself was sentenced to death by the FRC. But opposition to Arafat was not confined to the most extreme groups. The PFLP, the Popular Struggle Front, the Palestine Liberation Front, together with the PFLP–GC, formed what they called a "rejectionist front," which opposed any settlement with Israel for fear that it would end the revolutionary process and prevent the establishment of an Arab state in all of Palestine.[15] Since Syria also objected to the new PLO policies (in part, because its concern that a peace settlement would leave it without allies in its quest to reacquire the Golan Heights), it supported the rejectionists.

The differences among the Palestinian groups and with Syria were reflected in internecine warfare and terrorist attacks inside Israel and abroad. Violent assaults on civilians in Israel and abroad were designed to undercut the peace process by increasing tensions, provoking indiscriminate Israeli reprisals, and discrediting the PLO internationally. Rejectionist efforts to undermine the peace process were facilitated by the 1977 electoral victory of the right-wing Likud party in Israel.

Aside from opposing any dealings with the PLO, the Likud rejected the Labor party's willingness to trade land for peace. Instead, Likud took the position that all of the West Bank and Gaza rightfully belonged to Israel. To underscore its hard-line stance, Likud undertook a major effort to expand (and later "thicken") settlements. Likud spokesmen made it clear that "not one inch" of the Land of Israel would be yielded in any negotiations with the Arabs.* The peace accord with Egypt in 1979 did nothing to change this (the Sinai was not considered part of the Land of Israel).

The agreement with Egypt produced a loose temporary alliance against Egypt among the Palestinian groups and the Arab states (except Oman, Somalia, and the Sudan) called the Front of Steadfastness and Confrontation. The front never amounted to much because of internal disagreements involving Arab states (e.g., Syria and Iraq) and continuing discord between pragmatists and rejectionists inside the PLO.

As the 1980s began, the PLO found itself excluded from the peace process, militarily impotent, caught up in internal conflicts, and entangled in the Lebanese civil war. Under these circumstances it was not surprising that the PLO agreed to a cease-fire with Israel on the Lebanese border. What was surprising, however, was the PLO's gradual buildup of conventional arms (tanks, artillery, mortars, etc.) in southern Lebanon in the early 1980s. Since the nature and amounts of the PLO's conventional arms would be of little value against the Israel Defense Force (IDF), and since they were inconsistent with a protracted popular war strategy, they were of marginal utility, save perhaps boosting morale. What the conventional buildup did do was attract Israel's attention and set the stage for the 1982 war in Lebanon.

Everyone in the Israeli defense establishment was concerned about the potential damage that the PLO's conventional weaponry might inflict on the civilian population of northern Israel. In fact, similar concerns had resulted in periodic IDF raids, air strikes, and incursions into Lebanon in the past, the most notable being a major search and destroy effort called Operation Litani in 1978. The difference between these actions and the 1982 invasion was

*See the chapter by Nathan Yanai in this volume, "The Impact of the Intifada on the Likud Party within the Framework of Israeli Politics, 1987–1990," for a detailed analysis of the Likud position on the occupied territories.

that in 1982 the objective went beyond security (eliminating the PLO military presence in the south) to include more ambitious political aims. Foremost was the Likud government's ideological goal of retaining the West Bank. The principal architect of the invasion, Defense Minister Ariel Sharon, believed that the destruction of the PLO's military and political infrastructure would eviscerate its influence in the West Bank and thereby facilitate Israel's plan to spread settlements and consolidate control there. Sharon and his supporters further believed that the turbulent situation in Lebanon could be stabilized by reducing, if not eliminating, Syrian influence and by backing the emergence of a strong Maronite Christian president, Bashir Gemayel.

When the fog of war finally cleared, Israel found itself in an unenviable position. Although the IDF had moved to the outskirts of Beirut in a matter of days, it had engaged in some costly battles with Syrian ground forces, which many analysts felt could have been avoided if it had limited itself to the initial aim of securing southern Lebanon to a point forty kilometers north. Moreover, as the rapid movement of Israeli forces gave way to a prolonged siege of Beirut, the IDF opted for heavy artillery and air bombardments of PLO areas of the city in order to avoid the casualties that would be entailed by house-to-house combat in an urban labyrinth—a decision that, not surprisingly, generated both international and domestic criticism. To make matters worse, following an evacuation of PLO fighters from Beirut, Israel's Maronite allies entered the Palestinian refugee camps of Sabra and Shatilla in mid-September and proceeded to slaughter civilians. The IDF was blamed because it had allowed the Maronites access to the area, and in February 1983 a commission of inquiry recommended the dismissal of several officers, as well as the defense minister.

For over two years after these events, the IDF remained bogged down in southern Lebanon and managed to alienate most sectors of the Lebanese population. As casualties increased from guerrilla and terrorist attacks carried out by various Lebanese groups, especially the most extreme Shiites in Hezbollah, public and military morale in Israel eroded noticeably. Dispirited by the experience in Lebanon and the death of his wife, Prime Minister Menachem Begin resigned in August 1983. But it was not until new elections were held and a coalition government led by the Labor party's Shimon Peres was formed a year later that Israel withdrew its forces to a narrow security strip along the border.[16]

In retrospect, the political tally sheet of the 1982 war for Israel was hardly impressive. Although the PLO's military and political apparatus in the south was destroyed and the organization was once again engulfed in both internecine and inter-Arab conflicts, Arafat continued as a political force in the area and the PLO's influence in the West Bank was not expunged. Furthermore, the alliance with the Maronites backfired, as Bashir Gemayal was assassinated and succeeded by his brother, Amin, who not only distanced himself from Israel but also proved incapable of keeping order among the Maronites, to say nothing of Lebanon as a whole. Finally, Syria gradually reestablished its presence and influence in Lebanon.

Both Israel's successes and failures in the 1982 war played a part in setting the stage for the Intifada. Israel's success in expelling PLO fighters and most of the leadership further weakened the resistance. Although Arafat was able to regroup the top political leadership in Tunisia, what remained of his military capability was unimpressive, to say the least. Moreover, he was again caught up in severe disputes with the Syrians and rejectionist Palestinians as he sought to maneuver his way into the peace process.[17] Efforts to join with Jordan in this enterprise failed because Arafat, fearful of being outflanked by hard-liners, was unwilling to accept Security Council Resolution 242 (in effect recognizing Israel). On the eve of the Intifada, the PLO's image of indecisiveness and diminished political clout was underscored at an Arab summit in Amman (November 1987), where the Palestinian issue was virtually ignored. In many observers' eyes, the floundering of the PLO was a major factor leading Palestinians in the West Bank and Gaza to take matters into their own hands.[18] Ironically, then, Israel's success in weakening the PLO actually contributed to the Intifada.

The Israelis' failure to accomplish their other aims and to stabilize their position in southern Lebanon from 1982 to 1984 also affected the West Bank and Gaza. In both areas a more defiant younger population that was among the best educated in the Arab world had emerged. Unlike their parents, the young Palestinians were less intimidated by Israel. As they watched the PLO's tenacious seventy-day resistance prior to leaving Lebanon and the costs that guerrilla and terrorist attacks by Hezbollah and other groups inflicted on the IDF in the two years after the invasion, they saw vulnerability instead of invincibility.

The failures of both the PLO and Israel did not lead to a conscious strategic decision by inhabitants of the West Bank and Gaza to start an uprising. But they did contribute to changes in a psychological setting where there was already smoldering resentment because of dramatic expansion of Jewish settlements and various forms of socioeconomic deprivation. The general passivity, dependence on the PLO, and fear of the IDF that characterized the attitudes of the Arabs of the West Bank and Gaza gave way to a spirit of activism, self-reliance, and confidence.

The Intifada began spontaneously and soon spread throughout the West Bank and Gaza Strip. Although the PLO moved to exert control over events, credit for the uprising belongs to the people of the territories. The uprising did not begin as a new phase or tactic in the framework of the protracted popular war strategy. In fact, as events unfolded and the Intifada stressed nonviolent civil disobedience, public demonstrations and the like, it looked more like what Jerrold Green has called countermobilization as opposed to insurgency. While the Intifada has involved violence, it has been limited mostly to throwing stones and Molotov cocktails. Such acts, however, are clearly secondary and in no way constitute a rejuvenation of the armed struggle.[19] Whether the broader events of the Intifada can lead to such a successful rejuvenation is another question. To answer it, we need to return to the criteria used in our earlier assessment of the armed struggle to see what changes have taken place and what their implications are.

The Intifada and the Armed Struggle: The Environment

Important aspects of the human environment have changed in ways more favorable to armed struggle. Besides growing faster than the Jews, the Arab population in the territories has become much younger, with 75 percent under age twenty-eight. The younger generation is more militant, better educated, and less compliant than the older generations. Moreover, in many places the young people, often from lower classes, have become the de facto leaders of the Intifada, thus supplanting the leadership of the traditional notables.[20] Regardless of whether this departure from the normal deference to the older members of the upper classes (that is so much a part of the patriarchal social system) is a temporary phenomenon or the harbinger of a shift in values, it contributes to the potential for violent armed struggle.

Further enhancing this potential is the economic downturn and discrimination in the territories in the 1980s, which has been exacerbated by the Intifada. In the late 1960s and 1970s, it will be recalled, the Israelis had increased the standard of living in the territories, albeit not without Arab opposition to supporting taxation. Things changed, however, when the Likud came to power and started its extensive settlement program. The socioeconomic discrimination that accompanied the ambitious settlement process—land seizures, disproportionate water restrictions on the Arabs, restrictions on Arab business, and so on—have been well documented in the reports of Meron Benvenisti's West Bank Data Project.[21] That they fueled and intensified Arab resentment is equally well-known: Economic conditions that once had mitigated grievances changed to the point where they generated grievances and discontent.

If key changes in some elements of the human environment are more conducive to armed struggle, the same cannot be said of the physical setting. Both the small size of the area and topography continue to militate against the creation of bases and the concealment of sizable armed units that are essential for protracted popular warfare. The physical environment, in a word, remains a serious permanent impediment to protracted popular warfare.

Organization

The late 1970s and the 1980s saw the growth of various autonomous Palestinian institutions in the territories. These included libraries, universities, vocational schools, newspapers, cultural centers, unions, clubs, cooperatives, popular committees, and student committees. Although their activity was restricted by the Israelis and they formally avoided violence and political programs, such institutions facilitated closer ties among inhabitants of the territories. The student committees were particularly important because, as Yezid Sayigh notes, they became the backbone of a mass movement that was present in almost every village, city, and refugee camp. Many of the cadres were former prisoners who had learned political skills in Israeli jails.[22] Such institutional development was a positive step beyond the situation in the late 1960s and early 1970s. In fact, it was the kind of political evolution one would expect in the earliest phase of an insurgency using the protracted popular war strategy.

The gradual emergence of decentralized institutions in the territories did not mean the PLO's organizational status was good on the eve of the Intifada. To the contrary, although the PLO maintained its central apparatus in Tunis, its control over the people and events in the territories was basically loose and unstructured. Although individual groups like the PFLP and PDFLP did have cells and Islamic groups had organized some followers, none of this was integrally tied to a smoothly functioning central command echelon. No small wonder then that the Intifada started spontaneously and found the PLO playing a frantic game of catch-up to impose its control over events.

A survey among several dozen Gaza Strip residents who were active in organizing the Intifada in early December 1987 revealed a surprising lack of PLO influence in the early events. The early rioters, who were mostly young inhabitants of refugee camps with little education, said their main motivation was hatred of the occupation and despair created by the harsh social and economic conditions in the camps. Most indicated ignorance of the Palestinian National Charter and existing PLO policies. Few said they listened to PLO radio broadcasts.[23]

The fact that published plans of action in the form of leaflets did not appear until January 10, 1988, over a month after the Intifada began, also suggests that the uprising was spontaneous.

Leaflets were published under the logo of the Unified National Leadership of the Uprising (UNLU), a shifting group of local leaders from Fatah, the PFLP, the PDFLP, and the Palestine Communist party (PCP). However, it was not until the third leaflet that the PLO appeared on the heading.[24] Subsequent leaflets, according to Saul Mishal, were drafted in the territories, sent to the PLO for approval, broadcast on the radio, and later distributed.[25]

Ziad Abu Amr's assessment that the leaflets represent ad hoc efforts to deal with unfolding events and are not part of a clear and planned strategy of which each leaflet is an integral part is consistent with the notion that the PLO has struggled to keep up with (and eventually get out in front of) events. This somewhat loose connection between the PLO and local activists in the territories is not all bad, however. As far as the protracted popular strategy is concerned, local autonomy, flexibility, and initiative are important, as long as they are exercised within accepted general guidelines. It is just such guidelines that the leaflets seek to provide.[26] Besides their emphasis on several general themes (e.g., self-determination, creation of a Palestinian state, the leading role of the PLO, and demand for an international conference), the UNLU/PLO leaflets provide instructions on when to work, strike, and boycott, and who can work and travel.[27] While allowing local exceptions and adaptations, the leaflets have provided a sense of direction and have met with unprecedented compliance (compared to leaflets after the 1948 and 1967 wars).[28]

Such compliance, of course, is hardly happenstance. It has been made possible by organizational activities inside the territories. The multiplicity of social organizations that had emerged prior to the Intifada continued to proliferate and played various roles. National committees at all levels served as executive agencies to insure compliance with UNLU/PLO instructions and to look after the needs of the population.[29] Strike committees (later renamed the Popular Army), an offshoot of youth/action committees, are specifically responsible for ensuring obedience.[30]

The organizational pluses notwithstanding, it would be a mistake to leave the impression that the proliferation of groups and the PLO's more decentralized relationship with them is without costs. One such cost, which had become troublesome by the end of 1989, was the excessive use of violence against collaborators by local street gangs acting in the name of the PLO or one of its groups. The PLO is aware that a good deal of the violence has little or nothing to do with collaborators and much to do with local feuds and blood debts. Aside from pleas for restraint and discipline, the PLO issued a special leaflet near the end of 1989 calling for all strike committees and youths to be joined under a single umbrella.[31]

Although, on balance, the network of old and new institutions must be viewed as a distinct improvement over past political organizations inside the territories, two major problems had to be addressed before this network could become the foundation for renewed armed struggle. First, the overall organization must be able to meet basic socioeconomic needs of the people. If, as Abu Amr suggests, this is essential for widespread civil disobedience, it will be even more true for sustaining active support for violent armed struggle.[32] When and where adequate resources for such an undertaking will come from is by no means obvious. And, even if they do become available, the Palestinians still must resolve a second (and familiar) major problem—the continued factionalism that Yezid Sayigh calls the "main weakness."[33]

Unity

Up to this point, we have concentrated on the major organizational force behind the Intifada, the UNLU/PLO, and have noted that the UNLU has representatives from major PLO factions. The unprecedented cooperative action among followers of various groups, however, does not mean that harmony and unity of purpose reign. Two divisions account for this.

The first, and probably least severe, involves differences between Fatah and the left-wing groups, especially the PFLP. Discord between Fatah and the PFLP is, of course, long-standing. While he has grudgingly accepted PLO endorsement of Arafat's more moderate policies in recent years, PFLP leader George Habash is critical of recognizing Israel, opposed to cooperation with the PFLP's old ideological enemy, Jordan, and unhappy with the amount of authority exercised by Arafat. Consequently, he has sought and received support from Arafat's enemy, Syria. Differences such as this find their way into the common UNLU/PLO leaflets, which the various groups putatively take turns drafting. Even sharper differences can be seen in the omnipresent graffiti and leaflets issued separately by particular groups. For example, leaflets have been critical of Fatah-drafted leaflet nine, which was critical of Syria. Leaflet ten, which called for Palestinian deputies in Jordan to resign, was countermanded by a second leaflet issued by Fatah.[34]

More serious is the underlying discord between the UNLU/PLO and two groups of Islamic extremists—HAMAS, the militant arm of the older Moslem Brotherhood (Islamic Resistance Movement), and Islamic Jihad.[35] While the religious groups agree with the UNLU/PLO goals of creating a Palestinian state and weakening the military government through civil disobedience, they disagree on the extent and nature of the state and the process that will lead to it. The PLO's willingness to accept a two-state solution (i.e., both Israel and a Palestinian state) is utterly rejected by the religious camp because it views all of Palestine as a religious trust (*waqf*) that Moslems must liberate from the Jews. Moreover, the religious groups also object to the PLO's notion that a Palestinian state be secular, arguing instead that it must be an Islamic state based on the Shari'ah (Islamic Law). The divergence over goals and expectations contributes to disagreements over process. Whereas the PLO is pragmatic, wants a settlement with Israel, and directs appeals to moderate elements of the Israeli public, the religious camp is dogmatic, opposed to a final settlement that guarantees Israel's existence, and castigates Israelis with demonic phrases such as "brothers of monkeys," "bloodsuckers," "murderers of the prophets," "the epitome of wickedness," and so on. The fate of the Jews in the thinking of HAMAS is clear from the following comments of one of its Gazan leaders, Sheikh Khalil Quqa: "God has assembled the Jews in Palestine not to have them enjoy it as a homeland, but to make it a graveyard for them so that the world at large will be saved from their filth. In the same manner that any Moslem pilgrim redeems himself when he offers a sacrifice in Mina, so will the Jews be slaughtered on the rock of Al-Aqsa by pure hands such as those of the pilgrims."[36]

The differences between the UNLU/PLO and the religious groups are evident in both widespread graffiti and leaflets. The religious leaflets are issued separately from the UNLU/PLO and not surprisingly are infused with Islamic themes. The vast majority are produced by HAMAS; Islamic Jihad turns out very few. HAMAS and Islamic Jihad do not coordinate such efforts. The issuance of separate leaflets has led to frictions with the UNLU/PLO over strike days. While the religious groups have carefully avoided a rupture with the PLO and there has been some tactical coordination between Fatah and Islamic Jihad, they have not ruled out a future showdown with the PLO. In fact, reported violence between the UNLU/PLO and HAMAS necessitated the creation of conciliation committees in late 1989.[37] The main concern of the UNLU/PLO has to be the possibility that the Islamic groups (especially Islamic Jihad) may escalate the violence from stone throwing and Molotov cocktails to "hot" weapons, such as rifles, grenades, and bombs. Such a development, especially if it involves a new wave of terrorism, will undermine the gains of the Intifada and the PLO's moderate appeals to groups in both Israel and the international community (as the PLO found out from its own ill-conceived attack on a bus near Beersheba in March 1988).

While a UNLU/PLO decision to return to armed struggle might narrow differences with the Islamic camp, it is unlikely to close the gap. As in the past, we can expect strategic and ideological differences, as well as a struggle to control the destiny of the Palestinians, to lead to violence. This time, however, the intramural conflict may well have a deadly religious dimension spawned by desperation and frustration.

Popular Support

If disunity portends significant future problems, it has not undercut popular support in the short term. As indicated earlier, the scope and extent of active support for the Intifada surpasses past backing for the armed struggle. It has involved all social classes and locales in the West Bank and Gaza Strip. Moreover, it has engendered more support (albeit mostly passive) from Palestinians inside Israel.[38]

While the UNLU/PLO praises the activism and sacrifices of the people in the territories, it also recognizes that activism is limited by economic reality. Since existential needs must be met, actions like strikes, boycotts of Israeli goods and working for Israelis have been modulated and adapted to local needs.[39] To push the people beyond this, without compensating them for the loss of basic necessities, could easily lead to renewed disillusionment with the PLO. This raises an obvious question, namely, whether the much greater sacrifices that are associated with armed struggle would be forthcoming if the sacrifices of the Intifada are barely tolerable. My own guess is that there would be more active support for violence than in the past because socioeconomic treatment of the Palestinians is perceived to be more unjust and indiscriminate than ever, repression has increased, and the Palestinian community is younger and more radicalized. What I do not see is the capability to escalate the violence much beyond terrorism and to sustain such violence for a long period in the face of what are sure to be harsh reprisals from Israel.

External Support

Like popular support, external support has also increased during the Intifada. In fact, it would not be hyperbole to say that the Palestinians (if not the PLO) have gained the moral high ground internationally. Global media coverage of Israel's soldiers beating and shooting protesters and stone throwers has reversed the old image of Israel as David against the Goliath of collective Arab armies. Now it is the more powerful and better-armed Israelis who appear as Goliath suppressing unarmed Palestinian demonstrators who appear in David's role. The effect has been to generate increased *political* and *moral* support for the PLO. While such support had gradually grown as a result of Arafat's emphasis on diplomacy and perceived moderation after 1974, it nonetheless entered a dormant phase before the Intifada, particularly among the Arab states. What the Intifada has done is reenergize and add to the existing political and moral support, especially following Arafat's recognition of Israel. Since this favorable development, particularly outside the Middle East, is due largely to the PLO's accentuation of diplomacy and attenuation of violence, much of it could evaporate if there was a return to armed struggle. Moreover, since most Arab states either refuse to make contributions to the PLO, or delay or partially meet financial pledges they have made, it is hard to imagine them closing ranks and providing material and sanctuary support for such an undertaking.[40] It is even possible that they would be less disposed than ever, if a renewal of armed struggle saw the Islamic extremists playing a key role, because success by the extremists might inspire violent Islamic opposition groups at home.[41] In the final analysis, my conclusion is that potential external support for renewed armed struggle is no better than in the past. And, if the past is any indicator, material and sanctuary support will be insufficient and political support inconsistent.

The Government's Response

Of all the aspects of the Intifada, it is undoubtedly the government response that is best known. Since Israel is an open society, it has been unable to prevent an avalanche of information about Israeli policies and actions, despite efforts to restrict and censor the media. Moreover, both civilian and military critics within Israel have not been bashful when it comes to their thinking about the Intifada.

Israel has relied on a combination of political, economic, and military measures to quell the Intifada. Politically, it has sought to identify West Bank and Gaza leaders who might be willing to ignore the PLO and negotiate with Israel. This effort has failed for two major reasons. First, the PLO retains strong support in the territories and has warned of (and carried out) reprisals against those suspected of independent political dealings with Israel. Second, there are no anticipated gains commensurate with the risks of separate discussion with Israel because the Likud has ruled out any territorial concessions in advance. Basically, there is a deep chasm between the Likud's aim of permanent retention of the territories and the widespread support for an independent state among inhabitants of the territories.[42]

Since Israel is unable to placate the Palestinians on the political level, it has resorted to harsh punitive measures to contain the Intifada. These have included curfews, detentions without trial, deportations, destruction of homes, mass arrests, beatings, and various forms of economic punishment. While the first four measures were used in the past with some success (i.e., in the late 1960s and early 1970s), reliance on them during the Intifada has been much greater and frequently indiscriminate. The violent excesses are well-known to all those who follow foreign affairs and have met with sharp criticism inside and outside of Israel. Growing numbers of officers and men of the IDF have been among the internal critics. Not only have they voiced concern about increased Palestinian animosity toward Israel as a result of excessive violence, but they also worry about the longer-term impact on the morale and moral fiber of the IDF and the Jewish population. Equally troubling is the increased international criticism of Israel and sympathy for the PLO. The Israelis do not have to look to the experiences of others (e.g., the British in Northern Ireland in the seventies, and the Sri Lankan and Peruvian military policies in recent years) to learn the painful lesson that violent excesses intensify hatred and create support for opponents.[43] All they have to do is recall their own past. Until the deterioration of Israeli countermeasures against the Intifada is terminated and violent overreaction is curbed, the situation in the territories is unlikely to improve—unless the PLO decides on a return to armed struggle. Should that happen, the negative fallout from Israeli behavior will be mitigated because Palestinian violence will share the limelight with Israel's.

Conclusions

Having compared the situation at the height of the armed struggle in 1968–73 with the Intifada, I am convinced that a return to armed struggle would be unwise. While the steady deterioration of economic, social, and political aspects of the environment and regressive Israeli countermeasures create greater potential for armed struggle, a return to guerrilla attacks and terrorism is risky for several reasons. First, since the physical environment is no more favorable to guerrilla attacks and setting up bases than before, the only option would be a mixture of small-scale terrorist attacks and assaults on Israeli soldiers, both of which would play into Israel's hands and lend credibility to its oft-repeated charge that the PLO is nothing more than a terrorist organization. Second, despite the wide and active support for civil disobedience, it is by no means clear that the inhabitants of the West Bank and Gaza are willing to make the sacrifices that will be called for in the face of

Israeli reprisals. As we saw, the PLO has already recognized the limits to the people's willingness to sacrifice because of economic dependence on Israel. Third, while organizational improvements have been sufficient for the Intifada, they are by no means sufficient for sustaining armed struggle. Moreover, there is no reason to believe that the disunity that has always plagued the Palestinian resistance is going to disappear and give way to the integrated strategic planning and execution that is a hallmark of successful armed struggle. To the contrary, the UNLU/PLO-religious rift could easily lead to significant strife in the future.

In the final analysis, changes in the Palestinian situation suggest an environment conducive to civil disobedience but not to a rejuvenation of armed struggle. This does not mean that frustrated PLO leaders under pressure from rivals will not decide to intensify the armed struggle. They may very well do so. But, if the past is prologue, they will again fail.

Notes

1. On the specific incident that energized the Intifada, see Dan Avidan, "What Caused the Riots in the Territories," *Davar* (Tel Aviv), January 28, 1988, in *Foreign Broadcast Information Service Daily Report, Near East-South Asia* (hereafter *FBIS:NES*), No. 88019, January 29, 1988, pp. 40–41.

2. Ziad Abu-Amr, "The Palestinian Uprising in the West Bank and Gaza Strip," *Arab Studies Quarterly*, 10, no. 4 (Fall 1988): 399.

3. Further elaboration on these factors may be found in *Insurgency in the Modern World*, ed. Bard E. O'Neill, William R. Heaton, and Donald J. Alberts (Boulder, Colo.: Westview Press, 1980).

4. See the Palestine National Charter in Leila S. Kadi, comp. and trans., *Basic Political Documents of the Armed Palestinian Resistance Movement* (Beirut: Palestine Liberation Organization Research Center, 1968), especially Articles 1, 8, 14, 15, 19, 20, 21, 22, and 23.

5. *The Liberation of the Occupied Lands and the Struggle Against Direct Imperialism* (Fatah Pamphlet, n.d.), also quoted in Michael Hudson, "The Palestinian Resistance Movement: Its Significance in the Middle East Crisis," *Middle East Journal* (Summer 1969): 299. Fedayeen statements and literature have been replete and consistent with reference to the aim of destroying Zionism. See, for instance, *Free Palestine* (September 1970): 15; editorial in *Fatah* (Beirut), November 18, 1971; interview of Abu

Ammar with Yasser Arafat in *Free Palestine* (February 1971): 1; *Arab Report and Record* (London), January 1–15, 1969, p. 19, and January 16–31, 1971, p. 78; *Daily Star* (Beirut), May 17, 1971.

Disagreement on the meaning of a "secular, democratic, nonsectarian state" has been clearly evident within fedayeen ranks, with some groups striving to give the concept a meaningful content and others choosing to use it merely as a slogan for assuaging world opinion. See, for example, the accounts of a symposium of six fedayeen organizations on the question of the democratic Palestine state entitled *The Democratic Palestinian State* (n.p., March 1970). The same account can be found in *Al-Anwar* (Beirut), March 8 and 15, 1970. See also *Free Palestine* (March 1969): 6–8; *New York Times*, September 16, 1969; *New Middle East* (April 1970): 6. For three articles critical of the concept of the democratic state as articulated by the fedayeen, see Y. Harkabi, *Three Articles on the Arab Slogan of a Democratic State*, trans. Y. Karmi (n.p., n.d.). This booklet can be obtained from the Embassy of Israel. The articles reproduced therein can also be found in *Ma'ariv* (Tel Aviv), April 3, 17, July 10, 1970.

There has been inconsistency on the question of which Jews could remain in the new Palestinian state. Although the pre-1974 position of the *fedayeen* was that any Jew renouncing Zionism could stay, there have been suggestions that only those who were there before 1917 or, alternatively, 1947, could do so. The 1917 date seemed to be implicit in Article 6 of the Palestinian National Charter since that section clearly states that only those who resided in Palestine before the "Zionist invasion" were acceptable. Since the "Zionist invasion" is generally understood to date to 1917, the conclusion is obvious. See Kadi, *Basic Political Documents*, p. 137.

6. Obviously, the PLO did not characterize its attacks on civilians as "terrorism." But that is what they were. For a discussion of terrorism see O'Neill, Heaton, and Alberts, *Insurgency in the Modern World*, pp. 4–5.

7. Although some individuals and groups within the fedayeen movement seemed more inclined toward certain revolutionary models than others, there has been an attempt to study and borrow from all of them. That the Chinese, Cuban, Algerian, and Vietnamese experiences have influenced fedayeen thinking in a substantial way is evident from their publications, interviews, and statements. Of particular importance in this regard was a two-part series of pamphlets entitled *Revolutionary Studies and Experiences* (Beirut and Amman: Fatah, 1967–70). The following pamphlets are part of the series: *The Chinese Experience, The Vietnamese Experience*, and *The Cuban Experience* in part one, and *The Vietnamese Revolution* in part two. More accessible commentaries on the influence of these models may be found in Y. Harkabi, *Fedayeen Action and*

Arab Strategy, Adelphi Papers no. 53 (London: International Institute for Strategic Studies, 1968), pp. 7–8 and 13–17; Tom Little, *The New Arab Extremists*, Conflict Studies no. 4 (London: Current Affairs Research Services Center, 1970), pp. 11–12; the interview of George Habash cited in *Arab Report and Record* (London), March 1–15, 1969, p. 112; the interviews of K. Kudsi (Fatah) in *Free Palestine* (August 1969): 6, and (September 1969): 6.

8. A discussion of the protracted popular war strategy and the military focus strategy may be found in O'Neill, Heaton, and Alberts, *Insurgency in the Modern World*, pp. 28–33. In that volume they are referred to as the Maoist and Cuban strategies.

9. The poor topographical conditions for protracted popular war, especially guerrilla warfare, are striking to anyone who, like this writer, has served in Vietnam and visited Israeli military outposts in the West Bank.

10. On the PLO organization, see Bard E. O'Neill, *Armed Struggle in Palestine* (Boulder, Colo.: Westview Press, 1978), pp. 153–56, and Cheryl A. Rubenberg, "The Civilian Infrastructure of the Palestine Liberation Organization," *Journal of Palestine Studies* (Spring 1983).

11. A detailed review of Palestine disunity and various organizational structures created in an attempt to overcome it may be found in O'Neill, *Armed Struggle in Palestine*, pp. 125–53. Its contribution to the Jordanian civil war of 1970 is discussed on pp. 165–66.

12. On the PLO problems related to gaining active support in the territories in 1969–70, see O'Neill, *Armed Struggle in Palestine*, pp. 115–19. The reason for continued active support in Gaza was largely due to the fact that most Gaza residents are 1948 refugees from Israel.

13. O'Neill, *Armed Struggle in Palestine*, pp. 163–204, 209–10.

14. For a brief summation of Israel's counterinsurgency policies, see Bard E. O'Neill, "Israeli Defense Policy," in *The Defense Policy of Nations*, ed. Douglas J. Murray and Paul R. Viotti (Baltimore: Johns Hopkins University Press, 1982), pp. 391–93.

15. On the 1974 split, see Muhammed Y. Muslih, "Moderates and Rejectionists within the Palestine Liberation Organization," *Middle East Journal* (Spring 1976).

16. On the Lebanon war, see Trevor N. Dupuy and Paul Martell, *Flawed Victory* (Fairfax, Va.: Hero Books, 1986); Ze'ev Shiff and Ehud Ya'ari, *Israel's Lebanon War* (New York: Simon and Shuster, 1984); and Shai Feldman and Heda Rechniz-Kijner, *Deception, Consensus and War: Israel in Lebanon*, Paper no. 27 (Tel Aviv: Jaffee Center for Strategic Studies, Tel Aviv University, October 1984).

17. Besides opposition from the usual grouping of rejectionists, Fatah experienced a violent split in 1983, giving rise to a new Syrian-backed

Fatah breakaway faction led by Sa'id Musa Muragha (Abu Musa). Although various complaints were made by the rebels, the key issue was Arafat's "traitorous moderation." A detailed account may be found in Adam M. Garfinkle, "Sources of the Al-Fatah Mutiny," *Orbis* (Fall 1983): 603–40.

18. Abu-Amr, "The Palestinian Uprising," pp. 386–87, described the notion of armed struggle at that time as an empty slogan.

19. The use of violence by opponents of the government distinguishes insurgencies from sociopolitical protest movements such as those led by Ghandi in India, Khomeini in Iran, and Solidarity in Poland. Those interested in systematically analyzing such movements will find Jerrold Green's use of the concept "countermobilization" in the Iran case very helpful. See his "Countermobilization as a Revolutionary Form," *Comparative Politics* (January 1984). Since the Intifada has involved conscious acts of low-level violence, it is strictly speaking an insurgency—albeit at the bottom of the scale.

20. Yezid Sayigh, "The Intifada Continues: Legacy, Dynamics and Challenges," *Third World Quarterly* (July 1989): 29; Abu-Amr, "The Palestinian Uprising," p. 398.

21. See Meron Benvenisti, *1986 Report: Demographic, Economic, Legal, Social and Political Developments in the West Bank* (Jerusalem: West Bank Data Project, 1986), available from Westview Press, Boulder, Colorado. The problems discussed by Benvenisti have undercut improvements in the standard of living noted earlier in this chapter. For a discussion of these, see George Szpiro, "Israel and the Arabs in the Occupied Territories," *Swiss Review of World Affairs* (April 1987); Don Peretz, "Intifadah: The Palestinian Uprising," *Foreign Affairs* (Summer 1988): 965–67.

22. Glenn Frankel, "Israeli Prison in Gaza Was Finishing School for Rioters," *Washington Post*, January 3, 1988; Sayigh, "The Intifada Continues," pp. 24–27.

23. Avidan, "What Caused the Riots," pp. 40–41.

24. Abu-Amr, "The Palestinian Uprising," pp. 389–90.

25. Saul Mishal, "Intifada of Leaflets," *Ha'aretz* (Tel Aviv), June 23, 1989, in *Joint Publications Research Service—Near East/South Asia* (hereafter *JPRS/NES*), No. 89060, September 7, 1989, p. 16. Evidently, Mishal's analysis of the leaflets is considered credible by the PLO, judging from a long summary of it that appeared in *Filastin Al Thawrah* (Nicosia), July 23, 1989. See the reprint and translation in *JPRS/NES*, No. 89065, October 2, 1989. The only discomfort shown was toward Mishal's citations of the anti-Jewish rhetoric of the Islamic groups. Otherwise, the summary was straightforward.

26. Joel Brinkley, "Inside the Intifadah," *New York Times Magazine*, October 29, 1989, p. 29.

27. Abu-Amr, "The Palestinian Uprising," p. 393; Mishal, "Intifada of Leaflets," p. 17.

28. Mishal, "Intifada of Leaflets," p. 16, notes that leaflets are not unique, having been used after the 1948 and 1967 wars. What is new is their variety and frequency and the greater obedience they elicit.

29. Mishal, "Intifada of Leaflets," p. 17.

30. Sayigh, "The Intifada Continues," p. 38; Mishal, "Intifada of Leaflets," p. 22.

31. Ori Nir, "Hour of the Extremists," *Ha'aretz* (Tel Aviv), November 8, 1989, in *FBIS/NES*, No. 80219, November 15, 1989, p. 26.

32. Abu-Amr, "The Palestinian Uprising," p. 402. Brinkley, "Inside the Intifadah," p. 92, notes that Israeli punitive measures are feared and hence lead Palestinians to place limits on violent activity.

33. Sayigh, "The Intifada Continues," p. 48.

34. Abu-Amr, "The Palestinian Uprising," p. 393.

35. On the Islamic groups and their differences with the PLO, see Robert Satloff, "Islam in the Palestinian Uprising," *Orbis* (Summer 1989).

36. "Hamas Leader Interviewed on Islamic Movement," *Al-Anbar* (Kuwait), October 8, 1988, in *FBIS/NES*, No. 88198, October 13, 1988, p. 9; Mishal, "Intifada of Leaflets," pp. 18–19; Abu-Amr, "The Palestinian Uprising," pp. 394–95. Ironically, the Israelis favored the emergence of HAMAS as a counterweight to the PLO in the years prior to the Intifada. See Oren Kohen, "This Is the Hamas," *Hadashot* (Shel Shabat supplement), October 7, 1988, in *FBIS/NES*, No. 88198, October 13, 1988, p. 42.

37. Mishal, "Intifada of Leaflets," p. 19. On UNLU/PLO-HAMAS violence and the conciliation committees, see Ha'aretz (Tel Aviv), November 9, 1989, in *FBIS/NES*, No. 89218, November 14, 1989, p. 50.

38. See Nadim Rouhana, "The Political Transformation of the Palestinians in Israel: From Acquiescence to Challenge," *Journal of Palestine Studies* (Spring 1989): 46–48; Peretz, "Intifadah," p. 977; see also the chapter by Eli Rekhess in this volume, "The Arabs in Israel and the Intifada."

39. UNLU/PLO recognition of the limitations created by economic realities and dependence on Israel are noted by Brinkley, "Inside the Intifadah," p. 92; Mishal, "Intifada of Leaflets," pp. 20–21; and Sayigh, "The Intifada Continues," pp. 33–34.

40. In the short term, some Arab governments might provide limited support in order to placate internal opponents in much the same way that Indian leaders supported Tamil insurgents in Sri Lanka in order to retain political backing from the fifty million Tamils in India's state of Tamil-Nadu. But, like their counterparts in India, Arab leaders will be wary of long-term success by the insurgents, particularly the religious extremists. A victory by the Tamils could inspire separatism in India. A victory by Palestinian extremists might encourage their ideological/theo-

logical brethren in Arab states such as Syria, Jordan, and Egypt—all of which are presently concerned about religious extremism within their borders.

41. *Al-Watan* (Kuwait), November 13, 1989, in *FBIS/NES*, No. 89220, November 16, 1989, p. 5.

42. See the results and analysis of a 1984 public opinion survey of 3,306 Palestinians in the West Bank and Gaza Strip in Mohammed Shadid and Rick Seltzer, "Trends in Palestinian Nationalism: Moderate, Radical and Religious Alternatives," *Journal of South Asian and Middle Eastern Studies* (Summer 1988): 61–63. A more recent poll obtained similar results; see *Jerusalem Post*, December 25, 1987.

43. Ellen Laipson, "Palestinian Disturbances in the Gaza Strip and West Bank: Policy Issues and Chronology," *Congressional Research Service Report for the Congress*, February 2, 1988, pp. 9–11.

The PLO and the Intifada

Helena Cobban

Many Western and Israeli analyses of the relationship between the internal leaders of the Intifada and the Tunis-based leadership of the Palestine Liberation Organization (PLO) have tended to emphasize the political distance between Tunis and the occupied territories. For example, Rand analyst Graham Fuller wrote that "the West Bank has become a closed, self-contained political entity."[1] Other writers have judged that the PLO leaders were taken by surprise by the original eruption of the uprising in 1987 and have been trying to make up the lost ground ever since. These analyses are successful in capturing one aspect of the importance of the uprising to the development of the Palestinian national movement, namely the empowerment within the movement of the constituency resident within the bounds of the historic Palestinian homeland.[2] They are generally less successful, however, in capturing the dynamic nature of the interaction between the "resident" and the "exile" wings of the movement, since they generally rely on the model articulated by Menahem Milson, which considered the PLO as merely one other outside player attempting—in competition with the Israelis and the Jordanians—to influence the population of the occupied areas.[3]

The Milson model of the PLO leadership as one more outside

actor seems incapable, however, of accounting for the high degree of loyalty shown by the resident Palestinian population to the PLO since 1974, despite the physical distance between them and the PLO and the inability of the latter to provide any tangible rewards to this constituency. In this chapter, I will attempt to correct this shortcoming. Starting with an examination of the nature of the political leadership within the occupied territories, as demonstrated throughout the two years of the Intifada, I then analyze the intimate but complex relationship between this leadership (or those leaderships) and the various components of the exile-based PLO—a relationship that gives the PLO a different kind of link to the people of the occupied territories than that enjoyed by Israel or Jordan. I conclude by examining some of the consequences of the Intifada-inspired empowerment of the resident Palestinian constituency.

Political Life Inside the Occupied Territories during the Intifada

The Intifada (popular uprising) that started in the occupied territories in December 1987 was distinguished from its numerous, more ephemeral precursors primarily by the fact that within weeks of its original eruption it had become successfully institutionalized into an organized, near-unanimous challenge to Israel's presence in the territories that was sustained successfully throughout at least two years, with few signs, as of the end of 1989, that it was about to suffer any form of internal collapse.

The major organizing tool that ensured the continuation of the Intifada throughout its first two years was the series of leaflets that apparently started appearing in early January 1988. In a December 1989 article, philosophy professor Sari Nuseibeh described the early moves toward the institutionalization of the Intifada in the following terms:

> For two weeks the fire [of the revolt] raged in almost unfathomable proportions. Even the local grassroots committees, activists and leaders were caught off-guard . . . The first underground leaflet of the Intifada made a shy appearance . . . Then Communique No. 2 of the Intifada appeared. Rumours have it that it

was at this stage, through consultations with, and with the aid and blessing of, Abu Jihad [Fateh second-in-command Khalil Wazir], that the Unified Command was conceived and created . . . Communique No. 3 enshrining the birth of the Unified Command appeared. The uprising leaflets suddenly took on a special format, which continues to exist till this day.[4]

A document that may have been one version of Communiqué No. 2 was reportedly issued on January 13, 1988.[5] This document was issued in the name of "the National Command for the *Escalation* of the Uprising," and it was broadcast on a new clandestine radio station called Al-Quds Palestinian Arab Radio, operating under Syrian auspices; but it did make apparent reference to the body Nuseibeh referred to, the "Unified National Command." By January 20, the document Nuseibeh called Communiqué No. 3 had apparently been issued in the territories and was being broadcast by the PLO's Baghdad-based radio station.[6] This document was issued in the name of "the Unified National Command of the Uprising." This body's name came to be referred to with familiarity inside the territories as "al-Qiyada al Muwahhada" (the Unified Command, or Leadership), and to be commonly Anglicized in the form of "the Unified National Leadership of the Uprising"—UNLU.

By the time Leaflet No. 6 was broadcast on February 4, these documents had assumed a format that they were to retain through forty-three more editions appearing between then and early December 1989. Each started with a more or less extensive preamble that combined support for the PLO's current political stance with pep-talk-like exhortations and acclamations directed at the "glorious masses of the Intifada." The second half of each leaflet was then devoted to concrete instructions concerning how the Intifada's challenge to Israel's authority was to be sustained. These instructions would include general guidelines on such topics as strike hours, how to decrease consumption of Israeli products, how to deal with the challenges posed by collaborators, and so on, as well as a timetable of special events or remembrances for the days ahead. From No. 8 (February 11, 1988) onward, the sign-off at the end of the leaflet, at least as broadcast on the PLO radio, Voice of

Palestine, would attribute it to "the Unified National Leadership of the Uprising, the PLO," or "the PLO, UNLU." From No. 33 (January 22, 1989) onward, the sign-off became "the PLO–The Unified National Leadership of the Uprising, the State of Palestine."[7]

The instructions contained in the UNLU leaflets were characterized by a realistic sense of what the Palestinian communities living under military occupation in the West Bank and Gaza could actually sustain. The handling of the issue of commercial strikes provides one important example of this. Such strikes, which before December 1987 had been a frequent but sporadic part of the nationalists' political repertoire, became a constant staple of the late-1980s Intifada, defying the Israeli military's early attempts to break them by force and intimidation. But it should be noted that through the end of 1989, the UNLU never called for a total, open-ended commercial strike. Rather, commercial activities were limited to three hours every day, apart from certain pre-feast days.[8] Beyond the continuing restrictions on opening hours, the UNLU also required that shops observe the whole-day closures it called for on certain days as designated in the leaflets. By the end of 1989, the UNLU was designating about three to five days of total strikes per month. The Islamic Resistance Movement, HAMAS, was also designating about three other strike days per month. While Palestinian workers employed in Israel and Palestinian-owned manufacturing establishments were enjoined to observe the strike schedule in full, the latter group gradually came to be allowed to operate long hours on nonstrike days, in order to stimulate a "nationalist production" that could satisfy consumers who were being urged to boycott Israeli products.

The net effect of the degree of caution with which the UNLU addressed the strike issue (and of the UNLU's apparent ability to coordinate its strike timetable with HAMAS) was that merchants were able to keep their businesses ticking over at a minimal level, the general population was able to continue daily life in a modified and foreseeable way—and the nationalists continued to demonstrate their ability to exert control over this basic aspect of daily life. Other struggles for control that the UNLU entered against the military administration,[9] or into which the military was able to draw it, often seemed to result in an outcome in which neither side was able to declare total victory: These included the battle over opening the West Bank schools, and the "magnetic cards" battle in Gaza in the summer of 1989. The fact that the Israelis, despite the overwhelming preponderance of their firepower, were unable to "win" such confrontations, particularly in the all-important political aspect of driving a lasting wedge through the middle of the Palestinian population, further underlined the UNLU's achievement in sustaining "dual power" in the territories through the end of 1989. This achievement was directly attributable to the pragmatism displayed in the UNLU's instructions for nationalist activities.

As the timetable laid out in each of the UNLU leaflets approached its end, the question of the appearance, or failure of appearance, of the next leaflet assumed great importance for the Palestinians. The UNLU's ability to ensure that leaflets came out with no or little interruption in their schedule—despite repeated Israeli arrest campaigns in which it was claimed that "the ringleaders" had all been caught—gave the Palestinians continuing confidence in its leadership.

The UNLU leaflets can be considered the fundamental means by which the Intifada became institutionalized throughout the occupied areas. (That the Israelis also considered them such is indicated by the numerous attempts they apparently made to "spook" this important means of nationalist communication by issuing their own fake leaflets. However, the PLO's ability to back up the printed UNLU leaflets with broadcasts from outside made the major UNLU leaflets distinctive. At the more local level, for example in disputes concerning local issues in one town or another, the Israelis may have had some partial successes in sowing division through distribution of misleading flyers.) Any analysis of the nature of the political leadership that emerged in the occupied areas with the Intifada should thus include an analysis of two important features of the leaflets: their authors, and the nature of their authority, which produced a level of compliance with their instructions sufficient to ensure the continuation of the Intifada. A further question that requires analysis is the role played in the Intifada by publicly known political figures, primarily those resident in East Jerusalem.

UNLU and Other Political Organizations in the Territories

The basic membership of the UNLU comprised four individuals, one representing each of the four major secular-nationalist organizations active within the territories. These were Fatah, the Popular Front for the Liberation of Palestine (PFLP), the Democratic Front for the Liberation of Palestine (DFLP), and the Palestinian Communist party (PCP).[10] These organizations were all, to a greater or lesser extent, active participants in the work of the Tunis-based PLO (see the section on national leadership below).

While the Israelis were able on many occasions to detain one or more of the authors of the forthcoming leaflet—including one occasion on which they were reportedly able to detain three out of the four—they were never, through the end of 1989, successful in catching all four. The system of having a number of organizations represented in the UNLU had most likely originally been a *political* decision in order to coordinate the actions of the four organizations. But an important consequence of this decision was that there was never a single "command authority" for the Intifada within the territories that the Israelis could hope to decapitate; the relatively diffuse nature of the Intifada's command authority thus contributed to its survival.

While the UNLU was an inside-the-territories coalition of the four major secular-nationalist groups operating there, other secular-nationalist groups active in the Palestinian Diaspora were notably not represented in it and gave little evidence of having any significant following within the territories. These included the groups directly sponsored by Syria and Iraq—Saiqa and the Arab Liberation Front, respectively—and extremely small groups like the Palestinian Popular Struggle Front or the Palestine Liberation Front. The pro-Syrian Popular Front for the Liberation of Palestine–General Command (PFLP–GC) appeared not to have any significant organization active in the territories, but it retained some prestige there on account of two significant achievements within recent years. In 1985, the PFLP–GC had succeeded in negotiating the release of some fifteen hundred Palestinian political prisoners from Israeli jails in return for its release of four Israeli soldiers captured in Lebanon. The Palestinian "releasees" (*muharrarin*) came from all the political groups active in the territories, and those who returned to their home communities played an important role in building up the organizations that sustained the Intifada. Then in November 1987, a PFLP–GC operative managed to fly into northern Israel in a motorized hang glider, landing near an Israel Defense Forces (IDF) base. During the shootout that ensued, he killed six soldiers before being killed himself. This action badly damaged the aura of invincibility on which the IDF heavily relied for effectiveness within the territories, forming an important part of the psychological environment in which the Palestinians entered the Intifada.

Throughout the first two years of the Intifada, relations between the PLO and the Ba'athist regime in Syria remained extremely strained, as they had been since 1982.[11] The major issues that divided the two sides were approaches to the Arab-Israeli issue, with President Hafiz al-Assad of Syria remaining critical of the PLO's attempts to get itself into a restarted peace negotiation for which he judged that conditions were not yet ripe, and Lebanon, where the two sides seemed to lose few opportunities to challenge each other's continuing presence.

These PLO-Syrian disputes raged strongly in the political world outside the occupied territories, but within the territories the absence of any significant Syrian-sponsored organizations was an important factor enabling the UNLU to speak for the entire secular-nationalist camp there. The major organizational and political challenge to the UNLU came, instead, from the avowedly Moslem political organizations that claimed an organized following in the territories far more significant than that which they had in the Palestinian Diaspora.

The two major Moslem movements active in the territories were the Moslem Brotherhood and the Islamic Jihad movement. Both found their major source of popular support in Gaza, where circumstances such as the high proportion of socially disadvantaged families and refugees and the relative religious homogeneity of the population (that is, Sunni Moslems) combined to provide a particularly fertile breeding ground for Islamic millennialism. Throughout the late 1970s and early 1980s, the fundamentalists succeeded in increasing their popularity and influence in both Gaza and the West Bank, in line with the trend evident throughout the Moslem Middle East in the aftermath of Ayatollah Khomeini's victory over the Shah. One survey conducted in 1983–84 found that the "religiosity" of Gaza residents, as revealed in degree of Islamic observance, came to 57.8 percent of the population, while in the West Bank it came to 48.7 percent.[12] (It is not clear whether those surveyed for this study in the West Bank included that area's 15-percent-plus Christian population.) One of the authors of this survey also concluded that the survey data revealed that "the revivalist trend was most evident among the youth and the college-educated."[13]

The Moslem Brotherhood had had a presence in Gaza almost since its founding in Cairo in 1928. During the fighting that accompanied the establishment of the State of Israel in 1948, the Brotherhood sent volunteer units to help train and fight with local Palestinian militias. After the defeat of the Palestinians and other Arab armies, Brotherhood members who were stationed in the Egyptian army units occupying Gaza then turned their attention to building up cells of their movement among the local populace. Significantly, many of those Gaza residents who were recruited into, or worked with, the Brotherhood during the tumult of the late 1940s later turned their political energies elsewhere. Some later became leaders of local communist movements, while others—most notably Yasser Arafat and Khalil al-Wazir—were within the decade that followed to found the secular-nationalist organization Fatah.[14]

Throughout the four decades that followed 1948, the Moslem Brotherhood organization in Gaza, and its later offshoots in the West Bank and inside Israel itself, followed the lead of the mother organization in Egypt in espousing an essentially educational and social role for its adherents. Brotherhood publications consistently stressed that *all* of Palestine, including that part in which the State of Israel had been established in 1948, remained an Islamic land, and that not one inch of it could be negotiated away to "the Jews." But its program for realizing the goal of the liberation of Palestine was essentially gradualist, with the activist part of the program always postponed until after the satisfactory formation of a "Holy War generation" (*jeel jihadi*).[15] It was also, frequently, very hostile to secular forms of Palestinian nationalism. For example, one

Brotherhood publication widely circulated in the West Bank and Gaza, apparently in the mid-1980s, advocated efforts to "expose the traitors, agents and proponents of nationalism and . . . bring about Palestinian awareness of the true [religious, not nationalistic] nature of its battle with Zionism."[16]

Throughout the late 1970s and early 1980s, the Brotherhood engaged in numerous political and physical clashes with the secular nationalists. These included political battles for control of institutions, including student councils in the universities and numerous social institutions in Gaza, and a number of actual street battles in Gaza.[17]

At least part of the leadership of Fatah reportedly responded to the Brotherhood's growing challenge in 1979 by supporting the revival of another Moslem organization, the Islamic Jihad, which had originally been a splinter from the Brotherhood in the mid-1960s. While Jihad could compete for influence against the Brotherhood on the latter's own fundamentalist home turf, it was less hostile to the secular nationalists than the Brotherhood—and much more avowedly activist in its operations. Jihad was believed to have been responsible for many of the killings of individual Israelis that occurred in Gaza in the mid-1980s.

At the beginning of the Intifada, the secular groups represented in the UNLU attempted to include the two large Moslem movements in its deliberations. The UNLU communiqué of January 20, 1988, even welcomed the recent inclusion of the Islamic Jihad in its deliberations.[18] This relationship did not last long, but Jihad did continue to participate in the activities of the Intifada, in parallel with the efforts of the UNLU. In an interview in July 1989, a Gaza-based leader of the Islamic Jihad explained that there was a formula for relations between his organization and the UNLU "that works for now." He said this formula was based on the following two pillars: "Firstly, that no differences should be allowed to surface about the continuation of the Intifada and its activities, though political differences might continue. And secondly, coordination existed in practice, over such issues as assigning strike days."[19]

When asked about whether his movement wanted to replace the PLO in its leadership of the Palestinian people, this respondent answered that "the PLO has earned its legitimacy and sustained sacrifices. We will struggle [against it] in a democratic way after the establishment of the state." He described his movement's goal as being the elimination of the Israeli occupation and the establishment of a Palestinian state in the areas currently under occupation; but he stressed that this was only the immediate goal, whereas the "strategic goal" remained the establishment of an Islamic state "in all of Palestine." By supporting the idea of a Palestinian mini-state in the occupied areas as a step toward the liberation of "all of Palestine," the Islamic Jihad was thus much closer, politically, to ultranationalists within the PLO constellation, like the PFLP, than it was to the traditional Brotherhood position.

By contrast with Jihad, the Brotherhood spent the first few months of the Intifada sitting on the sidelines, continuing its campaigns for "proper Moslem social behavior," while the Intifada raged on around them. By August 1988, the most powerful local leader of the Brotherhood, Sheikh Ahmed Yasin, had clearly reached a momentous decision. That month, he announced the formation of a new body, the "Islamic Resistance Organization" (Harakat al-Muqawama al-Islamiya—HAMAS), which would take a much more active role in the Intifada than the Brotherhood had taken up until then. In an interview a year later, one young HAMAS leader in the West Bank revealed that "participation in the Intifada came as a result of a debate within the Islamic movement over whether it should wait for the emergence of an Islamic state somewhere or whether it should engage in direct confrontation with Israel." However, he said that the overall leadership of the Brotherhood (that is, its Cairo-based Supreme Guide) still placed HAMAS's participation in the Intifada firmly within the framework of the Brotherhood's traditional stress on educational efforts, saying that "the Islamic movement views the Intifada as a way to mobilize the masses to form the *jeel jihadi*, and at the same time as one form of jihad, as an introduction to armed jihad."[20]

The program of activities publicly espoused by Hamas from August 1988 on largely paralleled that of the UNLU, though with some significant differences. Like the UNLU, HAMAS laid out periodic timetables for its own strike days. After some early resistance in some West Bank communities to following the HAMAS strike calls, the West Bankers—Christians as well as Moslems—

all apparently joined the Gazans in observing both sets of strike days, though some analysts of the local scene cautioned that this should be interpreted more as signaling support for the idea of confronting Israel whenever feasible, rather than as a measure of support for the Brotherhood as such. On some issues, HAMAS's program was markedly different from the UNLU's. For example, after the military administration in the West Bank decreed the reopening of the schools in July 1989, the UNLU consensus at first called on school students to observe the schedule of general strike days, but HAMAS argued that the children had lost so much education that they should be exempted from the strikes. HAMAS was able to win the internal argument over this issue.[21]

The HAMAS of Sheikh Yasin had nevertheless moved a considerable distance from the long-held positions of the Brotherhood. This was evident at the level of its political program—a marked softening in its view of the PLO's secular-nationalist leadership. In a crucial April 1989 interview, Yasin said that he wanted to see the establishment of a Palestinian state and that this state "must be established on every inch of Palestine that we liberate, but without relinquishing our other rights." Asked if he supported the political steps taken by the PLO in late 1988, by which it announced its support for the partition of historic Palestine into Jewish and Arab states and its recognition of Israel, Yasin said, "I support and I oppose. I approve of the establishment of a state, but I refuse to relinquish the remaining territory of my homeland, Palestine." He also stressed that HAMAS "will not negotiate as a substitute for the PLO."[22]

HAMAS could thus be seen to have moved significantly closer to the mainstream PLO position at the political level. Yasin's late-April interview was particularly significant, since at the time he gave it the Israelis were putting the finishing touches to the elections proposal that Prime Minister Yitzhak Shamir announced in the middle of May 1989. According to statements made by Shamir's close aide, Yossi Ben-Aharon, the elections plan was aimed precisely at encouraging the emergence of a Palestinian leadership based in the occupied areas that would replace, rather than work with, the PLO in any negotiations. Yasin's refusal to play that role constituted one of the most important political victories that the PLO leaders won in 1989.

In May, too, Yasin was again arrested, and the authorities for the first time declared that HAMAS was "a terrorist organization." Over the following months, he would be charged with having caused the deaths of two Israeli soldiers and four Gazans accused of collaborating with the occupation.[23]

Compliance with the Intifada's Activity Programs:
The Role of Mass Organizations

An essential part in sustaining the Palestinians' Intifada of the late 1980s was played by a variety of mass organizations, which buttressed the ability of the different families and communities to follow the directives of the UNLU and the Moslem groups. (These organizations were also able to provide important input into deciding the content of the secular and Islamic leaderships' action programs.) The mass organizations consisted of both interest-based groups—labor unions, women's and student unions, merchant committees, professional unions—and geographically based groups, such as local popular committees and watch committees. Some of these organizations emerged during the Intifada, but many others predated it by years. It is undoubtedly true to say that if the Palestinians of the two occupied areas had not had a rich experience in mass organizational work before December 1987, the political leadership would have issued its leaflets in vain and the eruption of early December would have passed within weeks or days.

In both the West Bank and Gaza, the longest record in supporting the building of mass organizations had been held by the communists. In the West Bank, communist-supported labor unions and various women's organizations had existed since the 1920s, though most of the latter operated mainly as social welfare groups. After the Israeli-occupation authorities arrived in 1967, they closed down ten of the thirteen East Jerusalem based labor unions and arrested many unionists. In 1969, however, labor activists (mainly communists) were able to renew the license of the labor federation's dormant Nablus branch. Three years later, after a number of unions from throughout the West Bank affiliated, it was renamed the General Federation of Trade Unions Based in Nablus.[24]

Throughout the early 1970s, the Communists remained the most active party in broadening the membership of the union movement. Their ability to do this with less official harassment than other secular nationalists experienced stemmed from a number of factors: They did not, as the other nationalists did at that point, advocate or practice armed struggle against Israel, and their official ideology stressed Israel's right to exist within its pre-1967 borders; and they received some support from Arab and Jewish Communists inside Israel, who operated legally within the Israeli political system. By the late 1970s, other nationalist organizations, like the DFLP and the PFLP, were joining the Communists in building labor unions. Later, Fatah also joined the effort.

The union movement that emerged in the labor sector was highly political. Indeed, the multiplicity of political efforts invested in building the labor unions from the late 1970s on resulted not in one much-stronger labor federation, which would have been desirable from the labor-union point of view, but in at least four parallel labor federations, which were often in competition with each other. The same was true of the women's and student unions that emerged in the same period. In some sectors, too, the four parallel secular-based federations would be paralleled by other organizations loyal to the Moslem Brotherhood or other fundamentalists. This was the case in the student sector, where the four secular-based unions were on occasion able to bury their differences enough to work together in beating back a challenge from the Moslem organizations.[25]

Through 1982, however, the attitude of Fatah to mass organizing efforts was marked by ambivalence. Fatah was still committed to continuing to wage "armed struggle" against Israel; and the member of the Fatah leadership who was responsible for directing the movement's work inside the occupied territories, Khalil al-Wazir (Abu Jihad), was also in charge of all of its military activities. Through 1982–83, his approach to organizing in the occupied territories was thus based on the two pillars of building a clandestine military capability, with all the modi operandi that involved, and forging political deals with leading personalities in order to wage various elite-level political battles in the territories.

However, after the crushing of the PLO's major military capability in Lebanon in 1982 and, more particularly, after the reassessment of strategies that followed that defeat, Wazir shifted toward a fuller embrace of the concept of mass political work in the occupied territories. It was this shift, and the resulting efforts that Fatah's cadres inside the territories put into building up women's groups, student unions, and the omnipresent *shabiba* (youth) groups that, according to many accounts from inside the territories, tipped the balance and mobilized the majority of West Bank and Gaza communities into conscious participation in the nationalist political effort.

After the start of the Intifada, the occupation authorities deported or detained as many of the known activists of the mass organizations as they could, in an attempt to decapitate these organizations. But the principles of community action had become deeply enough internalized throughout the territories that the different kinds of communities were capable of generating new and appropriate local organizations. A more or less informal division of labor emerged in many areas: A merchants' committee would deal with commercial questions; youth committees would be responsible for engaging or diverting the military; the women of every neighborhood would act as watch committees or organize the distribution of emergency rations; labor committees would supervise strike observance or help organize efforts in the "alternative economy"; "reconciliation committees" of trusted community members would replace the work of the boycotted court system in resolving interfamily or intergroup disputes. For as long as they could, the numerous charitable associations operating in the West Bank worked with the local committees to alleviate the suffering caused by the Intifada, but in early summer 1989 the military closed them too, declaring their actions seditious.

The mass organizations that operated during the Intifada were distinguished by their focus on effectiveness at the local level, a feature that arose directly from the fact that they were adapted to a range of differing local conditions: in refugee camps, remote villages, or larger or smaller urban areas. In one West Bank village of twenty-five hundred, which I visited in the summer of 1989, a local activist reported that before the Intifada 70 percent of the village's workers were employed in Israel. "Now," he said, "only one busload of forty-nine or forty-two people travels into Israel for work, and they don't go on strike days." Meanwhile, the village council was employing seventy-six people in various capacities, and other workers had found jobs in the nearby town of Ramallah. The activist stressed that most of the villagers had meanwhile returned to their traditional reliance on agriculture. He reported that after the 1988 harvest, the village had been able to send a full truckload of olive oil to Gaza and another truckload of olives to West Bank refugee camps. He recalled that the villagers had first been stimulated to set up a system of popular committees by a fifty-five-day curfew the IDF had imposed on the village, and he explained that a village reconciliation committee now resolved all local disputes, a function that previously had been performed by a *mukhtar*, whose role had become largely discredited during the Intifada.

In the overcrowded refugee camps of Gaza and the sprawling suburbs of the West Bank towns, the population had become mobilized into forms of social organization that similarly reflected local needs and conditions. I did hear some views expressed in Gaza, to the effect that the UNLU appeared to take more careful note in its leaflets of the specific conditions in the West Bank than in Gaza. But taken as a whole, the ability of community activists to maintain local community organizations in all the different areas under Israeli occupation made a crucial contribution to allowing the national movement as a whole to withstand the occupation authorities' repeated efforts to decapitate it.

The Role of the Intellectuals

The Palestinian nationalist intellectuals, particularly those living in East Jerusalem, played a special role in the nationalist movement during the first year of the Intifada, and a different—possibly less important—role during its second year. The ability of the East Jerusalem intellectuals to engage in public political activity stemmed in great part from the fact that, ever since the Israelis annexed East Jerusalem and sizable areas of land lying around it in 1968, their part of the occupied territories had been ruled under Israeli civil law rather than by military order. This fact did not prevent the Israelis from imposing at least five curfews of some duration on different low-income neighborhoods of East Jerusalem within the Intifada's first two years, and subjecting its residents to many of the other humiliations suffered by compatriots living just down the road in the West Bank. Before and during the Intifada, the most prominent of the East Jerusalem intellectuals, Faisal Husseini, was detained for a number of periods of time under emergency regulations allowing for detention without charge or trial. The Israeli government withheld from the Jerusalem intellectuals permission to travel—to destinations abroad or even to the neighboring West Bank—according to the dictates only of its own political whim. The normal business or research activities of these intellectuals could be, and were, closed down at the stroke of a pen. Nevertheless, by virtue of their presence within the avowedly unified city, and their relatively easy access to its large body of Western diplomats, the Jerusalem intellectuals did have more freedom to carry out normal political activity than colleagues living in the West Bank—and much more than colleagues living in the distant obscurity of Gaza.

In the first weeks of the Intifada, in December 1987, the East Jerusalem intellectuals carried out one of the types of activity that had become customary for them: They presented a petition to the Western consuls decrying the military's violence in the occupied areas. By January, the political focus of the demands they made in their communication to the Western authorities (and to the Israeli government) had risen to a slightly higher plane. In a letter delivered personally to Secretary of State George Shultz in Washington on January 27, 1988, the editor of East Jerusalem's *Al-Fajr* daily, Hanna Siniora, and Gaza lawyer Fayez Abu Rahme, requested that "the international community . . . immediately authorize the provision of an international force to intervene in the occupied territories, to whose trusteeship our population can be delivered, as a first step towards the convening of an international peace conference."[26]

At that meeting, Siniora and Abu Rahme also handed Shultz a

copy of "the Fourteen Points," a document that Palestinian nationalist intellectuals and institutions from the occupied areas had released two weeks earlier. Most of the fourteen points were concerned with repealing or otherwise reversing the measures the IDF had taken to try to quell the Intifada so far. The document called for the release of the large number of prisoners the IDF had taken, the cancellation of deportation orders and the return of four Palestinians deported on January 13, the carrying out of a formal inquiry into the IDF's behavior in the territories, and the immediate application of the provisions of the Geneva Convention there. The highest level of political demand contained in the document was a call for the holding of municipal elections "under the supervision of a neutral authority."[27]

In a commentary on "the Fourteen Points," Siniora explained that they were concerned with questions of "the immediate oppression in the occupied territories," and that he, Abu Rahme, and the other signatories of the document could discuss their implementation. However, he stressed that for "the big negotiations" concerning an overall settlement of the Palestinian issue, the only Palestinian interlocutor was still the PLO.[28]

The refusal of the Palestinian intellectuals resident in the occupied areas to supplant the PLO in any national-level negotiations on a broad political settlement was shared by all other sectors of "resident" Palestinian society. But the division of labor Siniora had suggested, whereby the resident intellectuals might negotiate some immediate demands, pending the broader negotiations in which the PLO would take part, rapidly became overtaken by events, as the mounting casualty toll made the resident Palestinian communities feel that no mere move toward "municipal elections" could repay them for the pain they had suffered. The resident Palestinians judged that so long as the broader issue of sovereignty over the occupied territories remained unaddressed, any such lower-level political gain could easily be reversed by the occupation authorities—as had happened with the 1976 elections. A growing impatience with the idea of demanding municipal elections was clearly evident in the changing texts of the UNLU leaflets during February 1988. Whereas Leaflet No. 6 of February 4 called explicitly for the holding of municipal election, Leaflet No. 8, issued on February 22, made no mention of this demand at all.[29]

In late February, Secretary Shultz made a visit to Israel and East Jerusalem in order to revive the long-stalled peace process. He requested a meeting with Siniora and other Palestinian intellectuals in East Jerusalem's American Colony Hotel. At first, PLO chairman Arafat gave the intellectuals the go-ahead to attend the meeting; but later he changed his mind, apparently in response to warnings from organizers within the clandestine wing of the movement in the occupied territories that Shultz might use the meeting to portray the intellectuals as an alternative leadership to the PLO.[30] Thereafter, the intellectuals maintained their absence from formal diplomatic encounters with high-level American visitors, until after the United States decided, in December 1988, to open a formal diplomatic channel to the PLO leadership in Tunis. After that step had been taken, the intellectuals did attend meetings such as that held by Assistant Secretary John Kelly in Jerusalem in July 1989; but the major message they delivered was still that national-level issues could be negotiated only by the PLO.

In February 1988, it became evident to the Jerusalem intellectuals that there would be little immediate role for them in negotiating the kind of low-level, interim demands that, one month earlier, might still have brought the Intifada to an end. Thus, they turned their energies to whatever contributions they could make to sustaining the Intifada. A number of them had already learned valuable lessons from the success of a strategy they had pursued in April 1987. On that occasion, they had sought to broaden popular support for a hunger strike started by Palestinian political prisoners, by announcing a two-week timetable of near daily activities. The activities listed in the timetable—one day, a sit-in at the Red Cross, the next a day of wearing national dress, and so on—had drawn broad support. Within days, the students at Bir Zeit University had become engaged in demonstrations that drew live fire from the army, leaving two dead; the occupation authorities then decided to try to defuse the tensions by acceding to some of the striking prisoners' demands. The Jerusalem intellectuals drew positive lessons from that episode concerning the value of coordinating mass nationalist protest activities. Those lessons were then incorporated into the timetables of activities in the UNLU leaflets, leading Faisal Husseini to describe the April 1987 protests as a "dry run" for the Intifada.[31]

As it became clear that the Intifada of December 1987 would be of long duration, the resident intellectuals debated various long-term strategies for it. One idea that rapidly gained adherents was that of moving, within the context of the continuing Intifada, toward economic self-reliance. This would involve both boycotting Israeli products and increasing Palestinian economic capabilities. In early January 1988, Siniora proposed a boycott of Israeli cigarettes, but this proposal reportedly met with some derision from community activists who considered it a trivial diversion while they were daily risking death in the mass demonstrations. Nevertheless, by early February, it had become clear to nationalist activists at all levels that the Intifada could not bring victory if it relied solely on large-scale confrontations with an IDF that showed no signs of backing down from its decision to meet all such confrontations with superior force. The Palestinian activists realized they would have to dig in for a long contest of wills with the Israelis. Thus, the constituency for broadening the confrontation to include activities aimed at long-term economic disengagement grew larger.

Some of this emphasis was evident in the text of UNLU Leaflet No. 6, which said:

> Let all suitable organizations such as committees and units be formed in every area, on every street, and in every city, village, and camp in order to pave the road toward general civil disobedience. Disobedience means boycotting all enemy organs. It means boycotting the enemy economically and not paying taxes.
> Therefore let us climb another rung of the ladder by declaring this disobedience. Let us reinforce the spirit of sacrifice and common action following the war of molotov cocktails, stones and the raising of [Palestinian] flags. The disobedience will be a strong blow to the enemy, its economy, and its plunder of our people's wealth and resources.[32]

If it might have seemed, from this text, that the civil disobedience campaign was intended to *replace* the confrontation with Molotov cocktails and stones, by Leaflet No. 8 it was made clear that both efforts should be pursued concurrently. Leaflet No. 8 also reminded the resident Palestinians that "many basic needs can be secured from a small area of land before your house. This will raise your income, support your steadfastness, and decrease the burden of life under the occupation. . . . Let us recall that the Vietnamese achieved victory over the United States not through the rifle alone, but also through farming."[33]

Bir Zeit professor Ziad Abu Amr has noted the interaction that occurred between the resident intellectuals, most of whom operated like Siniora and Husseini within the domain of public diplomacy, and the continuing mass uprising. He judged that, "as these . . . intellectuals helped the Intifada continue, the Intifada, in turn, helped them modify their political outlooks and control the tempos of their political movement, activities, and writings in accordance with the spirit of the mass uprising."[34]

Some of the intellectuals also occupied themselves through the middle of 1988 in arguing that the time was ripe for the PLO to launch a decisive peace initiative. At a public meeting in Jerusalem at the end of July, Faisal Husseini and journalist Radwan Abu Ayyash, both of whom had recently been released from "administrative" detention, called for mutual recognition between the PLO and Israel and a two-state solution to the Palestinian-Israeli conflict.[35] Within days after this meeting, Husseini was imprisoned again, and the research center he headed was issued a twelve-month closure order. Among the documents seized from his premises during these actions was one, whose contents were later leaked to the Israeli press, that called for the declaration of a Palestinian state in the occupied areas and for mutual recognition between Israel and the PLO.[36] Bir Zeit professor Sari Nuseibeh was meanwhile busy writing an article, published in the PLO-supported weekly *Al-Yawm al-Sabi'*, based in Paris, arguing that "the Palestinian leadership is called upon now more than ever to take advantage of the historical opportunity to which the Intifada has given birth in order to bend the energy of the tremendous mass revolution and to translate it into a political product, to establish the independent state on the land which was occupied in 1967."[37]

Ideas broadly paralleling those articulated by Nuseibeh and Husseini had already been put forward by activists in the Palestinian Diaspora, most notably by Arafat aide Bassam Abu Sharif, in the document he circulated in Algiers in June 1988.[38] But undoubtedly, as members of the PLO's ruling body, the Palestine National Council (PNC), gathered in Algiers for their nineteenth session the following November, the fact that significant political figures associated with "the glorious Intifada" were also calling for an initiative undoubtedly helped Arafat to win the support he needed for the PLO's peace initiative.

The November PNC meeting granted formal PLO support for the first time to the 1947 United Nations resolution that divided historic Palestine between a Jewish and an Arab state. And in Geneva the following month, Arafat spelled out the PLO's recognition of Israel's right to exist and its renunciation of terrorism, thus paving the way for opening the official dialogue with the United States, which started in Tunis almost immediately thereafter.

The PLO leaders' twin victories—winning the PNC's backing for a significant peace initiative and opening the formal dialogue with the United States—changed the role of the Jerusalem-based intellectuals. Before November 1987, the intellectuals had played an important role in expressing the support of the newly enfranchised constituency of resident Palestinians for the political strategy for which the PLO leaders were trying to win a PNC mandate. After November 1987, the PLO leaders were no longer so dependent on that source of support. Similarly, before December 1987, the PLO leaders had relied heavily on the Jerusalem intellectuals not to make any move that might be interpreted as suggesting to the United States that they might constitute an alternative interlocutor, in place of the Tunis-based leadership. After December, this threat too receded. Meanwhile, the contribution the intellectuals had probably made to coordinating and strategizing for the institutionalization of the Intifada had also become, to a considerable degree, less important than it had been in the Intifada's early weeks, since many of the ideas they had proposed had become incorporated into the daily routine of both the UNLU and the community-based organizations.

The major political role left to the Jerusalem intellectuals during the second year of the Intifada was thus to pursue the contacts with Israeli individuals and groups, which was one of their special strengths. Faisal Husseini and Ziad Abu Ziad, an East Jerusalem lawyer who published a Hebrew-language periodical called *Gesher* (Bridge), were particularly effective in this regard, since they were able to talk with a broad range of Israelis, in Hebrew.

In the event that political talks should begin during 1990, the Jerusalem-based intellectuals would likely once more have an important role to play. And, if their behavior during the Intifada's first two years should prove any guide, they would continue to play it in close coordination with the PLO leaders.

National Leadership: The Parts Played by "Resident" and "Exile" Wings of the Movement

Did the Jerusalem-based intellectuals, by virtue of the activities already described, constitute an effective "new leadership" for the resident Palestinian communities, enabling these communities to function politically like the "closed, self-contained political entity" that Graham Fuller judged existed in the West Bank? The most crucial condition necessary, in order for such a description to hold, would be the existence of an effective, self-sustaining connection between the leadership of intellectuals and the mass movements of followers who sustained the Intifada on the ground. But the evidence, as of the end of 1989, strongly suggested that the relationship that had evolved between the Jerusalem-based intellectuals and the mass organizers during the Intifada's first two years fell far short of this description.

There were a number of exceptions to this general observation, Faisal Husseini being the clearest example. During interviews conducted in the summer of 1989, he evinced a clear familiarity with the debates then proceeding in various parts of the mass movement. Intellectuals thought to be connected with the "ideological," that is, non-Fatah, political groupings also generally showed themselves fairly familiar with developments in the mass organizations. (This was true of the non-Fatah secular nationalists, as well as of intellectuals connected with Moslem organizations.) In the special case of Beit Sahour, a small town with high general levels of education, the intellectuals in effect *were* the mass movement that took the town through its various campaigns of nonviolent resistance to the occupation.

These and similar isolated cases notwithstanding, however, the general judgment remains that most of the resident intellectuals—and particularly those whose names cropped up most frequently in diplomatic discussions in East Jerusalem—seemed little connected with the mass organizations. A content analysis of conversations they held among themselves would reveal, instead, far greater interest in such issues as 1) who was up and who down, politically, in the Tunis-based PLO leadership; 2) who attended or was slated to attend which diplomatic function in East Jerusalem; or 3) who attended or was slated to attend which meeting with Israeli figures. In this regard, their behavior and concerns suggested those of a branch of a Palestinian "State Department" far more than those of leaders of a mass-based movement. (The distance between the intellectuals and the mass movement was equally visible from the viewpoint of some sections of the mass movement, where the names of most of the prominent Jerusalem intellectuals evinced little recognition, even from activists deeply involved in mass organizing.)

Fairly clearly, too, and in line with this analysis, most of the intellectuals, as well as those "old notables" who were now associated with them, saw whatever mandate they enjoyed as emanating from Tunis, rather than from the mass movement in whose midst they lived. Such was the case for Hanna Siniora, in his account that it was Arafat who first gave and then withheld permission to attend the February 1988 meeting with Shultz in East Jerusalem. Such, too, was the case for al-Bireh deputy mayor Jamil Tarifi, who in July 1989 received (whether he wanted it or not) a sanction from the PLO in Tunis for a meeting he held with Prime Minister Shamir. In this latter case, it was significant that it was Salah Khalaf (Abu Iyad), Wazir's replacement as Number Two in Fatah, who simultaneously revealed and sanctioned Tarifi's meeting, rather than the UNLU or some other body within the territories.

If the intellectuals did not constitute a self-sustaining leadership for the residents of the occupied territories, could this instead be said of either the UNLU or the leaders of the mass and community organizations? In both cases the answer was similarly negative. In the case of the UNLU, both the original constitution of the body and its maintenance were by decision of the national-level leaderships of its constituent groups; and in all the groups with the possible exception of the PCP, such a decision could only be made by their exile-based leaderships. Some unaffiliated (but resident) observers of political developments in the occupied territories pointed to the fact that the UNLU differed significantly from previous territories-wide political leaderships, such as the Palestinian National Front of 1973–74 and the National Guidance Council (NGC) of 1978–81, precisely in that it no longer included any political "independents" in its membership. This fact, they concluded, served to increase the impact of the external PLO leaders on the situation inside.

In the case of the mass organizations, as has been noted earlier, these organizations had always been highly political, a major impetus for their work having come, once again, from the support of the PLO's constituent groups. Thus they, like the UNLU, remained heavily dependent on leadership from outside.

That the resident Palestinian communities should have proven incapable of generating a nationwide leadership independent of the exile-based PLO was due to a number of factors, but the most important of these remained the effects of more than twenty-two years of an Israeli policy that stifled the emergence of any effective territories-wide political leadership. At certain stages the Israeli authorities had tried to foster the emergence of an internal leadership that they could deal with or, later, that would act as a counter to PLO influence. This was the case to a certain extent during the early years of the occupation, when some in the military hierarchy tried to foster a "Palestinianism" that would look more to Israel than to Jordan for leadership. It was true far less ambiguously in the case of the attempt to build "Village Leagues" from 1981 on. One of the first solid political achievements of the Intifada was the announcement in February 1988 of the demise of the Village Leagues project. If this event passed with little notice, it was mainly because the project had failed, in practice, long before then.

A prime reason for the failure of the Israeli authorities' attempts to build a territories-wide political structure that they could deal with was the extreme stinginess with which they approached the task. They were asking Palestinian politicians to provide many valuable services for them, in terms of policing the local population, while they offered in return no assurances that the pragmatic aspirations of even the most cooperative of the Palestinians—assurances that investment projects could be freely pursued, historic rights to landownership and water resources respected, and so on— would ever be satisfactorily met. In the absence of such assurances, members of that fairly large group of Palestinians that, as of the late 1960s, might still have been prepared to broker a political deal with Israel found they had no alternative but to fall in behind the PLO's push for full independence.

Within the broad political framework of successive Israeli governments' unwillingness or inability to offer a workable deal to any potentially cooperative Palestinian leadership in the territories, the practical policies pursued by the occupation authorities frequently served to decapitate any emerging territories-wide leadership. This was the result of the policy of deportations that was followed, with some interruptions, throughout the two decades of the occupation. In the weeks following the June 1967 war, an estimated 15,000 men from Gaza were reportedly rounded up and trucked across Sinai to be deported to Egypt.[39] Explicit deportations from the more visible West Bank were more closely targeted. There, and in Gaza in the years that followed, many known community leaders and organizers were deported. Some 1,150 individuals are recorded as having been subject to individual or small-group deportation orders between September 1967 and May 1978.[40] Under the two Likud governments that were in power between 1977 and 1984, recourse to deportation was cut back significantly. In fact, between May 1980 and August 1985, only one deportation order was recorded.[41]

Then, in August 1985, the Labor-led National Unity government's defense minister Yitzhak Rabin resorted to deportations as a major part of the new policy in the occupied areas that the Palestinians termed "the Iron Fist." Between then and the start of the Intifada, fifty Palestinians were served with deportation orders.[42] The deportations that ensued constituted just one of the many ways in which the resident Palestinians suffered under the Iron Fist policy (which must be considered as an essential part of the backdrop against which the Intifada germinated). Like nearly all of those who preceded and succeeded them in political exile, the community leaders deported in the pre-Intifada phase were immediately incorporated into the command structures of various PLO member groups—in most cases, and especially within Fatah, this took place at levels considerably lower than that of the top leadership.

The net political effect of these deportations was thus similar to that of earlier waves of deportations: They drove the resident wing of the nationalist movement into deeper clandestinity and broader organizational dispersion, while increasing its reliance for overall leadership on that part of the movement working in the Diaspora. The relationship that emerged between the PLO's outside leadership and those local leaders who remained in the occupied areas has aptly been described by Faisal Husseini as being analogous to that between a military headquarters and its field commanders. "The field commander here can discuss tactics but not strategy," he said. "I am inside the Palestinian forest and can see the trees. But only the leaders outside can see where the fire is coming from."[43]

The authorities continued the policy of deporting community activists after the start of the Intifada. In the two years following December 1987, some sixty Palestinians were deported. Meanwhile, few inside the security establishment gave any sign that they had yet had any second thoughts about the effectiveness of this measure. (In September 1989, veteran security-affairs analyst Ze'ev Schiff wrote that "security people consider the deportation of Palestinian activists an extremely effective sanction. In many cases, this is correct from an operational point of view. . . . The question is whether it is also the wisest sanction from the political point of view. The fact is that a thorough examination of this question has never been made. Israel views the immediate result but ignores the long-term effect.")[44]

The links between the resident and exile wings of the Palestinian movement were thus extremely close at the political level. But there was another level, possibly even more important in determining people's behavior over the long run, at which the residents' commitment to the idea of unity with the Diaspora was also significant—the purely social level. For in addition to those resident Palestinians who had been formally deported from their home communities, hundreds of thousands of others who had been resident there from 1967 were subject to administrative exclusion from residence. These former residents, having fled during the 1967 fighting or left subsequently in order to pursue opportunities in education or employment that were denied them in the occupied areas, found after a census was taken in 1967 that they had lost their right to reside there. While some tens of thousands of those thus administratively excluded were permitted to reunify their families by returning, a far greater number, estimated by an Israeli source as numbering 200,000, found their applications were rejected.[45] While it is not known how many additional "administrative excludees" never even bothered to apply for family reunification, it is clear both from the number of those who applied and were rejected, and from the most cursory conversations with Palestinians in the territories, that every Palestinian there has immediate family members who are denied the right of permanent residence.

The occupation authorities were always well aware of the social consequences of their policy of wide-scale administrative exclusion of former residents. Indeed, they found that one of the strongest means of rewarding or punishing those living under occupation was through granting or withholding permits for family reunification, or for travel in or out of the occupied areas on family business. What perhaps they were unaware of was the political effects of their policy, for by the end of the 1980s the commitment of the resident Palestinians to the idea of unity with the Palestinian Diaspora had a much firmer underpinning at the social and family level than it did among many Diaspora Palestinians. By the end of the 1980s, many of those Palestinians who had grown up in refugee camps in Lebanon or Syria no longer had any close relatives living in the homeland, so their commitment to the idea of national unity existed at a more rarefied, ideological plane.

Some Consequences of the Intifada within the National Movement

The previous analysis stressed the extent to which the political leadership that became evident inside the occupied areas during the first two years of the Intifada was both linked and subordinate to the PLO's external political leadership. But it should also be stressed that, after the capabilities of the Palestinian constituency of the occupied areas were revealed during the Intifada, this constituency could not be treated by the national leadership as just another in the many geographical concentrations that made up the Palestinian people. In many respects, through their Intifada, the Palestinians of the territories had claimed for themselves a vanguard role, fighting directly on the front that the national leadership had already decided would be its principal front: a battle against the occupation of the West Bank and Gaza and for the establishment of a Palestinian state there, conducted by nonmilitary means.

In 1982, the Israelis' massive crushing of the PLO's military establishment in Lebanon brought home to the vast majority of the Palestinian exiles that—at least in the absence of concerted Arab military action—any hopes of attaining their ends through building up a military establishment in the Diaspora were illusory. By April 1983, at least one of the "historic leaders" of Fatah, Khaled al-Hassan, was articulating one of the consequences of this reality when he admitted that the major remaining source of the PLO leaders' international legitimacy, and its major hope for the future, now lay with the Palestinian population remaining in the historic homeland.[46]

According to many accounts from activists on the "inside," the events of 1982 were also decisive in changing their attitudes toward the liberation struggle. Faisal Husseini's assessment was that, "before 1982, people here would sit and wait for liberation from outside. After 1982, they started to ask what *they* could do to bring it about."[47] The results of this shift were clear from the Israeli security service records, which prior to 1982 had recorded Palestinian "disturbances" at an average rate of 500 per year; in the 1982–83 reporting year, this figure soared to 4,400 incidents, and it never dipped below the 3,000 mark in the period between then and December 1987.[48]

The period between 1982 and 1987 was thus one in which the resident Palestinians started seriously building up their own community-based challenge to the occupation. It then took the successful institutionalization of the Intifada to enable them and their compatriots in the Diaspora to realize the extent of their new empowerment. PLO Executive Committee member Yasser Abd Raboo, who was a prominent member of the DFLP, said in an interview in Tunis in June 1989 that the Intifada's success had broken the mold whereby, ever since 1948, Palestinians suffering in their own homeland had awaited deliverance from forces outside. "Now the resident Palestinians don't expect anything from anyone," he said "—including us. And that's better. . . . Now, the main question is how those outside can redefine their role. Those outside should become the 'echo' of those inside."[49]

Abd Raboo was probably more realistic, and more sanguine, about the political implications of the Intifada's success for the balance between the two wings of the national movement than were some of the other activists and leaders interviewed in the Diaspora. Quite possibly, he, as well as other representatives of the smaller UNLU factions, had reason to be so. The political composition of the UNLU, where power was split between four formally equal representatives, was different from that of PLO institutions on the outside, where Fatah enjoyed what by common consent amounted to two-thirds of the effective decision-making power, with all the six or seven other PLO member groups left to vie for the remaining third.

This disparity between the power balances in the resident and exile wings of the movement was sometimes a cause of tension. Some PFLP supporters on the inside, for example, voiced complaints that the outside (i.e. Fatah-dominated) leadership had crucially changed the text of one UNLU leaflet before "signing off" on it.[50] But by and large, the resident-exile power disparities did not seem to be too great a cause for concern to the Fatah leaders on the outside. One reason for this may have been that they knew that the political positions of at least two of the three smaller UNLU groups—the DFLP and the PCP—were more solidly in support of their own pursuit of a negotiated settlement and a two-state solution than was much of their own, Fatah, political base in the Diaspora. In August 1989, for example, Fatah held its fifth General Congress in Tunis. Since Fatah has always been a banned organization in the occupied areas, no resident activists were able to attend. In its political statement, the congress did "affirm the historic importance of the resolutions of the 19th PNC session"; but it also called for "continuing to intensify and escalate armed action and all forms of struggle to liquidate the Israeli-Zionist occupation."[51] With Fatah's Diaspora-rooted political machine putting brakes on the leadership's shift toward a political strategy, the relative empowerment of the DFLP and the PCP in particular, through the Intifada, bolstered the leaders' own pro-negotiations stance.

Another reason for the Fatah leaders' confidence may have been that, in any of the elections in the occupied territories that would likely form part of the peace process, any list that received Yasser Arafat's endorsement could easily outperform any put together by the small groups without his endorsement. At that stage, the charisma of Arafat's nationalist aura would likely count for far more than all the solid organizational credentials built up by the small groups in the territories.[52]

In elections or in any other major political challenge that might be posed in the future inside the territories, the major challenge to Fatah's control of national decision making would come, indeed, not from its secular-nationalist partners in the UNLU, but from the Moslem fundamentalists whose importance to national decision making had been underlined during the Intifada. This was another, even more fundamental, respect in which the political challenge faced by the Fatah leadership on the inside differed from that which it faced on the outside.

In the Palestinian Diaspora, the major challenge to the PLO's overall leadership of the national movement and its claim to be "the sole legitimate representative of the Palestinian people" had always, since the late 1960s, come from Arab governments or their direct Palestinian proxies. This was true of the campaign that the Jordanians waged against the Fatah/PLO leaders' right to represent the Palestinians from 1970 through 1974. (Inside the territories, the Jordanians' political challenge to the PLO continued long after 1974 but was publicly conceded when King Hussein withdrew his claim to represent the West Bankers in July 1988.) The same was also true of the challenge launched against Arafat's PLO leadership by the Iraqi-backed "Rejection Front" between 1974 and 1978. Then from 1983 through 1987, the Syrians mounted a sustained challenge to Arafat's legitimacy.

Throughout all those pre-Intifada political battles in the Diaspora, Moslem fundamentalists had never had any organized presence in the Palestinian political environment. After the Intifada underlined the primacy of the resident constituency within the movement, however, the fundamentalists, whose organizations there remained outside the PLO's decision-making structure, gained clearly identifiable influence over national decision making for the first time. Arafat himself admitted to the significance of this new state of affairs in February 1989, when he expressed the opinion that the fundamentalists now posed a greater potential threat to his leadership of the PLO than did the secular opposition groups headquartered in a still-hostile Syria.[53]

On occasion, the fundamentalist organizations clearly appeared to be trying to use the new influence with which the Intifada had endowed them to launch a direct challenge to the PLO leadership's legitimacy. This was the case, for example, when HAMAS elements painted public slogans declaring that "the Koran is the sole legitimate representative."[54] As of the end of 1989, however, the Islamic Jihad was still giving conditional support to Arafat's national leadership, and HAMAS was apparently still adhering to the assurance Sheikh Yasin had given in April 1989, that he would not seek to supplant the role of the PLO in any negotiations with Israel. While this latter position still fell short of endorsing the legitimacy of the Arafat leadership, it also signaled a decision to refrain from launching any direct challenge to it. Given the circumstances, this was a significant political victory for Arafat. But it remained to be seen how long, if a failure to register political movement should continue long after the end of 1989, the fundamentalists would continue to refrain from challenging Arafat. Indeed, if the occupied territories were where the new political trends in the Palestinian movement were being set from December 1987 on, then it looked as though, in the event that Arafat's political strategy should fail, a successor coalition to that which he had headed in the PLO leadership for twenty years might be formed by the PFLP and the fundamentalists, along with some disenchanted members of the Fatah base.

Conclusions

Far from having been caught off balance by the outbreak of the Intifada, the PLO leadership reacted to it just about as effectively as could have been hoped for from a leadership that was physically located 2,000 kilometers distant from the occupied areas and barred from easy communication with Intifada participants by a barrage of Israeli-enforced impediments. Within five weeks from the outbreak of the mass uprising, the external leadership had put into place an inside-the-territories coordinating mechanism that was able to institutionalize the Intifada and sustain a situation of effective dual power within the territories throughout two years of harsh Israeli countermeasures. Its ability to do this stemmed directly from the appropriateness of the organizing strategies that the PLO leadership—and in particular, Fatah's Khalil Wazir—had been pursuing in the territories throughout the previous four years.

The PLO leaders were also effective in harnessing the tremendous new power of the Intifada to the pursuit of the political strategy they (and a majority of the residents of the occupied areas) had favored for a number of years: to seek entry to a negotiation through which the occupation would end and a Palestinian state be established in West Bank and Gaza in its place. In this regard, note should be taken of the degree to which the Intifada had given new power not only to its direct participants in the occupied areas but also to the PLO leaders. By being able to invest their political aspirations for the first time, mainly in the Palestinian communities resident in the homeland, the PLO leaders were able to shake off the debilitating shackle of the "Arab consensus," to which they had been subject so long as they remained a Diaspora-based movement.

The PLO leaders were not able, during the first two years of the Intifada, to win the formal commencement of the negotiations they sought, far less its successful completion. But they were able to remove significant impediments which, before December 1987, had blocked its opening. These included, most significantly, King Hussein's lingering claim to represent the West Bankers and the Americans' refusal to talk to the PLO.

The Palestinians were unable, through the end of 1989, to force the Israeli government to agree to the formal negotiations over the long-term status of the territories that they sought. But they did succeed in bringing home to Israeli decision makers the fact that there could be no way of bringing the Intifada to an end through military means, without stretching Israel's national consensus beyond the breaking point. Thus, the National Unity government that emerged in early 1989 made it one of its first orders of business to combine its military efforts against the Intifada with a political initiative. Although the election plan launched by Prime Minister Shamir in the middle of May 1989 fell far short of the kind of negotiations the Palestinians were seeking, the fact that the same Shamir who sixteen months earlier had refused even to discuss the Palestinians' modest "Fourteen Points" was now putting forward his own (strikingly similar) proposal, showed that the Intifada had some ability to affect his actions.

After May 1989, the PLO leaders in Tunis were, in general, more eager than the activists on the ground in the occupied areas to explore the possibilities of the Shamir plan. Indeed, if in 1988 the net effect of the empowerment of the resident Palestinians on the leadership had been to help push the latter toward political moderation, then its effect throughout 1989 was largely to put a brake on the leadership's move toward moderation.

There were, it is true, some discernible differences between the political trends and imperatives operating between the resident Palestinian constituency and the outside leadership. But such differences never threatened the essential unity between the inside and outside wings of the national movement that had been underlined by both sides throughout the Intifada. And in that fact, after two years of the chronic suffering that accompanied the Intifada, lay the resident Palestinians' greatest achievement. For if, as seems to be the case, the real intention of Prime Minister Shamir when he launched his election proposal was to foster the emergence of an "inside" leadership that would challenge the PLO's claim to lead the Palestinians, then he failed utterly to achieve this.

Thus, as of the end of 1989, the battle of wills between Shamir and the PLO leadership remained unsolved. The PLO had been unable to impose meaningful negotiations on an unwilling Shamir; and he had been unable to find any group or even individual among the resident Palestinians who was willing to challenge the PLO's national leadership. This political standoff could not provide any stability for the occupied areas over the long run. But given the huge disparity between the two sides in all the measurable attributes of power, the PLO leaders' ability to sustain even this situation spoke highly of the resolution, political acumen, and internal discipline of their movement.

Notes

1. Graham E. Fuller, *The West Bank of Israel: Point of No Return?* (Santa Monica, Calif.: Rand, 1989), p. 25.
2. In 1984 I wrote that "the years from 1977 onward were marked by an accelerated shift in the center of gravity of the Palestinian movement from those of its components operating outside the Israeli-held areas closer towards those resisting Israel from within." Helena Cobban, *The Palestinian Liberation Organization: People Power and Politics* (New York: Cambridge University Press, 1984), p. 257.
3. Menahem Milson, "How to Make Peace with the Palestinians," *Commentary* 71 (May 1981): 30, 34, 35.
4. Sari Nuseibeh, "A true people's revolution," in *Middle East International*, December 15, 1989, p. 16.
5. " 'National Command' urges general strike 15 Jan.," on Al-Quds Palestinian Arab Radio in Arabic, January 14, 1988; as translated in *Foreign Broadcast Information Service: Daily Report Near East and South Asia* (hereafter *FBIS:NES*), January 15, 1988, pp. 3–4.
6. " 'Unified National Command' salutes 'Uprising'," Baghdad Voice of the PLO, January 20, 1988; as transcribed and translated in *FBIS:NES-88-013*, January 21, 1988, p. 6.
7. The texts of the leaflets as broadcast by the Voice of Palestine from Baghdad can generally be located in the *FBIS:NES* edition for the following working day.
8. Generally, the three hours of open shops would be held in the mornings, with the exception of the town of Bir Zeit, where for some reason the shops opened in the afternoons rather than the mornings.
9. Since the mid-1980s, the Israeli government has named the body

that directly oversees civilian affairs in the occupied areas (except East Jerusalem) the "Civil Administration." This administration is headed by former military officers and reports to the defense minister. Its actions, moreover, continued to be governed by the hundreds of military orders that have proliferated in the occupied areas since 1967 (more than 1,200 in the West Bank and at least 800 in Gaza). For these reasons, I consider the term "Civil Administration" something of a misnomer except inasmuch as it refers to a system for the administration of civilians. I prefer to continue using the less ambiguous term "military administration." For a brief survey of the administrative situation in the occupied territories, see *Briefing Papers on Twenty Years of Israel Occupation of the West Bank and Gaza* (Ramallah: Al-Haq/Law in the Service of Man, n.d.), pp. 2–9.

10. The information in the first section of this chapter, and much of the rest of it, is derived primarily from a series of in-depth interviews with more than forty individuals that I conducted, generally in Arabic, during a research visit to the occupied territories in the summer of 1989. Where possible I give attribution to those whose comments and judgments are directly cited. But because of the understandable fears that many of the interviewees entertained when discussing these issues, many of them agreed to speak only on condition that they not be identified.

For Sari Nuseibeh's confirmation concerning the composition of the UNLU, see Nuseibeh, "A True People's Revolution."

11. An account of these strains can be read in the my study, "The PLO from the Iran-Contra Affair to the Intifada," in *The Middle East from the Iran-Contra Affair to the Intifada*, ed. Robert O. Freedman (Syracuse: Syracuse University Press, 1991).

12. See Muhammad Shadid, "The Muslim Brotherhood Movement in the West Bank and Gaza," *Third World Quarterly* 10, no. 2 (April 1988): 663.

13. Shadid, "The Muslim Brotherhood Movement."

14. For details of the early history of the Brotherhood in Gaza, see Ziad Abu Amr, *The Roots of the Political Movements in the Gaza Strip, 1948–1967* (Akra, Israel: Dar al-Aswar, 1987), pp. 61–84.

15. Author's interview with second-level Brotherhood leaders in the West Bank, August 1989.

16. Quoted in Shadid, "The Muslim Brotherhood Movement," p. 669.

17. Details of some of the disputes in the West Bank can be found in chapters 6 and 7 of Emile Sahliyeh's excellent account, *In Search of Leadership: West Bank Politics since 1967* (Washington: Brookings Institution, 1988).

18. See " 'Unified National Command' salutes 'Uprising'," p. 7.

19. Author's interview, Gaza, July 1989.

20. Author's interview with a young HAMAS leader in the West Bank, August 1989.

21. See the article on schools reopening in the West Bank, *Jerusalem Post*, July 31, 1989, pp. 1, 8.

22. "Islamic Leader on Elections, Palestinian State," interview with Sheikh Ahmed Yasin, in *Al-Nahar* (Jerusalem), April 30, 1989, pp. 1, 4; as translated in *FBIS:NRS*, 89-084, pp. 39, 40.

23. "Hamas Founder Denies Charges," *Jerusalem Post International Edition*, January 13, 1990, p. 7.

24. Quoted in Lisa Taraki, "Mass Organizations in the West Bank," in *Occupation: Israel over Palestine*, ed. Naseer Aruri (Boston: Arab Association of University Graduates, forthcoming).

25. See Sahliyeh, *In Search of Leadership*, pp. 126–27.

26. Copy of letter as given to the author by Hanna Siniora, Washington, D.C., January 28, 1988.

27. The text of the fourteen points can be found in *The Middle East Ten Years after Camp David*, ed. William Quandt (Washington: Brookings Institution, 1988) pp. 484–85.

28. Conversation with Hanna Siniora and Abu Rahme at the Brookings Institution, Washington, January 28, 1988.

29. See *FBIS:NES-88-024*, February 5, 1988, pp. 3, 4; and *FBIS:NES-88-035*, February 23, 1988, pp. 5–6. These are the texts as broadcast on the PLO radio station. In the Al-Quds (pro-Syrian) radio version of No. 6, the demand for municipal elections is notably absent (see *FBIS:NES-88-025*, February 8, 1988, pp. 3–4).

30. Conversation with Hanna Siniora, Jerusalem, April 1988.

31. Interview with Faisal Husseini, Jerusalem, August 1989.

32. *FBIS:NES-88-024*, p. 3. This second paragraph was omitted from the version of the leaflet broadcast by Al-Quds.

33. *FBIS:NES-88-035*, p. 5.

34. Ziad Abu Amr, *The Intifada: Causes and Factors of Continuity* (Jerusalem: Palestinian Academic Society for the Study of International Affairs, 1989), p. 24.

35. See *FBIS:NES-88-146*, July 29, 1988, p. 23.

36. These leaked reports surfaced in the Israeli press in the first ten days of August. Translations of these reports, but not of the purported text of the actual document or documents, can be found in the *FBIS:NES* edition of August 9, 1988, pp. 32–34.

37. Sari Nuseibeh, "A Call for a Discussion of the State of the Intifada and Its Horizons," *Al-Yawm al-Sabi'* (Paris), August 1, 1988, pp. 18–19.

38. The text of the Abu Sharif document has been printed in Quandt, *The Middle East Ten Years after Camp David*, pp. 490–93.

39. Cobban, *The PLO*, p. 182.

40. A list of these deportees is given in Ann Lesch, "Israeli Deportation of Palestinians from the West Bank and the Gaza Strip, 1967–1978," *Journal of Palestine Studies*, no. 30, pp. 101–31, and no. 31, pp. 81–112.

41. See Joost R. Hiltermann, *Israel's Deportation Policy in the Occupied West Bank and Gaza*, 2d ed. (Ramallah: Al-Haq, August 1988), pp. 7, 106.

42. Hilterman, *Israel's Deportation Policy*, pp. 106–08.

43. Interview, Jerusalem, July 1989.

44. Ze'ev Schiff, "Israel Insists on Deporting Moderates," *Ha'aretz* (Tel Aviv), September 8, 1989, as quoted in *Israel Press Briefs*, no. 68, November 1989, p. 7.

45. Danny Rubinstein, "The Deportees," *Davar* (Tel Aviv), September 11, 1989, as translated in *Israel Press Briefs*, no. 68, November 1989, p. 15.

46. Quoted in Cobban, *The PLO*, pp. 257–58.

47. Interview, Jerusalem, July 1989.

48. Meron Benvenisti, *1987 Report* (Jerusalem: West Bank Data Base Project, 1987), p. 40.

49. Author's interview, Tunis, June 1989.

50. The substance of this complaint, which was voiced to me in Gaza in July 1989, was interesting. It was that the outside leaders had taken out of the text a reference to the Palestinians' long-sacred "right of return."

51. See " 'Text' of Fatah Political Program," in *FBIS:NES-89-153*, August 10, 1989, p. 2.

52. One of the East Jerusalem intellectuals summed up this judgment neatly in the summer of 1989: "al-Arafatiyeen fid-dakhil akther bi-katheer min al-fathawiyeen" (the Arafat supporters in the inside are much more numerous than the Fatah supporters).

53. Group discussion with Yasser Arafat, Tunis, February 1989.

54. The author saw many of these slogans painted in Nablus in July 1989.

Part Two

The Response of External Players to the Intifada

The American Response to the Intifada

4

David Pollock

This attempt to analyze American policy responses to the Palestinian uprising, or Intifada, must acknowledge three limitations at the outset. First, while the Intifada continues, that policy represents a "moving target"—moving slowly, perhaps, but not standing still ("gestating," in diplomatic jargon, rather than "stagnating").[1] Obviously, only tentative judgments can be rendered about a policy that is still unfolding, particularly when that policy is so deliberately both incremental and discreet. Second, and related to the preceding point, even the preliminary analysis offered here reflects a personal and partial view, especially since the major American decisions on the matter have been increasingly closely held at high policymaking levels.

Third, within that framework, this chapter is not meant to be a complete chronology of American policy, in part simply because the official record is, as always, very long and involved. On the diplomatic circuit, that record includes not only close consultation with Israel and Egypt but also periodic discussions with other Arab governments, Soviets, Europeans, and others; dialogue with the PLO; and working-level contacts with local Palestinians. At home, the record includes testimony in and reports to Congress, public statements and press briefings, meetings with concerned citizens, and so on. But the record is not merely long; it is also full of peripheral details that, important as they may be at the time, run the risk of obscuring the big picture. No attempt will be made here to do justice to every such detail; rather, the intent is to summarize the main trends.

Therefore, in the interests of brevity and analytical focus, U.S. diplomacy on several regional problems with some bearing on Arab-Israeli policy issues (including, for example, geographically broader or else more technical Middle Eastern security concerns) will be omitted entirely from this discussion. For the same reasons, even with regard to the Intifada itself, the presentation that follows largely excludes quiet U.S. diplomacy with Israel and with the PLO on issues of human rights or terrorism. Instead, the emphasis throughout will be on the middle ground between grand regional strategy and intricate detail: the central framework of American policy toward the new phase of the Arab-Israeli conflict that began with the inception of the Intifada in December 1987.

With all these caveats in mind, the following discussion will first sketch the relevant background of U.S. policy before the Intifada, proceed to examine the four subsequent stages of that policy, and then turn to some brief comments on its progress so far, and conclude on its future prospects in both short- and long-range perspectives.

Background

In the four years preceding the outbreak of the Intifada, U.S. policy had clearly put the Arab-Israeli "peace process" on a diplomatic back burner, without quite abandoning it altogether. American reluctance to get too deeply involved was motivated by a confluence of factors, all of which suggested caution verging on complacence. The experience of an ill-fated, if marginal, intervention in Lebanon from late 1982 through early 1984 had left a lasting negative impression. This derived, first of all, from the substantial and tangible risks (not to mention the cost in American lives) of direct U.S. involvement. It derived also from the demonstrably paltry rewards of attempting to broker any Arab-Israeli agreement—symbolized by the abortive U.S.-mediated Lebanese-Israeli accord of May 1983.

Moreover, after the withdrawal from Lebanon of the limited American military contingent in March 1984, the Arab-Israeli conflict seemed to settle into an uneasy but relatively manageable quiescence. Israel withdrew from all but a narrow border "security zone" in Lebanon by June 1985, leaving the protagonists in that country's unending civil war largely to their own devices. The discontent seething in the West Bank and Gaza remained mostly below the surface. The "cold peace" between Israel and Egypt seemed to be holding reasonably well. No other promising Arab diplomatic initiative beckoned for American support; nor was there any realistic prospect that the Arabs, thoroughly preoccupied by an economic slump and by the war against Iran, would turn their arms against Israel or their "oil weapon" against the United States.

Events inside Israel also militated against an activist American approach to Arab-Israeli peacemaking during that period. The Israelis, too, were preoccupied by purely internal affairs. This prolonged interlude started with the post-Lebanon political shakeup within the ruling Likud party, moved on with the fall 1984 election campaign that produced a virtual tie vote and a Likud-Labor National Unity government with a "rotating" prime ministry, and then continued through the next two years of primary focus on repairing the country's parlous economic situation. Under these circumstances, without a compelling reason to do otherwise, the United States was naturally inclined to encourage Israel to get its own house in order before attempting any more ambitious regional initiatives.

Finally, American policymakers were themselves distracted during the mid-1980s by Middle East issues other than Arab-Israeli ones: international terrorism, the Gulf war, and of course the "Irangate" controversy, which emerged in late 1986 and continued to reverberate in Congress and elsewhere well through the following year. By that time, other issues outside the region—Soviet-American relations, Central America, and assorted other Third World trouble spots, to name but a few—took precedence over the dormant Arab-Israeli conflict in U.S. foreign policy priorities.

As a result of all these factors, the Middle East policy emphasis in the second Reagan administration shifted even more strongly than before toward "strategic partnership" with Israel—almost regardless of any progress or lack thereof in some "peace process" in that area. The Palestinians, in particular, were widely considered to be only a minor or subsidiary factor in the equation.

All this is not to say, however, that Washington utterly neglected the peace process until the Palestinian uprising forced it back on the agenda. The record demonstrates otherwise; in fact, although not a high priority, there was a significant American foray into the Arab-Israeli peacemaking thicket in the year before the Intifada broke out. In early 1987, prodded by both Foreign Minister Shimon Peres of Israel and Jordan's King Hussein, and encouraged by early and still tentative signals of Soviet "new thinking," the United States quietly explored the possibility of reviving an international conference "framework" for peace talks between Israel and a combined Jordanian/Palestinian delegation. This approach seemed stymied by a classic Labor versus Likud deadlock over the issue in May of that year, but the United States kept probing for an opening anyway. In October 1987—two months *before* large-scale protests in Gaza ushered in the new era of Intifada—Secretary of State George Shultz actually traveled to the region to discuss alternative diplomatic strategies. But he made no progress in developing a formula—even a procedural one for initiating peace talks—that would be acceptable to Prime Minister Yitzhak Shamir of Israel as well as to King Hussein.

When, in the face of such frustration, the gathering storm in the territories finally broke in December, American policy underwent a series of adjustments, which would collectively constitute a response to the Intifada. Their common thread was a faster pace and higher profile of U.S. diplomatic activity, neatly captured in one simple statistic: While Shultz paid only one extended visit to the region in four full years before the Intifada, afterward he made three separate such trips in less than half a year. Thus, even if the uprising did not create American interest in an Arab-Israeli peace process ex nihilo, it certainly increased the urgency of that interest, and eventually channeled it in somewhat different directions.

The evolution of an official U.S. response to the new circumstances set in motion by the Intifada can be divided, for analytical purposes, into four chronological phases, straddling the last year of Ronald Reagan's and the first year of George Bush's presidencies: (1) initial reassessment, from December 1987 through February 1988; (2) the "Shultz Plan," from March 1988 through the end of that year; (3) policy planning for the new Bush administration, January through April 1989; and (4) the Palestinian election initiative, May 1989 to date. What follows is an attempt to outline the main features of each phase and also to explain what led from each one to the next.

Initial Reassessment, December 1987–February 1988

Americans, like most Arabs and Israelis themselves, were surprised by the Intifada, and it took everybody some time to take stock, assimilate, and then adjust to this new development. While the underlying tensions were fairly well understood, and some early warning signs of a possible explosion were evident (at least in retrospect), few were prepared for what still seemed a sudden and then unexpectedly lasting change in the political landscape. In fact, during the first few weeks of large-scale disturbances, there remained considerable uncertainty about just how wide, deep, and especially durable the uprising would prove to be—and therefore about its political significance.

Other, subsidiary questions demanded clarification. What were the precise, immediate causes of this outbreak, and what did they suggest about its future course? What was the role of "outside agitators," as opposed to local activists? How well organized, and how violent, would the campaign become? How would the Israeli army and government—and Israel's own Arab citizens—react?

As the Intifada continued, two things quickly became apparent. First, only time would provide definitive answers to what were already almost academic questions; but it seemed increasingly likely that the new wave of protests would be much more than a mere passing episode. And second, the very fact that the uprising was continuing, with no end in sight, suggested the desirability of an appropriate American diplomatic—as distinct from a purely rhetorical or palliative—response. In this initial phase, American public statements (and reportedly also private discussions) tended to concentrate on what might be called the humanitarian aspects of the uprising: concern over the suffering, loss of life, and moral dilemmas generated by the escalating violence. By February, however, official American thinking had evolved toward a more fundamental, political approach to address the issues underlying the Intifada, and not just treat their symptoms.[2] It was to gauge local reactions to this new proposal that Secretary of State Shultz embarked on the first in a series of "shuttle diplomacy" tours of the region at the end of that month.

The "Shultz Plan," March–December 1988

The major new feature of the U.S. proposal presented to the regional parties during the Intifada's first spring was an "interlock" between, on the one hand, the "final status" peace talks previously envisaged in the long-discussed international conference framework and, on the other hand, "interim arrangements" that might address the immediate causes of the uprising. The former aspect seemed designed to appeal especially to Jordan; the latter, rather paradoxically, to both Israel and the Palestinians. For Israel, "interim arrangements" sounded reassuringly like Camp David–style autonomy while avoiding any final, difficult decisions. For Palestinians, interim measures offered the prospect of at least loosening the bonds of Israeli occupation while more far-reaching solutions were considered. That prospect was enhanced (or so it was hoped) by what was informally called an "accelerated timetable" of just a few months for moving from negotiations on interim to more permanent aspects of an Arab-Israeli settlement.

As then Assistant Secretary of State Richard Murphy put it in October 1988, a "fundamental element" of U.S. policy was now to recognize "the indispensability of an initial agreement on transitional arrangements, tightly linked to an early start of negotiations on a final settlement."[3] This kind of linkage was admittedly problematic for the Israeli government; but, as Murphy had reasoned on another occasion, "While some Israelis have argued that the timetable and interlock mechanism are unacceptable deviations from the Camp David accords . . . can those people realistically believe that the clock can be turned back to 1978 and that negotiations can start from a basis which Jordan, Syria and others rejected categorically? This is an illusion which cannot and will not be fulfilled."[4]

With the benefit of hindsight, the "Shultz Plan" can fairly be described as a transitional one, from pre- to post-outbreak of the Intifada. It kept the existing idea of an international Middle East peace conference featuring King Hussein, but modified it on the margins to take the uprising into account—mainly by advancing the schedule and linking it to talks on the newly urgent issues "on the ground." That urgency was reflected in the visits that Shultz made to the region in order to promote the revised peace plan in late March/early April and again in mid-May 1988. Contributing to the stepped-up pace of these efforts was a subtle shift in the American domestic context of Middle East diplomacy: The Intifada had inspired a significant portion of Congress, and of the organized American Jewish leadership, to recommend greater attention to peacemaking on the part of the United States and Israel alike. This was publicly acknowledged to be a new factor. In two separate interviews in Israel in early April, Secretary Shultz referred to support for his initiative from members of Congress "on a bipartisan basis" as well as from "members of the American Jewish community."[5]

Nevertheless, if the timing was right for such efforts in that sense, it was wrong in other respects. Israel, struggling to cope with the new Palestinian challenge, was, if anything, more divided than ever, with Labor inclined to accept and Likud determined to reject Shultz's proposal. On the Palestinian side, there was still no authoritative spokesman with whom the United States could talk. In any case, all indications were that the Palestinians, still euphoric about their unaccustomed achievement, were hardly in the mood to talk about "half measures." As if that were not enough, Jordan delivered the coup de grace by announcing, at the end of July 1988, that it was in effect abandoning political responsibility for the West Bank. That role for Jordan, until then a key element in U.S. policy, had at last proven to be not an "option" but an optical illusion.[6]

American policy hastily tried to adjust to this new and major twist by deemphasizing both the international conference and the Jordanian part in it, while maintaining other features of the "Shultz Plan" largely intact. As Murphy put it, Jordan's "disengagement from the occupied territories has placed a greater obligation on the Palestinians themselves . . . [to] search for ways to open a dialogue with Israel."[7]

Unfortunately, as Secretary Shultz observed, as of September 1988 neither the Israelis nor the Palestinians seemed ready yet for political talks with each other—talks that would require, in the American view, a different approach by both sides:

> Palestinians must renounce terrorism and violence. They must accept the right of Israel to exist. . . . They cannot murder or threaten other Palestinians who maintain contact with Israeli authorities.
> Israel . . . cannot claim there is no one to talk to, while suppressing political expression and arresting or deporting . . . even those who speak in moderate terms.[8]

Despite these obstacles, the United States, according to Shultz, continued to advocate "direct negotiations, launched, if required, through an international conference" that could "support direct negotiations without interfering in them."[9]

But it was too late. By the autumn of 1988, any practical plans for the peace process ran afoul of the campaign season for national elections in both Israel and the United States, which fortuitously coincided in early November. In Israel, another inconclusive vote eventually produced another divided National Unity government—this time with the reins of foreign policy more firmly in Likud hands, leaving even less room for diplomatic maneuvering on a proposal already snubbed by that party. The "Shultz Plan" thus became a casualty of time and events, as the clock ran out on the Reagan years. There was still time, however, for one last surprising Middle East policy legacy to the next administration, bequeathed to President-elect Bush by his predecessor in mid-December 1988.

It was at that point that, in response to PLO chairman Yasser Arafat's public acceptance of the long-standing American conditions—including recognition of Israel's right to exist, acceptance of U.N. Resolutions 242 and 338, and renunciation of terrorism—the United States decided to open an "official, substantive dialogue" with the PLO. The rapid sequence of events leading up to this unprecedented and important step can actually be traced back to November, when the Palestine National Council meeting in Algiers resolved to declare Palestinian independence yet simultaneously recognize (with some remaining ambiguities) the legitimacy of a "two-state solution" in Palestine. Official American reaction was encouraging but noncommittal. Shortly thereafter, Washington turned down Arafat's application for a visa to address the U.N. General Assembly in New York on the grounds of his organization's involvement in international terrorism.

Subsequently, in statements at a special U.N. session in Geneva and then at a conclave with Jewish figures in Stockholm, Arafat further advanced his position. Finally, at a press conference back in Geneva, the PLO leader explicitly met the stated U.S. terms for bilateral talks and was immediately rewarded with a favorable American response.[10] It seemed that U.S. insistence on a more clear-cut declaration of intent, reinforcing both the pressures and opportunities created by the Intifada itself, had helped accomplish two goals: beginning a new chapter in PLO policy and therefore potentially in Arab-Israeli diplomacy as a whole, and opening a new channel for American involvement in regional peacemaking.

In the short term, however, the new U.S.-PLO relationship was predictably problematic for American-Israeli relations. In the eyes of many Israelis (and some others), the American decision to open an official dialogue with the PLO involved much more than mere procedure. Rather, as one perceptive private American analyst argued, "To talk to the PLO is to move a long way toward recognizing the legitimacy of Palestinian aspirations for a state. Hardline Israeli politicians know this—which is why direct talks with the PLO are absolutely anathema. Indeed, with the establishment of direct talks between the United States and the PLO, Israel now has, whether it wants them or not, indirect negotiations with the PLO."[11] Israeli spokesmen continued to contest not just the credibility but even the relevance of Arafat's organization, though they had little else to offer in the way of a political alternative. U.S. officials, for their part, admitted that they did not expect Israel to follow the American lead in this particular respect, although they had no ready blueprint for mediating even at a distance between these two potential partners for peace. The task of somehow squaring that circle was left, by an accident of the American political calendar, to the next administration in Washington, which took office in January 1989.

The New Bush Administration, January–May 1989

The inauguration of George Bush, the first incumbent vice president elected to the American presidency since Martin Van Buren, a century and a half before, promised a considerable measure of continuity in U.S. policy. Three previous new presidents during the preceding two decades had each launched a "new look" in American diplomacy in the Middle East, but Bush avoided that temptation. Other, more pressing global priorities, plus the obvious need for extensive preliminary diplomatic groundwork where the Arab-Israeli conflict was concerned, meant that the administration generally refrained from high-profile presidential involvement in the latter arena and avoided direct "on location" shuttle diplomacy by the Secretary of State. Behind the scenes, however, it guided lower but still senior levels in an active diplomatic campaign on Arab-Israeli issues, replete with the characteristic signals, "target dates," and confidential consultations of that craft.

Of course, continuity and quiet diplomacy could not mean a mere carbon copy of previous policy. Some old strands of that policy (like the "Jordanian option") had unraveled, and some new ones (like the dialogue with the PLO) had been added at the last minute, leaving the task of knitting the loose threads into a coherent fabric to the incoming administration. After a brief period of settling in, the new Bush policy team proceeded to pick up and then to rearrange those pieces, giving new impetus to the major thrust of existing American policy in the region.

Indeed, it may be precisely the underlying consistency of U.S. policy in this area that has misled some observers into exaggerating the significance of distinctions between the Middle East policy "style" of the Reagan and Bush administrations. Too much has been made by some pundits even of personality differences: between "warm" Shultz and "icy" Baker, for example, or between the "sentimental" Reagan and the "calculating" Bush. To be sure, there is significant scope in American policy toward the Arab-Israeli conflict for presidential decision. In fact, as William Quandt has convincingly argued, that issue, in part because of its unique mixture of foreign policy and domestic politics, is the arena for such leadership par excellence.[12] But considerations of personal style, temperament, or background are rarely if ever decisive in this regard. To say, correctly, that the major decisions ultimately rest with individuals is not to say that they make those decisions based on "gut instincts" or "personal chemistry" with foreign leaders. What counts for much more are the changing strategic and political realities—viewed inescapably through a personal prism, influenced perhaps by individual convictions and experiences, but acted upon, in the end, primarily on the basis of practical choices among competing interests and options. The parameters, in short, are those of politics, not personalities.

The political reality confronting the Bush administration was that the Intifada had greatly increased the salience of Arab-Israeli conflict management, without indicating a better means to that end. According to the new State Department director of policy planning, Dennis Ross, while events had created new pressures and possibilities for "practical movement," the incoming Bush administration still faced the "traditional barriers" to peacemaking: "On the question of substance, there was no change in the gap on the question of territories or sovereignty. On procedure, there was no change on the question of an international conference or on Palestinian representation."[13] To surmount those barriers, a revised approach was called for: rather than continue to pursue an ambitious but unattainable agenda, stress more modest but manageable goals; rather than promote an American peace plan, solicit suggestions from the parties. The effect would be to take smaller steps, but in a more precise direction. Or, as another U.S. official explained: "The gaps between the parties were too wide to generate a high-level, high profile American peace plan which might only serve to distract the parties from the key choices that they themselves would have to make. Rather, what was required was an effort that sought to create the conditions . . . for sustaining such a negotiation. This required an approach that avoided, as much as possible, the parties' bottom-line positions on the contentious issues . . . and that sought to change their views and perceptions toward one another."[14]

This incremental approach would not sacrifice principles on the altar of expediency; the principles were forcefully restated, to take one early and notable example, in Secretary of State James Baker's May 1989 address to the American-Israeli Public Affairs Committee (AIPAC), in which he called on the Arabs to demonstrate their readiness for peace and on the Israelis to "abandon their dream of a Greater Israel."[15] Such statements answered the demand for some larger vision of the American diplomatic destination, but the immediate task was now defined as one of helping the parties just get started on the right road. And those "parties" (to pin down an eternally elusive diplomatic circumlocution) now emphatically included the Palestinians as primary players—thanks in no small measure to the uprising they had managed to sustain.

In practice, this meant that Washington would drop both the international conference and the tight "interlock" between interim and final status arrangements and concentrate instead on getting to direct political talks between Israelis and Palestinians. This, it was hoped, would transform the Intifada into a political dynamic, substituting statements for stones and bargaining for bullets. And since Israel had the upper hand, it was from Israel that the United States sought agreement on a way to launch this transformation. While this tactic circumvented some of the difficulties that had bedeviled previous efforts, there was still much preparatory work to be done.

Right from the start, the issue of PLO participation in Arab-Israeli diplomacy had to be resolved, or at least finessed. When the Bush administration took office, in the words of one responsible official, "a reality that we confronted was the U.S.-PLO dialogue. Because the dialogue was adopted during the end of one administration and the transition to another, the dialogue had no focus or relationship to a process."[16] As policy was reformulated in early 1989, the decision was made to continue the dialogue and explore whether it could be better integrated with other features of American diplomacy but also keep its "relationship to a process," an arm's length one, given the Israeli government's refusal to deal openly or directly with the PLO. As another State Department staffer involved in Middle East policy put it in December 1989, "it was not then the intention of this government, and it is not now the intention of this government, to force a dialogue between Israel and the Palestine Liberation Organization."[17]

Still, if such a dialogue could not be forced, the prospect did have a certain persuasive power. Early in the new administration, U.S. officials hinted that, unless Israel came up with a workable proposal for a political dialogue with the Palestinians, then American diplomacy might shift in other directions less agreeable to the Israeli government—back to an international Middle East peace conference, or forward to formal PLO participation in the peace process. In March 1989, for example, Secretary Baker observed that, "if you can't have direct negotiations that are meaningful . . . [without] the PLO, we would then have to see negotiations between Israel and representatives of the PLO."[18] The effect of this official American posture, coupled with corresponding shifts on the margins of American public and in Congress and organized American Jewish groups,[19] was to reinforce the incentives for an Israeli diplomatic response to the Intifada. The situation was aptly summarized in one Washington "think tank" report: "The U.S.-PLO dialogue . . . greatly alarmed the Israelis. . . . Moreover, American Jewish leaders were . . . urging Shamir to launch some kind of peace initiative which Israel's friends in the United States could support."[20]

As a result, when Shamir visited Washington in March 1989, he brought with him the outline of an initiative along those lines. By May of that year, the Israeli cabinet formally presented a four-point proposal that responded to the American requests. The first three points covered the familiar desiderata of enhancing Egyptian-Israeli peaceful relations, expanding the peace to include other Arab states, and improving conditions for Palestinian refugees through an international aid program. The fourth point, by contrast, offered something new that appeared both fundamental and practical at the same time—an election in the West Bank and Gaza for Palestinian representatives to political talks with Israel. And it was this element that the United States seized upon as a point of departure toward the more distant goals. To quote Assistant Secretary of State John Kelly, such an election would be "a way station to negotiations on transitional arrangements which are themselves a way station to . . . a political settlement defining how the Israelis, Palestinians and other Arabs will relate to each other and live together over the long term."[21] With this framework in mind, getting to that first "way station" became the operational objective of the next phase in the American policy response to the Intifada. To recapitulate, the new Bush policy team had "asked Prime Minister Shamir for an initiative that would give us something to work with. He did that precisely."[22] The next challenge, clearly, would be to make that initiative actually bear fruit.

The Palestinian Election Plan, May 1989–March 1990

That challenge, as of late 1990, has still not been met; but nearly a year of painstaking American effort has at least cleared away some of the obstacles and clarified the ones that remain. Taking procedural matters first, U.S. policy patiently maneuvered to the point where, by the autumn of 1989, "the dialogue and elections have supplanted the conference," even in Soviet calculations. As for substantive issues, some would have to wait. Only after an Israeli-Palestinian dialogue was under way would it be possible to "change the psychological realities and make the unthinkable of today the thinkable of tomorrow."[23]

For example, according to Ambassador John Kelly, the new assistant secretary of state for Near Eastern and South Asian affairs, while American policy was "supportive of . . . land for peace . . . that does not mean that we expect the government of Israel to accept that point . . . before negotiations." And while "the United States is committed to moving to final status," and supports "self-government for Palestinians in a manner acceptable to Palestinians, to Israel and to Jordan," it also recognized "the reality that we cannot move directly to final status. The gap between the parties is too great to allow it. Elections, in our view, constitute an integral part of the process leading to transitional arrangements and final status."[24] The benefits of getting started, in other words, were worth the cost of postponing the day of reckoning on the more difficult dilemmas.

In the region, attitudes toward U.S. acceptance of Israel's election initiative combined understanding with skepticism. As one team of unofficial American analysts put it, "Israeli gratitude for American support of elections coexisted uneasily with fears that U.S. tactics were actually leading in another direction. The Palestinians, for their part, could not quite grasp why the United States had accepted Arafat in December and now, six months later, was arguing for a process that put Arafat into the shadows again. Both the Israelis and the Palestinians were lobbying for U.S. advocacy of a particular position as the key to moving the other side."[25] Washington, for its part, firmly resisted those blandishments. When, for example, the PLO argued for a formal "presence" in the diplomatic run-up to a Palestinian election, American officials successfully insisted that this would actually be counterproductive. And when, in July 1989, the Likud Central Committee appeared to place its own newly restrictive conditions on the election proposal, the United States "spent a couple of weeks working very hard with the Israelis to get a reaffirmation, since we had invested quite a bit in this initiative."[26]

The rationale for that American investment was clear. Indeed, Kelly explained, the attraction of the Israeli initiative was precisely that it deferred some of the most divisive issues even as it offered an unprecedented forum for direct Israeli-Palestinian negotiations: "We are trying to encourage Palestinian representatives from the territories and representatives of the Israeli government to work out these issues. This is the really dramatic and new opportunity that the Israeli government proposal has offered. . . . This is the first formal, legal government proposal from Israel in a decade. You can argue about elements of it, but we think it is an opportunity."[27] In practice, all sides not only could but did argue, with each other and among themselves, about various elements of the elections proposal so that, by the fall of 1989, it became clear that an even more preliminary phase of formal discussions would be required to sort out the competing point-by-point lists of agendas, assurances, and preelection arrangements. (Egypt, to oversimplify just a bit, countered Likud's "four constraints" of July 1989 with a ten-point table of "conditions," to which Israel eventually and indirectly responded with a list of six "assumptions".) In the resulting "battle of the points," the formula that was finally found—the five-point "Baker plan" released in November—was for a tripartite meeting of American, Israeli, and Egyptian foreign ministers to prepare for direct talks between Palestinians and Israelis, which would include detailed consideration of election "modalities."

By February 1990, Secretary Baker felt able to tell the Senate Foreign Relations Committee that "we have had results. Working closely with both Israel and Egypt, we have hammered out a framework for an Israeli-Palestinian dialogue in Cairo" as a first step. "If," continued the secretary, "the parties are prepared to approach this process in a practical and broadminded way, we can make progress."[28] The immediate thrust of U.S. diplomacy, according to numerous published reports and commentaries, was to promote compromise solutions to the key "procedural" problems blocking the start of an Israeli-Palestinian political dialogue. These included the composition of a Palestinian delegation acceptable to both sides, with the corollary questions of involvement by Palestinians both from East Jerusalem and from outside the territories; the indirect role of the PLO, if any, in sanctioning these discussions; and the agreed scope of their agenda. Both sides wanted specific American assurances on all these points, but any such assurances could not be mutually contradictory if the process were to work at all.

On the Jerusalem issue, for instance, the United States, believing that "the Arabs of East Jerusalem should be allowed to vote," was exploring "various formulas that are talked about under which this could be done," and which might nevertheless be acceptable to Israel.[29] On the PLO issue, the United States sought to obtain that organization's tacit acquiescence to the Cairo talks without driving the Israelis away from the bargaining table. Indeed, the continuing U.S.-PLO talks were "designed to help determine if the PLO is serious about pursuing a practical process of elections.[30]

In practical terms, therefore, the United States was supporting the Egyptians' efforts to promote, in consultation with the Palestinians, the dialogue they hoped to launch in Cairo; at the same time, American policy recognized that any solution even to these procedural problems presupposed agreement by the mainstream of both halves in Israel's Likud/Labor governing coalition. A renewed internal Likud showdown erupted over these issues at another fractious Central Committee meeting in February 1990; but the United States withheld official comment while suggesting a desire to proceed with what was, after all, the Israeli government's own initiative. As one perceptive Israeli journalist admiringly summed up the American role in this unfolding scenario: "[Secretary Baker] is displaying the patience and endurance of a marathon runner . . . Baker and his Middle East specialists are tireless in their quest for compromise formulas which would not splinter the PLO or break up Israel's National Unity government. They do not believe in an alternative Palestinian leadership from among local residents of the territories. At the same time, they have learned to entertain a healthy doubt about the option of a Peres-led narrow government and the capacity of such a government to deliver on the diplomatic front."[31]

Nevertheless, by the time those words were penned, there were signs that the administration's much-tried patience was beginning to wear thin. Many had begun to wonder whether, as Shamir reacted to partisan pressures and presumably his own private misgivings, Israel's initiative was degenerating into a delaying tactic. The Israeli government, which had accepted Baker's five points in principle in November, was still dissatisfied with the precise terms of reference for a tripartite foreign ministers meeting, let alone for an Israeli-Palestinian conference in Cairo. A new series of signals (at least as perceived in Israel) suggesting American impatience now emanated from Washington. Among them, in January 1990, was a well-publicized proposal by Senate Republican Minority Leader Robert Dole—not immediately disavowed by the White House—to cut aid to Israel, Egypt, and other "favored" countries, in order to free additional funds for the transition toward democracy in Eastern Europe. This was soon followed by public administration objections to any use by Israel of U.S. assistance for the purpose of settling Soviet Jewish immigrants in occupied territory.

Accompanying these were press reports linked to anonymous "officials" that additional American aid might be contingent on Israeli flexibility for the sake of progress toward peace.

Needless to say, American policy had to take Israel's delicate internal political equation into account throughout this effort. The United States, recognizing the intrinsic sensitivity of the issues as well as the need for a common denominator despite Israel's domestic divisions, had endeavored to make a virtue of necessity, working to ensure the widest possible official Israeli consensus behind a promising peacemaking strategy, as a kind of insurance against renewed diplomatic deadlock. As one key American official put it in a revealing comment made in November 1989, "Some may feel that the Likud in Israel is the only party that is holding up progress in the peace process. I categorically reject that assertion. It is Likud and Labor working together in a coalition government that has permitted this process to go forward."[32] By February of the following year, however, Washington's chronic concern over Israel's coalition constraints became acute again when Ariel Sharon, leader of the "constraints camp" that sought to limit Shamir's diplomatic room for maneuver, accused the prime minister of betrayal and dramatically resigned from the cabinet. As Secretary Baker testified in Congress that the United States had done about all it could to advance the peace process until Israel responded,[33] another showdown over the issue loomed inside the Likud and between the Likud and Labor halves of the Israeli government.

At just this sensitive juncture, the diplomatic process became further entangled in still another emerging issue: Soviet Jewish immigration. A quantum leap in the number of these immigrants to Israel, arriving at the rate of over 5,000 each month in early 1990, aroused the attention of Arabs and Israelis alike, in characteristically exaggerated and opposite ways: the former seeing in it the danger of another Palestinian displacement of historic proportions; the latter, a historic opportunity to set back the clock on the so-called Arab/Jewish demographic time bomb. Prime Minister Shamir's comment on January 13 that "a big *aliyah* [Jewish immigration] requires a big Israel" had already provoked a wave of rhetorical outrage in the Arab world, embarrassment in Moscow, and consternation in Washington. Among the unintended consequences was a further delay in direct flights between Moscow and Tel Aviv.

More to the point here, concerns about the issue raised by Shamir's remark inspired a spate of statements by American officials in late February and early March invoking the established prohibition against any use by Israel of U.S. assistance to finance settlements in occupied territory. Other statements seemed to oppose Jewish settlements in East Jerusalem specifically, reminding Israel of the longstanding U.S. policy that the city's status remained to be negotiated.[34] After some quick "clarifications" all around, the matter appeared to fade. Yet some distrust lingered on all sides, contributing to the strained atmosphere in which the next controversy—the one that finally brought down Israel's increasingly divided National Unity coalition—played itself out.

By that time, the immediate diplomatic obstacles had narrowed to this: Could one or two Palestinians deported from the West Bank, and one or two with a "second address" in East Jerusalem, be part of a delegation to preliminary talks with Israel in Cairo? The United States and Israel's own Labor party were pressing Shamir hard for an affirmative answer. When he still stalled, Labor threatened to pull out of the government. Shamir responded by dismissing Peres first; the other Labor ministers resigned all at once; and finally, on March 15, what was left of Israel's government fell in a close no-confidence vote, in which half the religious party contingent abandoned Shamir. After the consultations required by law, President Chaim Herzog gave Peres, rather than Shamir, the first chance at patching together a new coalition that would command a parliamentary majority. But at the end of March, the outcome remained shrouded in uncertainty, leaving Israeli policy in the hands of a caretaker government with neither a popular nor a parliamentary mandate.

For the United States, as for the other interested parties, the result of all this was a kind of temporary diplomatic time-out while Israel reshuffled its domestic political cards. American officials declared, to no one's surprise, that they hoped to work on the peace process with whatever new Israeli government emerged.[35] The American principles underlying that process, though, remained in place, prompting a capsule review of their progress and prospects.

The American Response to the Intifada:
An Interim Assessment

The American response to the Intifada has been notable as much for the diplomatic "underbrush" it cleared away (to borrow an apt term from William Quandt) as for the painstaking, and so far admittedly limited, progress in building a new foundation for peace. No longer does the United States advocate either a "Jordanian option" or an early international Mideast peace conference. No longer is Washington bound to boycott the PLO; and, most important of all, no longer does it seem resigned to, if not content with, the Arab-Israeli status quo. In the meantime, the parties themselves have responded, unevenly and still not unequivocally, to the new circumstances and also to the new U.S. policy emphasis those circumstances indicate: direct political talks between Israelis and Palestinians. What clearly remains to be demonstrated, from an American vantage point, is their openness to concrete compromises in this direction that would justify even more intense U.S. involvement.

More than two years into the Intifada, the snail's pace of diplomacy should not obscure the significant incremental movement that has already taken place. The United States helped prod the Palestinians to moderate both their basic posture toward Israel and their "procedural" requirements and expectations, and they have. By the same token, the United States helped prod Israel to create a new plan oriented directly toward the Palestinians, and it did. Though the plan itself is modest, and though even those modest goals have not yet been achieved, progress in this context, as Secretary Baker noted, must be "measured in small steps."[36] Or, as one previous American participant in U.S.-Arab-Israeli diplomacy summarized the situation in March 1990:

> Through delicate, largely quiet diplomacy, the Administration coaxed the Palestinians and Israelis to the brink of direct talks over a sensible first step: West Bank and Gaza elections to choose Palestinian representatives politically acceptable to Israel in future stages of negotiation.
>
> Making peace in the Middle East is . . . achievable only in

episodic stages. The Bush Administration understands this, and also understands the narrow limits of America's ability to determine diplomatic outcomes. It deserves equal understanding—and admiration—for the progress it has made thus far.[37]

Quite naturally, neither Arabs nor Israelis have, to put it mildly, always displayed such understanding or admiration. Their contradictory criticisms of American policy are, of course, nothing new; the contemporary scene is vaguely reminiscent of the time, twenty years ago, when then Secretary of State William Rogers was asked, tongue-in-cheek, whether rejection of his peace plan by both Israelis and Arabs proved that the plan was on target, and he gamely responded that indeed he thought it did. Today, some Israelis who protest American objections to settling Soviet Jews in occupied territory seem to forget the considerable American contribution to getting those Jews out of the Soviet Union in the first place. Conversely, some Arabs who complain that the U.S.-PLO dialogue lacks sufficient speed, stature, or substance seem to ignore the fact that, for the sake of sustaining that dialogue, the United States has so far been inclined to overlook some provocative actions or declarations by certain Palestinian factions.

Much of this debate, in my opinion, misses the point. Charges and countercharges about Jewish settlements or terrorism, however sincere, pale by comparison with the larger political issues at stake. More important still, Arab and Israeli complaints about American "pressure" or "tilt" in one direction or the other, however genuinely felt, risk losing sight of the shared goal: progress toward peace, which will inescapably involve wrenching compromises by both sides.

In this highly charged atmosphere, cautious persistence is an appropriate, probably indispensable, guide for policy, and it has been the hallmark of the American response to the Intifada over the past two years. The demise of the Jordanian option, coupled with the start of a U.S.-PLO dialogue, did not produce a radical shift in American policy, only a careful adjustment suitable to circumstances. Similarly, the delays imposed by Israel's internal divisions did not produce a rupture, either in American-Israeli relations or in U.S. efforts to implement the Israeli plan for a Palestinian election. And if that plan ultimately fails, it is unlikely to be replaced by an abrupt or lasting withdrawal (notwithstanding the obvious temptations) of American involvement.

It is true that, as the new decade dawns, momentous changes in Eastern Europe and the Soviet Union continue to push Arab-Israeli issues into the background of global policy discussions in Washington. Even within the region, the Intifada itself appears to be settling into an uneasy equilibrium. The number of Palestinians still being killed by Israelis is now surpassed by the number killed by other Palestinians as "collaborators" (the "intrafada," as one anonymous wag grimly tagged it). But many factors conspire to keep the issues symbolized by the uprising on the agenda. And while the headlines focus on other areas, quiet U.S. diplomacy on the Middle East continues—and continues to be the indispensable catalyst for funneling the pressures of circumstances into diplomatic channels. Moreover, the United States is likely to persevere in this effort. To understand why this is so, and what the short-term options might be, requires some further reflection.

What Next for U.S. Policy?

From an American standpoint, the Arab-Israeli arena retains many of the old dangers of instability, perhaps even at more dangerous and unconventional levels of armament, in a volatile and still mutually hostile region. And yet, recent developments have created new opportunities for progress toward an Arab-Israeli settlement, along with a new danger: that the opportunity may be missed. Though the precise outlines of such a settlement remain unclear, the long-term trend of events points toward the attainment of Palestinian political rights compatible with Israel's security. Yet neither side of that equation is inevitable, and both can be fully realized only gradually. That situation implies a need for cautious but committed and carefully balanced American encouragement, which will surely remain a necessary, though insufficient, condition for the next halting steps. In the meantime, those who advocate, from whatever point of view, a different American approach have yet to make a compelling case that their own ideas are either realistic or desirable.

In this connection, some have argued that the Intifada already calls for a more fundamental shift in American policy toward the Arab-Israeli conflict, at least in its long-term conceptual design. For instance, according to one unofficial but widely read analysis sponsored by the Defense Department, the eventual, almost unavoidable outcome of the processes unleashed by the Intifada will be a West Bank/Gaza Palestinian state, probably one headed by the PLO. And, argues the author:

> The United States will play a critical role in the process. . . . The American Jewish community, increasingly active and outspoken on the Intifada question, could have a major impact on the White House in supporting a more active U.S. role in pushing the Shamir government to face realities . . . [a]lthough the United States clearly cannot dictate terms to Israel or to the PLO. . . . Without that sense of political direction—*even if it is not publicly articulated*—trust in a blind process between unwilling partners will not work.
>
> . . . A Palestinian state on the West Bank is overwhelmingly the probable long-term outcome of the present struggle. . . . In the end, U.S. and Israeli policy must be increasingly informed not by what seems preferable in the abstract, but by what seems most likely in the real world.[38]

I submit, however, that such a shift is premature, simply because the path leading to the long term is littered with too many imponderables and possible detours. Perhaps a better model is the step-by-step process that led, five years after a major war, to Egyptian-Israeli peace: starting small and open ended; building slowly upon concrete progress and growing mutual confidence; and leaving a large measure of latitude to the local players, even as the United States urged them on and intervened constructively to bridge the inevitable diplomatic gaps. The analogy is, of course, flawed, maybe more deeply than most, but the underlying American attitude of "one step at a time" is hardly less valid for the current, even more complex Palestinian conundrum.

Throughout this long and frequently frustrating period, on other occasions of deadlock in Arab-Israeli diplomacy, various interested parties have warned of the dangerous consequences of delay, often including the possibility of drastic and presumably ominous changes in their own policies. Yet such threats ring a bit hollow, precisely because they invoke alternatives that are unpalatable. For the United States, in particular, the list of useful options is a limited one. If current efforts fail, one possibility might be to resurrect the international conference option, but a conference arranged against the will or better judgment of some participants would surely be at best ineffective and at worst self-defeating, if indeed it could be convened at all. Similar problems would afflict an attempt to "leapfrog" over current procedural stumbling blocks by proclaiming another comprehensive American peace plan.

A more realistic alternative might be simply to suspend intensive American diplomacy on the Arab-Israeli dispute, in the spirit of "a plague on both your houses." In that case, the operative question would be: yes, but for how long; how long, that is, before domestic or international factors made a reconsideration desirable? It may be, however, that just such a pause is now required, until internal and external pressures, including the ever-present specter of a more violent explosion in the territories or on Israel's borders, drive the parties back toward the bargaining table—almost certainly, given their own proven inability to reach agreement by themselves, through Washington's good offices.

Long-term Prospects

Despite this rather gloomy short-term prognosis, from a broad historical perspective, the prospects for Arab-Israeli peace are actually quite promising. After a generation or more of almost unrelieved hostility, some things have clearly changed—and for the better. Egypt and Israel have now been at peace, not just on paper, but also to a considerable extent in practice, for more than a decade. What is more, the Egyptians have managed this feat while fully and formally reintegrating themselves into the Arab world. The Palestinian national movement has reached a historic turning point in accepting coexistence with Israel. Israel itself, which made a series of major and tangible sacrifices for the sake of peace with

Egypt, is today more, not less, secure for having done so. Internally, too, Israel's political system, for all its many and varied distractions, is focused perhaps more than ever before on its further fateful choices along this road. And the United States has retained or regained the confidence or at least the ear of all interested parties and, moreover, remains committed to continuing involvement in regional conflict resolution.

To be sure, the same record offers some more humbling historical lessons as well. Some of the major players, whether traditional ones like Syria or new claimants like Iraq, have remained outside the "peace process" orbit altogether, and show little desire to move in. Pockets of religious extremism on both sides of the Arab-Israeli divide may be more of a threat to pragmatic political discourse now than in the past. More important, none of the positive trends sketched above is absolutely irreversible. And the time it took to get this far should be proof against the common trap of assuming that the Arab-Israeli conflict is poised for some immediate dramatic movement, either for peace, for war, or for any particular intermediate condition. On balance, however, U.S. policy planners taking the long view would be justified in concluding that, at a minimum, some progress is possible and that additional American efforts in this area would not be entirely in vain.

But neither will such efforts suffice without creative local input. Those who still believe that the United States will one day "deliver" Israel, simply by holding hostage the small fraction (about 10 percent) of its national economy that comes from Washington, are laboring under an unfortunate illusion. So are those, at the other extreme, who believe that American support for Israel will forever remain as solid as it is today, no matter what Israel itself does or fails to do. And closer to their common home, Palestinians and Israelis who think they can ultimately "beat" the other side, either "in the bedroom" or in the prison barracks, are similarly self-deceived—unless they would willingly turn their shared historic patrimony into another Lebanon. The Intifada has already reminded American policymakers, and many Arabs and Israelis as well, that time is really on no one's side. The sooner all sides come to grips with that fact, the more easily will the abiding

American interest in promoting an Arab-Israeli "peace process"—an interest at once idealistic and pragmatic—advance from rhetoric to reality.

Author's Note

The views of the author are his own and do not necessarily reflect the official viewpoint of the U.S. Information Agency or the U.S. government.

Notes

1. The phrase is from an address by Ambassador John Kelly, assistant secretary of state for Near Eastern and South Asian affairs, September 15, 1989, in Washington Institute for Near East Policy, "U.S. Policy and the Middle East Peace Process: Fourth Annual Policy Conference," proceedings (hereafter WINEP Proceedings), p. 4.

2. For background on this development, see, e.g., articles in *New York Times*, January 5, 1988, p. 10; January 22, 1988, p. 1; and February 5, 1988, p. 8.

3. Statement before the Subcommittee on Europe and the Middle East of the House Foreign Affairs Committee, October 13, 1988, in U.S. State Department *Bulletin* (hereafter DSB), December 1988, p. 43.

4. Speech to the Council on Foreign Relations, June 14, 1988, in DSB, September 1988, p. 45.

5. DSB, June 1988, pp. 3, 6.

6. For background on this question, see David Pollock, "Jordan: Option or Optical Illusion," *Middle East Insight* (February 1985): 21–27.

7. Address at the Center for Strategic and International Studies, Washington, December 8, 1988, in DSB, February 1989, p. 58.

8. Address at the Washington Institute for Near East Policy, September 16, 1988, in DSB, November 1988, p. 12.

9. Ibid., p. 11.

10. For official statements and interviews on this matter, see DSB, February 1989, pp. 51–57.

11. Graham Fuller, *The West Bank of Israel: Point of No Return?* (Santa Monica, Calif.: Rand, August 1989), p. viii.

12. See William B. Quandt, *Decade of Decisions: U.S. Policy toward the Arab-Israeli Conflict, 1967–1976* (Los Angeles: University of California Press, 1978), Introduction and Conclusion.

13. Dennis Ross, presentation to the Washington Institute for Near East Policy, September 16, 1989, in WINEP Proceedings, p. 11.

14. Speech by Aaron D. Miller at the Center for Strategic and International Studies, Washington, December 7, 1989, in *American-Arab Affairs* (Washington) 31 (Winter 1989–90): 30–31.

15. See full coverage and excerpts in, e.g., the *Washington Post* and the *New York Times*, May 23, 1989.

16. Ross, WINEP Proceedings, p. 10.

17. Miller, speech, p. 30.

18. Cited in Fuller, *The West Bank*, p. 45.

19. For good overviews on this subject, see Alvin Richman, "American Attitudes toward Israeli-Palestinian Relations in the Wake of the Uprising," *Public Opinion Quarterly* 53 (Fall 1989): 415–30; and Steven M. Cohen, *Ties and Tensions: An Update—The 1989 Survey of American Jewish Attitudes toward Israel and Israelis* (New York: American Jewish Committee, 1989).

20. Harvey Sicherman, Graeme Bannerman, Martin Indyk, and Samuel Lewis, *The Arab-Israeli Peace Process: A Trip Report*, Research Memorandum no. 13 (Washington: Washington Institute for Near East Policy, January 1990), p. 2.

21. Kelly, WINEP Proceedings, pp. 3–4.

22. Ross, p. 12.

23. Ibid., pp. 11, 13.

24. Kelly, pp. 3–4.

25. Sicherman et al., p. 16.

26. Ross, p. 13.

27. Kelly, (question and answer session), p. 7.

28. *New York Times*, February 26, 1990.

29. Kelly, p. 9.

30. Ross, p. 13.

31. Akiva Eldar, *Ha'aretz* (Tel Aviv), February 12, 1990.

32. Deputy Assistant Secretary of State Dan Kurtzer, presentation to the Washington Institute for Near East Policy, November 17, 1989, published in *Policy Forum Report* 1, no. 8 (December 1989): 3.

33. *Washington Post*, March 3, 1990.

34. *New York Times*, March 8, 1990.

35. Ibid., March 16, 1990.

36. Ibid., January 22, 1990.

37. Samuel W. Lewis, "Mideast: Still Not Ready for Peace," *New York Times*, March 22, 1990.

38. Fuller, pp. 52–55.

The Soviet Union and the Arab-Israeli Conflict since the Intifada

Robert O. Freedman

The Intifada came at a difficult time in Soviet-Palestinian relations. By December 1987 the new Soviet leader, Mikhail Gorbachev, had already embarked on a major effort to improve Soviet-Israeli relations. Thus, there had been a sharp increase in the number of Soviet Jews allowed to leave the Soviet Union, with 8,155 departing in 1987 as opposed to only 914 in 1986. In addition, in April 1987, Israel's most implacable foe, Syrian leader Hafiz Assad, was told by Gorbachev that the absence of Soviet-Israeli relations was "abnormal," and in July 1987 a Soviet consular delegation arrived in Israel.[1] Consequently, with Soviet-Israeli relations on the upswing, the Soviet reaction to the Intifada was far more restrained than it otherwise might have been. Indeed, despite the Intifada throughout 1988 and 1989, Soviet-Israeli relations continued to improve, and while Moscow hailed the decision of PLO leader Yasser Arafat to recognize Israel and renounce terrorism in 1988, and even elevated the PLO mission in Moscow to embassy status in January 1990, the Soviet gestures to the PLO were essentially symbolic in nature, and the growing ties between Israel and the Soviet Union, although still not extensive enough to persuade the Israelis to allow the Soviet Union to play a central role in the Middle East peace process, were to cause increasing friction between Moscow and the PLO, despite Soviet efforts to display an evenhanded policy between Israel and the Palestinians.

Gorbachev, who had taken power in the Soviet Union in March 1985, was the most energetic Soviet leader since Khrushchev and the most willing to undertake domestic reforms since Lenin instituted the New Economic Program of the 1920s. As the new Soviet leader consolidated his hold on power in 1985 and 1986, he came to see that the economic problems facing the Soviet Union were so great that a respite was needed in the arms race with the United States so that resources could be diverted from Soviet military to civilian needs. To accomplish this task he had to persuade the NATO powers, and especially the United States, that the "Soviet threat" had diminished. This would not only improve the chances for new arms control agreements but also give encouragement to the advocates of reduced military spending in NATO nations and undermine the support for such projects as the U.S. Strategic Defense Initiative. Gorbachev set about trying to win over the NATO states in four ways. First, there was the rhetoric about "new thinking" in Soviet foreign policy (see extract below). Second, Gorbachev made a number of concessions in Third World conflict areas, such as Angola, Cambodia, and Afghanistan and, as mentioned above, made a significant effort to improve relations with Israel. Third, Gorbachev backed off from the previous Soviet hard-line position opposing arms control negotiations so long as the United States continued its deployment of cruise missiles and Pershing II missiles in Europe. Instead, Gorbachev actively promoted an intermediate-range missile agreement that was to be signed in 1987. Fourth, he instituted what became known as *glasnost* in the Soviet Union where, for the first time in the history of that nation, the Soviet media were allowed to report events as they actually occurred, rather than either covering up problems, such as train wrecks and airplane crashes, or reporting events through the prism of Marxist-Leninist ideology. Gorbachev evidently decided that if there was to be real reform in the Soviet Union—he used the word *perestroika*—people first had to realize just how critical the situation actually was. The policy of glasnost was also aimed at mobilizing the Soviet intelligentsia behind Gorbachev; his decision to bring Andrei Sakharov back to Moscow from internal exile in

Gorky in December 1986 may be seen as a major step in signaling to the intelligentsia that he was giving more than lip service to glasnost. Needless to say, the return of Sakharov, who was the Soviet Union's most famous dissident, also had major public relations value in the West and contributed to improving the Soviet image in NATO states, as did the rehabilitation of posthumous Nobel Prize winner Boris Pasternak.[2]

It should be emphasized, however, that the "new thinking" in Soviet foreign policy did not begin in 1985 with the advent of Gorbachev. Indeed, some of the hard-line policies taken in his first year in power, such as intensifying the Soviet war effort in Afghanistan and sending SAM-5 missiles to Libya, led a number of Western observers to comment that his policy was "Brezhnevism without Brezhnev."[3] By the beginning of 1987, however, with Gorbachev having consolidated his position, the "new thinking" in Soviet foreign policy was officially in place. It was at this time that Moscow, after several false starts in 1985 and 1986, also began in earnest to improve relations with Israel. Essentially, the "new thinking" had five major principles.[4]

1. The danger of nuclear war impels the superpowers to realize that human survival should take precedence over the interests of states, classes, and ideologies.
2. There is a need to abandon such concepts as "spheres of influence," "vital interests," "positions of strength," and the "zero-sum game" approach to the Third World.
3. A new concept should lie at the heart of international relations, the "balance of interests" which would take into account the legitimate interests of the USSR, the United States, and regional states.
4. Primary reliance should be placed on political means for the resolution of regional conflicts.
5. There is an organic connection between regional conflicts and confrontation between the superpowers and, hence, there is a need for joint action by the superpowers to settle the most serious regional conflicts because there will be no possible détente in U.S.-Soviet relations if there is no settle-

ment of the most serious regional conflicts, especially in the Middle East.

In looking at the "new thinking," it is clear that there is indeed much that is new. First, the linkage between superpower relations and Third World conflicts is a marked departure from the Brezhnev period when the Soviet leadership felt it could act freely in the Third World, in places like Angola and Ethiopia, without having a major effect on détente. Second, there is a downgrading of Marxist-Leninist ideology in Gorbachev's approach to world affairs. Since it did not seem possible to separate ideology's internal role in the Soviet Union as the legitimizer of the rule of the Communist Party of the Soviet Union (CPSU) from its role in shaping the Soviet view of world affairs, Gorbachev's domestic critics within the party, already angry at his other reform efforts that threatened their power, took issue with the policy change on ideology. Leaders of self-proclaimed Marxist-Leninist states in the Third World such as Fidel Castro of Cuba and Assad and Muamer Kaddafi of Syria and Libya, fearing a loss of Soviet support under Gorbachev, also criticized the new policy. In addition, the downgrading of the importance of ideology removed a major obstacle to the improvement of Soviet-Israeli relations, since "Zionism" was no longer portrayed as an implacable enemy of the USSR. This, in turn, led the increasingly independent Soviet media to take not only a more balanced view of Israel but also a more balanced approach toward the Arab-Israeli conflict as a whole. Third, the new Soviet emphasis on a "balance of interests" in reaching settlements in Third World conflicts became a major theme employed by Gorbachev as a device to entice the United States and Israel to agree to include the Soviet Union in a Middle East peace conference. Finally, while Soviet concern about the outbreak of a war in the Middle East that could negatively affect Soviet-American relations had long predated Gorbachev, the new Soviet leader went further in his efforts to prevent such a war than any of his predecessors by publicly admonishing Syrian leader Assad to settle the Arab-Israeli conflict politically, and not by war.

In sum, therefore, when the Intifada broke out, Moscow was

well into its "new thinking" and the process of improving its relations with Israel. In part, this was caused by the larger Soviet goal of improving Soviet-American relations. At the same time, however, it should be noted that Moscow continued its competition with the United States in the Middle East, albeit in a lower key. The Soviet effort to improve ties to Israel was also due to Gorbachev's desire to play an active role in a Middle East peace settlement, which Moscow continued to hope would be arranged by means of an international peace conference in which the Soviet Union would play a major role. Nonetheless, when the Intifada erupted on December 8, 1987, Moscow seemed as surprised as the Israeli government, although the Soviet Union quickly moved, from a propaganda point of view, to exploit it. Thus a Soviet government report linked the Israeli "repression" of the protestors with the newly signed U.S.-Israeli military cooperation agreement,[5] and Moscow also sought to exploit the U.S. abstention on a U.N. Security Council resolution condemning Israeli actions on the West Bank and Gaza.[6] Yet, aside from condemnation of Israeli policy, and constantly linking the United States to Israeli actions, Moscow took no substantive action in regard to the uprising until mid-January, despite Arab urgings.[7] To be sure, there were Palestinian solidarity meetings, a World Federation of Trade Unions (WFTU) declaration, a statement by Soviet Moslems, an Afro-Asian Peoples Solidarity Organization condemnation, and even a message from Gorbachev to Arafat noting that the "violent measures Israelis were using against the Palestinians aroused anger and indignation in the Soviet people".[8] Interestingly enough, however, the Gorbachev message also noted that "one must not ensure one's own rights and security by flouting the rights of others"—a statement foreshadowing Gorbachev's later remarks to Arafat in Moscow that the PLO, in its quest for a state, had to take into consideration Israel's security needs. In addition, perhaps concerned that its consular delegation in Israel might be terminated by Israeli officials demanding a reciprocal Israeli mission in Moscow—just when it was of the highest importance for Soviet officials to have accurate, firsthand information on events in Israel—Moscow agreed in principle in mid-January 1988 to receive an Israeli consular delegation, although no date was set for its arrival.[9] And, in a press briefing, Soviet Foreign Ministry spokesman Genady Gerasimov stated that the resumption of Soviet-Israeli relations would be possible "within the process of a Middle East settlement."[10]

The major Soviet response to the uprising came six weeks after it had begun. On January 20, Soviet Foreign Minister Edward Shevardnadze wrote a letter to the U.N. Secretary General, in which he called for the Security Council to begin consultations at the foreign minister level, to both establish and start up a mechanism for an international conference on the Middle East.[11] This was an effective propaganda ploy for Moscow, given the fact that both Israel and the United States rejected the Shevardnadze proposal, while the Arab states generally supported it.[12] Nonetheless, the United States was galvanized by the Palestinian uprising to the point that Secretary of State Shultz, after first dispatching Philip Habib and Richard Murphy to the Middle East, set out himself on what was to be the first of three trips in the winter and spring to bring about a peace agreement. Moscow's negative public reaction to the peace efforts of the American envoys generally emphasized two points. First, U.S. efforts were just another attempt to make a "separate deal," like the Camp David agreement, and divert attention from the Palestinian uprising.[13] Second, with Moscow increasingly supporting Arafat and the PLO following the Algiers Palestine National Council (PNC) conference (the estrangement between Arafat and Gorbachev, caused by the Hussein-Arafat agreement, had ended with the agreement's abrogation), the USSR asserted that U.S. efforts to claim that the uprising was "spontaneous" were merely an effort to undermine and discredit the PLO.[14] Indeed, on the latter point, Popular Front for the Liberation of Palestine (PFLP) leader Naef Hawatmeh, invited to Moscow in early February by the Afro-Asian Peoples Solidarity Organization and interviewed in *Izvestia*, noted: "The aim of all these allegations is clear—to discredit the PLO as allegedly not enjoying authority and influence among the population of the occupied territories and instill mistrust of this organization. To our deep regret, some Arabs have fallen into this propaganda trap."[15] In addition, Soviet propaganda, which all along had been linking Israel's repression of the Palestinians on the West Bank and Gaza to U.S. support of Israel, exploited the U.S. plan to close the PLO mission to the United Nations as yet another anti-Palestinian and anti-Arab action undertaken by the United States.[16]

Meanwhile, the Soviet position in the Middle East was strengthened by Gorbachev's announcement in early February that he was pulling Soviet troops out of Afghanistan. The Soviet occupation of Moslem Afghanistan had been highly unpopular in the Moslem world, especially in its Arab segment, while such nations as Saudi Arabia and Iran also perceived a strategic threat from the Soviet occupation. Consequently, the Soviet withdrawal could be expected to improve relations with the Arab world, and Gorbachev sent special envoys to virtually every Arab state to inform them of the withdrawal and seek their aid in assisting it, by using their influence to get Pakistan and the United States to agree to Soviet conditions for the withdrawal at the Geneva talks.[17] Reportedly, in his messages to Arab heads of state, Gorbachev also warned them against accepting George Shultz's Middle East peace plan, while stating that the withdrawal from Afghanistan "would help the USSR devote more time to other Middle East problems like the Gulf war and the Palestinians."[18]

Meanwhile, Shultz was having a difficult time during his journeys to the Middle East. While no side, including Syria, gave an out-and-out "no" to his plan (which consisted of a foreshortened autonomy period and talks between Israel and its neighbors at a ceremonial international conference), there was little support for it outside of Israeli Labor party leader Shimon Peres and President Hosni Mubarak of Egypt, with Prime Minister Yitzhak Shamir of Israel, Syria, and Jordan, to say nothing of the PLO, which denounced the plan, opposing it. As it became clear that both the Palestinian uprising was continuing and Shultz's efforts had proved unsuccessful, and with another U.S.-Soviet summit again on the horizon, Moscow took a more active role in Middle East diplomacy, as it again sought to convene an international conference. Thus, in its description of the meeting between Shevardnadze and the seven-man Arab committee that traveled to Moscow in mid-March to discuss the Middle East, Tass, while emphasizing that Israel had to withdraw from *all* occupied territory, nonetheless also stated that the participants agreed on the need to ensure the right of *all* states and peoples of the region to a safe existence and also expressed the view that in evaluating the U.S. (peace) proposals, the main criterion should be the extent to which "they accord with the task of achieving a comprehensive and lasting Middle East settlement with due regard for *the balance of interests of all the parties* involved in the conflict."[19] The Tass report also noted that the sides agreed that the international conference "should be a permanently functioning forum within the framework of which talks would be held and *mutually acceptable decisions taken*" (emphasis added). Then Gorbachev himself, meeting in early April with the general secretary of the Italian Communist party, Alessandro Natta, appeared to further soften the Soviet position on renewing diplomatic relations with Israel when he stated that "within the framework of preparing to hold the [international] conference, a way will be found also toward renewing normal relations between the USSR and Israel." And, in an obvious effort to demonstrate that the conference would not be a coercive one, Gorbachev also reportedly noted that "the most varied multilateral and bilateral talks could take place within it," and, instead of calling for PLO representation at the conference, referred only to representatives of the Palestinian people.[20]

The main Soviet signal to Israel was to come during PLO leader Arafat's visit to Moscow in early April. During talks with Shevardnadze and Gorbachev, the PLO leader was told that Israel's interests, including its security concerns, had to be taken into consideration in any peace settlement, along with those of the Palestinians, Specifically, Gorbachev noted, according to a Tass report:

> The Palestinian people has extensive international support and this is the earnest of the solution of the main question for the Palestinian people—the question of self-determination. Just as *recognition of the State of Israel and account for its security interests*, the solution of this question is a necessary element of the establishment of peace . . . in the region on the basis of the principles of international law.
>
> The Soviet Union, Mikhael Gorbachev said, persistently works for a just and all-embracing settlement *with due account*

for the interests of all—both Arabs, including Palestinians, and Israel. It is prepared to interact constructively with all the participants in the peace process.

The Soviet view of the essence of the settlement, he said, is the following:

The withdrawal of Israeli troops from territories occupied in 1967—the West Bank of the Jordan, the Gaza Strip and the Syrian Golan Heights—is the key precondition of a settlement.

The Palestinian people *has the right to self-determination in the same measure as it is ensured for the people of Israel.*

How will the Palestinians exercise this right is exclusively their own business.

An international conference under the aegis of the United Nations organization is the most effective mechanism of a settlement. *Recognition by all its participants of resolutions 242 and 338 of the United Nations Security Council and the lawful rights of the Palestinian people, including the right to self-determination, should become the legal basis of the conference.*

The conference should be attended by representatives of all sides drawn into the conflict, including the Arab people of Palestine, and also the permanent members of the United Nations Security Council.

The conference presupposes most diverse forms of interaction of its participants. As to the role of the permanent members of the United Nations Security Council, it will be to create a constructive atmosphere for the conduct of talks at the conference. For this purpose, in particular, they can collectively or individually table proposals and recommendations.

The invitations to all participants in the conference are to be sent by the United Nations Secretary General.

Mikhail Gorbachev showed an understanding attitude to the idea of a single Arab delegation at the international conference.[21]

While Gorbachev's comments may have been aimed at convincing Israel it had nothing to fear from an international conference, it would appear that Arafat, despite his assertion that this was "the most successful of all his visits" and that there was "complete unity of views," did not like all that he heard.[22] Thus, not only did the Tass statement note that there was a "businesslike atmosphere" (the usual Soviet term for low-level agreement), but Arafat, after leaving the USSR, also asserted that Gorbachev did not ask him to recognize Israel, a claim that would appear to be inconsistent with both the tone and content of the Tass statement.[23] Two of the issues that may have irked Arafat were Gorbachev's unwillingness to state that the PLO was the sole legitimate representative of the Palestinian people or to use the term "Palestinian state," as the Soviet leader limited himself to the more ambiguous term "self-determination." These may well have been further tactical gestures to the Israeli leadership, which was united on its opposition to the PLO and to a Palestinian state, if on little else, as well as to the United States, which also opposed the PLO and a Palestinian state. Indeed, in an interview with the Kuwaiti newspaper *al-Siyasah*, a Soviet Foreign Ministry official, Alexander Ivanov-Golitsyn, in response to a question about a Palestinian state, noted that "it was the first time the Soviet leadership did not discuss a Palestinian state. This is not a rescindment of the Soviet stand, but we believe some flexibility should exist."[24] He then went on to state in response to a question about Palestinians who were dispossessed in 1948: "We as realistic politicians can only discuss the establishment of a state in the West Bank and Gaza. Palestinians living abroad can return to this state. Israel is a fait accompli. Talking about the repatriation of the 1948 Palestinians is something extreme."

Gorbachev's gesture to Israel during the Arafat visit was accompanied by a further low-level improvement in state-to-state relations between the USSR and Israel. Thus the Soviet Party Youth Organization, Komsomol, invited a group of Mapam (a left-of-center party, but noncommunist) youth to visit the USSR[25]; Soviet ham radio operators were permitted to talk to their counterparts in Israel[26]; a famous Soviet singer, Alla Pugachova, gave concerts in Israel[27]; and the Soviet Union began to allow Soviet Jews to visit Israel as tourists.[28] There was a brief cooling of ties after the assassination of Abu Jihad, which the Soviet media blamed on Israel and linked to the signing of a memorandum on security cooperation between the United States and Israel (appearing to be yet another example of Soviet disinformation aimed at weakening the

U.S. position in the Arab world).[29] Still, Moscow also welcomed the short-lived reconciliation between Assad and Arafat that was precipitated by the assassination, with Moscow Radio, in Arabic, hailing it as "a very important event."[30] Possibly, because Moscow also felt it had to demonstrate a tougher Middle Eastern stance in the aftermath of the Abu Jihad assassination (he was, after all, a close comrade of Arafat, who had just visited Moscow), Soviet negotiators took a hard line on the Middle East during Shultz's visit to Moscow in late April. Whatever the reason, Richard Murphy reportedly told Israel's U.N. ambassador, Moshe Arad, that the talks were "not productive" and that the Soviets were "rigid" in their attitudes.[31]

By the beginning of May, however, with the summit less than a month away, Moscow again began to send signals to Israel. Thus, Shimon Peres made a surprise visit to Hungary—the first such visit by a major Israeli leader to a Soviet bloc state (other than Rumania) since the 1967 war. Peres, who had been interviewed by the Hungarian government newspaper in April (a month after the formal establishment of the diplomatic interest sections agreed upon in 1987),[32] met with a number of top Hungarian officials, including Hungary's new prime minister, Karoly Grosz.[33] Given the close ties still existing in May 1988 between the USSR and Hungary, it is difficult to believe that the Soviet Union had not approved the visit, despite Shevardnadze's assertion at a news conference in mid-May that "the visit by the Israeli foreign minister to Hungary has no bearing on Soviet-Israeli relations. This was an independent step, taken within the framework of bilateral relations."[34]

From Hungary, Peres went on to Madrid, to a meeting of the Socialist International where, as in 1987, he had meetings with Soviet officials. This time he was reportedly assured by Soviet Middle East specialist Alexander Zotov that the proposed international conference would not have the authority to impose a settlement.[35] Interestingly enough, to make sure Shamir got the same message (lest he perhaps assume that Peres was using the meeting for partisan political purposes), Edgar Bronfman, president of the World Jewish Congress, who was visiting the USSR, was given a message to carry to the Israeli prime minister that emphasized the same point.[36] Meanwhile, to improve the atmosphere further, there was another marked increase in the exodus of Soviet Jews, with 1,086 leaving in April and 1,145 departing in May—both monthly figures higher than any month since 1981.[37]

As the date of the summit neared, Moscow stepped up its diplomatic activity. On May 18 Peres met with the Soviet ambassador to the United States, Yuri Dubynin, in Washington, and was read a Soviet position paper on the Middle East.[38] Once again, Peres was told that in Moscow's view an international conference could not impose a settlement, and also that any negotiations had to be based on U.N. Resolution 242.[39] While Dubynin again pressed the issue of Palestinian self-determination, he also promised to look into the delay in the Soviet issuing of visas for Israel's consular delegation that was due to go to Moscow. A week later, Peres's adviser, Nimrod Novick, was told by Genadi Tarasov, deputy director of the Soviet Foreign Ministry's Middle East department, that Moscow would issue visas for the Israeli consular delegation after the superpower summit.[40] Peres, predictably, sought to get the maximum political benefit from the Tarasov statement, stating that the USSR had come a long way in its relations with Israel, while Shamir's supporters, also predictably, sought to minimize the move, with Yossi Ben-Aharon, director general of Shamir's office, accusing Peres of "constant theatrics" in depicting the USSR as moving toward a more favorable attitude toward Israel.[41] It should be noted that Shamir and his Likud backers were not the only ones skeptical about the amount of genuine movement in the Soviet position. A number of U.S. officials, including Secretary of State Shultz, expressed skepticism, with one American close to the Middle East negotiations remarking that Peres was engaged in "wishful thinking."[42]

It was perhaps to quiet such skeptics that Gorbachev, in his press conference following the summit (where little progress was made on the Middle East, although Reagan pressed the issue of Soviet Jewry) went further than ever before in seeking to reassure Israel that Moscow would take its interests into account at an international conference:

> We stand for a political settlement of all issues, *with due account for the interests of all sides concerned and, of course, for*

the principal provisions of the relevant U.N. resolutions. We are talking about the fact that all the Israeli-occupied lands be returned and the Palestinian people's rights be restored. We said to President Reagan how we view the role of the United States, but we cannot decide for the Arabs in what form the Palestinians will take part in the international conference. *Let the Arabs themselves decide, while the Americans and we should display respect for their choice.*

Furthermore, *we ought to recognize the right of Israel to security and the right of the Palestinian people to self-determination. In what form—let the Palestinians together with their Arab friends decide that. This opens up prospects for active exchanges, for a real process.* Anyway, it seems to me that such an opportunity is emerging.

I will disclose one more thing: We said that *following the start of a conference—a normal, effective conference, rather than a front for separate talks—a forum which would be inter-related with bilateral, tripartite, and other forms of activity, we will be ready to handle the issue of settling diplomatic relations with Israel.*

We are thus introducing one more new element. This shows that we firmly stand on the ground of reality, on the ground of recognition of the balance of interests. Naturally, there are principal issues—the return of the lands, the right of the Palestinian people to self-determination. I should reiterate: *We proceed from the premise that the Israeli people and the State of Israel have the right to their security because there can be no security of one at the expense of the other. A solution that would untie this very tight knot should be found.*[43]

When one analyzes the Soviet leader's statement, it appears to be a Soviet version of an "evenhanded" position on the Arab-Israeli conflict. Thus, while he called for the return of all lands occupied by Israel and the Palestinian people's rights of self-determination, he did not stipulate a specific role for the PLO at the conference, leaving that for the Palestinians and the Arabs to decide. In addition, he stated that Soviet-Israeli diplomatic relations could be restored following the start of the conference, and that the USSR recognized Israel's right to security. To be sure, much of what

Gorbachev said was vague; nonetheless, the tone toward Israel was positive, something recognized even by Shamir who noted in New York that Gorbachev was a "great man and a great leader,"[44] and that the tone of Soviet statements had changed.[45] He questioned, however, whether the substance of the Soviet position had changed, and he indicated that, having been invited to meet with Shevardnadze in New York, he would, as in the past, press for increased emigration of Soviet Jews to Israel and the restoration of diplomatic relations.

The Soviet leadership, in deciding to arrange the Shevardnadze-Shamir meeting, seems to have been motivated by one major consideration. With Shamir's Likud party gaining in the polls against Labor, there was a good chance that Shamir would form Israel's next government, and Moscow may well have wished to signal its willingness to deal with him. The Soviets sent Shamir a further signal during the talks, which both sides publicly characterized as "useful and constructive," by announcing the time of the forthcoming Israeli consular visit to Moscow in mid-July.[46] This enabled Shamir to demonstrate to the Israeli public that he too could obtain benefits from Moscow, not just Peres. Several days later Israel agreed to renew, for an additional three months, the visas of the Soviet consular delegation in Israel, thus enabling Moscow to keep a diplomatic presence in Israel,[47] and on July 28 the Israeli diplomatic delegation arrived in Moscow.[48]

Meanwhile, as Soviet-Israeli relations improved, Soviet-Syrian relations became strained. Although Syria was the primary Soviet ally in the Arab world, its quarrels with Iraq, Egypt, and the PLO (the rapprochement between Assad and Arafat after the assassination of Abu Jihad had been short-lived) continued to hamper Soviet efforts to achieve Arab unity, and Syria's continued confrontational approach to Israel raised the prospect of an Israeli-Syrian war at a time not desired by Moscow. Thus, throughout 1988, the USSR continued to repeat the message Gorbachev had given Assad in 1987: in the nuclear age political solutions had to be found for regional conflicts.[49] For their part, the Syrians publicly noted that there had been no change in Israeli policy and that Syria had to receive more weapons to keep up with the weapons supplied to Israel by the United States or, like the new Israeli satellite, developed by Israel itself.[50] There were a number of reports of major arms deals between the Soviet Union and Syria in 1988 which, if true, would indicate that Moscow had decided to continue to arm Syria with modern weaponry so as to maintain its influence in that country even as Moscow was improving ties with Egypt and Israel and urging Damascus to refrain from going to war.[51] The Soviet Union did deny, however, that it was supplying poison gas equipment to Syria as had been charged by the *New York Times*,[52] and Soviet commentators minimized the agreement reached with Syria in May 1988 that gave the USSR quasi-base rights for its fleet to use the Syrian port of Tartus. *Krasnaya Zvezda* called it a "material and technical supply point," including "two tenders and two storehouses on dry land," which was to be used by the Soviet fleet for preventive maintenance and for rest and relaxation for Soviet sailors.[53] Interestingly enough, however, possibly because it was not getting all the weaponry it wanted from the Soviet Union, Syria was rumored to be trying to acquire M-9 missiles from China.[54]

In mid-June, an Arab summit convened; Gorbachev's message to the summit called for Arab unity on a "constructive and realistic basis"—a change in the previous Soviet call for Arab unity on an "anti-imperialist basis"—and he called both for Palestinian self-determination and for free development and safe existence for all states and peoples in the region.[55] As far as the summit itself was concerned, Soviet Middle East commentators hailed what they perceived as the unity in the Arab world displayed by the conference, unity highlighted by the fact that Kaddafi attended an Arab summit for the first time in fifteen years.[56] The summit also met the Soviet policy goals of calling for an international conference on the Middle East, with the PLO represented on an equal footing, which supported Palestinian self-determination and national independence, called for the complete withdrawal of all Israeli troops from the occupied territories, and criticized U.S. support of Israel.[57] Nonetheless the summit did not reject the Shultz Plan and, although giving the PLO oral support, did not provide it with the funding it requested to support the Intifada. In addition, the degree of Arab unity was something less than the Soviet commentators had indicated, as Arafat, in a *New Times* interview, somewhat caustically noted.[58] Indeed, with the rise of *glasnost*, such journals as *New Times* felt free to break with the *Pravda* and Tass lines on the summit, with Middle East specialist Leonid Medvenko asserting: "My impression was that effective unity as regards the Palestinian uprising was patently lacking. Not just cooperation, but even mutual understanding between the Arab patriotic organizations is only just beginning to take effect."[59]

So matters stood until King Hussein changed the diplomatic equation in the Middle East by publicly severing Jordan's connection with the West Bank at the end of July. Whatever the king's motivations, his action, together with pressure from the leaders of the Intifada on the West Bank and Gaza, led the PLO in less than four months to call for an independent Palestinian state at the Palestinian National Council (PNC) meeting in Algiers in mid-November 1988. In the interim period, Moscow took a cautious stand. Unwilling to alienate Jordan, with which relations had been slowly improving, and concerned about the continuing divisions within the PLO, the Soviet leadership issued no formal statement on the king's action, and Soviet commentators were circumspect in their analysis of it. The *al-Ittahad* interview in late August with Karen Brutents, deputy director of the CPSU Central Committee's International Department, however, appeared to reflect Moscow's hopes as to the most desirable outcome: "It is difficult now to discuss this action. . . . its results are unclear and . . . the Palestinian stand on it is not specified. . . . however, if the Jordanian move consolidates the Palestinian stand, leads to an active and effective Palestinian participation in the international peace conference, and secures further Jordanian support for this direction, then the results of this move will be positive."[60]

During the three-and-one-half months between the king's severing of ties with the West Bank and the November Algiers PNC, Moscow played host to a number of different Palestinian groupings, from the mainstream Fatah to the Marxist Democratic Front for the Liberation of Palestine (DFLP), as strategy was being worked out for the PNC. That Moscow was in favor of the PLO declaring publicly its support for a two-state solution for the Arab-Israeli conflict was in little doubt, because precisely this solution had been part of the Soviet Middle East peace plan since 1976.

Writing in *Izvestia* in mid-September, as Palestinian thinking moved toward a two-state solution, *Izvestia* commentator Konstantin Geivandov made this point clear:

> The Palestinian uprising on the Israeli-occupied West Bank of the Jordan River and in the Gaza Strip, now in its 10th month, could not better illustrate the new realities that have arisen in recent decades in this region of the Middle East. And against that backdrop, the step taken by the Jordanian leadership in announcing an end to its administrative and legal ties to the West Bank of the Jordan was a logical one—logical in so far as it is intended to help some people rid themselves of persistent illusions and remind others of their historical responsibility.
>
> First, King Hussein's decision dashed the hopes of those who were counting on the "Jordanian scenario" to settle the Palestinian problem and identified the real people who must be dealt with in negotiations on this problem, i.e., the Palestinians. Second, it offered the Palestine Liberation Organization (PLO) the status of sole legitimate representative of the Palestinian people, a fact that was confirmed at the recent Arab summit meeting in Algiers, and it made possible a whole series of political and diplomatic initiatives aimed at securing the Palestinians' right of self-determination.
>
> One would like to believe that the PLO will use the existing situation for the good of its people. Specifically, an extraordinary session of the Palestine National Council is planned for October, at the PLO's initiative, for the proposed purpose of discussing ways and means of restoring the Palestinian Arabs' national rights. *The possibility of declaring an independent Palestinian state and creating a government in exile is one such means that is under discussion. In the given case, what is intended?*
>
> First of all, let us return to the 1947 United Nations Resolution No. 181 on the partition of Palestine, which became the legal foundation for the appearance of the State of Israel. But this resolution stipulated the creation of two states from the partition of Palestine: Jewish and Arab. And each was assigned territory of appropriate dimensions. The second part of this U.N. resolution has yet to be fulfilled, and it must be acknowledged

that the leaders of certain Arab states are by no means the least to blame for this. *Therefore, it is proposed that if the PLO, in acting to gain the Palestinians' right to self-determination, now declares the creation of an independent Arab state on the grounds of Resolution 181, it will rectify an injustice permitted more than 40 years ago. Moreover, the PLO's recognition of Resolution 181 would lay the groundwork for the observance of international law in the Arab-Israel conflict.*[61]

When the PNC was held in mid-November (possibly a tactical mistake because holding it after the November 1, 1988, Israeli election, instead of in October as originally planned, cost the PLO a chance to influence Israeli public opinion prior to the election),[62] the decision taken was for a declaration of a Palestinian state, renunciation of terrorism, and the acceptance of U.N. Resolution 242 (which implicitly recognizes Israel's right to exist) on the proviso that an international peace conference be held. The vote in favor was 253–46 with the DFLP and the PFLP opposing the acceptance of 242 but agreeing to go along with the consensus,[63] reportedly, in part, because of intensive lobbying by the Soviet Union.[64]

In any case, the PLO action did not go far enough to meet U.S. conditions for talks with the PLO, which included the unambiguous acceptance of U.N. Resolution 242, renunciation of terrorism (the PLO document obfuscated this somewhat), and recognition of Israel's right to exist. Interestingly enough, Moscow itself exercised some ambiguity in reacting to the PNC declaration, perhaps in an effort not to alienate either Israel or the United States, both of whom continued to oppose a Palestinian state, and also to mollify the Israelis who were angered by the Soviet vote to exclude Israel from the U.N. General Assembly in October. The official Soviet government statement noted only that the USSR recognized the declaration of the state, not the state itself.

Resolutions adopted by the extraordinary session of the Palestine National Council held in Algiers have met with interest and approval in the Soviet Union. Taken together, these resolutions, which are infused with the lofty sense of realism and responsibility demonstrated by the leadership of the Palestine

Liberation Organization, are a great contribution to the process of a just political settlement in the Middle East.

As a result, a situation has developed in which all parties directly involved in the conflict proceed from a recognition of the fact that the path to peace and peaceful co-existence among Arabs and Israel lies through negotiations based on Security Council Resolutions Nos. 242 and 338, and of the equal rights of Jewish and Arab states to exist in Palestine. It is important that the highest representative body of the Palestinian people proclaimed its adherence to generally accepted principles of international intercourse.

The Soviet Union has unfailingly supported the Palestinian people in its efforts to secure its inalienable national rights, including the right to create an independent state of its own. Our people understand the feelings of political uplift and enthusiasm that the Palestinians and their brother Arabs are expressing in connection with the decisions taken by the Algiers session of the Palestine National Council. The Soviet Union, true to the fundamental principle of freedom of choice, *recognizes the proclamation of a Palestinian state, guided by the understanding that the achievement of a comprehensive settlement will also result, in practice, in the culmination of the historically important process of that state's creation.*

The way is being cleared for the immediate convening of an international conference on the Middle East. The Soviet Union appeals to all interested states to step up efforts aimed at accelerating preparations for this conference. The United Nations and the U.N. Security Council and its permanent members have a particularly great role to play in this matter. The common task is to not miss the chance that has presented itself, to get down to practical work with the goal of establishing an enduring peace in the Middle East, with the result that the Palestinian people will find a homeland, the Israeli people will find dependable security, and the entire region and international community will extinguish one of the most dangerous hotbeds of tension.[65]

Moscow also hailed Egypt's decision to recognize the Palestinian state formally, claiming that it was a serious blow against Camp

David and a contribution to the strengthening of Pan-Arab unity.[66]

Meanwhile, the United States, still considering Arafat a terrorist, denied him a visa to visit the United States to address the UN—an action severely criticized in the Arab world, and in Moscow.[67] Gorbachev, in a major address to the United Nations in December, took the opportunity to criticize the United States for its action and expressed Moscow's "solidarity" with the Palestine Liberation Organization, which had taken a "constructive step facilitating the search for an untangling of the Middle East knot." In another part of his speech, however, Gorbachev made his most extensive statement to date on the deideologization of international relations. This section of his speech is important, given the negative effect it was to have on Moscow's relations with the radical self-proclaimed socialist states of the Arab world (and not only of the Arab world), who feared that with this policy change Moscow would have less reason to support them.

> The deideologization of interstate relations has become a requirement of the new stage. We are not renouncing our convictions, our philosophy or traditions. Neither are we calling on anyone else to give up theirs. Yet we are not going to shut ourselves up within the range of our values. That will lead to spiritual impoverishment, for it would mean renouncing so powerful a source of development as sharing all the original things created independently by each nation. In the course of such sharing, each should prove the advantages of his own system, his own way of life and values, but not through words or propaganda alone but through real deeds as well.
>
> That is indeed an honest struggle of ideology, but it must not be carried over into mutual relations between states. Otherwise we will simply not be able to solve a single world problem; arrange broad, mutually advantageous and equitable cooperation between peoples; manage rationally the achievement of the scientific and technical revolutions; transform world economic relations, protect the environment, overcome underdevelopment or put an end to hunger, disease, illiteracy and other mass ills. Finally, in that case, we will not manage to eliminate the nuclear threat and militarism.[68]

Meanwhile, Arafat was continuing to gather support for his Palestinian state, and the United States became increasingly isolated because of its denial of a visa to the PLO leader. The UN overwhelmingly (154–2) voted to move to Geneva, Switzerland, for a special session where Arafat could freely address the organization.[69] In Geneva, however, Arafat, in a speech and press conference statement, finally met the American conditions for a U.S.-PLO dialogue,[70] and the dialogue was begun in mid-December with a meeting between the American ambassador to Tunisia, Robert Pelletreau, and PLO leader Yasser Abd Raboo.[71] Moscow's reaction to this event was ostensibly positive, but the Soviet leadership may well have been concerned that just as the United States had successfully mediated peace between Egypt and Israel in the 1973–79 period and in the process moved Egypt from the Soviet to the American orbit, it would have a similar effect on the PLO by mediating peace between the Palestinians and the Israelis. It was possibly for this reason that the official Soviet statement on the U.S. decision to begin a dialogue with the PLO followed its praise of the American action as an "important positive step" with a call for convening the international conference—a move to try to preempt any unilateral role by the United States in the peace process.[72]

Meanwhile, just as U.S.-PLO relations had begun to improve, so too did Soviet-Israeli relations. This was due, however, less to Soviet actions—the Israeli consular mission in Moscow was severely circumscribed in its activities[73]—and more to Israeli policies. Thus at the beginning of December, Israel promptly returned a group of four hijackers who had flown to Israel after seizing a busload of children as hostages and releasing them in return for an aircraft. Moscow warmly praised Israel for its role in the affair and Israel, for the first time since the 1967 war, was positively treated in the Soviet press.[74] Gorbachev himself, during his U.N. visit, which took place after the hijacking, was photographed by *Agence France Press* shaking hands with Israel's U.N. ambassador Yochanan Bein.[75] Gorbachev reportedly told Bein, "I want to thank the Israeli people for the efficient cooperation we received with regard to the hijacked airplane. . . . Please tell the Israeli government and the people of Israel that there is a lot of good will and friendship in the Soviet Union toward Israel."[76] Gorbachev had to cut short his stay in the United States because of a massive earthquake in Armenia, and here again Israel proved helpful to the USSR. Sending medical teams and four tons of medical supplies, the Israelis set up a field hospital in the city of Kirovakan. Their team, which was praised in the Soviet press, found and saved three women who had been buried alive in the rubble.[77] Nonetheless, despite Israel's assistance in these two episodes, there was little letup in Soviet criticism of Israeli actions in the Middle East. A *Pravda* article on December 30, for example, took a dim view of the policies of Israel's newly formed coalition government. Interestingly enough, however, on the same day *Izvestia* published an article critical not only of Israeli "terror in the occupied territories" but also of a meeting of Islamic fundamentalists who were planning to wage a *jihad* (holy war) against Israel and of Damascus-based PLO factions that were trying to undermine Arafat's leadership in the PLO.

While Moscow was castigating Israel for its policy in the occupied territories, Shevardnadze was meeting with Soviet consular officials to set forth a new policy toward Soviet émigrés that had the potential to further improve Soviet-Israeli relations. Shevardnadze told the consular officials that instead of viewing émigrés as traitors, they should be treated as potential assets for the improvement of ties between the Soviet Union and the émigrés' new homelands. Shevardnadze also urged consular officials to encourage business contacts between the USSR and firms owned by these "compatriots."[78] Given the fact that at this time more than 170,000 Soviet émigrés lived in Israel, the new Soviet policy had major implications for Soviet-Israeli relations. Indeed, less than a week after the consular conference, Shevardnadze met Israel's new foreign minister, Moshe Arens, in Paris, where both were attending a conference on the control of chemical weapons. In talks that Arens termed "very friendly, open and sincere," Shevardnadze reportedly promised to upgrade Israel's consular delegation in Moscow and to allow Israeli diplomats to conduct political talks there.[79] The Soviet foreign minister also indicated that the Israeli consular delegation could move from its crowded quarters in the Dutch embassy to the old Israeli embassy building, which had been occupied by Israel before the severing of relations in 1967. In addition, Shevardnadze, who again urged Israel to participate in the international peace conference as soon as possible since "all parties' interests" would be taken into account there,[80] also noted in a *Figaro* interview that he agreed with Arens that Israeli-Soviet contacts should be stepped up in order to achieve a settlement in the Middle East.[81] Other signals of an improvement in Soviet-Israeli relations at the time included an end to the jamming of Kol Israel (Radio Israel) broadcasts to the USSR,[82] the granting of visas to 175 Israelis to attend a Soviet-Israeli basketball game in Moscow,[83] and the offer by the Soviet ambassador to Egypt to help establish a dialogue between Israel and the PLO.[84] In addition, in its clearest signal to the Arabs to date, Genadi Tarasov, interviewed in Kuwait's *Al-Anba*, noted that since Israel was a party to the Middle East conflict, there had to be dialogue with it. Tarasov then listed three objectives to be obtained from the Soviet-Israeli meetings:[85] (1) the most important, "that the Israelis become familiar with the USSR stand from the original sources, as it is well known that there are some in Israel and in the West who try to cast doubts on the USSR stand"; (2) "to become familiar with the Israeli stand from the original source as well"; and (3) "to try to influence the Israeli stand as much as possible and encourage it to become constructive and realistic with respect to a Middle East settlement."

While Moscow intensified its contacts with Israel, it was not neglecting the PLO. Indeed, less than two weeks after the Paris discussion between Shevardnadze and Arens, Soviet and PLO officials, meeting in Tunis, reached an agreement "making Soviet-Palestinian consultations more regular and intensive."[86]

Shevardnadze was to meet Arens again in February, during the Soviet foreign minister's trip to the Middle East that coincided with the pullout of the last Soviet troops from Afghanistan, and which included visits to Syria, Jordan, Egypt, Iraq, and Iran, as he sought to consolidate Moscow's position in the region following the withdrawal. His first stop was Syria, which at least symbolically, was honored as "the Soviet Union's leading partner" in the Near East both by Shevardnadze's words and by being the first stop in his tour.[87] Yet with the Soviet media reporting the visit as taking place in an atmosphere of "friendly frankness,"[88] there clearly remained significant differences between the two sides, as Shevardnadze emphasized the need for Syria to improve its ties with the PLO, Iraq, and Egypt. He also urged a meeting between the representatives of Jordan, Syria, Egypt, Lebanon, and the PLO[89] (a suggestion he repeated in Jordan, his next stop) as a means of coordinating Arab efforts.

Indeed, as Shevardnadze noted in his dinner speech to Assad: "There can be no two views: a fair settlement cannot be achieved without having secured the unity of the Arab countries."[90] Perhaps also reflecting concern about the development of the U.S.-PLO dialogue, Shevardnadze called for the preparation of an international conference on the Middle East in no more than nine months.[91] As to the key issue of Syria's desire for military parity with Israel, although Shevardnadze did talk to Assad about "the development of ties in various fields, including the military field,"[92] he also repeated to Assad what Gorbachev had told the Syrian leader in 1987, that the Arab-Israeli conflict had to be solved peacefully.

> We see how much peoples can give each other when they cooperate in the creation of a modern economy, the use of national resources, and the professional training of young people.
>
> We see how much people are deprived of by war and hostility. The bitter memory of the past, embodied in the ruins of Kuneitra, echoes like a sharp pain today. But however unbearable it may be, it cannot but be overcome by concern for the future, which is concern for peace and not for war.
>
> We see how different cultures, which stood in opposition in the past, have now merged into a single civilization, calling for the search for the path that should lead us to the supremacy of values common to all of mankind.
>
> The present generation will have to fulfill a historic mission and lay the foundations for a secure future for all mankind. To bring this about, one must master the difficult art of living in peace and respect for one another while preserving one's national, political, spiritual, and religious values in all their diversity and originality. Movement toward this noble goal is only possible given the rejection of strong-arm approaches in politics and the transfer from confrontation to dialogue, from rivalry to codevelopment and the search for a balance of interests. Man-

kind has been given no other alternative. This relates to global as well as regional affairs. The reality of today's interdependent world is such that any flare-up in one region throws a worrisome atmosphere over our whole planet.

The new thinking is powerfully knocking at the door of the Near East, too. Through suffering, its peoples have achieved the right to a peaceful and safe life. It is time to build the bridges of mutual understanding and peaceful coexistence in this region too.[93]

While Assad could not have been too happy with the Soviet foreign minister's message, Shevardnadze, himself, proved unsuccessful in forging a Syrian-PLO reconciliation during his visit to Damascus, as Soviet efforts to arrange an official invitation for Arafat to visit Syria to meet with Shevardnadze fell through.[94] Arafat did meet the Soviet foreign minister, however, in Cairo, in what must have appeared as a double blow to Syria. Not only did the Shevardnadze visit to Cairo (the first by a Soviet foreign minister in fifteen years) cap the Soviet-Egyptian rapprochement, but it also further legitimized Egyptian leader Hosni Mubarak's policies, including the maintenance of peace with Israel. Not only did Shevardnadze meet Arafat and Mubarak in Cairo, but he also met Foreign Minister Moshe Arens of Israel there as well, thus putting Egypt, not Syria, at the center of Middle East diplomacy. Indeed, Shevardnadze was lavish in his praise of Egypt, as he noted: "In the Soviet Union, it is assumed that Egypt, as a major country of the Arab world with rich historical, cultural, and political traditions, is called upon to occupy a fitting place in the community of nations. On the Soviet side a positive assessment is made of Egypt's role in the Nonaligned Movement; its constructive and carefully weighed approach to solving urgent international problems is noted; and acknowledgment is expressed of Egypt's support for Soviet peace initiatives."[95] The Soviet foreign minister also highlighted the Soviet-Egyptian rapprochement: "We can with full justification place the full normalization of Soviet-Egyptian relations, which has now become a fact, on a level with the greatest political achievements of the recent period, which have so greatly promoted radical changes in the nature of world politics and in the maintenance of a dialogue common to all mankind."[96]

Shevardnadze also used his visit to Egypt to emphasize the new thinking in Soviet foreign policy, especially its deideologization:

> Traditional and—we'll be blunt—obsolete standards and outlooks are being reviewed. It is indicative that in this common channel the Soviet Union, aspiring to the democratization of interstate communication, is reducing, or even completely excluding from it the previously predominant ideological component. The world can be saved from nuclear, ecological, economic and other catastrophes only by acting together and being guided by the priority of values common to mankind. We have a vital interest in the construction of international relations on innovative designs, and we are gladdened that the ideas and proposals M.S. Gorbachev set out in his speech at the United Nations General Assembly session are meeting with a well-disposed and committed response, as has been shown by our conversation with President H. Mubarak. This is also not the least important factor in strengthening our hope that Egypt, as one of the authoritative and influential members of the international community and the Nonaligned Movement, will continue to actively assist the process of improving the situation, including that in the vicinity.[97]

While Soviet-Egyptian relations had clearly improved as a result of Shevardnadze's visit, the Soviet foreign minister's talks with Arens had a more mixed outcome. Although Shevardnadze reportedly agreed to continue high-level meetings between the USSR and Israel and to set up meetings of "experts," Aryeh Levin, Israel's chief diplomatic representative in the USSR, noted after the talks, "It's going to take some time before we begin understanding each other."[98] The cause of disagreement, not unexpectedly, was Moscow's continued call for an international conference and insistence that the PLO participate in all phases of any new peace initiative. The Soviet foreign minister did, however, emphasize the need to also focus on security guarantees for Israel. In his statement in Cairo at the end of his talks with Arens, however, Shevardnadze took a hard line against Israel, going so far as to threaten sanctions if Israel continued "in massive violation of the rights of the civilian population [of the occupied territories]," and again urged Israel to agree to an international conference and to a dialogue with the PLO. If Israel took these actions, Shevardnadze stated, "Our two countries could take yet another step forward towards re-establishing full diplomatic relations, and the beginning of the conference would be a starting point for resumed relations."[99]

Following the conclusion of the Shevardnadze visit to Egypt, the chief Soviet concern about the Middle East appeared to be that the United States would exploit its new dialogue with the PLO to bring about an Israeli-Palestinian agreement in a diplomatic process that would again exclude the USSR. Fortunately for Moscow, however, growing opposition to the dialogue in the United States Congress, an unwillingness on the part of Israel's Shamir-led government to talk to the PLO, and a hesitancy on the part of the new Bush administration to get actively involved in the Palestinian-Israeli conflict, made a U.S.-mediated agreement seem increasingly unlikely. Instead, the United States moved to endorse the Israeli election plan, first suggested by Defense Minister Yitzhak Rabin in January 1989, and then endorsed by both Shamir and the Labor party in May. Since the plan made no mention of a Palestinian state, although it did affirm that in the talks between Israel and the Palestinian body elected in the West Bank and Gaza, any proposal for a final settlement to the conflict could be brought forward,[100] the PLO rejected it. Moscow, in its first reaction to the publication of the plan, supported the Palestinian rejection. *Pravda*, on May 17, noted that the plan rejected the creation of an independent Palestinian state and cited the Palestinian complaint that it was "an attempt to stamp out the fire of the Palestinian uprising." Soviet Foreign Ministry spokesman Gennady Gerasimov, speaking just before the plan was formally issued (it had been discussed for two months in the press), had gone even further in his criticism, noting "elections without the PLO's participation were not elections but a sham aimed at setting up puppet representative bodies with which Israel could reach a peace."[101]

Unofficially, the Soviet officials were reported to be taking a more moderate position, with a U.S. State Department team, which had just completed talks with Soviet officials in Moscow, telling Peres that the USSR did not reject the election proposals but continued to advocate the convening of a noncoercive international conference.[102] Indeed, Shevardnadze reportedly went so far as to state that the Shamir plan was "worthy of discussion."[103] It would appear, however, that the Shevardnadze statement was aimed more at mollifying the United States, which, in the new spirit of Soviet-American cooperation, might be expected to invite the USSR to play a more active role in Middle East diplomacy, than at genuinely considering the Shamir plan as a viable means to reach a peace agreement. Rejecting the Shamir plan, which had the endorsement of the United States, would, therefore, have been counterproductive to Moscow's larger interests. An even more negative interpretation of the Soviet strategy was given by Yossi Ben-Aharon of Shamir's office, and one of his foreign policy advisers: "True, the Soviet Union made some positive mention of the element of elections in our four-part [peace plan] menu. But they garnished it with so many side dishes as to alter the taste beyond all recognition. On top of it all, the Soviets said that the purpose of the elections was to permit the Palestinians self-determination."[104]

Gorbachev himself, speaking a week later in Paris, seemed to bear out Ben-Aharon's analysis, as the Soviet leader endorsed French president François Mitterand's rejection of the Shamir peace initiative. Both Gorbachev and Mitterand came out for an international conference.[105] This was also the position of the Arab summit, which had met in late May, and Moscow warmly praised the outcome of the summit which, in addition to calling for an international conference, also endorsed U.N. resolutions 242 and 338 as the basis for a settlement. *Pravda* put a particularly positive evaluation of the summit, noting: "Reference to 242 and 338, which stipulate the right of all the region's states to an independent and secure existence, is viewed as 'de facto' recognition of Israel at the Pan-Arab level and it is seen as clearing the way for a broad, peaceful dialogue."[106]

As Israel stressed the Shamir peace plan, the USSR continued to press for an international conference. The two countries also were at loggerheads on a number of other issues: For example, Israel strongly protested the Soviet sale of SU-24 fighter bombers to Libya in April (since Libya was still pledged to destroy Israel), complaining that the aircraft had the range to reach Israel, which

Moscow denied.[107] For its part, Moscow sharply criticized Israel's seizure of Lebanese Hezbollah leader Sheikh Obeid in mid-July, with a Soviet government statement asserting: "The act of violence perpetrated by Israel is unquestionably a flagrant violation of Lebanon's sovereignty and no motives can justify it. It constitutes an act of international terrorism."[108]

While these clashes were taking place in the spring and summer on the state-to-state level, below the surface in such areas as cultural, religious, and humanitarian relations there was sharp improvement in Soviet-Israeli ties. Thus, when disaster again struck the USSR, this time in the form of a train crash on the Trans-Siberian Railway, Moscow gratefully accepted Israeli offers of aid for the burn victims of the crash, a team of doctors, and specially developed burn medicine and synthetic skin.[109] Upon the return of the medical team to Israel, it was met by the head of the Soviet consular team in Israel, Georgy Martirosov, who stated that the team saved the lives of a number of people, including two children, and that its actions had contributed to a "positive atmosphere" between the USSR and Israel.[110]

In another form of humanitarian assistance to Moscow, Israel treated sixty-one Armenian victims of the December 1988 earthquake who arrived in Israel on the first El-Al plane ever to make a flight to the USSR. Forty-eight people were given special artificial limbs, twenty underwent operations for crush injuries, and one, a nine-year-old boy, was given a special splint to aid his crushed arm until he was old enough for a prosthesis.[111]

In addition to the humanitarian assistance provided by Israel, subgovernmental relations of all kinds blossomed in the spring and summer of 1989. For the first time since 1967, Israelis were allowed to visit the USSR on tourist visas;[112] an Israeli journalist delegation traveled to the USSR on an official invitation; and there was an exchange of visits between Israeli and Soviet rabbis with the chief rabbi of Tel Aviv, upon his return from the USSR (where the rabbis were given red-carpet treatment by Soviet officials), calling on the Jews of the world to say a special blessing for the well-being of Gorbachev.[113] In addition, the Soviet Union opened up its archives on the Holocaust to Israeli researchers;[114] the Israeli Philharmonic orchestra was invited to play in Moscow and

Leningrad;[115] Israeli films were shown in Moscow's film festival for the first time;[116] the Moscow Youth Theater, the first Soviet theater troupe to perform in Israel, participated in the Haifa Festival;[117] Soviet Jews went to Israel to study, and Israeli teachers went to teach in newly established Soviet Yeshivot (religious schools);[118] an agreement was reached for exchange visits of the Israeli Habimah and Soviet Taganka theaters;[119] for the first time, Soviet scholars participated in the Israeli-based World Congress of Jewish Studies;[120] and, perhaps most important of all from a symbolic point of view, the world-famous Bolshoi Ballet arrived in Israel in September.[121] At the same time, Moscow opened it gates to Soviet Jewish emigration, with 4,557 Jews emigrating in April, 3,779 in May, 4,354 in June, 4,537 in July, and 6,756 in August, with an increasing number of the Jews traveling to Israel, as it became more difficult to enter the United States because of U.S. funding limitations.[122]

One particularly important aspect of the subgovernmental blossoming of Soviet-Israeli relations during this period was the increased activity of a number of Soviet republics in contacts with Israel. In May a twelve-member official Estonian delegation arrived in Israel,[123] and a Lithuanian delegation arrived the following month to participate in Israel's Maccabiah athletic contests.[124] In July an Azerbajzhani folk dance troupe arrived in Israel, accompanied by the republic's culture minister, Polad Buil-Buil, who said he would consider a twin-city relationship between Baku and Haifa "if there's no interference from above."[125] In August two delegations arrived from Soviet Georgia. One was headed by Georgia's trade minister, Vaza Dzingickadze, who said that the purpose of the trip was to develop trade between Georgia and Israel, including the establishment of joint companies, barter agreements, and the purchase of agricultural produce and medical equipment from Israel.[126] A second delegation was headed by the Georgian minister of culture, Valery Estiani, who signed a cultural agreement with Israel and arranged for an Israeli arts fair to take place in Tbilisi, Georgia, and a Georgian arts fair in Jerusalem.[127]

While the visits of delegations from the four Soviet republics were welcome to Israel as further signs of warming Soviet-Israeli relations, they also reflected the wishes of the republics, each of which was pushing for more autonomy from Moscow, to demonstrate their increasing freedom of action. On occasion, this led to Israel being a factor in the conflict between Moscow and its peripheral republics, as in the case of Estonia when Israeli Agriculture Minister Avraham Katz-Oz, who had been invited to attend an Estonian flower exhibition, was denied a Soviet visa.[128]

Trade was another interest in the efforts of the Soviet republics to establish relations with Israel, as the decentralization of the Soviet economy under Gorbachev's *perestroika* gave the republics more freedom in arranging foreign trade.[129] But it was not only the peripheral republics but also the central government in Moscow that was showing interest in developing trade ties with Israel, as a lead article in the *Jerusalem Post* on July 27, 1989, indicated. Reportedly, senior Soviet officials told the Israeli consul in Moscow, Aryeh Levin, that Moscow wanted to import Israeli fruit and vegetables and acquire Israeli technological expertise in food production, desert reclamation, and solar energy.[130] In August, Marina Kisseleva, a contributing editor of the Soviet Union's new business magazine, *Moscow Business*, visited Israel to prepare an article on Soviet-Israeli trade relations.[131] The same month, a Soviet company signed a contract with Israel's high-tech medical equipment company, Elscint, for the joint production of ultra-sound medical equipment in Kiev,[132] and an Israeli-Soviet agricultural company, Agromir, was established as a joint venture.[133] As trade relations developed, there were reports of negotiations for a major deal in which the USSR would provide Israel with oil and coal in return for a solar-power station to be constructed by an Israeli firm in the Soviet Union,[134] and at the end of September, Soviet and Israeli officials signed an agreement to set up bilateral trade offices in Moscow and Tel Aviv.[135]

Glasnost also played a role in the development of Soviet-Israeli relations in the spring and summer. While Soviet officials had been available for interviews in the Israeli media for several years, now it was the Soviet media's turn to interview Israeli officials. In May Peres gave an interview to *Izvestia*'s Cairo correspondent in which he stated that the lack of Soviet diplomatic ties with Israel was "part of a past that is no longer relevant,"[136] and *Izvestia* interviewed Peres, Ezer Weizman, and Ehud Olmert about the peace process in June.¹³⁷ In August, Israel's foreign minister, Moshe Arens, appeared on Soviet television and used the opportunity to assert that "total diplomatic agreement" should not be a precondition for the restoration of diplomatic ties and that Moscow had to make the first move since it had severed relations in 1967.¹³⁸

By September, it appeared as if Moscow was, at least in a limited way, making such a move. Genghis Iatematov, chairman of the Cultural Committee of the Supreme Soviet, secretary of the Soviet writers union, and a close adviser to Gorbachev, arrived in Israel for a ten-day visit on September 9 and, soon after arriving, called for the Soviet Union and Israel to renew full diplomatic relations immediately, without any preconditions.¹³⁹ He also stated that the public debate in the USSR about the Middle East and the resumption of diplomatic relations with Israel (such a debate had appeared in *Izvestia* in late August and early September) was an indication of the dramatic changes that had taken place in the Soviet Union. For his part, Shamir noted that closer relations between the USSR and Israel could bring great benefits to the Soviet Union.¹⁴⁰ While Iatematov, in a Jerusalem press conference prior to his departure, stated that the views he had been expressing about renewing diplomatic relations were his own private feelings, the fact that he also praised the decision of the Hungarians to restore full diplomatic relations with Israel—a decision that had taken place during his visit to Israel—seemed to be a further signal to the Israelis that Moscow wanted closer relations.¹⁴¹ Indeed, relations between the two countries appeared to improve further at the end of September when Arens met Shevardnadze at the United Nations. The Soviet leader both praised the dialogue that had developed between the two countries and stated that the Soviet airline Aeroflot had been authorized to begin talks with El Al about establishing direct flights between the two countries¹⁴² (a preliminary agreement was to be signed on October 18). The Israelis had long desired such flights, since they would facilitate Soviet Jewish emigration to Israel. This development held great promise for Israel since the United States had now placed a limit on the number of Jews it would accept as refugees. Shevardnadze also offered to host Israeli-PLO talks in Moscow, noted that there were "reasonable elements" in the Shamir peace plan, and announced that he might meet with Shimon Peres, who had just been invited to the Soviet Union for a "private" visit by the Soviet Peace Committee.[143]

In looking to explain the apparent turn in Soviet policy, there are two possibilities to consider. By September, it appeared as if the Middle East peace process was again on track as President Hosni Mubarak of Egypt offered his own ten-point plan to facilitate Israeli-Palestinian talks, which was hotly debated in the Israeli government throughout September. As in past situations of this kind, when the Arab-Israeli peace process showed some promise, Moscow may well have wanted to participate and may have feared it was again on the verge of being frozen out of an important Middle East diplomatic effort. In addition, with Soviet-Egyptian relations rapidly improving, Moscow had no desire to affect them negatively by openly criticizing Mubarak's peace efforts. Indeed, Shevardnadze publicly noted at the UN that "there are also many interesting elements in the proposals of Mr. Mubarak"[144]—a diplomatic and noncommittal evaluation of the Egyptian leader's plan that, if accepted, would have sidetracked the Soviet plan for an international conference.

A second explanation for the apparent turn in Soviet policy toward Israel may lie in the fact that Moscow had perhaps come to realize that to play a serious role in the diplomatic process in the Middle East, closer relations with Israel were a sine qua non. Indeed, even when the Israeli inner cabinet rejected the Mubarak plan by a six-to-six vote, evenly divided along party lines (Labor versus Likud), Moscow continued to demonstrate its interest in improving ties with Israel. Thus on October 17, for the first time, Moscow refused to support an Arab-sponsored resolution aimed at ousting Israel from the General Assembly. The Soviet representative abstained in the vote, as did Czechoslovakia's and East Germany's. Interestingly enough, however, the Soviet representative sought to justify his abstention in such a way as to give minimal offense to Arab states that would, predictably, be angered by it: "The reason we abstained is that we are coming to a new formula concerning the universality of international organizations. This means the Soviet Union will seek to participate in all international organizations and recognizes that this should apply to all countries. . . . The change of vote does not reflect in any way that we have changed our assessment of Israel, in which, so far, unfortunately we have seen no changes. But I hope this will send a signal to the government of Israel that it is high time to listen to the world community."[145]

The increasingly evenhanded Soviet policy toward the Arab-Israeli conflict, however, caused severe criticism of Moscow in the Arab world. To help counter this criticism, Moscow Radio broadcast an Arabic language interview with the number two leader in the PLO, Abu Iyad, who stated: "We condemn all statements which raise doubt about Soviet-Palestinian relations and which are exploited by those who seek to harm the friendly relations between the USSR and the Palestinian Arab people."[146]

As the USSR sought to play a more evenhanded role in the Palestinian-Israeli conflict, a series of developments were to make Moscow's task more difficult. First, the United States began to press Gorbachev on three issues relating to Israel: 1) the reestablishment of full diplomatic relations; 2) the abrogation of the U.N. "Zionism is racism" resolution, which Moscow had helped to pass in 1975; and 3) the finalization of the agreement on direct flights between the USSR and Israel. Second, the pace of Middle East diplomacy once again slowed to a crawl as a result of conflict within Israel's National Unity government, whose Likud component was to take an increasingly negative view of Moscow's role in Middle East diplomacy. Finally, the upsurge in Soviet Jewish emigration to Israel, which had resulted from U.S. immigration limits, soon precipitated major Arab protests against Soviet emigration policy. These protests escalated in intensity when Shamir, in mid-January 1990, sought to justify Israel's holding on to the occupied territories because of the influx of Soviet Jews, leading Moscow to postpone indefinitely direct flights between Moscow and Tel Aviv. During this period, despite the ups and downs of Soviet-Israeli political relations, cultural, economic, and other forms of subgovernmental "people-to-people diplomacy" continued to flourish, and in the November 1989–January 1990 period alone, three Israeli cabinet ministers made visits to Moscow.

As the Bush administration sought to foster the peace process, it urged the Soviet Union to agree to resume diplomatic relations with Israel. Given the fact that Bush and Gorbachev were scheduled to meet at the summit in early December, Moscow, which continued to seek a number of benefits from the United States and was now concerned that Washington might take advantage of the collapse of pro-Soviet regimes in Eastern Europe, could not simply disregard the American urgings. Thus on the eve of the summit, the first deputy foreign minister of the Soviet Union, Yuli Vorontsov, gave a detailed justification of Moscow's position in a major interview in *Izvestia*:

> We recognize the state of Israel both as a political reality and de jure. . . . [but] for as long as Israel does not agree to move toward a settlement, to take steps toward convening an international conference, what would the resumption of diplomatic relations symbolize? Would it not be perceived in Israel and indeed in the world in general, as abandonment of support for the Palestinians' just struggle? And there is no cause to doubt that there are people in Israel who would like to see our policy precisely from this standpoint. . . .
>
> But . . . the absence of diplomatic relations does not impede the development of contacts between our peoples or the strengthening of cultural ties. . . . Nor are political contacts suffering. When the need arises, they are pursued at the most diverse levels, including meetings between the two countries' Foreign Ministers. We seriously hope that the evolution of the Israeli position will ultimately allow our relations to be properly arranged.[147]

At the summit itself, the Middle East was not the top priority, although the two leaders did discuss it. A *Tass* report noted: "The U.S. President voiced an opinion that the restoration of diplomatic relations between the USSR and Israel might facilitate a Middle East settlement. The U.S. President was told in turn that the Soviet Union does not object in principle to the restoration of relations with Israel, but it must take place within the framework of a Middle East settlement."[148]

Meanwhile, Shamir was taking a dim view of Soviet justification for not establishing full diplomatic relations with Israel. His media advisor, Avi Pazner, told the *Jerusalem Post* on December

1, "Israel cannot accept conditions for diplomatic ties. The USSR knows full well that Israel is not a special case and should not be made to pay a price for diplomatic ties."[149] The U.S. assistant secretary of state for the Middle East, John Kelly, who visited Israel immediately after the summit to brief Israeli leaders on the Bush-Gorbachev talks, did note a possible modification in the Soviet position, stating that Gorbachev had told Bush that the USSR would renew full diplomatic relations with Israel as soon as an Israeli-Palestinian dialogue got off the ground. Kelly also noted that Bush and Gorbachev had agreed that the two superpowers could not determine or impose a solution in the Middle East.[150]

Soon after the summit, the United States raised another issue with Moscow pertaining to the Arab-Israeli conflict—the U.N. resolution equating Zionism and racism. On December 11 at a speech at Yeshiva University in New York, Vice President Dan Quayle called on the Soviet Union to cosponsor a motion at the United Nations to repeal the "Zionism is racism" resolution.[151] Before Quayle's speech, the USSR had appeared to give some hint of being ready to move on the issue. Thus Alexander Golitsyn, political counselor at the Soviet Embassy in London, had denounced the 1975 U.N. resolution in early November 1989. Speaking at a conference, he asserted: "If we recognize the state which brings Jews from the four corners of the world, we must recognize the ideological movement on which it is founded. . . . The condemnation of Zionism as racism was part of the ideological war at the time when everything relating to Israel was presented in the USSR in an unfavorable light. But now it was time to get rid of ideological conflicts in international relations and in relations among people."[152] Similarly, in its commentary on the passage of a joint Soviet-American U.N. resolution on international cooperation, Tass noted, also in early November, "Most importantly we are committed to work together through the U.N. system to depoliticize its proceedings and promote an atmosphere of realism and practicality."[153]

If Moscow was indicating its agreement to depoliticize the UN in early November, it was to change its position a month later. Possibly because it was under Arab criticism for its increasingly close economic and cultural ties with Israel, or because it had failed to support a PLO effort on the eve of the superpower summit to have the PLO observer status at the UN raised to that of a state, Moscow publicly opposed the U.S. move to repeal the "Zionism is racism" resolution.[154] Vladimir Petrovsky, the deputy foreign minister, stated at a news conference that trying to repeal the resolution would "bring a confrontation which goes far beyond the Middle East and would have a negative effect on the whole state of the United Nations. We have no need of this kind of action."[155]

The third major issue on which the United States was pressing Moscow was on direct flights between the Soviet Union and Israel. With the United States now placing limits on Soviet Jewish emigration at a time of rising popular anti-Semitism in the USSR, both the United States and Israel felt that direct flights to Israel were the best way to handle the increasing number of Soviet Jews who wanted to leave the Soviet Union. Shevardnadze, in his talks with Arens in September, had noted that Aeroflot had been authorized to begin talks with El Al on the subject, and in November and early December, detailed discussions took place in Moscow between representatives of El Al and Aeroflot. On December 7, El Al reported an agreement, but an official at the Soviet Ministry for Civil Aviation stated that no agreement had been signed.[156] Although the lack of direct flights was not hampering the exodus per se (a record 71,196 Jews were to leave in 1989), it did slow the potential emigration to Israel which, nonetheless, had risen rapidly in the last three months of 1989, with 1,565 Jews arriving from the USSR in October, 1,936 in November, and 3,590 in December.[157] Indeed, the head of the Jewish Agency's Aliyah (immigration) Department, Uri Gordon, had predicted that with direct flights about 1,000 Soviet immigrants per day could land in Israel.[158] As might be expected, the rise in Soviet Jewish immigration to Israel was opposed by the PLO and many Arab states. Moscow took note of this criticism in early January as an Arabic language broadcast to the Middle East stated:

> As far as those who are propagating the question of the emigration of Soviet Jews, they are not seeking to expose its essence, but to misrepresent Soviet policy and to undermine the relations of the Soviet Union with the Arabs. There has been absolutely no arrival *en masse* of Soviet Jews to Israel—a mat-

ter which, as is alleged, may lead to a fundamental alteration of the demographic situation in Arab occupied lands. . . .

The rights of Soviet citizens to leave the USSR without restriction and to live where they want . . . is called for by the nature of the time, international conventions, and the quest to practice relations with other countries and peoples on a civilized basis.[159]

Unfortunately for Moscow, its efforts to play down the significance of the Soviet Jewish immigration to Israel were torpedoed by Shamir himself. Speaking at a Likud party rally in mid-January, he claimed that Israel needed the occupied territories to house the incoming Soviet Jews. "What is clear is that for a big immigration, we need a big and strong state. . . . we need the space to house all the people."[160] The Shamir statement precipitated a crescendo of criticism. Not only were the Arabs outraged, but there was also strong criticism from the U.S. government and from sectors of the American Jewish leadership as well.[161] For its part, the Soviet government, under heavy criticism from the Arab world, publicly rebuked Israel, with Vorontsov calling in the head of the Israeli consular delegation, Aryeh Levin, telling him, "We oppose any use of citizens leaving the USSR, at great risk to them, to push Palestinians off land belonging to them."[162] Israel quickly responded, saying it had no policy of settling immigrants on the West Bank and Gaza,[163] and Arens criticized the Vorontsov statement, noting "the Soviet message was not expressed very politely and we are sorry about it, especially because it is based on misunderstanding over the position of the Israeli government."[164] Moscow was to exploit the Shamir statement, however, to delay direct flights to Israel indefinitely. Tarasov, Shevardnadze's assistant for Middle East affairs, after four days of meetings with PLO leaders in Tunis, stated, "We have at present no plans to establish direct air links and all rumors . . . to this effect do not correspond to reality."[165] He did, however, rule out any measures to prevent Soviet Jews from emigrating, and he appealed to the international community as a whole to stop the movement of Soviet Jews to the occupied territories: "To get the facts clear, every Soviet citizen—Jew, Russian, Ukrainian, Azerbaizhani—has the right to leave the country and come back. He is free to leave the country for any destination he wants. The International Community at large should apply steps which would preclude the possibility of setting up settlements."[166] The USSR was to follow up Tarasov's last point by bringing the issue to the U.N. Security Council and trying, albeit unsuccessfully, to get the United States, during Secretary of State Baker's visit to Moscow in early February 1990, to jointly condemn the settlement of Soviet Jews on occupied territory.[167] In sum, therefore, Moscow continued to play a balancing act—letting Soviet Jews emigrate, with large numbers moving to Israel (thus pleasing Israel and the United States), but prohibiting direct flights, which would have led to an even more rapid increase in Israel's population and possibly to an increase in the number of settlers on the West Bank and Gaza (thus pacifying the Arabs).

While Soviet Jewish immigration to Israel was accelerating, the diplomacy of the peace process appeared to be moving ahead glacially. Although the Israeli cabinet in early November was to approve by a nine-to-three vote Secretary of State Baker's five-point plan to facilitate the holding of elections under Mubarak's ten-point plan, there remained strong divisions between Labor and Likud over the interpretation of the American assurances that went along with the entire diplomatic process. At the same time, Foreign Minister Arens was taking an increasingly negative public stance toward Soviet participation in the Middle East peace process. Thus, in mid-December, he belittled the role Moscow could play in the Middle East: "The Soviets want to be involved in the peace process, yet the Soviets do not see the Middle East as most important for them. After events in Europe, the idea of viewing the Soviets as a superpower equal to the U.S. needs examination."[168] Three weeks later Arens stated that Moscow had nothing to contribute to the diplomatic effort aimed at holding elections on the West Bank,[169] and the Israeli Foreign Ministry in late January was reported to have planned to oppose the lifting of the Jackson-Vanik amendment (which severely limited trade with the USSR),[170] although two days later a Foreign Ministry spokesman told the *Jerusalem Post* that Israel would not oppose the abolition of Jackson-Vanik.[171]

While diplomatic relations between Israel and the USSR remained chilly, other aspects of the relationship blossomed. The Israeli

Habimah Theatre, which had originated in the USSR, returned there for a triumphal visit in early January 1990;[172] Soviet Parliament member Leonid Shkolnik became the first member of the new Soviet Parliament to visit the Knesset (he was in Israel to attend the Third International Conference of the Jewish Media);[173] and for the first time since 1964, a chess team from the USSR participated in a chess championship in Israel.[174] At the same time, Soviet Jewish tourists continued to come to Israel in large numbers (25,000 in 1989), and a memorial was established in Israel for the 200,000 Jewish soldiers of the Soviet army who died in World War II.[175]

Economic and scientific ties also flourished. In late November, the Israeli agriculture minister, who had been denied a visa in September, arrived in Moscow by invitation of the Soviet Academy of Sciences. During his visit he reached an agreement whereby Israel would sell $30 million in agricultural produce to the USSR and would assist Moscow in water planning, cotton production, and the establishment of dairies and construction of chicken coops. As part of the agreement, there would be an exchange program of 1,000 children from each country visiting the other.[176]

In January, two Israeli cabinet ministers went to Moscow, Zvulun Hammer, minister of religion, and Ezer Weizman, minister of science. (Peres, however, had postponed his trip three times, possibly because he was seeking a meeting with Gorbachev, which the Soviet leader was as yet unwilling to grant.) Weizman, having just been excluded from the inner cabinet by Shamir because of his contacts with the PLO, was certainly persona grata in Moscow.[177] He had an extended meeting with Shevardnadze in which, according to Weizman, the foreign minister promised to upgrade relations with Israel from the consular level to that of chargé d'affaires and promised to talk to Iran about the fate of Israeli soldiers missing in Lebanon.[178] While in Moscow, Weizman also signed a scientific cooperation agreement with the Soviet Academy of Sciences. Yet, with Weizman in Moscow, Gorbachev once again sought to demonstrate the USSR's evenhandedness between Israel and the PLO, as Moscow upgraded the status of the PLO mission in Moscow to full embassy status and appointed an ambassador to the PLO Executive Committee.[179]

Indeed, the Tass report describing the Shevardnadze-Weizman

meeting juxtaposed Shevardnadze's call for an international conference "as the main way to achieve a genuine and lasting peace in the Near East," with a call for the participation of the PLO "at every stage of the peace process." It then went on to explain that Moscow's view of the important role of the PLO was the reason for its decision "to turn the PLO mission in Moscow into the Embassy of the State of Palestine."[180]

From the point of view of the PLO, however, the Soviet move may have appeared primarily symbolic. With Soviet Jews continuing to flock to Israel in record numbers, and with new regimes in East Germany, Czechoslovakia, and Poland cutting off military assistance, the PLO's international position was weakening. As an aide to Arafat noted, "The deep changes in the Eastern Bloc, which was our chief international ally for the past twenty-five years, will prevent it from playing any Middle East role for at least another five years. The PLO is now working to build new international bridges as an alternative for the absence of an active East Europe."[181] In any case, the Soviet elevation of the PLO's Moscow mission to embassy status is a good point of departure for evaluating Soviet policy toward Israel and the PLO since the start of the Intifada.

Conclusions

In analyzing Soviet policy toward the Intifada, there are two central conclusions to be drawn. First, despite the Intifada, Soviet-Israeli relations continued to improve in a large number of areas, from people-to-people diplomacy to Soviet Jewish emigration to Israel, although Moscow continued to rebuff Israeli efforts to have the USSR restore full diplomatic relations. Second, Soviet support for the PLO remained limited, and while the USSR was to step up its contacts with the PLO after the beginning of the U.S.-PLO dialogue in December 1988, the very fact that it was simultaneously improving its ties with Israel weakened the Soviet-PLO relationship, given the PLO's zero-sum view of the triangular relationship among itself, Israel, and the USSR. This was the case, despite such symbolic Soviet actions as elevating the PLO mission in Moscow to embassy status.

Soviet-Israeli relations, which had begun to improve in 1987 prior to the Intifada, improved still further in 1988 and 1989 despite the Intifada, which the USSR strongly criticized Israel for repressing. On the diplomatic front, Moscow's actions in 1988 included permission for an Israeli consular delegation to come to the Soviet Union, public comments by Gorbachev to Arafat that Israel's interests had to be taken into account in any peace settlement, the assertion by a senior Soviet diplomat that in a Palestinian-Israeli settlement Palestinian refugees could only return to the West Bank-Gaza state, not to Israel proper, and Shevardnadze's meeting with Prime Minister Shamir in New York. At the same time, Moscow sharply increased the number of Soviet Jews leaving the USSR, with 18,965 leaving in 1988. In addition, beginning in December 1988 and for the first time since the 1967 war, the Soviet Union gave Israel favorable media coverage, praising its prompt return of a group of hijackers and its aid to the Soviet victims of the Armenian earthquake.

In 1989, despite the formation of a Likud-led National Unity government at the end of 1988, Soviet-Israeli relations improved still further. Besides a major increase in cultural and athletic interactions and other such forms of diplomacy as exchange visits of scholars and chief rabbis, by January 1990 the pace of diplomatic contacts had quickened as well, with no fewer than three meetings between Shevardnadze and the new foreign minister, Arens, and visits by three Israeli cabinet ministers to Moscow. The two countries, however, still differed strongly over the Middle East peace process: There was a negative Soviet reaction to the Shamir peace proposal and Israel sharply protested the Soviet sale of SU-24s to Libya. Nonetheless, Moscow continued to urge Israel's main enemies, PLO leader Arafat and President Assad of Syria, to settle their conflicts with Israel politically, and Assad was also told that Moscow would not support his efforts to gain military parity with Israel.

Interestingly enough, for the first time, in 1989, a number of Soviet Union republics were to play a role in Soviet-Israeli relations, as they both demonstrated their increasing autonomy from Moscow and also sought to gain trade benefits. For its part, the central government in Moscow also began the process of reestablishing trade relations with Israel. In September the two countries signed a Chamber of Commerce agreement, and in November, with the Israeli agricultural minister in Moscow, a large-scale agreement on the Israeli sale of agricultural produce to the USSR was signed. Another sign of improving Soviet-Israeli relations in 1989 was the sharp increase in the number of Soviet Jews both leaving the USSR (71,000) and, because of immigration limits in the United States, arriving in Israel (12,000). While Moscow facilitated the exit of almost all Jews now wanting to leave, it backed off from its promise of direct flights, in part because of rising Arab opposition and in part because of a statement by Shamir that appeared to use the sharp increase in the number of Soviet Jews arriving in Israel to justify continued occupation of the West Bank and Gaza. Moscow's shift to a more evenhanded approach to the Arab-Israeli conflict was also shown in 1989 when it abstained on the Arab motion to exclude Israel from the U.N. General Assembly, but it was not yet willing to join the United States in repealing the U.N.'s "Zionism is racism" resolution of 1975.

In seeking to explain the improvement of Soviet-Israeli relations despite the Intifada, there appear to be four major factors to consider: Middle East politics, Soviet-American relations, the Soviet interest in expanded foreign trade, and, to a lesser extent, the impact of Soviet public opinion, which for the first time was becoming a factor in the formulation of Soviet foreign policy. When Gorbachev took office, the Middle East peace process appeared to be well underway as a result of the Hussein-Arafat agreement of February 1985 and U.S. efforts to broker a Palestinian-Jordanian negotiating team acceptable to Israel. Consequently, Gorbachev, a far more flexible leader than his predecessors, felt an opening to Israel was necessary for Moscow to enter the peace process, from which it had been excluded since 1973. While the peace process came to a halt because of the rise in Middle East terrorism and the break between Hussein and Arafat, Moscow continued its contacts with Israel, because it was seeking Israeli support for an international peace conference, which Gorbachev, like his predecessors, felt was the best way to resolve the Arab-Israeli conflict (and enhance the Soviet position in the Middle East in the process). Moscow stepped up its efforts throughout 1988 and 1989 to try to persuade Israel to enter an international conference—holding out the bait of resuming full diplomatic relations—despite the Intifada.

Moscow's opening to Israel was due not only to its interest in joining the Middle East peace process but also to its desire to influence public opinion in the United States. Following the CPSU party conference in February 1986, with his position in the Communist party reinforced, Gorbachev set about to undertake major economic and political reforms in the USSR. To succeed in his program, however, particularly at a time of declining hard currency earnings due to the drop in oil prices, Gorbachev clearly wanted to slow down the arms race to free resources for Moscow's lagging economy. He was also interested in getting credits from the United States, as well as investments in joint ventures, and this necessitated changes in the Jackson-Vanik and Stevenson amendments (the latter limited U.S. credits to the USSR). Given the fact that Moscow has long overestimated Jewish influence in the United States, and that it understands the close tie between American Jewry and the State of Israel, Soviet gestures to Israel, which included in 1988 and 1989 a large number of cultural and athletic exchanges, coupled with the increased exodus of Soviet Jews, seemed aimed at improving the Soviet image in the United States for arms control purposes and positioning Moscow for U.S. trade benefits. Indeed, the fact that the chief rabbi of Tel Aviv, after returning from a trip to the USSR, called on Jews all over the world to pray for Gorbachev, indicated just how successful the Soviet leader's playing of the "Israeli card" has been in his efforts to improve relations with the United States

Trade has also emerged as a factor, albeit a limited one, in Soviet-Israeli relations. With the Soviet economy experiencing serious shortcomings, particularly in the sphere of food production, trade with Israel, both by the Soviet central government and by its increasingly assertive republics, may provide a mechanism whereby some of these shortages can be partially alleviated. For example, Israeli experience in growing crops in saline soil will be of major assistance to the Central Asian republics. In addition, Israel's high-tech medical equipment industry may help the USSR improve the quality of its health-care delivery system.

Finally, one now cannot overlook the impact of Soviet public opinion on the making of Soviet foreign policy. With Gorbachev seeking to transfer power from the party to a popularly elected parliament, and Shevardnadze now making an annual report to Parliament on Soviet foreign policy, the attitudes of the Soviet "man in the street" are becoming a factor, if not yet a major one, in Soviet foreign policy. While some of this popular opinion is clearly anti-Semitic, other Soviet citizens have been favorably impressed by Israeli help to the USSR during the 1988 hijacking affair, in the Armenian earthquake relief effort, and in the aftermath of the Trans-Siberian train accident. Reinforcing the pro-Israeli turn in Soviet public opinion—at least on the intelligentsia level—is the fact that in the pre-Gorbachev period the Soviet media portrayed the Arab-Israeli conflict in terms of good and evil, with Israel the evil party. Under Gorbachev, a much more balanced portrayal of Israel is being depicted, with top Israeli politicians now being regularly interviewed. In turn, a more negative view is portrayed of some of Moscow's Arab allies, like Syria, who are the recipients of extensive Soviet aid, which many Soviet citizens would prefer to be used at home. It is too early to determine whether Soviet public opinion will become a significant element in Soviet foreign policymaking, although the victory of progressives in the 1990 Soviet elections is a positive sign.

As far as the Palestinians are concerned, Moscow took what might be called an instrumental position toward the Intifada. Perhaps hoping that the Intifada would pressure the United States and Israel into accepting an international conference, through most of 1988 Moscow downgraded the status of the PLO, calling instead for "representatives of the Palestinian people" to attend and qualified Palestinian representation at the conference still further by raising the possibility that a single Arab delegation might attend. In addition, Moscow downgraded its previous call for a Palestinian state to just "self-determination."

The Soviet approach to the PLO began to change following King Hussein's abdication of responsibility for the West Bank in July 1988 and the PLO's subsequent decision to come out for a two-state solution for the Palestinian-Israeli conflict, a decision Moscow warmly endorsed, although it initially only recognized the declaration of the state, not the state itself. Once the United States began a dialogue with the PLO, however, Moscow apparently became concerned that the United States would work out another "separate deal," as it had between Egypt and Israel in 1979. Consequently, Moscow stepped up its contacts with the PLO and attacked the Shamir election plan because it sought to avoid a role for the PLO. In addition, Shevardnadze called for the establishment of a PLO-Israeli dialogue as another price of establishing Soviet-Israeli diplomatic relations, and Moscow's first deputy foreign minister, Yuli Vorontsov, justified Moscow's failure to establish full diplomatic relations with Israel prior to its agreement to an international conference that would include the PLO, because it would be perceived as "abandonment of support for the Palestinians' just struggle." While Moscow was unwilling to support the PLO's call for statehood status at the United Nations, it did raise the status of the PLO's mission in Moscow to that of an embassy. However, much of what Moscow did for the PLO was essentially symbolic, and the Soviet effort to develop a more balanced policy toward the Israeli-Palestinian conflict seemed, by early 1990, to be tipping more and more toward Israel. While Moscow did not yet have full diplomatic relations with Israel, it had extensive contacts with the Jewish state in virtually all other areas. In sum, therefore, Moscow's interest in a better relationship with Israel superseded its indignation at Israel's suppression of the Intifada. In this area, at least, Moscow's "new thinking" appeared to be more than just rhetoric.

Notes

1. For an analysis of Gorbachev's policy toward Israel in the 1985-87 period, see Robert O. Freedman, "Soviet Policy toward the Middle East," in *The Middle East from the Iran-Contral Affair to the Intifada*, ed. Robert O. Freedman (Syracuse: Syracuse University Press, 1991), chap. 2.

2. For an analysis of Gorbachev's policies toward the Middle East as an element in his overall foreign policy, see Robert O. Freedman, *Moscow and the Middle East since the Invasion of Afghanistan* (Cambridge: Cambridge University Press, 1991) chap. 4.

3. See *Soviet Foreign Policy*, ed. Robbin F. Laird (New York: Academy of Political Science, 1987).

4. For the major source of information on the "new thinking," see

Gorbachev's own book, *Perestroika: New Thinking for Our Country and the World* (New York: Harper & Row, 1987). See also Paul Marantz, *From Lenin to Gorbachev: Changing Soviet Perspectives on East-West Relations* (Ottawa: Canadian Institute for International Peace and Security, 1988).

5. *Pravda*, December 20, 1987.
6. *Pravda*, December 24, 1987.
7. A meeting between Voronstov and a group of Arab diplomats on December 26, 1987, to discuss "the dangerous situation in the Israeli-occupied Palestinian territories" was reported in *Tass*, December 28, 1987, in *Foreign Broadcast Information Service Daily Report: USSR* (hereafter *FBIS:USSR*), December 29, 1987, p. 42.
8. Moscow Domestic Service, January 16, 1988, in *FBIS:USSR*, January 19, 1988, p. 37.
9. Tass, January 26, 1988, in *FBIS:USSR*, January 27, 1988, p. 9; Jerusalem Domestic Service, January 20, 1988, in *FBIS:USSR*, January 20, 1988, p. 19. Perhaps as a signal to Moscow, the Israeli Foreign Ministry in December had granted only a one-month extension to the visas of the Soviet consular delegation in December, 1987 (author interviews at Israeli Foreign Ministry, July 1988, and U.S. Embassy, Moscow, January 1988).
10. Tass, January 19, 1988, in *FBIS:USSR*, January 20, 1988, p. 5.
11. *Izvestia*, January 22, 1988, in *FBIS:USSR*, January 22, 1988, p. 23.
12. See article by Pavel Demchenko in *Pravda*, February 2, 1988.
13. *Pravda*, February 26, 1988.
14. *Pravda*, February 9, 1988.
15. *Izvestia*, February 6, 1988, in *FBIS:USSR*, February 12, 1988, p. 36.
16. Tass, February 11, 1988, in *FBIS:USSR*, February 18, 1988, p. 24.
17. Tass, International Service, February 19, 1988, in *FBIS:USSR*, February 22, 1988, p. 39.
18. KUNA (Kuwait), February 23, 1988, in *FBIS:USSR*, February 24, 1988, p. 29.
19. Tass, March 18, 1988, in *FBIS:USSR*, March 21, 1988, p. 30. A Tass report on April 4, 1988, in *FBIS:USSR*, April 5, 1988, p. 22, noted that the USSR had no "fundamental objections" to the intermediate steps preferred by the U.S., but "such steps can yield a positive result only in the context of a comprehensive settlement."
20. See Moscow Domestic Service, April 3, 1988, in *FBIS:USSR*, April 4, 1988, p. 13. See also Reuters, *Jerusalem Post*, March 31, 1988.
21. Tass, April 9, 1988, in *FBIS:USSR*, April 11, 1988, p. 26, my emphasis.
22. Moscow Domestic Service, April 9, 1988, in *FBIS:USSR*, April 11, 1988, p. 27.
23. See Associated Press report, *Jerusalem Post*, April 13, 1988.

24. *Al-Siyasah* (Kuwait), April 26, 1988, in *FBIS:USSR*, May 2, 1988, p. 35.

25. Cited in Michael Yudelman, *Jerusalem Post*, March 8, 1988. Three days later, the *Jerusalem Post* reported a meeting between an Israeli and a Soviet diplomat at the UN, in which the Soviet diplomat reportedly stated that the PLO terrorist attack on an Israeli bus in early March was a "tremendous mistake," and openly wondered if the PLO had any coherent policy.

26. Cited in Jonathan Karp, *Jerusalem Post*, April 15, 1988.

27. For a wry comment on the Pugachova tour, see Yosef Begun, *Jerusalem Post*, April 14, 1988. Begun, a former Refusenik, called for more Israeli artists to tour the USSR.

28. Gorbachev's purpose in allowing such tourism may have been to lessen the pressure from Soviet Jews to permanently leave the country. Ten thousand Soviet Jews were to visit Israel in 1988.

29. Tass, April 22, 1988, in *FBIS:USSR*, April 25, 1988, p. 38. For the text of the memorandum of agreement, see *Jerusalem Post*, April 22, 1988.

30. Moscow International Service, in Arabic, April 25, 1988, in *FBIS:USSR*, April 26, 1988, p. 23.

31. Menachem Shalev and Wolf Blitzer, *Jerusalem Post*, April 29, 1988.

32. For a description of the interview, see Associated Press report, *Jerusalem Post*, April 15, 1988.

33. For a description of the Peres visit, which Hungary played down, see Menachem Shalev and Lisa Billig, *Jerusalem Post*, May 10, 1988, and Henry Kamm, *New York Times*, May 10, 1988.

34. Tass, May 12, 1988, in *FBIS:USSR*, May 13, 1988, p. 7.

35. *Jerusalem Post*, May 11, 1988.

36. Bernard Josephs, *Jerusalem Post*, May 16, 1988.

37. David Remnick, *Washington Post*, June 9, 1988. See also Philip Taubman, *New York Times*, May 18, 1988.

38. For the reported text of this document, see *Jerusalem Post*, June 10, 1988.

39. Wolf Blitzer, *Jerusalem Post*, May 19, 1988.

40. Jerusalem Post Diplomatic Staff Report, *Jerusalem Post*, May 25, 1988.

41. Glenn Frankel, *Washington Post*, May 25, 1988.

42. Wolf Blitzer, *Jerusalem Post*, May 20, 1988.

43. *Pravda*, June 3, 1988, in *FBIS:USSR*, June 3, 1988, p. 9, emphasis added.

44. Elaine Sciolino, *New York Times*, June 7, 1988.

45. Wolf Blitzer, *Jerusalem Post*, June 9, 1988.

46. For reports on the Shamir-Shevardnadze talks, see Don Oberdorfer,

Washington Post, June 10, 1988; Elaine Sciolino, *New York Times*, June 10, 1988; and Menachem Shalev, *Jerusalem Post*, June 12, 1988. According to Israeli Foreign Ministry sources, however, Shevardnadze was "disappointed" by his talks with Shamir.

47. Menachem Shalev and Asher Wallfish, *Jerusalem Post*, June 13, 1988.

48. Associated Press report, *New York Times*, July 29, 1988, and Gary Lee, *Washington Post*, July 29, 1988. It should also be noted that the chief rabbi of the city of Rehovot in Israel, Rabbi Simha Kook, was given a visa to visit the Soviet Union in late June 1988, despite the fact that he put on his visa application that the purpose of his visit was to "teach Jewish law and visit synagogues" (*Jerusalem Post*, June 24, 1988).

49. See Gorbachev's message to Assad on the twenty-fifth anniversary of the March 8, 1963, Ba'athist Revolution in Syria (Tass, March 7, 1988, in *FBIS:USSR*, March 7, 1988, p. 30, and Deputy Foreign Minister Yuli Voronstov's talk with Assad in Damascus in July (*Pravda*, July 21, 1988).

50. The clearest exposition of the Syrian position is found in a Tass interview with the outspoken Syrian defense minister, Mustapha Talas, in *FBIS:USSR*, October 6, 1988, pp. 18–19.

51. *Davar* (Tel Aviv) on July 11, 1988, reported that Moscow was sending Sukhoi-24 ground-attack bombers to Syria (*FBIS:NESA*, July 11, 1988, p. 25); on July 6, 1988, the *Jerusalem Post*, citing Israeli Defense Ministry sources, said Moscow was sending more SS-21 ground-to-ground missiles to Syria. The SU-24 deal was also reported by *Al-Ittihad* (Abu Dhabi) on August 29, 1988, along with a sale of MIG-29 aircraft (*FBIS:USSR*, August 29, 1988, p. 18). Defense Minister Yitzhak Rabin in an interview on Israeli television on August 30, 1988, discussed a sale "at the beginning of 1988" of tanks and SS-21 missiles and possibly other aircraft (*FNIS:NESA*, August 31, 1988, p. 23).

52. See *Argumenty i Fakty*, September 3–9, 1988, in *FBIS:USSR*, September 2, 1988, p. 6. The story originated in the visit to Damascus of the Soviet chief of chemical warfare. It is possible, given Iraq's use of poison gas and its enmity toward Syria, that the Syrian government wanted countermeasures against Iraq. It is also possible, however, that Syria was actively engaged in the development of chemical weapons itself as a countermeasure against Israel's nuclear capability.

53. *Krasnaya Zvezda*, September 15, 1988, in *FBIS:USSR*, September 16, 1988, p. 18. For another view of the Tartus "facility," see Robert Pear, *New York Times*, August 28, 1988.

54. See Ya'acov Lamdan, *Jerusalem Post*, December 12, 1988, citing the Lebanese weekly *al-Muharrar*, and report by David Ottaway, *Washington Post*, June 23, 1988. Reportedly, Syria's debt to the USSR for military purchases totaled $16.5 billion by the end of 1988.

55. In *FBIS:NESA*, June 7, 1978, p. 1.

56. Radio Moscow, June 10, 1988, in *FBIS:USSR*, June 13, 1988, p. 39; Tass, June 9, 1988, in *FBIS:USSR*, June 10, 1988, p. 35; and *Pravda*, June 12, 1988.

57. For the summit communiqué, read by the Arab League secretary general Chedli Klibi on Algerian television, see *FBIS:NESA*, June 10, 1988, pp. 11–14. For reports describing the atmosphere of the summit, see Youssef Ibrahim, *New York Times*, June 10, 1988, and George D. Moffet, *Christian Science Monitor*, June 10, 1988.

58. Arafat was interviewed by Leonid Medvenko, "A Time to Throw Stones and a Time to Collect Them," *New Times* 36 (1988): 18.

59. Ibid., p. 17.

60. *Al-Ittihad*, August 23, 1988, in *FBIS:USSR*, August 25, 1988, p. 11.

61. *Izvestia*, September 18, 1988 (translated in *Current Digest of the Soviet Press (CDSP)* 40, no. 38 [1988]: 17), emphasis added.

62. A terrorist attack on the eve of the election, in which several Israelis were killed when their bus was firebombed, hardened Israeli attitudes against the PLO. Soviet press spokesman Gennady Gerasimov condemned the attack, although he also condemned "state terrorism." However, in a clear rebuke of the perpetrators of the attack, he stated, "With respect to this specific act, one also has to ask: who gains from this, particularly on the eve of the parliamentary elections in Israel?" *Pravda*, November 1, 1988 (translated in *CDSP* 40, no. 44 [1988]: p. 19).

63. The text of the political program of the PNC was printed in the *New York Times*, November 17, 1988. See also Youssef Ibrahim, *New York Times*, November 15, 1988.

64. See George D. Moffett, *Christian Science Monitor*, November 15, 1988.

65. *Pravda*, November 19, 1988 (translated in *CDSP* 40, no. 46 [1988]: 19–20), my emphasis. Gerasimov gave a legalistic argument for the Soviet Union's limited recognition stating, "Our practice knows no precedents when a state would be recognized while its territory was under foreign occupation and which had no government at the moment of recognition." (Tass, English, November 24, 1988, in *FBIS:USSR*, November 25, 1988, p. 5), emphasis added.

66. Radio Moscow, November 21, 1988, in *FBIS:USSR*, November 22, 1988, p. 24.

67. See *Izvestia*, November 29, 1988.

68. *Pravda*, December 8, 1988, in *FBIS:USSR*, December 12, 1988, p. 12.

69. *Washington Post*, December 3, 1988.

70. See Arafat's press conference statement, *New York Times*, December 15 1989. See also Robert Pear, *New York Times*, December 15, 1988,

and David Ottaway and John Goshko, *Washington Post*, December 15, 1988.

71. See Patrick Tyler, *Washington Post*, December 17, 1988.

72. *Pravda*, December 18, 1988.

73. Interview with Aryeh Levin, head of the Israeli consular mission in Moscow, Jerusalem, Israel, January 4, 1988.

74. For a Soviet account of the hijacking, see Vitaly Bordunov, "A Drama Brought to an Early Finale," *New Times* 50 (1988): 46–47. Aryeh Levin himself was interviewed and photographed for the same article.

75. See Walter Ruby, *Jerusalem Post*, December 9, 1988.

76. Ibid.

77. See David Remnick, *Washington Post*, December 22, 1988.

78. Moscow Domestic Service, in Russian, January 4, 1989, in *FBIS: USSR*, January 5, 1989, p. 3.

79. See Michael Zlatowski and Menahem Shalev, *Jerusalem Post*, January 9, 1989.

80. Tass International Service, in Russian, January 8, 1989, in *FBIS: USSR*, January 9, 1989, p. 11.

81. *FBIS:USSR*, January 12, 1989, p. 8.

82. Tass, January 5, 1989, in *FBIS:USSR*, January 5, 1989, p. 3.

83. Tass, January 11, 1989, in *FBIS:USSR*, January 12, 1989, p. 7.

84. *Ha'aretz* (Tel Aviv), December 29, 1988, in *FBIS:USSR*, December 28, 1988, p. 8.

85. *Al-Anba* (Kuwait), January 7, 1989, in *FBIS:USSR*, January 10, 1989, p. 34.

86. Moscow Domestic Service, January 18, 1989, in *FBIS:USSR*, January 19, 1989, p. 30. According to interviews conducted by the author in PLO headquarters in Tunis in February 1989, contacts had indeed been stepped up.

87. Shevardnadze's dinner speech in Damascus, *Tass*, February 19, 1989, in *FBIS:USSR*, February 21, 1989, p. 20.

88. *Pravda*, February 20, 1989, citing Shevardnadze's talks with Syrian vice president Abd al-Halim Khaddam, the former Syrian foreign minister.

89. Shevardnadze dinner speech, *FBIS:USSR*, February 21, 1989, p. 21.

90. Ibid.

91. Shevardnadze news conference, Tass International Service, February 19, 1989, in *FBIS:USSR*, February 21, 1989, p. 23.

92. Ibid.

93. Shevardnadze dinner speech, *FBIS:USSR*, February 21, 1989, p. 20, emphasis added.

94. The author was in Tunis interviewing PLO officials when the Soviet effort was made and related to him.

95. *Pravda*, February 21, 1989, in *FBIS:USSR*, February 21, 1989, p. 28.

96. Tass, February 20, 1989, in *FBIS:USSR*, February 21, 1989, p. 29.
97. Ibid., p. 30.
98. Patrick Tyler, *Washington Post*, February 23, 1989.
99. The text of Shevardnadze's comments was published in the *Jerusalem Post*, February 26, 1989.
100. The text of the Israeli government peace plan was published in the *Jerusalem Post*, May 15, 1989.
101. Tass, International Service, May 10, 1989, in *FBIS:USSR*, May 11, 1989, p. 6.
102. Menahem Shalev, *Jerusalem Post*, May 14, 1989.
103. David Ottaway, *Washington Post*, June 2, 1989.
104. Asher Wallfish, *Jerusalem Post*, June 30, 1989, and Wolf Blitzer, *Jerusalem Post*, June 18, 1989.
105. Michael Zlotowski, *Jerusalem Post*, July 6, 1989.
106. *Pravda*, May 29, 1989 (translated in *Current Digest of the Soviet Press* 41, no. 22: 18).
107. *Izvestia*, April 7, 1989.
108. *Pravda*, July 21, 1989 (translated in *Current Digest of the Soviet Press*, 41, no. 31: 30).
109. Kenneth Kaplan, *Jerusalem Post*, June 13, 1989.
110. Kenneth Kaplan, *Jerusalem Post*, June 18, 1989.
111. For stories about Israeli aid to the Armenian earthquake victims, see Sabra Chartrand, *New York Times*, June 29, 1989, Michael Eilan and Andy Goldberg, *Jerusalem Post*, June 29, 1989, Leslie Susser, *Jerusalem Post*, August 16, 1989, and Joel Brinkley, *New York Times*, August 16, 1989.
112. *New York Times*, July 27, 1989.
113. Haim Shapiro, *Jerusalem Post*, May 14, 1989.
114. Ernie Meyer, *Jerusalem Post*, September 18, 1989.
115. Lea Levavi, *Jerusalem Post*, June 20, 1989.
116. Reuters, *Jerusalem Post*, June 22, 1989.
117. *Jerusalem Post*, April 24, 1989.
118. Charles Hoffman, *Jerusalem Post*, August 8, 1989.
119. Joseph Hoffman and Andy Goldberg, *Jerusalem Post*, July 21, 1989.
120. Charles Hoffman, *Jerusalem Post*, August 17, 1989.
121. Helen Kaye, *Jerusalem Post*, September 11, 1989.
122. Emigration statistics from the National Conference on Soviet Jewry, New York City.
123. *Jerusalem Post*, May 15, 1989.
124. *Jerusalem Post*, June 30, 1989.
125. Ya'acov Friedler, *Jerusalem Post*, July 13, 1989.
126. Judy Maltz, *Jerusalem Post*, August 17, 1989.
127. *Jerusalem Post*, August 2, 1989.

128. *Jerusalem Post*, September 8, 1989. (Reportedly a Soviet official stated, "We decided to teach them [the Estonians] a lesson. We're just sorry it was at your expense.") A similar problem may have been the cause of the confusion over reports about an invitation to Ariel Sharon to visit Soviet Georgia (see *Jerusalem Post*, August 17, announcing the visit, and August 20, citing Soviet denials of the invitation).

129. Ukrainian and Moldavian republic ministers also visited Israel in July (see Judy Maltz, *Jerusalem Post*, July 31, 1989).

130. Menahem Shalev, *Jerusalem Post*, July 27, 1989.

131. Harold Rose, *Jerusalem Post*, August 10, 1989.

132. *Jerusalem Post*, August 11, 1989.

133. *Jerusalem Post*, August 14, 1989.

134. Larry Dorfner, *Jerusalem Post*, September 21, 1989.

135. Michael Zlotowski, *Jerusalem Post*, September 27, 1989.

136. Menahem Shalev, *Jerusalem Post*, May 12, 1989.

137. *Izvestia*, June 7, 1989, in *FBIS:USSR*, June 9, 1989, pp. 9–10.

138. Dan Petreanu, *Jerusalem Post*, August 15, 1989.

139. Menahem Shalev, *Jerusalem Post*, September 12, 1989.

140. *Jerusalem Post*, September 13, 1989.

141. David Makovsky, *Jerusalem Post*, September 22, 1989.

142. Walter Ruby, *Jerusalem Post*, September 29, 1989.

143. Ibid.

144. Ibid.

145. Paul Lewis, *New York Times*, October 18, 1989.

146. Moscow International Service, in Arabic, November 4, 1989, in *FBIS:USSR*, November 6, 1989, p. 25.

147. *Izvestia*, November 30, 1989, in *FBIS:USSR*, November 30, 1989, p. 12.

148. Tass, December 6, 1989, in *FBIS:USSR*, December 7, 1989, p. 10.

149. Menahem Shalev, *Jerusalem Post*, December 1, 1989.

150. Menahem Shalev, *Jerusalem Post*, December 6, 1989. This was, in reality, little in the way of a modification of the Soviet position because the PLO continued to demand an international conference, and any Palestinian-Israeli dialogue would inevitably lead to an international conference, if, as seemed most likely, the PLO was the primary factor influencing the Palestinians in the dialogue. In an interview in Tunis in February 1989, Arafat told the author that an international conference was necessary to gain general Arab support for a settlement and isolate Syria if it failed to agree.

151. Walter Ruby and Wolf Blitzer, *Jerusalem Post*, December 12, 1989.

152. David Horowitz, *Jerusalem Post*, November 3, 1989.

153. Tass, November 3, 1989, in *FBIS:USSR*, November 6, 1989, p. 8. It

should also be remembered that less than a year before, Gorbachev had given his deideologization speech at the United Nations (see ibid.).

154. Caryle Murphy, *Washington Post*, December 1, 1989. The United States strongly opposed the PLO move, and Moscow, with more important issues at stake, presumably did not want to alienate the United States over aid to the PLO effort, which had also received limited Arab support.

155. Paul Lewis, *New York Times*, December 16, 1989. In response to a question by the author as to the rationale for the Soviet position on the "Zionism is racism" resolution in light of Moscow's new emphasis on "deideologization" at the UN, Petrovsky replied, "We no longer see Zionism as racism but to revoke the resolution now would bring confrontation to the UN at a time when we are working for universal cooperation." (Petrovsky had just given a lecture, on February 27, 1990, at the Brookings Institution in Washington, D.C., on "New Trends in International Relations," in which he discussed the depoliticization of the UN.)

156. For reports on the progress of these talks, see *Jerusalem Post*, November 7, 13, 17, December 4, 8, 1989.

157. Research Bureau, National Conference on Soviet Jewry.

158. Charles Hoffman, *Jerusalem Post*, December 12, 1989.

159. Moscow Radio, in Arabic, January 5, 1990, in *FBIS:USSR*, January 9, 1990, p. 33.

160. Joel Brinkley, *New York Times*, February 5, 1990.

161. At the National Jewish Community Relations Council meeting in Arizona in mid-February, there was strong criticism of the settlement of Soviet Jews in the occupied territories.

162. *Jerusalem Post*, January 30, 1990.

163. Sabra Chartrand, *New York Times*, January 31, 1990.

164. Associated Press report, *Washington Post*, January 31, 1990.

165. Reuters report, *Jerusalem Post*, February 4, 1990.

166. Ibid.

167. Don Oberdorfer and Al Kamen, *Washington Post*, February 9, 1990.

168. David Makovsky, *Jerusalem Post*, December 12, 1989.

169. David Makovsky, *Jerusalem Post*, January 2, 1990.

170. David Makovsky, *Jerusalem Post*, January 28, 1990.

171. Joshua Brilliant, *Jerusalem Post*, January 30, 1990.

172. For a background analysis of the visit, see Helen Kaye, *Jerusalem Post*, December 28, 1989.

173. *Jerusalem Post*, January 10, 1990.

174. Yitzhak Liss, *Jerusalem Post*, November 24, 1989. International Chess Grandmaster Edward Gurfeld reportedly stated upon completing the competition, "I am very happy that we made something of a break-

through by coming here on the first direct commercial flight between Russia and Israel [since 1967]." David Rudge, *Jerusalem Post*, December 6, 1989.

175. *Jerusalem Post*, November 13, 1989.
176. *Jerusalem Post*, December 4, 1989.
177. A Moscow Radio Domestic Service report praising Weizman for his position favoring talks with the PLO also praised him for his World War II "combat operations against Hitlerite troops in North Africa, India and the Near East"—thus implicitly refuting the charge, frequently made in the pre-Gorbachev Soviet media, that Zionism actively cooperated with the Nazis (Moscow Radio, January 1990, in *FBIS:USSR*, January 11, 1990, pp. 32–33.
178. David Makovsky, *Jerusalem Post*, January 11, 1990.
179. *Tass*, January 10, 1990, in *FBIS:USSR*, January 11, 1990, p. 31.
180. Ibid.
181. Reuters report, *Jerusalem Post*, January 21, 1990.

The Arab World and the Intifada

F. Gregory Gause III

The reaction in the Arab world to the Palestinian uprising represents a synthesis of two competing political trends, which have battled for predominance in the Arab Middle East for the past half century. Rhetorical and diplomatic support for the Intifada among Arab states and Arab publics has been steady, enthusiastic, and heartfelt. The Palestinian cause has always been a central item of the Pan-Arab agenda, largely because of the widespread identification among Arab publics, both elite and mass, with it. Support for it has been seen as an obligation upon all Arab states, not a matter of choice. For example, the three major Arab state players in the Arab-Israeli dispute—Jordan, Syria, and Egypt—each had good reasons to be leery of the Intifada. It threatened to further complicate Egypt's relations with Israel, and perhaps with the United States. It represented a setback to Syrian and Jordanian efforts to play a larger role in Palestinian politics, at the expense of the Palestine Liberation Organization (PLO). In addition, the example of mass popular upheaval in the occupied territories was an unsettling precedent to the neighboring Arab governments. Despite these possible problems, Syria, Egypt, and Jordan have all felt constrained to express continuing support for the Intifada.

However, the way Arab support has been manifested reflects

the continuing dominance of raison d'état, as opposed to transnational ideological agendas, as the guiding principle of Arab state foreign policies. Therefore, the practical measures taken by the Arab states regarding the Intifada have differed substantially. Egypt has stood behind the PLO and urged it to adopt a policy of negotiations and compromise. Syria has attempted to use the heightened emotions and involvement of Palestinians to subvert the conciliatory policy and the leadership of Yasser Arafat. Jordan, while strongly supporting the new PLO policy line, has in effect taken itself out of the Palestinian political arena through its July 1988 decision to sever existing political and administrative links with the West Bank.

This synthesis between Pan-Arab obligation and state (or regime) interests in dealing with the Palestinian issue reflects a larger consensus in the Arab world, which developed since the 1970s. Common Arab interests and all-Arab political frameworks, like the Arab League, would be respected and acknowledged. No state could long "opt out" of the Arab political agenda. However, that agenda would not be allowed to impede the pursuit of individual state interests on vital matters.

This study discusses how the synthesis has been played out in two separate arenas: all-Arab responses to the Intifada as expressed in Arab League and Arab summit forums, and the individual responses of the frontline states of Syria, Jordan, and Egypt. An emerging challenge to this dominant synthesis, which sees the Palestinian uprising as part of the regionwide movement of Islamic political awakening and support for it as an Islamic, as opposed to an Arab nationalist, obligation, will also be examined.

The All-Arab Response

The Arab League summit meeting held in Amman on November 8–11, 1987, appeared at the time to be a turning point in inter-Arab politics. Differences over the Iran-Iraq war had apparently been bridged, as both Syria (Iran's major Arab ally) and Iraq attended the meeting. The summit voted to allow individual Arab states to reestablish diplomatic relations with Egypt, paving the way for Cairo's return to the inter-Arab political scene and eventually to the Arab League. The summit did adopt a number of resolutions regarding the Palestinian question. These included support for "enabling the Palestinian Arab people to exercise their inalienable national rights," and a call for the PLO, "the sole legitimate representative of the Palestinian people," to participate on an equal footing with other parties in a proposed international peace conference.[1] However, it was clear from the tone and tenor of the proceedings that the Palestinian issue was not at the top of the inter-Arab agenda. Threats emanating from the Gulf war and from the resurgence of Islamic opposition movements, and efforts to heal inter-Arab rifts dominated the meeting. The host, King Hussein, who in February 1986 had halted a political dialogue with the PLO over a joint negotiating position, seemed to go out of his way to embarrass and slight PLO leader Arafat.

The Intifada, which began one month later, refocused the attention of Arab publics on the Palestinian issue, and their governments soon followed. The Arab League foreign ministers met in Tunis on January 23–24, 1988, in a special session to discuss the uprising. The meeting pledged to set up a special fund, to be administered by the PLO, to support the uprising, though no specific financial commitments were announced. (Syria, feuding with Arafat, urged that the fund be administered by the Arab League, not the PLO, but was voted down.) A ministerial committee composed of the foreign ministers of Tunisia, Saudi Arabia, Algeria, Iraq, Syria, and Jordan, along with a representative of the PLO and of the Arab League, was established to pursue diplomatic initiatives at the United Nations and with other states aimed at supporting the Palestinian political agenda.[2]

As the Intifada continued, the Arab states scrambled not only to support it, but also to be seen publicly as supporting it. On June 7–9, 1988, an extraordinary Arab summit meeting was held in Algiers, called specifically to discuss the Palestinian situation. The summit reiterated past resolutions of support for the PLO as the "sole legitimate representative of the Palestinian people" and for Palestinian rights to self-determination in an independent state with Jerusalem as its capital. It called for a U.N. trusteeship for the occupied territories and for the convening of an international conference under the auspices of the five permanent members of the

Security Council, in which all the parties to the conflict, including the PLO, would be represented. The summit also explicitly urged the United States to recognize the PLO.[3] The ministerial committee set up at the January 1988 foreign ministers meeting did in fact submit a specific proposal to the United States for an official U.S.-PLO dialogue in November 1988, after the Palestine National Council (PNC) meeting and just before the United States initiated such a dialogue.[4] In these matters the Arab states were expressing support for the political program of the PLO, as set forth both in the PLO working paper circulated at the conference and in the message sent to the summit by the Unified National Leadership of the Uprising.[5]

The summit meeting also committed itself to "support the uprising, for consolidating its effectiveness and ensuring its continuation and escalation."[6] No specific amounts of financial aid commitments were mentioned in the summit declarations, but it was subsequently revealed by Palestinian sources that the summit agreed to provide the PLO $128 million immediately, and then somewhere between $40 million and $43 million per month to support the Intifada.[7] Payments were assigned by country according to the percentage formula used for determining annual contributions to the Arab League budget.

It is in the area of financial aid that the Arab states moved from declaratory and diplomatic support to the commitment of scarce resources to the Palestinian cause, and it is in that area that the most tension arose between the PLO and the Arab states as a group. As early as August 1988 a top-ranking PLO official, Salah Khalaf (Abu Iyad), complained that the Arab states, with the exception of Saudi Arabia and Iraq, had not even begun to fulfill their financial commitments to the PLO undertaken at Algiers.[8] Similar complaints were made by Faruq Kaddumi, the PLO's "foreign minister," in December 1988 and by Yasser Arafat himself in April 1989, when he urged the Arab states "not to be stingy with the Palestinian revolution. . . . I am tired of asking for these commitments to be honored."[9] In another forum Arafat again rebuked the Arab states for failing to keep their promises of aid, stating that the total amount of Arab aid given to the Palestinian revolution over twenty-five years was $1 billion, in comparison to the $3 billion of annual aid given by the United States to Israel.[10]

The Intifada occurred at a time of general economic downturn in the Arab East. The oil glut, which had driven oil prices below ten dollars per barrel in 1986, had yet to abate. The amount of aid available from the oil-producing states was not only greatly reduced by the oil glut, but the competition for those aid dollars was also fierce. The lion's share of aid from the Arab Gulf oil states was going to support the Iraqi war effort, as those regimes saw the prospect of an Iranian military victory as more immediately threatening to their own security than failure to meet their commitments to the PLO.

The question of financial support was still much on Arafat's mind as he addressed the Arab summit that convened in Casablanca May 23–26, 1989. He charged that none of the original Algiers commitment of $128 million had been paid, and that only Saudi Arabia, Iraq, the United Arab Emirates, and Libya had contributed to the monthly maintenance fund. He asked Arab states to levy a special tax on Palestinians within their borders to support the Intifada and implied that popular donations collected in the Arab states to support the Palestinian cause frequently did not reach the PLO.[11] In an interview published in the Arabic weekly al-Majalla in July 1989, Jawid al-Ghusayn, the chairman of the Palestine National Fund, reported that payments on the Algiers commitments began to pick up in the early part of 1989. (The Iran-Iraq war had ended in July 1988, and oil prices began to rise at about the same time.) He stated, however, that the original $128 million commitment had never been met and that following the Casablanca Arab summit, new aid contributions were received from Saudi Arabia, Iraq, the United Arab Emirates, Kuwait, and Libya.[12] As late as August 1989, the conference of Fatah, Yasser Arafat's organization, called upon the Arab states to "fulfill their agreed upon financial commitments" to support the Intifada.[13]

While financial aid was a continuing bone of contention with the Arab states, the PLO did win important political and diplomatic victories in the Arab arena during 1989. Every Arab state, even Syria, recognized the new Palestinian state whose independence was declared at the PNC meeting of November 1988. Only Syria, among the major Arab states, withheld recognition of Arafat's selection as president of the new state by the PLO Central Committee in April 1989. At the Casablanca Arab summit of May 1989, Arafat received a general Arab endorsement for the resolutions adopted by the November 1988 PNC meeting, support for the PLO diplomatic initiative aimed at convening an international conference, and backing on the specific issue of elections in the occupied territories proposed by the Israeli government. The summit, like the PLO, supported the idea of elections, but only under international supervision following Israeli withdrawal, and only as part of a process leading to a comprehensive settlement.[14]

In sum, at the all-Arab level, the Intifada in general and the PLO in particular received considerable rhetorical, political, and diplomatic support. This was a reflection of the widespread support among both Arab elites and mass publics for the Palestinian cause. The tension between particular state interests and Pan-Arab obligations played itself out largely in the field of financial support for the PLO. In that area the states were much more reluctant to provide the levels of support requested by the PLO at a time of general economic austerity and the financial demands generated by the Iran-Iraq war. With the end of that war and the upturn in oil prices, more aid was apparently forthcoming from the oil states. Two oil states stand out for their continuing financial support for the PLO during the period: Saudi Arabia, which, despite the regional economic downturn, still had considerable financial resources; and Iraq, which, amid the pressures of its war with Iran, wanted to maintain a leading role in inter-Arab politics.

While the Arab states balanced Arab obligation and individual interests in dealing with the Intifada, Islamic opposition groups in the Arab world were urging a more radical approach. An example of this trend can be found in the political platform of the Islamic Front candidates in the November 1989 Jordanian election. Their platform rejected all United Nations resolutions on the Palestinian issue, including the original 1947 partition resolution. International conferences and negotiations with the "Zionist enemy" were ruled out. Moreover, the platform called for an opening of the Jordanian-Israeli border as a "forward position from which to liberate Palestine."[15] Efforts by Islamic opposition groups to appropriate the Palestinian cause from their nationalist rivals and from the ruling regimes have not yet met with much success. However, an uncompromising "Islamic" approach to the Palestinian issue has been advanced in both the Palestinian and the larger Arab communities. Its attractiveness can only increase in the absence of progress toward a settlement.

Hashemite Kingdom of Jordan

The Jordanian reaction to the Intifada was in many ways the most interesting of all the Arab states. Jordan was the Arab state most potentially threatened by the uprising, both in terms of its own foreign policy goals in the occupied territories and in terms of the large Palestinian community resident in the East Bank.[16] It is also the Arab state that has been most affected by the events in the West Bank and Gaza. The king's decision of July 1988 to sever formally Jordan's legal and administrative ties to the West Bank, established by his grandfather King Abdallah as a result of the Jordanian conquests in the 1948–49 war with the new Israeli state, can only be understood in light of the Intifada. It was a profoundly important step in the political evolution of Jordan. It refocused political energies in the country away from the diplomatic maneuverings of the Arab-Israeli peace process and toward specific East Bank issues. In that way the disengagement decision set the stage for the riots of April 1989 and the subsequent return of parliamentary life in Jordan with the elections of November 1989.

On the eve of the Intifada, Jordanian-PLO relations were in their customary state of mutual suspicion and fear, characteristic of the relationship since the bloody fighting of "Black September" 1970. Twice during the 1980s, King Hussein and Yasser Arafat had attempted to reach a joint position upon which to enter Arab-Israeli negotiations. Both efforts failed. The king had brought the second round of these negotiations to an end in February 1986, accusing the PLO of bad faith over its refusal openly to accept UN Security Council Resolution 242. Jordan subsequently closed down PLO offices in the country, sponsored a spectacularly unsuccessful rival to Arafat for Palestinian leadership (a Palestinian military official named Atallah Atallah, known by his nom de guerre Abu Za'im), and reoriented Jordan's regional policy toward closer cooperation with Syria, an avowed enemy of Arafat.[17]

The beginning of the Intifada did nothing to improve Jordanian-Palestinian relations. The Jordanian government made it clear that it would not allow Palestinians on the East Bank to engage in activities similar to those of their West Bank cousins. In late December 1987–early January 1988, authorities arrested a number of Palestinians associated with the Popular Front for the Liberation of Palestine (PFLP), either for their involvement in demonstrations (according to the PFLP) or for their planning of demonstrations (according to Jordanian officials).[18] Throughout the spring there were sporadic demonstrations and protests in support of the Intifada, some in conjunction with U.S. secretary of state George Shultz's visit to Amman in early April 1988.[19] In March 1988 Jordanian prime minister Zayd al-Rifai officially protested to PLO officials the impression left by Call Number Ten of the Unified National Leadership of the Uprising that the PLO encouraged West Bank representatives in the Jordanian Parliament to resign their seats.[20]

The outbreak of the Intifada did lead to a renewal of consultations between high-ranking PLO and Jordanian officials in December 1988 and January 1989, but no political initiatives emerged from these talks. PLO representatives, including Arafat and Khalil al-Wazir (Abu Jihad), characterized the level of coordination with Jordan at this time as "rather low" and "not at the required level." However, both sides evidenced a willingness to continue consultations about practical matters resulting from the uprising, despite their political differences.[21] The political atmosphere improved somewhat over the next few months as it became clear that Palestinians on the East Bank were not actively opposing the Jordanian regime and that the Jordanian government would not become involved in American-sponsored diplomatic initiatives opposed by the PLO.

The king's position on Arab-Israeli diplomacy remained unchanged during the first months of the Intifada. He continued to support the calling of an international conference on the Middle East, in which Jordan and the PLO would be represented by a joint delegation. In an interview with the Egyptian daily *al-'Ahram* in December 1987, he called on the PLO to resume negotiations with Jordan based upon the Hussein-Arafat agreement of February 1985 aimed at constituting such a joint delegation.[22] Shultz was unable, during his several visits to Amman in the spring and summer of 1988, to convince the king to enter a direct negotiating process with Israel, without the PLO and without the cover of an international conference.

A number of factors came together in the summer of 1988 to cause the king's decision to disengage from the West Bank, a historic shift in Jordanian policy. First, his own diplomatic initiatives were going nowhere. The United States, while adopting the principle of an international conference, was making no effort to push the idea actively. While Washington expressed support for an earlier initiative by Hussein to set up a $1.25 billion development fund for the occupied territories, to be administered through Jordan as a means of increasing Jordanian political influence there, the United States was willing to commit only $50 million to the project. Hussein's secret consultations with Israeli Labor party leader Shimon Peres in April 1987, which yielded an agreement on the principles for convening an international conference, had no impact. Peres was unable either to convince the National Unity government in Israel to accept the proposal or to bring the government down over the issue.[23]

Second, the king found little Arab support for his initiative. No Arab country was willing to contribute to his development fund, which had been condemned by the PLO. The Algiers Arab summit of June 1988 reiterated its support for the PLO as the sole legitimate representative of the Palestinian people and for the PLO position on an international conference, despite Hussein's urging in his speech to the summit that more flexibility be shown. The king also found himself once again denying to the Arab summit that he was attempting to reestablish his control of the West Bank at the expense of the PLO.[24]

Finally, it was clear that there was no support for a unilateral Jordanian initiative among public opinion on either the West Bank or the East Bank. Rumors circulated in Amman in late July 1988 that a high-ranking Jordanian delegation had secretly toured the West Bank, with the cooperation of Israeli authorities, and found no local support for a Jordanian move.[25] The Unified Leadership of the Uprising subsequently called Hussein's disengagement decision "one of the most important achievements of the great popular uprising."[26] The Palestinians on the East Bank also were not pressing the king to take the diplomatic initiative. Conversely, their relative quiescence during the Intifada demonstrated that twenty years of Israeli occupation had created substantive political differences between the East and West Bank communities, lessening the prospect of a violent East Bank Palestinian reaction to a disengagement from the West Bank. Also, Jordanians of East Bank origin were becoming increasingly impatient with what they saw as the government's obsession with the Palestinian question, at the expense of the immediate material and political interests of the East Bank community. These feelings eventually surfaced in the April 1989 riots.[27]

Finding no international, regional or domestic support for a continued Jordanian role in the occupied territories, Hussein took his historic step. On July 28, 1988, the Jordanian Council of Ministers dismantled the Jordanian development fund for the occupied territories, citing its desire "to enable the PLO to shoulder its responsibility fully . . . as the sole legitimate representative of the Palestinian people."[28] On July 30, 1988, the king dissolved the Jordanian Parliament, half of whose seats were allocated to West Bank representatives. In a speech broadcast on the evening of July 31, 1988, Hussein told his country and the world that Jordan was severing its political and administrative links to the West Bank. He portrayed this decision as coming at the behest of Palestinian and general Arab opinion:

> Of late, it had become clear that there is a general Palestinian and Arab orientation which believes in the need to highlight the Palestinian identity in full, in all efforts that are related to the Palestinian question and its development. It has also become obvious that there is a general conviction that maintaining the legal and administrative relationship with the West Bank—and the consequent special Jordanian treatment of the brother Palestinians living under occupation through Jordanian institutions in the occupied territories—goes against this orientation. It would be an obstacle to the Palestinian struggle.[29]

The king asserted that his grandfather, King Abdallah, had responded to the wishes of the West Bank Palestinians in 1950 for unity with Jordan and that he now was responding to the wish of the PLO, "the sole and legitimate representative of the Palestinian people, to secede from us as an independent Palestinian state." The king went on to caution that his move affected only the West Bank, not East Bank Jordanians of Palestinian origin: "All of them have citizenship rights and commitments, just like any other citizen regardless of his origin." He warned that safeguarding Jordanian national unity is "a sacred matter that will not be compromised" and stressed that "order and discipline" must be the basis of a stable and productive national unity. He also declared openly that "Jordan is not Palestine" and warned against Israeli-inspired efforts to portray it as such. Finally, he said that Jordan was still a "basic party" to the Arab-Israeli conflict and "will not relinquish its commitment to participate in the peace process," repeating his call for an international conference.

The impact of Hussein's sweeping moves was enormous. First, it signaled the end to any possibility of a "Jordanian option" in the Arab-Israeli peace process, where Jordan would negotiate a territorial compromise with Israel on the West Bank. While some contend that Hussein's move was simply another tactical maneuver in his contest for influence with the PLO, and thus not negating a future "Jordanian option," such analyses have been emphatically denied by the king and his closest advisers. At an English-language news conference on August 7, 1988, the king said, "we are not playing at tactics and our decision is a decision that . . . we will adhere to." Later in the same news conference, he reiterated that "Jordan does not have any sovereignty over the West Bank, sir. The West Bank belongs to the Palestinians." He also said that Jordan would not participate in a joint Palestinian-Jordanian delegation to any peace conference, as the PLO was the representative of the Palestinians.[30] In an interview some months later with an Arabic weekly, Jordanian foreign minister Marwan al-Qasim responded to comments that the decision was merely tactical: "Never. This is a decisive and clear strategic decision and it is a shame that there is anyone who says different."[31] Jordanian diplomatic behavior has borne these statements out.

Second, the decision signaled a new relationship among the Jordanian government, Palestinians on the East and the West Bank, and the PLO. The king was clear that East Bank Palestinians would be expected to behave as loyal Jordanian citizens; those who could not do so would be expected to seek citizenship in whatever Palestinian entity emerged. His implicit message was that he would not tolerate Palestinian political activity on the East Bank. Fear among East Bank Palestinians over the eventual political effects of the decision is believed by many to have contributed to the weakening during late 1988 and early 1989 of the Jordanian currency, the dinar, as East Bank Palestinians sought to move their capital out of the country. The resignation in December 1988 of prominent East Bank Palestinian Tahir al-Masri, who had served as Jordan's foreign minister, was also seen as a signal of unease among East Bank Palestinians. However, the subsequent improvement in Jordanian-PLO relations and changes in the Jordanian domestic political and economic scenes have served to reassure, at least somewhat, that community.

Many of the necessities of daily life in the West Bank had been handled through Jordanian institutions, among the most important being international travel on Jordanian passports and Jordanian certification of secondary school degrees—both of which are essential for Palestinians seeking to find work outside of the occupied territories. As a result of the decision, Jordanian passports were declared valid for West Bank and Gaza Palestinians for only two more years. Jordan would continue to approve secondary school certificates, provided that West Bank schools continued to use the Jordanian curriculum. Twelve thousand West Bank and Gaza public employees had their salaries paid either partially or in full by the Jordanian government; these salaries were stopped in August 1988. Jordan continued to provide full salaries only for West Bank and Gaza religious functionaries in the department of *awqaf* (religious endowments), which administers the Islamic holy sites under occupation, and in the office of the chief *qadi* (religious judge), where births, deaths, marriages, divorces, and inheritance settlements are recorded.[32] Jordan abolished its cabinet Ministry of Occupied Territory Affairs and transferred the remaining responsibilities to the Foreign Ministry's Department of Palestinian Affairs.

As a result both of the uncertainties introduced into the daily life of West Bank Palestinians and of the clear assertion that Palestinians on the East Bank owed their loyalty to the Jordanian government, not the PLO, the PLO's first reactions to Hussein's decision were negative. Yasser Arafat canceled a previously scheduled trip to Amman and publicly stated that Hussein had not consulted with the PLO before taking these steps.[33] However, many Palestinians hailed the step as a positive development, removing the possibility of a "Jordanian option" and ending the international uncertainty over who really represented the Palestinians in the occupied territories. The positive reaction of the Unified National Leadership of the Uprising was already mentioned (see note 26). Both high-ranking PLO official Salah Khalaf and PNC chairman Sheik Abd al-Hamid Sa'ih said the decision was a boost for the PLO.[34] Jordan displayed its good faith in meetings with a high-level PLO delegation sent to Amman in mid-August 1988 to discuss the effects of the decision,[35] and slowly the initial suspicions harbored by Arafat and others in the PLO of Hussein's intentions began to fade.

Hussein went out of his way to reassure Arafat and the PLO that he sought a cooperative relationship. In September 1988, he told an interviewer that his country would not involve itself in any peace process unless asked to do so by the PLO.[36] In late December 1988, Jordanian authorities closed the offices of Atallah Atallah (Abu Za'im), whom they had sponsored as a rival Palestinian leader to Arafat.[37] Jordanian officials expressed strong support for the resolutions of the November 1988 PNC meeting in Algiers and for the Palestinian declaration of independence.[38] In May 1989, Hussein rejected the election plan put forward by Prime Minister Shamir of Israel, which assigned a negotiating role to Jordan, stating that only the PLO can speak for the Palestinians.[39] Foreign Minister al-Qasim of Jordan stressed in a number of interviews during 1989 that Jordan sought no role in representing West Bank Palestinians and that it supported the PLO call for an international conference based on UN Security Council Resolutions 242 and 338.[40]

The PLO response to Jordanian policy in the postdisengagement period has been positive. On November 26, 1988, Arafat visited Amman and praised the king for his support of the Palestinian cause.⁴¹ He subsequently met with the king on March 25, 1989 (in Ismailia, with President Hosni Mubarak of Egypt), on April 15, 1989, before the king's visit to Washington, and on August 21–22, 1989 (the latter two meetings in Amman), to consult on moves in the peace process. During the August 1989 meeting, Arafat also gave the king an indirect vote of confidence in the wake of the April 1989 riots, by ordering the reopening of Palestine National Fund offices in Amman.⁴² This move was particularly significant, as the flight of Palestinian capital in the wake of the disengagement was seen as a major cause of the fall in value of the Jordanian dinar. In late June 1989, Hussein said that "Jordanian-Palestinian relations today are better than at any time before."⁴³

This improvement in PLO-Jordanian relations has had a direct impact on the domestic political stability of Jordan. Palestinians for the most part did not participate in the April 1989 riots, which were sparked by government austerity measures adopted as part of negotiations with the International Monetary Fund. The king praised the PLO for the "pacifying nature" of its behavior and asserted that "the Palestinian brothers played a positive role and were completely distanced from the riots."⁴⁴ The riots led to the king's decision to revive parliamentary life in Jordan, with the freest elections since the 1950s occurring on November 8, 1989. While some Jordanians affiliated with smaller Palestinian organizations, like the PFLP and the Democratic Front for the Liberation of Palestine (DFLP), ran in the election as independents, the PLO took great pains to publicly distance itself from any involvement in the elections.⁴⁵ East Bank Palestinians apparently did not participate in great numbers in the voting, but neither did they attempt to disrupt it or use it as a platform for antiregime activity.

While dissociating itself from the West Bank, Jordan has, as the king promised, remained an active player in Arab-Israeli diplomacy. The king has consulted frequently with both Arafat and President Mubarak on issues related to the peace process, traveled to Washington in April 1989 for talks with President Bush, and has consistently urged the PLO to continue its pursuit of a negotiated settlement through an international conference. Jordan has not ruled out the possibility of a future confederation of the occupied territories and the Hashemite kingdom but has emphasized that such a confederation could only come about with the support of the PLO and the Palestinians in the territories. The king also made a brief foray into Israeli domestic politics, publicly (and to little effect) urging Israelis on the eve of their November 1988 elections to support the Labor party. A number of incursions by Palestinians across the Jordanian-Israeli border occurred in the spring and summer of 1989, but Jordanian authorities moved quickly to apprehend those involved and maintain their tacit border security cooperation with Israel.[46] Although still involved in the Arab-Israeli dispute, Jordan has remained adamant that it will not speak for or negotiate about the Palestinians in the occupied territories.

In the case of Jordan, the tensions between Pan-Arab obligations to the Palestinian cause and state interests have, to a great extent, been resolved by the disengagement agreement. Previously, the king's continuing interest in playing some role in the occupied territories placed him at odds with the general Arab consensus that only the PLO could speak for the Palestinians there. This conflict with the PLO reflected on the domestic stability of the regime in the East Bank, where the Palestinian community was pulled between emotional loyalty to the PLO and the practical reality of living in a Jordanian state. By giving up his claim to the West Bank, the king has removed the major bone of contention between him and the PLO and thus has been able to assert more confidently his right to rule Jordanians of Palestinian background on the East Bank. The stability of his regime has thus been strengthened by the disengagement agreement. He is also more able to play an active role in Arab-Israeli diplomacy without exciting the suspicions of the PLO and the rest of the Arab world and, therefore, is more able to respond to the Pan-Arab obligation to support the Palestinian cause without threatening his own domestic stability.

Syrian Arab Republic

For Syria, the Intifada has been a major challenge. Syrian policy since 1983 has aimed at weakening and discrediting the leadership role of Fatah and Yasser Arafat within the Palestinian movement, in order to subject the PLO to the larger strategic vision of the Syrian leadership. In particular, Hafiz Assad mistrusted what he saw as Arafat's willingness to accept a compromise solution to the Palestinian problem, brokered through the United States and its local Arab allies, which would leave Israel the dominant power in the region. He asserted that Syria represented the "real" interests of the Palestinian movement, because only Syria remained true to the Pan-Arab political agenda and rejected "capitulationist" compromise with Israel. However, the clear identification of the leaders of the Intifada (except the Islamic organizations) with the PLO and with Arafat's policy line dealt the Syrian strategy a blow. The Assad strategy demanded continued opposition to Arafat, but Pan-Arab obligations required support for the Intifada. In the two years of the uprising, Syria has sought to manage that tension but has not been able to resolve it.

By the end of 1987, Syrian-Palestinian relations had been through five difficult years. Syria sponsored a rebellion among Fatah elements in Lebanon against Arafat, led by Sa'id Musa al-Maragha (Abu Musa), in the spring of 1983. Syrian troops drove Arafat out of Tripoli, his final Lebanese stronghold, in December 1983. Damascus used political pressure and terror to help sabotage the Jordanian-PLO negotiations of 1985–86. Upon breaking off those talks in February 1986 the king aligned his regional policy closely with Syria. As the Intifada began, PLO forces were battling for control of the Palestinian refugee camps in Beirut against the Syrian-allied Amal movement and the Syrian-supported Palestinian dissidents.

The Intifada was a catalyst for both sides to reconsider their relationship: the PLO believing that the uprising had given them new strength with which to deal with Syria as an equal, and Syria hoping that this new element could lead to a PLO agreement to adopt the Syrian strategic line. Thus, at the beginning of 1988, there were numerous reports of contact between Arafat and Assad through various intermediaries.[47] In January, Amal declared a unilateral cease-fire in its battle with the PLO, ostensibly out of respect for the Intifada. Arafat publicly attributed this decision to Syria, saying he hoped that "a new leaf has been turned in our relations with the Amal brothers and with the Syrian brothers."[48] The April 16, 1988, assassination of Khalil Wazir (Abu Jihad) provided the occasion for the renewal of direct Syrian-PLO contacts.

Wazir was buried in Damascus in an emotional ceremony, and Arafat paid his first visit to the Syrian capital since 1983. These discussions apparently led to some agreement, as a number of Fatah officials remained behind in Damascus to continue the dialogue, and Salah Khalaf reported that Syria had agreed to release 2,000 pro-Arafat Palestinians from Syrian jails.[49]

This rapprochement was short-lived. Even while Syria was attending the June 1988 Arab summit meeting called to express support for the Intifada and the PLO, the Syria-supported Abu Musa faction was battling pro-Arafat forces for control of the Palestinian camps in Lebanon. In July 1988, the Syrian drive for control of these camps was completed, and the Fatah fighters were evacuated south to PLO positions in Sidon. The PLO Central Council, meeting in Baghdad on August 3, 1988, held the Syrian leadership "fully responsible for the destruction of our camps and the expulsion of our people."[50] At the same time, Yasser Arafat accused Syria of using its negotiations with the PLO as a cover to prepare for the attack on the camps.[51] Syrian media outlets and Syrian-supported Palestinian factions meanwhile resumed their propaganda attacks against Arafat and his policy line, accusing him of being a "capitulationist" and comparing him with former Egyptian president Anwar Sadat.[52] Reports circulated that hundreds of pro-Fatah Palestinians in Syria were arrested.[53]

The tension between the Pan-Arab obligation of supporting the Intifada and the Palestinian cause and the Syrian state interest of opposing Arafat and the current PLO leadership became particularly acute with the declaration by the November 1988 PNC meeting of Palestinian independence and statehood. This move met with widespread approval in the Arab world as a whole and among Palestinians generally. However, it was also a victory for Arafat, and the political program adopted at the meeting signaled the PLO's willingness to consider a negotiated settlement not subject to Syrian veto. For a Syrian regime whose rhetoric was based on the premise that it was the last true repository of Pan-Arabism, opposing what had been for decades a major goal of the Pan-Arab agenda would have been very difficult. In fact, the Syrian state media reported official support for the declaration of Palestinian independence, while criticizing what it saw as concessions to Israel. Syria attempted to constrain Arafat's freedom of maneuver by calling for a unification of Palestinian ranks, while allowing its client Palestinian organizations (the Abu Musa faction, al-Sa'iqa, the Palestine National Salvation Front, the Popular Front for the Liberation of Palestine-General Command) savagely to attack Arafat and the resolutions of the PNC.[54] Indeed, hostility between the two sides reached the point in April 1989 that an unattributed commentary on the Voice of the PLO radio station, which broadcasts from Baghdad, called for the assassination of President Assad.[55]

The Arab summit meeting at Casablanca in May 1989 again confronted the Syrian leadership with the challenge of reconciling the Pan-Arab obligation to support the Palestinian cause with Assad's interest in opposing the PLO policy line. The pressure on the Syrians was all the greater at this time. They were facing a crisis situation in Lebanon for which they desperately needed Arab support. Iraq, freed somewhat to reenter the inter-Arab arena by the cease-fire in the Gulf war, was attempting to put together an anti-Syrian bloc on the Lebanon issue while actively supporting Syria's Lebanese nemesis, General Michel Aoun. Syria had finally dropped its long-standing opposition to the return of Egypt to the Arab League, and this further reduced Syrian political clout on the inter-Arab level. The Syrian need for financial support from the Gulf oil states, supporters of Arafat and the PLO, was also acute, as the ten-year aid program agreed to at the 1978 Baghdad summit had come to an end.[56]

Faced with all these pressures, Syria once again sought to come to some understanding with the PLO. This time, however, it was Arafat who had the upper hand. According to Arab press reports, he set four conditions for a Syrian-PLO summit meeting before the Casablanca conference: (1) an official Syrian invitation to him as president of Palestine (the Syrians, unlike most Arab governments, had not officially acknowledged his election by the PLO Central Committee on April 2, 1989); (2) public Syrian support for the November 1988 PNC resolutions and the political line of the PLO; (3) freeing of Palestinian prisoners in Syria; and (4) the presence of Algerian and Soviet representatives at any meeting to serve as guarantors of agreements reached.[57] These stipulations proved too much for the Syrians to accept, and Syria went to the Casablanca summit without a previous agreement with the PLO.

At Casablanca, Assad agreed to a summit resolution that expressed wholehearted support for the Arafat policy line and the resolutions of the November 1988 PNC. In exchange, he deflected Arab pressure for an early withdrawal of Syrian troops from Lebanon and avoided an open break with the oil states. For the PLO this compromise was a major victory, as Syria could no longer publicly object on Pan-Arab grounds to the PLO policy line.[58] While the Syrian regime has been more restrained in its criticism of Arafat and the PLO since that time, it has, as before, stressed the importance of unity among Palestinian factions, clearly intending that unity to be on the platform of its own client organizations.[59] And, as before, it has permitted those client organizations to maintain their vituperative criticism of Arafat. On November 11, 1989, the Abu Musa group announced that it would try the PLO leader for treason, for recognizing Israel and abandoning "the revolution's principles."[60] In return, pro-Arafat forces have continued to express their hostility toward Damascus. The general congress of Fatah, meeting in August 1989, criticized "conspiracies hatched by the Syrian regime and carried out by its agent tools."[61]

In sum, the Assad regime has settled into a policy of waiting on the Palestinian question. It continues publicly to support the idea of an international peace conference, while questioning if the circumstances are ripe for its convening and charging that Israel will never agree to the real compromises necessary for it to succeed.[62] Damascus has not relented in its opposition to Arafat and his policy line but is forced by regional circumstances to hold its fire, hoping that he will fail and keeping its own Palestinian forces in reserve to take advantage if he does.

Syrian policy toward the Palestinian question in general and the Intifada in particular has been one of state interest clothed in the rhetoric of Pan-Arab obligation. Syria has been constrained by the pressures of inter-Arab politics, both in terms of the general Arab support for the PLO and in terms of specific Syrian political interests in Lebanon, to agree to support PLO positions in Arab League and Arab summit forums. Confronted in Casablanca with a serious dilemma, Damascus opted to trade its adherence to the pro-PLO summit resolutions for general Arab acceptance of its Lebanese policy. In that sense, Pan-Arab factors have forced some small modification of Syria's Palestine policy. However, the Assad regime shows no signs of abandoning its opposition to the current PLO policy line or the current PLO leadership, an opposition based on its own view of the leading role Syria must play in the strategic future of the region.

Arab Republic of Egypt

More than any other Arab country, Egypt has faced the difficulties of reconciling Pan-Arab obligations to support the Palestinian cause and particular state and regime interests. The Egyptian-Israeli peace treaty led to Egypt's expulsion from the Arab League and isolation within the Arab world. That isolation gradually broke down during the 1980s, largely as a result of the need felt by many Arab regimes for an Egyptian balance to the power of Iran and its revolution. Egypt has expressed strong support for the Intifada and for the policy line of the PLO throughout the period under study, but always in the context of its existing policy of maintaining peace with Israel and strong ties with the United States. For the Mubarak government, the Intifada has not been a reason to change Egypt's own definition of its foreign policy interests, but rather an occasion to help move the PLO, and through it the rest of the Arab world, closer to Egypt's understanding of how the Arab-Israeli conflict should be settled. Cairo is attempting to resolve the tension between the sense of Pan-Arab obligation to the Palestinians and individual state interest by altering the former to conform with the latter.

The continuing support from Egyptian public opinion for the Palestinian cause was manifested at the beginning of the Intifada by a number of demonstrations, some of which turned violent, in Egyptian universities and elsewhere expressing solidarity with the Palestinians. In one such demonstration, outside the al-'Azhar Mosque, two prominent Moslem activists were arrested.[63] The security risk of allowing the Islamic opposition to mobilize public sympathy for the Intifada and turn it against the government strengthened President Mubarak's determination to play, and to be seen domestically to play, an active role in supporting the PLO. Egyptian-PLO relations had, by the end of 1987, weathered a brief period of strain. The April 1987 PNC meeting had strongly criticized Egypt, leading Mubarak to respond by closing PLO offices in the country. However, the main PLO office in Cairo was reopened in late November 1987, after the Amman Arab summit resolution permitting Arab states to reestablish bilateral relations with Egypt. (Jordan had done so in 1984; most other Arab states followed suit in late 1987 and early 1988.) Egyptian Foreign Minister Ismat Abd al-Majid told an interviewer in late December 1987 that "there are absolutely no critical differences between us and the PLO." Arafat publicly called for Egypt's return to the Arab League in early January 1988.[64]

Mubarak saw the Intifada as the kind of galvanizing political event that could shake up solidified positions and lead to new diplomatic opportunities, and he immediately sought to take advantage of it. In an interview with the *Washington Post* published on January 22, 1988, he proposed a six-month moratorium on both Palestinian demonstrations in the territories and on Israeli settlement activity, during which time steps would be taken to guarantee political rights and plans would be drawn up for an international peace conference. At the same time, he rejected Prime Minister Shamir's call for reopening autonomy talks based on the Camp David Accords, saying that events had overtaken the terms of that agreement.[65] Neither the PLO, still heady with the renewed power and prestige the Intifada brought it, nor the Israeli government responded to Mubarak's suggestion.

For the rest of 1988, as the American presidential campaign made any U.S. initiative unlikely, Mubarak concentrated on quiet diplomacy in the Arab world and with the PLO. Egypt strongly backed proposals circulated before the November 1988 PNC meeting for a Palestinian declaration of independence and formation of a provisional Palestinian government.[66] Cairo expressed wholehearted support for the resolutions of the November PNC, particularly its acceptance of U.N. Security Council Resolutions 242 and 338 and its endorsement of a negotiation strategy based on an international conference. After some hesitation, the Mubarak government also officially recognized the new Palestinian state.[67] Arafat arrived in Cairo immediately after the PNC meetings. He and Mubarak clearly coordinated on the next steps to take on the international level.[68] Egypt also played a behind-the-scenes role in urging the United States in December 1988 to open a dialogue with the PLO. Foreign policy adviser 'Usama al-Baz said that Mubarak sent three messages to President Reagan in the four days before the American decision. The Egyptian president also spoke by telephone with Secretary of State Shultz hours before the decision was announced.[69]

With a new administration in office in Washington and with major changes in the PLO's official position, Mubarak was ready in 1989 to renew his public diplomacy. In preparation for his April 1989 visit to Washington, Mubarak met with Arafat and King Hussein in Ismailia on March 25, 1989. The three leaders announced their common support for the convening of an international peace conference. Mubarak signaled his continuing support for the PLO by allowing other Palestinian offices in Cairo and Alexandria, closed after the 1987 PNC meeting, to reopen in April 1989.[70] His first meeting with President Bush yielded a public relations, if not a diplomatic, coup, as the new American president used the occasion to call for an end to the Israeli occupation of the West Bank and Gaza. This announcement played well in the Arab world and reflected positively in the region on Egypt's role as a supporter of the Palestinian cause.

During this trip, Mubarak refused an offer by Prime Minister Shamir for an impromptu summit during the overlap of their Washington visits, in order not to be identified with Shamir's plan for elections in the occupied territories. However, from April 1989 the peace process came to focus on this plan, as the Bush administration adopted it as a possible "next step." Both the Unified National Leadership of the Uprising and the PLO Executive Committee rejected the Shamir plan, for it ruled out the idea of a Palestinian state in the occupied territories and negotiations with the PLO. Given American support for it, however, Mubarak sought to reconcile the PLO to some aspects of the election idea and use that as a first step on the road to an international conference. In August 1989, he sent a list of ten points, phrased as questions concerning the election proposal, to the Israeli government. The ten points included proposals that Israel agree to allow Palestinians in East Jerusalem to vote in the elections, that construction or expansion of Jewish settlements in the territories be frozen during the election period, and that Israel publicly commit itself to the principle of trading land for peace. An Israel-Palestinian committee, formed with Egyptian and American help, would supervise preparation for the elections.[71]

Mubarak followed up his ten points with intensive consultations with Arafat aimed at putting together a Palestinian delegation acceptable to the PLO, which could meet with the Israelis.[72] Arafat visited Cairo no less than four times during the months of September–November 1989. The ten points did not receive enthusiastic support from the PLO, largely because they failed to mention either an independent Palestinian state or the PLO. The PLO Executive Committee, meeting on September 14, 1989, welcomed the idea of elections in the territories under international supervision *after* an Israeli withdrawal and stated its refusal to allow any party to bypass the PLO.[73] Arafat, while leery of being identified too closely with the ten points, continued to work with Mubarak on setting up a Palestinian delegation that could meet with the Israelis. Publicly Arafat supported the idea of Israeli-Palestinian dialogue, but only as a first step toward convening an international conference.[74]

These negotiations with Arafat did generate a list of possible Palestinian participants acceptable to the PLO. Mubarak carried these names with him to Washington on October 2, 1989, for meetings with President Bush and Secretary of State James Baker.[75] Baker indicated strong support for the Mubarak initiative, but he has also been sensitive to objections raised by Prime Minister Shamir. Israel has expressed its unwillingness to meet with a Palestinian delegation including PLO members or Palestinians not resident in the occupied territories, as well as its refusal to discuss with a Palestinian delegation anything but the proposed elections.[76] Baker responded to the Israeli demands by calling for a meeting of the Israeli and Egyptian foreign ministers with him in Washington, aimed at constituting a Palestinian delegation. The PLO insists that it must be a participant in all stages of the negotiating process and that any dialogue or election must be the first step in a process leading to an international conference.[77] In December 1989,

Egypt accepted Baker's latest proposal, and a meeting of the American secretary of state with the foreign ministers of Egypt and Israel was scheduled for January 1990 in Washington.[78]

Egypt clearly hoped to initiate a Palestinian-Israeli dialogue, even if limited to a discussion of the proposed elections, in order to overcome the psychological and diplomatic hurdle of direct contacts. From that point, Mubarak hoped to be able to move the negotiating process quickly toward an international conference. The prospects of achieving that kind of breakthrough, however, appeared dimmer than they were in the fall of 1989. It was likely, however, that Egypt would continue its efforts to bring the PLO and the Israelis together. Such an effort held out the promise for Egypt of reconciling its own state interests in peace with Israel and strong ties to the United States with its Pan-Arab obligations to support the Palestinian cause. A complete breakdown of the peace process and an abandonment by the PLO of its current conciliatory policy would put Egypt once again in the difficult position of having its state interests and its Pan-Arab responsibilities on the Palestinian issue leading in contradictory directions.

Conclusions

The Arab reaction to the Intifada has reflected a synthesis between specific state interests and a general sense of Pan-Arab obligation to support the Palestinian cause, in which state interests are dominant but Pan-Arab obligation cannot be ignored. In no case has this Pan-Arab obligation overridden existing state interests. Egypt did not abrogate the peace treaty with Israel over the latter's treatment of the Intifada. Jordan did not open its borders to Palestinian groups seeking to attack Israel. Syria did not drop its hostility toward Arafat and the conciliatory line of the PLO. In an economic environment of tight money, many Arab states have not been willing to meet the financial commitments they made to support the Intifada.

However, the fact of the Intifada and the Pan-Arab obligation to support it has had some impact on Arab state policy in this area. The most noticeable has been in Jordan. Largely because of the Intifada, King Hussein came to the conclusion that the stability of his regime—in both the domestic and the regional contexts—could not be maintained if he continued to assert a role in the occupied territories. The disengagement decision thus brought his own particular interest in regime stability in line with the general Arab obligation to support the PLO. Syria's Assad was constrained both by general Arab sentiment and by his particular interests in Lebanon to accept publicly the Casablanca Arab summit conference resolutions that strongly supported the Arafat policy line. Egypt has worked to shift the PLO, and thus the Arab consensus, more toward its own views of an acceptable settlement, in order in the future to avoid the dilemma it faced after Camp David, when its state interests and the Pan-Arab consensus on the Palestinian issue were mutually exclusive. The Intifada also strengthened the PLO as an actor in inter-Arab politics, after a number of defeats in the 1980s, and provided an impetus for the PLO to receive general Arab approval of its policy line in the Algiers and Casablanca summits.

The dominant synthesis in the Arab world, where individual state interests dominate but Pan-Arab obligations cannot be completely ignored, is now being challenged by increasingly powerful Islamic movements. Much like Nasserist Pan-Arabism in the 1950s and 1960s, the current Islamic resurgence asserts that state and regime interests must be subordinated to certain overriding ideological goals. One of these goals, according to many in the Islamic movements, is reclaiming all the historical land of Palestine for Moslem rule. The future of the Arab-Israeli peace process depends in large measure on how this dialectic between the dominant synthesis and the Islamic challenge works itself out in both the Palestinian community and in the larger Arab world.

Notes

1. Resolutions of the summit regarding the Palestinian issue can be found in *Journal of Palestine Studies* 17, no. 3 (Spring 1988): 176–77.
2. *Foreign Broadcast Information Service Daily Report: Near East and South Asia* (hereafter *FBIS:NES*), January 25, 1988, p. 7.
3. *FBIS:NES*, June 10, 1988, pp. 11–14; June 13, 1988, pp. 4–5.
4. *Middle East Journal* (chronology section) 43, no. 2 (Spring 1989): 250.
5. Both documents can be found in *Journal of Palestine Studies* 18, no. 1 (Autumn 1988): 271–75.

6. *FBIS:NES*, June 10, 1988, p. 12.

7. These figures are taken from the speech given by Yasser Arafat to the Arab summit conference in Casablanca in May 1989, in *FBIS:NES*, May 26, 1989, p. 14; and from an interview with Jawid al-Ghusayn, the chairman of the Palestinian National Fund, in *FBIS:NES*, July 13, 1989, p. 4. The figures are confirmed in the resolutions of the Casablanca summit, *Journal of Palestine Studies* 19, no. 1 (Autumn 1989): 132–34.

8. *FBIS:NES*, August 15, 1988, p. 4.

9. *FBIS:NES*, December 29, 1988, pp. 11–12; April 7, 1989, p. 4.

10. *FBIS:NES*, April 18, 1989, p. 1.

11. *FBIS:NES*, May 26, 1989, p. 14.

12. *FBIS:NES*, July 13, 1989, p. 4. al-Ghusayn also reported that only Saudi Arabia had fully met its financial commitments to the PLO set out in the ten-year plan of financial aid agreed upon at the 1978 Baghdad Arab summit.

13. *al-Hawadith*, no. 1711, August 18, 1989, p. 25.

14. Resolutions of the Casablanca Arab summit can be found in *Journal of Palestine Studies* 19, no. 1 (Autumn 1989): 132–34.

15. The text of the platform can be found in *FBIS:NES*, October 27, 1989, pp. 24–25.

16. It is generally assumed that Jordanian citizens of Palestinian origin make up a majority of the inhabitants of the East Bank. King Hussein, at the time of the Jordanian disengagement from the West Bank, contended publicly that only 40 percent of the East Bank population was of Palestinian origin (*FBIS:NES*, August 8, 1988, p. 33). His contention is supported by the recent research of Valerie Yorke, "Jordan Is not Palestine: The Demographic Factor," *Middle East International*, no. 323 (April 16, 1988), pp. 16–17. Some of this discrepancy might result from the ambiguous position of those Palestinian residents of the East Bank who remain in officially recognized refugee camps. In any event, whether 40 percent or 60 percent or some other number, Palestinians represent a substantial part of the East Bank population.

17. An excellent account of Jordanian-PLO relations in the period between the Camp David accords and the Intifada can be found in Emile Sahliyeh, "Jordan and the Palestinians," in *The Middle East: Ten Years after Camp David*, ed. William B. Quandt (Washington: Brookings Institution, 1988).

18. *FBIS:NES*, January 4, 1988, p. 6; January 27, 1988, p. 38.

19. See reports in *Middle East Journal* (chronology section) 42, no. 3 (Summer 1988): 454–55, 468.

20. Ibid., p. 452.

21. See, for example, Palestinian statements in *FBIS:NES*, January 5, 1988, p. 2; January 7, 1988, p. 7; February 1, 1988, pp. 54–57.

22. *FBIS:NES*, December 15, 1987, p. 47.

23. A text of the Peres-Hussein agreement can be found in Appendix G of Quandt, *The Middle East*.

24. A brief summary of Hussein's remarks to the summit can be found in *Middle East Journal* (chronology section) 42, no. 4 (Autumn 1988): 650.

25. The author heard these rumors during a research trip to Amman in late July 1988.

26. *FBIS:NES*, August 8, 1988, p. 4.

27. For an excellent account of Jordanian domestic politics during the 1980s, particularly the sentiments of East Bank Jordanians, see the chapter on Jordan in Valerie Yorke, *Domestic Politics and Regional Security: Jordan, Syria and Israel*, (Aldershot, England: Gower Publishing for International Institute for Strategic Studies, 1988).

28. *Middle East Journal* (chronology section) 43, no. 1 (Winter 1989): 70.

29. The full text of the king's speech can be found in *FBIS:NES*, August 1, 1989, pp. 39–41. Subsequent quotes are taken from this text.

30. *FBIS:NES*, August 8, 1988, pp. 32–35; *Middle East Journal* (chronology section) 43, no. 1 (Winter 1989): 71. Jordanian officials later said that they would consider a joint Jordanian-Palestinian delegation if all the concerned parties, including the PLO, accepted the arrangement. See the speech by Crown Prince Hassan bin Talal, *Jordan's Approach to the Peace Process*, (Washington: Washington Institute for Near East Policy, September 12, 1989).

31. *al-Watan al-Arabi*, No. 107-633 (March 31, 1989), p. 24.

32. The official Jordanian decisions on these matters are reproduced in *FBIS:NES*, August 5, 1988, p. 27; August 22, 1988, pp. 33–34. The figure of 12,000 is taken from *New York Times*, August 5, 1988, p. 1. King Hussein said that thirty-two hundred Jordanian civil servants were involved in the decision but that numerous others who were not Jordanian civil servants received some of their salary from Jordan, and they were also affected (*FBIS:NES*, August 8, 1988, p. 33). Yasser Arafat contended that the PLO assumed the burden of supporting 19,000 former Jordanian employees who were affected by the decision (*FBIS:NES*, May 26, 1989, pp. 13–14).

33. *Middle East Journal* (chronology section) 43, no. 1 (Winter 1989): 71; *FBIS:NES*, August 4, 1988, p. 3; August 12, 1988, p. 4.

34. *FBIS:NES*, August 10, 1989, pp. 3–4.

35. *FBIS:NES*, August 12, 1988, pp. 38–39, and August 15, 1989, pp. 38–39.

36. *Middle East Journal* (chronology section) 43, no. 1 (Winter 1989): 75.

37. *FBIS:NES*, December 28, 1988, p. 37.

38. *FBIS:NES*, November 16, 1988, p. 34.
39. *FBIS:NES*, May 18, 1989, p. 33.
40. See, for example, *al-Watan al-Arabi*, no. 107-633 (March 31, 1989), p. 24, and *al-Hawadith*, no. 1703 (June 23, 1989), pp. 22–23.
41. *FBIS:NES*, November 28, 1988, p. 42.
42. *FBIS:NES*, August 23, 1989, p. 30.
43. *FBIS:NES*, July 3, 1989, pp. 30–33.
44. *FBIS:NES*, April 28, 1989, p. 40.
45. See the statement by Abd al-Razzaq al-Yahya, PLO representative in Jordan, in *FBIS:NES*, September 28, 1989, pp. 3–4.
46. *FBIS:NES*, October 6, 1989, p. 34, and October 11, 1989, p. 34; *Middle East Journal* (chronology section) 43, no. 3 (Summer 1989): 464, and 43, no. 4 (Autumn 1989): 661.
47. *FBIS:NES*, December 31, 1987, pp. 3, 30, and January 5, 1988, p. 2.
48. *FBIS:NES*, January 29, 1988, p. 7.
49. *Middle East Journal* (chronology section) 42, no. 4 (Autumn 1988): 640–41.
50. *FBIS:NES*, August 4, 1988, p. 6.
51. *FBIS:NES*, August 12, 1988, p. 8.
52. See, for example, *FBIS:NES*, August 25, 1988, pp. 32–33, and August 30, 1988, p. 3.
53. *Middle East Journal* (chronology section) 43, no. 1 (Winter 1988): 73.
54. For the Syrian official reaction, see *FBIS:NES*, November 17, 1988, p. 42. For the criticism of the Syrian client groups, see, for example, *FBIS:NES*, November 16, 1988, p. 7, December 16, 1988, p. 10, and May 4, 1989, pp. 2–3; *Middle East Journal* (chronology section) 43, no. 2 (Spring 1989): 252–53, no. 3 (Summer 1989): 466.
55. *FBIS:NES*, April 20, 1989, pp. 2–3.
56. For an account of Syria's aid relationship with the Arab oil states, see *Middle East Economic Digest* 33, no. 35 (September 8, 1989), p. 6.
57. *FBIS:NES*, May 12, 1989, p. 2.
58. See, for example, the interview with Jamal al-Surani, the secretary (al-'amin al-sirr) of the PLO Executive Council, in *al-Hawadith*, no. 1721 (October 1989): 38.
59. See the statement by Syrian foreign minister Faruk al-Shar' in *FBIS:NES*, July 31, 1989, pp. 36–38.
60. *New York Times*, November 12, 1989, p. 26.
61. *FBIS:NES*, August 10, 1989, pp. 1–4.
62. See the statement broadcast on Damascus radio on April 12, 1989 in *FBIS:NES*, April 14, 1989, p. 40.
63. *FBIS:NES*, January 4, 1988, pp. 9–10, and January 13, 1988, p. 20.
64. *FBIS:NES*, December 28, 1987, p. 13, and January 15, 1988, pp. 8–9.

65. *Washington Post,* January 22, 1988, p. 16.

66. See *FBIS:NES,* January 12, 1988, pp. 20–21, and August 22, 1988, p. 9; *Middle East Journal* (chronology section) 43, no. 1 (Winter 1989): 72.

67. *FBIS:NES,* November 18, 1988, p. 8, and November 21, 1988, pp. 7–8.

68. *FBIS:NES,* November 22, 1988, pp. 5–6.

69. *FBIS:NES,* December 15, 1988, p. 9.

70. *FBIS:NES,* April 25, 1989, p. 4.

71. A list of the ten points can be found in *New York Times,* September 18, 1989, pp. 1, 8.

72. After meeting with Israeli Defense Minister Rabin in Cairo on September 18, 1989, a visit immediately preceded and immediately followed by meetings with Arafat, Mubarak told the press, "We are doing our best and hope we will form a Palestinian delegation acceptable to both parties, and then a dialogue could begin in Cairo" (*FBIS:NES,* September 19, 1989, pp. 1–3).

73. *FBIS:NES,* September 15, 1989, p. 3. For the generally negative view of the ten points taken by the Unified National Leadership of the Uprising, see *FBIS:NES,* September 25, 1989, p. 6.

74. *New York Times,* September 22, 1988, p. 8; *FBIS:NES,* November 3, 1989, p. 5.

75. For a list of the names, see *Middle East Economic Digest* 33, no. 40 (October 13, 1989), p. 12. Mubarak confirmed that he was taking such a list to Washington in an interview with the *Washington Post,* September 24, 1989, p. 1.

76. *New York Times,* November 16, 1989, p. 3.

77. These points were included in the statement of the PLO Executive Committee issued after their meeting of November 5, 1989, in Cairo (*FBIS: NES,* November 7, 1989, p. 1).

78. *New York Times,* December 7, 1989, p. 11. The scheduled meeting never occurred. The political crisis in Israel, which led to the fall of the National Unity government and its replacement by a Likud-led right-wing coalition, along with the upsurge in Jewish emigration from the Soviet Union, consumed Israeli political energies during the first half of 1990. The Iraq-Kuwait crisis of August 1990 pushed the Palestinian issue off the Middle Eastern diplomatic stage.

Impact of the Intifada on American Jews and the Reaction of the American Public and of Israeli Jews

George E. Gruen

The Intifada, as the three-year-long sustained popular Palestinian struggle to shake off the Israeli occupation in the territories is now generally known, has profoundly affected the American Jewish community.

On the one hand, despite whatever misgivings many individual Jews may have concerning specific policies or actions of the Israeli government, the overwhelming majority of American Jews remain firm in their support for the State of Israel and are deeply committed to the security and survival of their brethren in the Jewish state. On the other hand, and at the same time, there has been within the American Jewish community much soul-searching, wringing of hands, and greater and more sustained questioning of Israeli policies than at any other time in the four decades of American Jewish-Israeli relations, more so even than during the painful period of the 1982 war in Lebanon.

This chapter is necessarily impressionistic, since much of the evidence is anecdotal. It cannot be rigorously scientific and my conclusions must therefore be tentative, for several reasons.

The number of Jewish respondents in the regular national opinion polls is too small to draw scientifically valid conclusions. The only direct comparison of a significantly large national Jewish sample (1,018) with a comparable general American sample (1,100) was a poll conducted by the *Los Angeles Times* in April 1988.[1]

The only systematic survey of American Jewish attitudes has been a series of questionnaires administered over the past seven years by Steven M. Cohen, professor of sociology at Queens College of CUNY, on behalf of the American Jewish Committee.[2] These are referred to here as the National Survey of American Jews (NSAJ). Finally, a Survey of American Jewish Leaders (SAJL) was conducted by Cohen in the fall of 1989 on behalf of the Israel-Diaspora Institute of Tel Aviv University, with financial support from the Jewish Community Federation of San Francisco and the American Jewish Committee.[3]

Some questions have been raised about the representativeness of the Cohen sample. Skepticism has also been voiced over the inherent difficulty—even with the most carefully constructed sample—in eliciting true and meaningful answers on emotionally charged issues about which the respondents are often deeply conflicted.

In his summary of the *Los Angeles Times* poll, conducted in the fourth month of the Intifada, Robert Scheer concluded that the violence dismayed both Jews and non-Jews, but also engendered views that are far more nuanced, contradictory, and complex than most analysts had thought. Specifically, he found that American Jews are not so preoccupied with Middle East issues, homogeneous in their thinking, or as different from their non-Jewish neighbors as had generally been assumed. The portrait of American Jewry that emerges from the survey, he wrote, is "an active, committed Jewish community increasingly polarized and concerned about the direction of events involving Israel."[4]

Another difficulty in assessing the direct impact of the Intifada on American Jewish attitudes to Israel is that the uprising did not occur in a vacuum. It is therefore difficult to determine whether certain shifts in attitude were exclusively the result of the Intifada or whether other factors contributed to the changes. Various events affecting Israel-Diaspora relations in recent years have also had either a short-term or a more gradual influence over time on the attitudes of American Jews to Israel.

For example, during the first two years of the Intifada, the long simmering issue of "who is a Jew?" erupted several times as a major source of controversy as a result of Orthodox attempts to enact legislation to disqualify the validity within Israel of conversions to Judaism performed by non-Orthodox rabbis abroad. Many American groups, including for the first time communal leaders in the philanthropic establishment, active in federation and United Jewish Appeal (UJA) campaigns on behalf of Israel, went to Jerusalem in unprecedented numbers after the November 1988 Knesset elections to lobby Israeli politicians against reported concessions by the two major parties (Labor and Likud) to Orthodox demands in the course of coalition bargaining.[5] This illustrated a further development of the trend I noted in an earlier work, *The Not-So-Silent Partnership*, of American Jews in recent years to question Israeli policies and intervene directly with Israelis to make their views heard.[6]

When Cohen asked his sample of American Jewish leadership whether they approved or disapproved of "expert American Jewish lay and professional leaders being involved in" various aspects of Israeli life, he found an overwhelming readiness to intervene on the "who is a Jew?" issue: 88 percent approved while only 11 percent disapproved—and on "immigrant absorption in Israel" (84 percent to 12 percent). On the other hand, Cohen found a great reluctance to become involved in "Israeli security policies": 67 percent disapproved, while only 25 percent approved such intervention. American Jewish leaders were most conflicted and divided over the appropriateness of intervention on "Israelis' treatment of Palestinian protesters"—53 percent approved, 39 percent disapproved, and 9 percent were not sure, and over the issue of "electoral reform/adopting a constitution in Israel"—50 approved, 40 disapproved, and the rest were not sure.[7]

Another example has been the debate over policy with regard to Soviet Jewish emigration. Until the recent agreement under which Russian Jews could apply directly to come to the United States, there were heated debates in the American Jewish community and between American Jews and Israelis as to whether and to what extent Israel's need for immigrants should have priority over the principle of freedom of choice, and how this should be reflected in practical decisions regarding both U.S. governmental and American Jewish communal aid for those who left the Soviet Union with visas to Israel but in Europe decided to come to the United States.

The repercussions of the Jonathan Jay Pollard spy affair have continued to rankle. More fundamentally, demographic and political changes in Israel, notably the coming to power of the nationalist Likud party in 1977, the 1982 war in Lebanon, and the growing polarization within Israel, as well as the perception of a rightward drift within the Israeli public, have all had long-term effects on American Jewish attitudes toward Israel.

The polling data indicate that the American community as a whole and the predominant majority of the leadership tend to be liberal. This is reflected in the fact that although median household income of the leadership is $125,000, 69 percent said they considered themselves Democrats, and only 13 percent thought of themselves as Republicans. (The rest said they were independents.) It is striking that the year after the 1988 presidential campaign in which liberalism was portrayed by George Bush as a dirty word and even Governor Dukakis was afraid to identify himself with the term, 47 percent of American Jewish leaders said that their usual stand on political issues was "liberal," 43 percent regarded their position as "middle-of-the-road," and only 10 percent identified themselves as "conservative."[8] One colleague put it aptly, when he said American Jews earn like Episcopalians but vote like Puerto Ricans.

Thus to the extent that Israel adopts policies and engages in actions that appear contrary to liberal democratic principles of justice, fairness, and equity in its treatment of the Arabs, and adopts hardline political attitudes, one can expect growing discomfort in the American Jewish community and eventual distancing from Israeli society. The one caveat is that to the extent that Israel's actions appear necessary to meet legitimate security needs, such as to counter Arab terrorism and other threats to public safety, American Jewry will grit its teeth and defer judgment to the Israelis.

Another question is to what extent the more critical image of Israel lately being projected by opinion leaders, such as government officials, editorial writers, and columnists on television and in print, will translate into a further weakening of what had been the generally favorable public image of Israel. As Steven Cohen and Sid Groeneman note in a recent paper: "According to one widely held theory, Israel became very popular among American Jews in the late 1960s and early 1970s because it functioned as a source of ethnic pride. If so, then to the extent that Israel becomes, or is simply perceived to be, less well liked among the broader American public, Israel will decline as a source of pride—indeed in the present context be transformed into an embarrassment for some—thus reducing her attractiveness to American Jews."[9]

Financial Support for Israel

Despite some worrying signs of gradual erosion, direct involvement in pro-Israeli activities and support for Israel by American Jews continue to be manifested in various ways. For example, direct financial contributions to pro-Israeli Political Action Committees (PACs) grew steadily in recent years and reached record amounts during the 1988 election campaign in the United States. A recent survey found that the numbers of pro-Israel PACs and the financial contributions they have raised for members of Congress is today exceeded only by the PACs on behalf of the real estate industry.[10]

According to Stanley B. Horowitz, president of the United Jewish Appeal, contributions to UJA have more or less kept even despite the Intifada. Cash collections to the regular overseas campaign, the great bulk of which goes to Israel (the rest is used for the programs of the American Jewish Joint Distribution Committee), for the fiscal years ending June 30, came to $337 million in 1986, $358 million in 1987 (before the start of the Intifada), fell slightly to $335 million in 1988, and rose slightly to $339 million in 1989.[11]

Total cash collections for both the regular and the emergency campaign for Soviet Jewry, which amounted to $368 million for the year ending June 30, 1989, jumped to $426 million in the year ending June 30, 1990.[12] Moreover, "Operation Exodus," the UJA's current special campaign to aid the absorption of the unprecedented massive numbers of Soviet Jewish immigrants coming to Israel, had by the end of October 1990 obtained pledges for more than

$450 million—exceeding the initial $420 million goal—and had already transmitted $128 million in cash to Israel.[13]

This demonstrated once again that when confronted with a genuine Israel-related emergency, American Jews continue to be quick and generous in their response. The Yom Kippur War campaign made 1974 the UJA's banner year for large contributions. When Israel is faced with a struggle for survival or to meet the challenge of swiftly rescuing Jews threatened with pogroms in Russia, American Jews set their political divisions aside and unite to support Israel.

The sharply increased giving for the current emergency has also reversed, at least for the moment, the long-term trend of Jewish communities spending a greater percentage of their charitable income for domestic local and national needs.

An American Jewish Committee–sponsored poll in 1988 reported that 55 percent of the Jews said they contributed to the overall UJA/Federation campaign. However, the *Los Angeles Times* poll found that only 41 percent of all Jewish respondents said they had given $100 or more. The figures were analyzed by Milton Goldin in a recent article, "Politics and Philanthropy: The State of American Jewish 'Giving.' "[14] Goldin contends that the significant change is not manifested in the amount of money but rather in the declining percentage of Jewish philanthropy flowing to Israel. He quotes from Arthur Hertzberg's article "The Illusion of Jewish Unity" that contributions to Israel "have given way to larger allocations of funds to build community centers and hospitals and old age homes and day schools for the benefit of Jews in America." Hertzberg adds that now Israel receives 40 percent of the total of funds raised in combined UJA-Federation campaigns compared to the roughly 60 percent it received less than twenty years ago.[15]

Rabbi Harold S. Kushner recalls that in the years he served on the allocations board for UJA-Federation in the Boston area, the percentage allocated to Israel and other overseas concerns declined in the course of a decade from roughly 50 to 40 percent. The stated reason was not any political disaffection from Israel but a sense of greater urgency in meeting local Jewish needs. For example, a convincing case was made that unless we spent more money on Jewish education now, when the younger generation grew up their identification with the Jewish community would become increasingly tenuous and their commitment to Israel would inevitably also be eroded.[16]

Goldin claims in his article that the number of Jewish givers to both Israeli and American Jewish causes has been declining at an increasing rate over the last fifteen years. He concludes that "while the *intifada* has brought issues in Jewish giving to a head, major problems in Jewish philanthropy have as much to do with sociological change in America as with events in Israel." These sociological changes include growing rates of intermarriage and the acceptance of America Jews into the mainstream of American academic, civic, and cultural institutions, which increasingly have become the beneficiaries of large grants by wealthy American Jews.[17]

Another major reason for this change has been the increasing pressure within the communities to spend money on unmet domestic Jewish and general communal needs, especially as the Reagan administration's policies resulted in curtailed funding for domestic social programs. The UJA's special "Passage to Freedom" campaign, which raise $50 million in 1989 for the resettlement of Soviet Jewish emigrés, was one such new priority. This was less successful than the current "Operation Exodus," because "Passage to Freedom" was caught up in ideological and practical disputes as to how much should be allocated to bringing Russian Jews to the United States, and how much should be passed on to Israel to absorb the rising wave of Russian immigrants choosing to go directly to Israel.[18]

Of course many of the contentious issues relating to philanthropy preceded the Intifada. Already in 1986 UJA's national chairman, Martin Stein, warned Prime Minister Yitzhak Shamir that if the Law of Return were altered, major decreases in contributions from Conservative and Reform donors would follow.[19] In fact, in February 1989, well after the uprising began, "Planeloads of prominent American Jews descended on Jerusalem; dignitaries and spokesmen on behalf of the Jewish-Israel lobby in Washington threatened to stop or seriously cut their annual commitments."[20] Goldin points out that it was not the Intifada that brought these visitors but the "who is a Jew" controversy, which was prompted by Israeli religious parties' proposed redefinition of legitimate conversions to Judaism.[21]

This anger would not necessarily be translated into less philanthropy for Israel as a whole but rather into the shifting of money from the Jewish Agency, the primary Israeli channel for UJA funds to Israel, to other more specialized channels for philanthropy to Israeli causes. These include the trend toward targeted direct giving to the Conservative and Reform institutions in Israel and to grass roots social action groups in Israel, funded by the New Israel Fund, whose donors have increased from 80 to 12,000 in a decade and whose income has grown steadily and dramatically from $131,000 in 1980 to more than $5 million in 1989.[22]

This has been paralleled by increased giving in response to the independent appeals conducted in the United States by a plethora of Israeli educational, religious, health, and social welfare institutions.[23] This renewed emphasis on targeted giving may reflect a growing sophistication and a more critical approach to philanthropy among younger American Jews. They no longer give, as their parents did, simply in response to the emotional appeal of Israel, but they reach their decisions only after making a more careful study of the specific causes and institutions they wish to strengthen. Cohen's Leadership Survey confirmed that American Jewish leaders were troubled over Israeli bureaucratic inefficiency. By a plurality of 47 percent to 31 percent they agreed with the statement "Because of infighting and mismanagement, Israelis waste an excessive amount of philanthropic aid they receive from American Jews."[24]

It should be noted that additional millions of American dollars flowed to Israel in 1988 in response to the unofficial fund-raising trips to the United States by Israeli officials from all across the spectrum of Israeli politics, seeking campaign contributions for their respective parties before the November 1988 Knesset elections.

American Jews Firmly Support U.S. Aid to Israel

Moreover, irrespective of whether they had any preferences among Israeli political parties, or whether they disagreed with specific Israeli government policies, the overwhelming majority of American Jews have continued to voice their support for the maintenance of the current high levels of military and economic aid to Israel by the U.S. government. There continues to be strong opposition in the Jewish community to any threat of punitive action against Israel by the American administration.

In April 1988—four months into the Intifada—the *Los Angeles Times* asked Americans whether "the United States Government should step up its military aid to Israel, or keep it at about the same level, or do you think the government should cut down military aid to Israel?" Among the general, non-Jewish public, opinion was divided. About one-third (34 percent) favored cuts. A plurality, 47 percent, favored keeping aid at current levels, while only 8 percent supported an increase. By way of contrast, the Jewish response was overwhelmingly positive. Some 90 percent of all affiliated Jews, irrespective of denomination, backed continued or increased military aid for Israel. Even among those Jews who described themselves as unaffiliated, more than three-quarters were for either current levels (64 percent) or increased (12 percent) aid to Israel. Only 10 percent of the unaffiliated Jews said they favored some cuts in U.S. military aid to Israel.[25]

Although a majority of the Jewish leadership sample disagreed with Prime Minister Shamir's rejection of the concept of territorial concessions for peace, they were unwilling to support even slight American pressure on Israel. Fully 89 percent disagreed with the statement "The U.S. Congress should cut aid to Israel by a little bit just so the hard-line Israelis will understand that American support for Israeli has its limits." Only 7 percent agreed with this proposition.[26]

It is remarkable that the $3 billion in U.S. aid to Israel, the highest foreign aid appropriation for any single country, continued to sail through Congress virtually unscathed during 1988 and 1989, despite the Intifada and the budget-cutting pressures on Congress.

The first serious challenge to the $3 billion figure was launched by Senate Minority leader Robert Dole (R-Kansas) in January 1990. But his action was not prompted specifically by the Intifada and was not limited to Israel but was in response to the urgent need for additional funds to help the new regimes in Eastern Europe. It also reflected the administration's annoyance with Congress over the practice of earmarking specific sums for individual countries, thereby denying the executive branch the flexibility the president wanted in allocating foreign aid.

Senator Dole's suggestion, in an op-ed article in the *New York Times*, of a 5 percent cut for major current aid recipients has raised a storm of controversy. In an editorial the following day, the *Times* suggested that Dole could better find the necessary funds elsewhere in the $1 trillion-plus federal budget rather than in the relatively modest $15 billion total for foreign aid. As for the proposed specific cut in aid to Israel, the *Times* asked rhetorically, "Would reduced aid speed the Middle East peace talks?" The paper acknowledged that "Mr. Dole and others in Congress are fed up with Prime Minister Shamir's glacial pace," but reducing aid would be counterproductive because it "could cause Mr. Shamir to dig in his heels and rally Israelis behind him."[27]

One source of American Jewish dollars that has been negatively affected at least in part by the Intifada has been tourism. The decline in the number of Jewish tourists to Israel from the United States in 1988 was probably the result of exaggerated fears by potential tourists for their safety, heightened by the television coverage of the violence, especially during the early months of the Intifada. Vacation travelers generally shy away from places of turmoil and perceived danger.

Overall tourism numbers gradually began to recover, starting in April 1989.[28] Tourism to Israel from the United States in the period January–March 1990 increased 18 percent over the previous year, while April set a record for worldwide tourism to Israel. The figure of 181,000 was 35 percent higher than in 1989 and 5 percent above April 1987, which had been the previous peak year for tourism.[29] The improvement can be attributed to two factors: there was a sharp decrease in the level of Intifada violence directed against Israelis, and the media were so preoccupied with developments in Eastern Europe that there was virtually no television coverage of the territories. The widespread Palestinian riots following the killing of seven Palestinians by a deranged Israeli and the abortive terrorist attack by the Libyan-backed Palestine Liberation Front on a beach near Tel Aviv occurred in May 1990.

These incidents brought brief TV coverage to the area but were soon eclipsed by the attention given to the Gorbachev-Bush summit. However, American tourism to Israel again sharply declined in the fall of 1990 as a result of increasing Palestinian-Israeli clashes and fears of war as a consequence of Iraq's invasion of Kuwait and President Saddam Hussein's repeated threats to unleash a chemical warfare attack against Israel.

Whatever the reason, Israelis have bemoaned the failure of American Jews to come in larger numbers, either as immigrants or even as tourists. Israelis have tended to see the physical distance of American Jews as a psychological removal and a failure to express full solidarity with them in their time of distress.[30]

Attitudes within the Jewish Community at Large

In the 1989 National Survey of American Jews (NSAJ) conducted by Steven Cohen for the American Jewish Committee, a 62 percent majority of American Jews polled expressed a feeling of "closeness" toward Israel (22 percent very close, 40 percent fairly close), contrasted with 31 percent who said they felt somewhat distanced. These figures are virtually identical with those for 1986, the year before the outbreak of the Palestinian uprising. In 1986, 62 percent said they felt close to Israel (20 percent very close and 42 percent fairly close; 33 percent did not feel close).

There was, however, a 5 percent increase between 1986 and 1988 of those who said they are often "troubled" by the policies of the current Israeli government (40 percent in 1986 and 45 percent in 1988). Nevertheless, the growth in the number of those who feel troubled does not seem to affect significantly the overall support Jews have given to Israel, specifically since the Intifada began. In fact, 82 percent of the people who claim to have disagreements with Israel said these differences on specific policies do not interfere with their overall feelings of closeness toward Israel.[31] Furthermore, 72 percent said that the recent violence has not made them feel less warmly about Israel.[32] When asked when their opinions were formed, more than half said that they were formed even before the Six Day War in 1967.[33]

When Cohen polled the Jewish leadership in the fall of 1989, nearly two years after the outbreak of the Intifada, he found them to be even more supportive of Israel than Jews in general. More than three-quarters (76 percent) said they felt "very close" to Israel and another fifth (19 percent) said they felt "fairly close."[34]

Although Jewish support for Israel remains strong, the emergence of a dissenting minority, visible in the polls, raises again some basic issues about the proper relationship between Israel and American Jews. The principles of this relationship were set out in the discussions held in 1950 between Jacob Blaustein, a prominent American industrialist and president of the American Jewish Committee, and Prime Minister David Ben-Gurion. The agreement, on both sides, was one of mutual support and a pledge of noninterference in each other's domestic and political affairs.[35] The question today, as it was then, is whether public criticism of each other's policies and actions should be regarded as a violation of this principle of noninterference.

In the *Los Angeles Times* poll, Jews were asked whether they believed other Jews should criticize Israel in public. A little more than half agreed that it was acceptable. In the same poll, when the general public was also asked this question, 49 percent agreed that Jews should criticize, while 30 percent felt they should not. In the NSAJ poll, 43 percent admitted that they had heard Jewish friends speaking critically of Israeli policy in the West Bank and Gaza.[36] Yet what seems strange is that these numbers do not seem fully reflected in the responses to the polls. For example, in the last NSAJ poll in early 1989, a majority of 65 percent said that they felt that Israel's handling of the uprising has been appropriate (except for a few incidents), while 12 percent disagreed and 23 percent were not sure how to answer.[37]

This contrasts with the views of the general public, who were far more critical of Israeli actions. Eytan Gilboa, a Hebrew University scholar who has closely studied American public opinion toward Israel and the Arab-Israel conflict, found that in seven polls conducted during the first half of 1988 more than one-third of the non-Jews felt Israel's reaction had been too harsh. (The critical responses ranged from 28 to 50 percent.)[38]

The American Jewish population is split when it comes to specific aspects of the Palestinian question and its relation to the future of Israel. On these issues, the opinions are as divided as they are in Israel itself, between the Likud and others of the "nationalist camp" on the right, who oppose yielding sovereignty over territory, and the Labor Party and other parties on the left who favor territorial compromise. In general, the American Jewish opinions lean toward the dovish side. For example, the 1989 NSAJ shows that only 22 percent approved of an Israeli annexation of the West Bank, while 31 percent disapproved and 47 percent said they didn't know.[39] On the issue of supporting the concept of land for peace, 38 percent agreed, 30 percent disagreed, and 31 percent said they were not sure.[40]

The sense of ambivalence and unease in the American Jewish community over developments in Israel during the past three years has been reflected in expressions of anguish over some reportedly excessive Israeli military actions taken to quell the disturbances and a reluctance to support certain Israeli governmental policies, especially where they appear to run counter to American peace efforts.

One indication of this distress is the marked increase in expressed concern over the adverse effect on Israel's future of continued Israeli occupation of the territories. For example, in the replies to Cohen's series of NSAJ polls, in 1986 only 6 percent of the sample thought that the occupation would "erode Israel's Jewish character." In 1988 that number had more than tripled, to 20 percent. In 1989 it dropped to 16 percent, but the number who expressed confidence that the occupation would not erode Israel's Jewish character continued to decline, from 63 percent in 1986 to 56 percent in 1988 and 52 percent in 1989. Conversely, the number of American Jews who were unsure had increased from one-quarter (24 percent) to one-third (32 percent) of all respondents between 1988 and 1989 as the Intifada continued.[41]

On a related question, in 1986 only 11 percent thought that the occupation would "erode Israel's democratic and humanitarian character." By 1988 that figure had risen to 30 percent. Although in 1989 it dropped slightly to 26 percent, the number who disagreed also went down—from 41 to 38 percent—and those who were unsure increased—from 29 to 35 percent.[42]

While many Jews have kept their misgivings to themselves or have limited their criticisms to discussions among family and Jewish friends, there has been an increasing readiness within the community to criticize the policies of Prime Minister Shamir, not only in private but also in public. Those who have recently voiced their misgivings and dissent openly have come not only from among the ranks of well-known traditional left-wing critics of the Zionist State, such as Noam Chomsky, and liberal Zionist reformers, such as Michael Lerner, editor of *Tikkun*. They have increasingly included active supporters of Israel from among the mainstream of the Jewish community.[43]

The Intifada accelerated a trend that had already begun during the controversy surrounding Israel's involvement in Lebanon in 1982. As J.J. Goldberg, a reporter for New York's *Jewish Week*, noted in his review of significant developments affecting American Jews in the 1980s, "Lebanon was an irrevocable watershed in American Jewish relationships with Israel, and with each other. Before Lebanon, questioning Israeli policies seemed confined to a few intellectuals and radicals at the community's fringes; after Lebanon, public criticism of Israel penetrated the inner sancta of community life."[44]

Increasing Contacts between U.S. Jews and Palestinians

Another significant development since the outbreak of the Intifada has been the greater readiness of mainstream American Jewish communal figures to become involved in informal talks with Palestinians, including some who are rather closely identified with the Palestine Liberation Organization (PLO). These discussions have ranged from the unpublicized meetings of the Jewish Women's Leadership Consultation on Israel, chaired by Blu Greenberg, to participation in public forums such as the conference at Columbia University and a convocation at the Washington Cathedral, both held in March 1989.[45]

The Columbia conference, "The Road to Peace: Co-Existence between Israelis and Palestinians," was cosponsored by the dovish Israeli monthly *New Outlook* and the pro-PLO Palestinian daily *Al-Fajr*, published in Jerusalem, together with the American Friends of Peace Now and the American Council for Palestine Affairs. The

Washington convocation was sponsored by the United States Interreligious Committee for Peace in the Middle East, a coalition of Jewish, Christian, and Moslem leaders endorsed by more than 1,000 clergy. While the group's founder, Ronald Young, had for fifteen years been engaged in efforts to bring about Israeli-Palestinian reconciliation from the time he had been the American Friends Service Committee's representative in the Middle East, what was noteworthy was that his current interfaith peace effort included fourteen rabbis on its forty-member board. (The group held a similar major two-day convocation at the New York Cathedral of St. John the Divine in February 1990.)

Hard-liners continue to dismiss the value of such informal talks, which bring together American Jews, Israelis, Palestinians and Arab-Americans. Indeed, supporters of Prime Minister Shamir's Likud party and other right-wing critics contend that such discussions are inherently dangerous and may undermine Israel's bargaining position in eventual negotiations.

Speaking in almost apocalyptic terms, Foreign Minister Moshe Arens warned American Jewish leaders not to allow the world to drive a wedge between them and Israel. In a speech to the Presidents Conference in New York on March 16, 1989, Arens chastized the five American Jews who had met with Arafat, saying he could not understand "why any Jew, or any self-respecting person," would do that. He also accused the left-wing Knesset members who had attended the Columbia peace conference the previous week of "putting pressure on the Israeli government via other governments."

Arens virtually equated public dissent from Israel's government policies with betrayal of the Jewish people. Noting pointedly that during the Holocaust "American Jewish leadership did not do everything it could have done or should have done," Arens concluded, "Let that be an object lesson that we never again fail to live up to our responsibilities." He implied that erosion of support for Israel among American Jews posed a greater danger than did the Intifada: "Firebombs, rocks and knives are dangerous to *individual* Israelis, not a danger to Israel's existence. But," he warned ominously, "there's no need for me to tell you what political ramifications it could bring about if there was a sense of political isolation."[46]

Other voices on the right have been even more vehement in their attack on American Jewish critics of current Israeli policy. The late right-wing Kach party leader Rabbi Meir Kahane, in an April 1989 op-ed column in the *New York Times*, expressed his disgust for "those liberal Jews who instinctively feel guilty about everything—whether they had anything to do with what's wrong or not."[47] The Likud-Herut USA also compared current Jewish organizational leaders with those during World War II, charging that they had a history of neglecting Jewish needs: "Jewish left-wingers led in the assault on the government of Israel, thus legitimizing latent hostility on the part of many of their non-Jewish colleagues."[48]

Other actions have been organized, such as demonstrations in support of Israel and its government's policies. During Shamir's visit, a new right-wing group issued an indictment called "Against Incomplete Reporting." In their "open letter" published in the *New York Times* on April 1, 1988, they attacked the media, and its manipulation by the PLO to "undermine the moral integrity of Israel, defame the Israeli government and bias world opinion."[49] In the fall of 1989, more than 500 persons attended the national conference in Boston of CAMERA (Committee for Accuracy in Middle East Reporting in America). This grass-roots group, created at the time of the negative media treatment of Israel's military involvement in Lebanon during the war in 1982, monitors and responds to what it regards as instances of anti-Israel bias in press, radio, and television coverage. However, despite the expected criticisms from the right, the recent Palestinian-Jewish meetings have aroused far less general controversy in the community than, for example, did the secret meetings of a five-member delegation of prominent American Jewish individuals with Yasser Arafat and his aides in Stockholm in the fall of 1988 in an effort to persuade the PLO to moderate its official position. This was probably because the five Americans, led by Rita Hauser, U.S. chair of the International Center for Peace in the Middle East, met with Arafat before he had formally recognized Israel's right to exist and while the U.S. government was still officially refusing to meet with the PLO.

In contrast, the March 1989 public meetings came shortly after the United States had opened its own dialogue with the PLO following Arafat's official declaration in mid-December 1988 ostensibly recognizing Israel's right to exist and renouncing terrorism. While many were still skeptical, there are increasing numbers of American Jews who, like Hauser, saw a momentum of hopefulness in the proliferation of communications between and among Israelis, American Jews, Palestinian nationalists, and Arab-American leaders.[50]

Although mainstream Jewish participants in both March 1989 conferences were known as "doves," Carolyn Toll Oppenheim notes, their public participation enables other, more "establishment" figures in the American Jewish community to begin a similar process of holding such discussions in private. Rabbi Balfour Brickner, long active in liberal causes, stressed the significance of the breaking of the taboo on talks with Palestinians who identify themselves as supporters of the PLO. "Many people in this room remember when meetings like this were held in secret—some thought it was dangerous," Brickner told the Convocation at the Washington Cathedral; "now we're out of the closet." Reflecting on the shift in American Jewish thinking, Brickner continued, "we who were so scorned a minority—called left, liberal—find ourselves entering the mainstream. The value of these conferences is to create the atmosphere for us and the larger world of the possibilities of peace. If we can conceive of it together that is of enormous value."[51]

In discussing trends within the American Jewish community with regard to Israel, Steven Cohen has found a pattern of gradual decline in the intensity of sympathy and support for Israel among the younger generation (thirty-five years and under) of American Jews, who have never personally experienced the precariousness of Jewish existence and have grown up at a time when Israel has been portrayed as a dominant military power in the Middle East. This contrasts with the pervasive and passionate support for Israel among older Jews (sixty-five and over) who lived through the time of the Holocaust and the difficult struggle for Israel's creation in 1948 and the subsequent threats to its existence. Cohen presents various tentative hypotheses to explain this phenomenon and notes that further investigation is required to give definitive explanations. Cohen concludes that while persons under thirty-five had somewhat greater misgivings about Israeli responses to the Intifada, he found no evidence to attribute the greater coolness and distancing of some of the young from Israel specifically to the impact of the

Intifada. For one thing this has been a gradual process, and it began long before the outbreak of the Palestinian uprising.[52]

Mitchell Bard, editor of *Near East Report*, argues that even this decline may be only temporary and the result of the "life-cycle effect." He points out that younger Jews are at a stage where they are "altogether more self-absorbed and less interested in public events or in Judaism." Bard suggests that "it is quite possible that those who feel less close to Israel today may grow more attached with age."[53]

Jewish Leadership Supports U.S. Peace Effort

When Secretary of State George Shultz decided in February 1988 to travel to the Middle East to pursue an intensive new American effort to break the long stalemate in the Arab-Israeli conflict, his initiative was generally welcomed by the American Jewish community. Indeed, encouragement by American Jewish leaders, who were deeply distressed by the daily television images coming from Israel of violent clashes resulting from the Palestinian uprising, had reportedly played a significant role in persuading Shultz to resume an active American role in reviving the moribund peace process.

The Reagan administration and Shultz had retreated to the sidelines after the frustrating outcome of earlier American efforts, notably the failure of the September 1982 Reagan initiative to find support from the governments of Israel, Syria, or Jordan; the brutal Shi'ite terrorist attacks upon the American Embassy and Marine barracks in Beirut; and finally the abrogation, under intensive Syrian pressure, of the Lebanese-Israeli agreement that had been concluded in May 1983 through American efforts.

American Jewish leaders were not prepared to pressure Israel to accept specific American proposals. This was in keeping with their traditional view that since the Israelis had to bear the risks of any concessions, a peace agreement should be the result of direct Israeli-Arab negotiations. At the same time, however, there was growing concern within the Jewish leadership that the Israel government headed by Prime Minister Shamir not obstruct the latest American efforts to reach a peace settlement.

To bring this message home to Shamir, on the eve of his visit to

Washington in March 1988, thirty senators, including many of Israel's staunchest supporters, sent a letter to Secretary Shultz "to express our support for your effort to break the dangerous Middle East stalemate that has led to the current cycle of violence and counterviolence." Noting that all American efforts were based, as was the Egyptian-Israeli Peace Treaty, on United Nations Security Council Resolution 242, which they said "can be summarized in three words: land for peace," they stated that they were "dismayed" to read that Shamir had reportedly declared (*New York Times*, February 26) that "this expression of territory for peace is not accepted by me." The senators went on to declare: "We hope that the Prime Minister's statement did not indicate that Israel is abandoning a policy that offers the best hope of long-term peace. Israel cannot be expected to give up all the territory gained in 1967 or to return to the dangerous and insecure pre-1967 borders. Resolution 242 does not require it to do so. On the other hand, peace negotiations have little chance of success if the Israeli Government's position rules out territorial compromise."

What was most extraordinary was that this letter had been drafted by two Jewish senators, Carl Levin (D-Mich.) and Rudy Boschowitz (R-Minn.), who have been among the most ardent supporters of Israel. Three other Jewish senators who signed the letter were Frank Lautenberg (D-N.J.), Howard Metzenbaum (D-Ohio), and Warren Rudman (R-New Hampshire). Although the letter also criticized the Arab states, with the exception of Egypt, for failing to make peace with Israel, urged Jordan not to drop out of the peace process, and supported Israel's refusal to negotiate with the PLO, the headlines focused on the news that "Senators Criticize Shamir's Position on Mideast Peace."[54]

While concern over the harmful effects of the continuation of the Intifada was reflected in the senators' letter, the well-publicized split between Likud and Labor in Israel over the concept of territory for peace, which had forced Secretary Shultz to hold separate meetings with Prime Minister Shamir and Vice Premier and Foreign Minister Shimon Peres during his latest peace mission to the area, may have emboldened the senators to take the unusual step of publicly criticizing the Likud leader.

Since there was no longer a unified Israeli official position, they could argue that they were not acting in opposition to the State of Israel. Rather, they were supporting a principle that, they stressed, had been "the foundation of United States diplomacy in the region through five Administrations" and, moreover, that "successive Israeli leaders have declared their dedication to the Camp David Accords including resolution 242's 'land for peace' formula and have indicated that it would apply to the West Bank and Gaza." Thus, they implied, it was Shamir who was deviating from this consensus. (In fact, Prime Minister Menachem Begin, who had led the Likud to power in 1977 and had signed the Camp David Accords, had long argued that the withdrawal provisions of Resolution 242 had been satisfied when Israel gave up the entire Sinai, more than 80 percent of all the territories captured in the 1967 war.)

The remaining two Jewish members of the Senate did not sign. Senator Arlen Specter (R-Penn.) said that he had been asked but had refused to do so, explaining that it was "a very bad idea" for persons in Washington "to give advice to people in Israel thousands of miles away." He said that if any senators disagreed with Mr. Shamir's *publicly* stated position, they should tell the Israelis *privately*. Senator Chic Hecht (R-Nevada), who had not been approached to sign the letter, said the comments in the letter were ill advised. "The people of Israel elected their own leadership," he said, adding that "Israel is our most important ally in the Middle East and we should not interfere."[55]

Reaction in the organized Jewish community was mixed. Abraham H. Foxman, national director of the Anti-Defamation League of B'nai B'rith, called the senators' intervention "well-intentioned, but premature and counterproductive." He believed the letter could undercut attempts to achieve a peace settlement and also might deepen the rivalries between Likud and Labor. But Hyman Bookbinder, the recently retired longtime Washington representative of the American Jewish Committee, said the senators had acted appropriately because the issue was actively being debated in both Israel and the United States, and the senators' expression of views was a legitimate part of this process.[56]

It is interesting to note that at this time Israeli Jews were about evenly split when asked whether they agreed that, "because of the aid it gives Israel," the United States has "the right to try to influence Israeli policy." In a poll conducted in Israel in March 1989 by the Smith Research Center for the *New York Times*, 47 percent of Israeli Jews felt the United States had the right to try to influence Israeli policy. Similar results were obtained when a *New York Times*/CBS Poll asked a sample of the general American public the same question in May 1989. Some 43 percent said yes, 44 percent said no. The number of undecided was 12 percent in the American sample, 6 percent in Israel.[57]

When the thirty senators wrote their letter to Shultz critical of Shamir's opposition to territorial compromise, they were reflecting misgivings and frustrations over the stalemated peace process that had become widespread among their constituents. For example, the *New York Times*/CBS poll asked a national American sample in May 1989, "Do you believe Israel has done enough to prove that it is interested in peace, or hasn't it done enough?" Even though this question was asked a few weeks after Prime Minister Shamir had met President Bush in Washington and announced a new four-point Israeli peace initiative, only 17 percent of the respondents thought Israel had done enough to prove its interest in peace. A full 70 percent of the American public still felt it had not. This contrasts sharply with the response of a sample of Israeli Jews, who had been asked the same question two months earlier by the Smith Research Center on behalf of the *New York Times*. A majority of 54 percent felt Israel had done enough to prove its interest in peace, while 40 percent believed it had not. The latter number roughly correlates with the percentage of Israelis highly critical of Shamir and supportive of Labor and other left-of-center parties.[58]

The Roper polls of 1988 and 1989 show a drop in sympathy for Israel (48 percent in 1987, 36 percent in 1989)[59] in contrast with an increase in sympathy for the Arabs, from 8 percent in 1987 to 13 percent in 1989. Alvin Richman,[60] Senior Public Opinion Analyst at the State Department, in his report on the polls since the uprising, notes that as the sympathy for Israel decreases, the number of neutral answers increases (roughly one-half on the average). It is not clear to what extent the amount of undecided responses is a result of indifference or a declining confidence in Israel's willingness to seek peace in the Middle East.

A national poll conducted by the *New York Times* and CBS

News in June 1990 found that "Americans continue to side with Israel in the Middle East conflict, though by a lesser margin than at any time since the question was asked, beginning in the early 1970s. Forty percent of Americans say they are more in sympathy with Israel, while 19 percent say they sympathize more with the Arab nations." The figure for sympathy with the Arabs was at a record high; it has earlier briefly reached 15 percent in September 1982 but dropped down to 5 percent in 1984. A February 1990 Roper Poll had found 35 percent favoring Israel and 11 percent favoring the Arab nations.[61]

The only consolation friends of Israel could draw from the American poll results was that Americans were almost as skeptical as were the Israelis on the question of whether the Palestine Liberation Organization "has done enough to prove that it is interested in peace with Israel." Only 14 percent of the American public and 7 percent of the Israeli Jews believed the PLO had done enough; 70 percent of the Americans and 90 percent of the Israelis did not.

But this is scant comfort when one considers that only 17 percent of the Americans polled felt Israel had done enough, while 70 percent majorities were critical of both Israel and the PLO. These are sobering numbers, for they indicate a significant erosion from the traditional American view that Israel held the moral high ground, because its leaders and people eagerly sought peace while the surrounding Arab states were sworn to Israel's destruction.[62]

Much of the change in American opinion was attributed by the editors of the CBS News/*New York Times* Poll to "a greater acceptance of Palestinians in Israel and to dismay with Israel's handling of its internal situation." Nearly half of the public (47 percent) in June 1990 favored giving the Palestinians a homeland on the West Bank and Gaza, only 25 percent opposed. The percentage of those who agreed that the United States should "be more sympathetic to the concerns of the Palestinian minority in Israel than it is now" went up from 26 in 1988 to 38 in 1990. Conversely, the percentage who disagreed declined from a plurality of 49 in 1988 to 37 in 1990.[63]

It is interesting to compare the general American public's view with the response of the Jewish leadership to a somewhat similar question asked by Cohen toward the end of 1989 about the fairness of Israel's treatment of Israeli Arabs and Arabs on the West Bank. With regard to the former, 36 percent felt they were somewhat unfairly treated and 8 percent felt they were very unfairly treated. A majority (51 percent) of American Jewish leaders believed the Arabs on the West Bank were unfairly treated; 38 percent said somewhat unfairly and 21 percent said very unfairly.[64]

Reactions to the Opening of the U.S.-PLO Dialogue

In its April 1988 poll, the *Los Angeles Times* found a sharp divergence between Jews and non-Jews on whether the United States should negotiate with the Palestine Liberation Organization. A majority of non-Jews (52 percent) said the United States should reverse its long-standing policy and talk with the PLO and a third (34 percent) said no. In contrast, a large majority of American Jews (61 percent) opposed U.S.-PLO talks, and fewer than a third (29 percent) were in favor of such a shift on the part of the American government.[65]

Eytan Gilboa cites three other national polls in early 1988 that gave similar results. The percentage of the general public favoring U.S.-PLO talks to help achieve peace ranged from 53 percent to 62 percent, those opposing from 26 percent to 35 percent. There was no breakdown of the sample by religion.[66]

On December 14, 1988, Secretary of State Shultz announced that the United States was prepared to open "a substantive dialogue with PLO representatives" in Tunis after Chairman Yasser Arafat of the PLO had made a public declaration that explicitly met the long-standing American conditions, namely, acceptance of UN Security Council resolutions 242 and 338, recognition of Israel's right to exist in peace and security, and renunciation of terrorism.[67]

Although the Israeli government was unhappy with the American decision, the organized leadership of the American Jewish community did not launch a campaign of criticism against this historic development. While there was widespread skepticism within the Jewish community as to the genuineness of Arafat's "conversion" to moderation, the organizational comments concentrated on asking Washington to probe the PLO's intentions.

A typical statement was issued by Theodore Ellenoff, president of the American Jewish Committee, saying that "we hope and expect that in its dialogue with the PLO, the US will call on the PLO to match words with deeds." Specific actions the AJC asked the United States to demand from the PLO were an end to attacks on Israeli civilians, urging the Palestinians in the territories to call off the violent aspects of the uprising "to give the peace process a chance," and a formal revocation of the PLO charter's provisions calling for the dissolution of Israel. The committee also declared that it was crucial for the United States to seek to coordinate its strategy with Israel on the next steps in resuming the peace process, and it expressed confidence that the United States under the Bush administration would continue to be "sensitive to the security concerns of Israel" as had the Reagan administration. Finally, the committee praised Shultz, saying that by his firm stand in denying a visa to Arafat to address the UN General Assembly in New York, "Mr. Shultz helped Arafat withstand the pressures from his own hard-liners and successfully prodded him to meet more fully the long-standing U.S. conditions for starting a dialogue."[68]

Why was the official American Jewish response so restrained, especially in view of the cited polling data showing strong opposition within the community to such a step? One explanation is that Shultz had proven himself to be a genuine friend of Israel. American Jews were ready to take him at face value when he emphasized in his announcement of the U.S.-PLO dialogue that "the United States commitment to the security of Israel remains unflinching." Shultz had also insisted that the talks with the PLO did not "imply an acceptance or recognition by the United States of an independent Palestinian state." He reiterated that the status of the West Bank and Gaza could not be determined by unilateral action of either side but only through a process of negotiations. Therefore the United States "does not recognize the declaration of an independent Palestinian state." Another likely reason was that the Jewish leadership saw no point in picking a fight with the outgoing Reagan administration.

Finally, the April 1988 poll had been taken before the PLO at its Algiers conference in November 1988 endorsed, albeit vaguely, a two-state solution, accepting Israel's existence, and Arafat made the point explicit in his Geneva press conference. Consequently there was also the hope among at least some in the Jewish community that perhaps the PLO was beginning to change and that it might therefore be helpful to the peace process for the United States to explore this possibility fully. This latter reason also helps explain the failure of Deputy Foreign Minister Binyamin Netanyahu's efforts in early 1989 to enlist the support of the major American Jewish community relations organs in a campaign to lobby the Bush Administration to break off the dialogue with the PLO.[69]

A related factor is the degree to which American Jews share the general American belief in the virtue of talks, even with unsavory characters. A poll conducted by Penn and Schoen Associates in mid-January 1988 concluded that "even though the American people view the PLO negatively and believe it remains committed to the destruction of Israel, they still overwhelmingly favor negotiations. Americans have a bias toward trying a reasonable approach; they feel you can discuss anything, no matter how intractable or emotional the issues may be."[70] Penn and Schoen found that among respondents who were familiar with the PLO (72 percent of the sample), two-thirds regarded the PLO as a "terrorist organization" rather than a "national liberation movement" (66 percent versus 17 percent). Nevertheless, most Americans approved the United States having "contact" with the PLO (55 percent) and "inviting" it to an international conference to help resolve the Middle East dispute (59 percent). However, a similar proportion (62 percent) said in 1988 that the PLO should not be accorded recognition as the "official representative of the Palestinian people" until it "recognized Israel and disavowed terrorism."

Alvin Richman, senior public opinion analyst in the U.S. Department of State, reports that "surveys taken in early 1989, after the start of the U.S.-PLO talks, show about two-thirds of the public (67 percent) approves of them, even though nearly that number (61 percent) still regard the PLO as a terrorist organization."[71]

When asked their opinion on U.S. negotiations with the PLO in an April 1988 poll, 62 percent supported the inclusion of the PLO in American negotiations to "bring about peace in the Middle East," and 35 percent felt the United States should not deal with the PLO "because they are terrorists and they refuse to recognize Israel's right to exist."[72] A poll taken in January 1989, shortly after Arafat's speech to the United Nations and his subsequent news conference, found that the number favoring American talks with the PLO had risen to 67 percent, 17 percent disapproved, and 16 percent said they were not sure.[73]

The National Survey of American Jews (NSAJ) conducted by Cohen in January and February 1989 found that 38 percent of American Jews agreed that "it is good that the United States decided to talk with the PLO," while 28 percent disagreed and 38 percent said they were not sure. The extent to which American Jews share the general American belief in the value of talks and are eager for the United States to be involved in the peace process is reflected in the significant fact that fewer than three out of ten American Jews expressed clear opposition to Washington's decision.[74] In the Jewish leadership survey toward the end of 1989, Cohen found that 63 percent approved and only 29 percent disapproved of American diplomats "having private discussions with those PLO officials who are often viewed as 'moderates'." Nearly three-quarters (74 percent) approved of Israeli officials doing so, but only a third approved of "American Jewish communal leaders" carrying on such dialogues, while 59 percent disapproved.[75]

Confusion on Specific Solutions to the Conflict

On specific questions concerning possible solutions for peace, the 1989 Roper poll showed that 59 percent of those questioned felt unqualified to respond. When asked the reasons, 35 percent admitted that they hadn't followed the situation closely enough to render a decision.[76] Similarly some of the "unsure" answers in the Jewish polls may also reflect ignorance of the details of Israeli politics. When the NSAJ asked the participants whether Shimon Peres and Yitzhak Shamir were from the same party, 34 percent admitted they did not know.[77] (As might be expected, the Jewish leadership is much more knowledgeable about the details of Israeli affairs.)

The *Los Angeles Times* poll that measured the attitudes of both Jewish and non-Jewish Americans in April 1988 found similar results. American Jews were split—31 percent in favor to 43 percent opposed—on the question of whether Israel should "give up the occupied territories in exchange for Arab recognition of Israel as part of a settlement." Presumably a higher percentage would favor trading some territory for peace. When Cohen asked a national Jewish sample around the same time in April 1988 whether they agreed that "Israel should offer the Arabs territorial compromise in the West Bank and Gaza in return for credible guarantees of peace," he found 38 percent agreed, 30 percent disagreed, and 26 percent said they were not sure.[78]

The *Los Angeles Times* found a far higher percentage who said they had not heard enough to make an intelligent choice among non-Jews (37 percent) than among Jews (8 percent). Of the non-Jews who considered themselves informed, the paper found 28 percent approved the land for peace formula, while 22 percent disapproved. (If one excludes the uninformed and those who were unsure, the concept of territorial compromise was supported by a majority of 56 percent to 44 percent.)

Israeli author Yael Dayan was quoted in *Newsweek* on the dilemma American Jews faced.[79] The roughly 50–50 split in Israeli opinion on the peace process has led Americans to be "agnostic" about the occupied territories, she said: "They're ill-informed and frightened, afraid to decide even in their own minds between those who say we can't give up the territories and those like me who say we're strong enough to compromise."

But despite their ambivalence on pressing the land for peace formula, 61 percent of the Jews in the *Los Angeles Times* poll favored the then current Shultz peace initiative, including the convening of an international peace conference, as did a similar percentage of non-Jews. Only 17 percent of the Jews were opposed. Strongest opposition came from the Orthodox, but even they supported the Shultz initiative by 41 to 23 percent. The remainder of the Jews said they were unaware or unsure.[80]

These numbers suggest that many Jews favor active American diplomatic efforts to solve the Arab-Israeli conflict, even where the stated American position may be at some variance from the official Israeli position. It should be noted that both the Reagan and Bush administrations have repeatedly declared their opposition to any imposed solution, claiming that they would not exert pressure upon Israel and that they were committed to maintaining Israel's security.

Reluctance on Pressing Israel to Talk to the PLO

On the question of whether *Israel* should talk to the PLO, the American public remains divided. In both April 1988 and April 1989 the Roper Poll asked the following: "Israel has agreed to meet with local Palestinian representatives but refuses to negotiate with the PLO, claiming that it is a terrorist organization. Do you think Israel is right or wrong in refusing to negotiate with the PLO?" The percentage of those agreeing with Israel's stand went down from 44 to 42, while those feeling that Israel was wrong went up from 27 to 32 percent. Presumably the slight increase in those favoring Israeli-PLO talks reflected Arafat's more conciliatory declarations and the U.S. decision to open its own talks with the PLO.[81]

When Cohen asked the national Jewish sample in February 1989 whether they agreed that "Israel should talk to the PLO without any further preconditions," only 19 percent agreed, 69 percent disagreed. However, when the proposition posed was "If the PLO recognizes Israel and renounces terrorism, Israel should be willing to talk with the PLO," a clear 58 percent majority of American Jews agreed and only 18 percent disagreed. The rest said they were not sure.

Interestingly, when the latter question was asked in April 1989, a full two-thirds (67 percent) agreed and 17 percent disagreed. The shift was reflected mainly in an increase in the number of those who were not sure, presumably because they were receiving mixed signals: The U.S. government was acting on the proposition that the PLO had in fact recognized Israel and had renounced terrorism, while the Government of Israel kept insisting that Arafat had only engaged in a tactical maneuver to gain American recognition. The continuation of the violent aspects of the Intifada, including murderous attacks by Muslim fundamentalists, coupled with terrorist attacks by radical leftist Palestinian factions from outside, left most American Jews still skeptical of Palestinian peaceful intentions.[82]

Cohen noted the "striking parallels" between Israeli and American Jewish public opinion on this matter. A *New York Times*–commissioned poll, published on April 2, 1989, found only 18 percent of Israelis favoring Israeli negotiations with the PLO on the basis of Arafat's recent declarations. However 58 percent of the Israelis said they favored Israeli government talks with the PLO if it "officially recognizes Israel and ceases terrorist activity"—precisely the same figure as the percentage Cohen found among American Jews who favored such talks.

One conclusion to be drawn is that the divisions in Israeli thinking on the Arab-Israel issue are largely reflected in the American Jewish community. For the Americans, however, there is a more delicate additional issue, namely, whether actively and publicly to urge the Israelis to take a particular course of action.

American Jewish Dilemma: Whether to Criticize Israeli Policies

As noted, American Jews have naturally been eager for the peace process to be resumed and for a political solution that would bring the Intifada to an end. In February 1989, after the Intifada had gone on for more than a year and Shultz's diplomatic efforts had failed to bear fruit, there was much concern in Jewish community leadership over whether Prime Minister Shamir's government was really prepared to undertake the necessary innovative policies to promote the peace process. One indication of this concern was the heated debate during the annual plenum of the National Jewish Community Relations Advisory Council (NJCRAC) in Washington in mid-February over an amendment to the group's Middle East strategic goals. Theodore Mann, former chair of NJCRAC, past chair of the Conference of Presidents of Major American Jewish Organizations, and past president of the American Jewish Congress, proposed an amendment on behalf of the Congress that would have the NJCRAC "express to the Israeli leadership our unalterable commitment to their security, as well as our continuing deep concern over the profound consequences of a continuation of the status quo in the territories."

The proposal was narrowly defeated by a 157–151 vote of the

umbrella group, whose members include 13 national Jewish organizations and 117 local community relations councils.[83] The matter was then referred back to the Israel Task Force of NJCRAC, which after further debate adopted compromise language that expressed American Jewish concern but muted the implied criticism of Israeli policy. The relevant section dealing with the Intifada in NJCRAC's *Joint Program Plan, 1989-90* states: "The Jewish community relations field should . . . continue to interpret to the general community the complex challenges faced by Israel in its ongoing efforts to restore order in the West Bank and Gaza Strip; continue to monitor the impact of the extended violence in the West Bank and Gaza Strip on the Jewish community and American public opinion and seek appropriate ways of communicating these findings to Israeli leaders; share with the Israeli leadership and people the field's deep solidarity with them and unalterable commitment to their security; convey to Israeli leadership a concern *which the field shares with them* over the status quo in the territories" (emphasis added).

One reason behind this trend toward greater public questioning of Israeli policies is a concern for the overall moral integrity of the Jewish state. When asked by the *Los Angeles Times* about the order of priority in determining their Jewish identity, 50 percent of the Jews named "a commitment to social equality" as number one. Religious observance and support for Israel were each cited by 17 percent.[84]

The tensions over the moral fiber and character of Israeli society were indicated in the polls. When asked by the *Los Angeles Times* if they felt that the occupation "will erode Israel's democratic and humanitarian character," 35 percent felt that it would, compared with 45 percent who felt it would not. (The non-Jewish sample was split 35 percent to 32 percent, with a higher percentage registering uncertainty than among the Jewish sample.)[85] As already stated, the NSAJ showed a similar division: 26 percent agreed, 38 percent disagreed, and 35 percent were not sure.[86]

One effect of the controversy on what concessions Israel should be prepared to make for peace was reflected in the growing resistance among Diaspora Jews to giving the Shamir government a blank check endorsement. To buttress his position on the eve of his trip to Washington to meet with the new Bush administration, Shamir convened a solidarity conference in Jerusalem in March

1989. To gain maximum support, the conference was ostensibly nonpartisan and cosponsored by Labor as well as Likud. The fundamental differences were papered over by a lowest-common-denominator declaration that served as an oblique method of gaining general support for Israel while evading specific issues. A key sentence reads, "We are unified by our common heritage, the moral values that flow from it and our love for Israel which transcends the diversity of our views." Despite the short notice, 1,500 leaders from American and European communities attended.

Reportedly fewer than half of the British Jews invited responded to the invitation while a few of the leaders decided to boycott the conference entirely. Sir Isaiah Berlin was quoted in the London *Jewish Chronicle* as saying, "Talking to [Shamir] is like talking to a stone wall."[87] Some American Jewish liberal activists spearheaded by *Tikkun* magazine's editor, Michael Lerner, expressed disdain for Shamir's tactics. A full-page advertisement in the *New York Times* on April 5, 1989, timed to coincide with Shamir's visit to the White House and signed by many prominent liberal individuals, the late Abbie Hoffman and women's rights activist and author Betty Friedan, for example, read, "NO, MR. SHAMIR. Don't assume that American Jews support your policies towards the Palestinians."

However, when during his Washington visit Mr. Shamir unveiled his four-point peace plan, including a proposal for elections among the Palestinians in the territories, American Jewish leadership breathed a sigh of relief. They were eager to welcome a positive initiative that also won approval in principle from President Bush and Secretary of State James Baker. Of course differences quickly reemerged both in Israel and with American Jewry over the complex details of implementation.[88]

To counteract such critical comments, in advance of Shamir's subsequent trip in mid-November 1989, the Conference of Presidents of Major American Jewish Organizations published an advertisement in the *New York Times* and the *Washington Post* addressed to the prime minister and timed for his arrival in Washington. The letter declared their "unity and solidarity" for the government's "search for lasting peace and security" and a wish for the prime minister's success in his talks with President Bush and Secretary of State Baker. This vague, general statement was the most the member organizations of this umbrella group could agree on. The earlier draft, which endorsed the official Likud position, included many hard-line statements such as no talks with the PLO and insistence that the discussion with the proposed Palestinian Arab delegation "must limit itself to the election procedures," was published in the *New York Times* on the same day by B'nai B'rith International. (Seymour D. Reich, president of B'nai B'rith, was also the current chairman of the Presidents Conference.)[89]

More significantly, a letter delivered to Shamir on the eve of his appearance before the General Assembly of the Council of Jewish Federations in Cincinnati at the same time reflected a growing frustration with Likud policies among some American Jewish leaders, as well as an attempt to avert what had happened during earlier visits. For example, Shamir had used the standing ovation he received while addressing a UJA meeting to show the U.S. administration and the Israeli public that he had overwhelming Jewish support for his policies. This letter noted that "profound differences" on how to proceed with the Middle East peace process existed in Israel and the U.S. Most of the forty-one signatories were *past* officials of major American Jewish organizations. The letter centered on Shamir's rejection of the land-for-peace principle as a basis for negotiations and pointed out that most American Jews do not reject territorial compromise.

The issuance of the two documents at the same time reflects the fact that, although many individual Jewish leaders are upset with Shamir's policies, the current leaders of mainstream organizations are still reluctant to criticize Shamir in public. Reportedly the current top officials of major Jewish organizations were not asked to sign, since the sponsors of the letter realized that they would not feel free to act without the approval of their boards.[90]

A dovish mainstream group called Nishma (Hebrew for "let us listen") was formed in 1987 at the time of the visit to the United States of four former Israeli generals, who head the 600-member Israeli Council for Peace and Security, which contends that Israel's security can be safeguarded even with territorial compromise. Nishma works to provide a broader forum for the group's viewpoint by arranging briefings for Jewish leaders and distributing articles.[91] Earl Raab, past director of the San Francisco Community Relations Council and cochairman of Nishma, says that American Jews who are critical of Israeli policies supporting the status quo should "flaunt their strategic differences with the majority [National Unity] Government." He contends that this would help rather than hurt Israel, "as long as spokesmen for the center bound their criticism with the need to support Israel."[92]

Not all Jews were prepared to be so limited in their criticism. Since the outbreak of the Intifada, several liberal and leftist organizations and groups of individuals, many of whom had been critical of Israel for years, voiced sharp public opposition to American support for the current Israeli government and its policies through full-page newspaper advertisements. One, sponsored by an ad hoc group calling themselves "Jews Opposed to the Occupation," included Noam Chomsky, a long-time critic of the Israeli establishment, and others covering a wide occupational and geographical spectrum. They asked fellow American Jews to "join with world opinion and the growing dissident movement in Israel in condemning the Israeli government's brutal actions against the Palestinian uprising" and called upon the American government to end military, political and economic support for the occupation.[93] Other statements expressed a similar sentiment: basically, a dissociation from Israeli policies and a call for an international peace conference.[94]

Filmmaker Woody Allen, a self-professed nonactivist, felt the need to "take a public stance" and express his perplexity over Israel's handling of the Intifada in an Op-Ed column in the *New York Times*: "As a supporter of Israel and as one who has always been outraged at the horrors inflicted on this little nation by hostile neighbors . . . I am appalled beyond measure by the treatment of the rioting Palestinians by the Jews."[95] He went on to say that those who "are rooting for Israel to exist and prosper" have an obligation to speak out and put an end to "this wrongheaded approach."

Beyond criticism there has been direct political action. A notable example was the establishment in July 1989 of the Jewish Peace Lobby, headed by Jerome Segal, then a professor at the University of Maryland.[96] The group, which includes some well-known rabbis, scholars, writers, and public figures, claims to have been formed to provide an alternative to the American Israel Public Affairs Committee (AIPAC).[97] The peace lobby supports the right of Israel to live at peace within secure and well-defined boundaries; the right of the Palestinian people to self-determination, including the right to an independent state, which would live at peace with Israel; and the right of the Palestinian people to be represented by leadership of their choice, including representation by the PLO or by the provisional government of the State of Palestine, should such a government be established.

Whether the organized leadership accurately reflects views of the grass roots in the Jewish community remains in dispute and is the subject of increasing debate.[98] As discussed, in the spring of 1989, Columbia University hosted a conference entitled "The Road to Peace," cosponsored by both Arab and Jewish groups. At that conference Ester Leah Ritz, a member of the board of the Jewish Agency and Council of Jewish Federations, said she believed that "the gap between the Jewish community and its leadership is growing and there is a great silent majority . . . there must be a relationship with the Palestinian people leading to a two-state solution, but the silent majority is not ready to take that step. The 'peaceniks' of American Jewry cannot . . . isolate themselves from the rest of the community." (Ritz was among the forty-one Jewish communal leaders who wrote the letter to Shamir.)[99]

Arye Naor, who was cabinet secretary in the first Begin government, disagrees. Naor claims that North American Jewry is changing, that the "number of activists interested in the details of Israeli politics is declining, while the rest tend increasingly to the extreme."[100] While speaking with different Jewish groups on a trip to the United States at the end of 1989, Naor reports that he heard increasingly hard-line suggestions such as the "transfer" of the Palestinians east of the Jordan River. He does not believe this means that "American Jewry" is becoming more radical. Rather, it is a result of an opposite process—that more and more Jews are keeping aloof from Israel's policies. He sees a gradual erosion of American Jewish participation in discussions and activities concerning Israel. He attributes this decline to the absence of reasonable solutions to the problems in the West Bank and Gaza consistent with American Jews' commitment to a democratic Jewish state.

As a result, they prefer to remain quiet. "The more the right-wing radicals express their point of view, the less the liberals are interested in participating," Naor concludes.

He warns that as a result of American Jewry's "wish to defend Israel or at least not to criticize it," Israel "is becoming less significant in [its] self-identification." As an illustration of his thesis that "Israel is being pushed to the sidelines," Naor cites the fact that at the recent conference of the Union of American Hebrew Congregations in New Orleans, only four out of 125 working meetings were concerned with Israeli issues, and UAHC President Rabbi Alexander Schindler devoted only five minutes to Israel in his 75-minute opening speech. When asked, Rabbi Schindler dismissed Naor's conclusion. The Reform movement and he personally remained deeply concerned about Israeli affairs, Schindler said. He had publicly denounced Defense Minister Rabin's declared policy of beatings of Palestinian protesters, and the UAHC had both before and shortly after the outbreak of the Intifada reiterated its position that the status quo was not viable and that Israel should be prepared to trade territory for peace. He said he devoted about ten minutes to Israel in his speech, but since he had nothing new to say on the subject, he dedicated the bulk of his speech to the many other pressing issues facing the Reform movement.[101]

Conclusions

A good example of the dilemmas facing the dovish mainstream of American Jewish leadership in weighing whether to engage in public criticism of specific Israeli policies is the media coverage given to the letter of the forty-one Jewish communal leaders. The headlines and the leads in the *New York Times*, the *Washington Post*, and other major media outlets focused on the paragraph in the open letter to Prime Minister Shamir that said, "When you are presented to the General Assembly [of the Council of Jewish Federations] and all rise to greet you with every courtesy that is due the Prime Minister of Israel, we respectfully ask of you this: Do not mistake courtesy for consensus, or applause for endorsement of all the policies you pursue."

But the major papers either buried near the bottom of the story or totally ignored the immediately preceding paragraph in the Jewish leaders' letter. Yet it is the sentiment expressed in this paragraph that, despite the divisions over land-for-peace and widespread anguish over the Intifada, continues to reflect the basic consensus of solidarity with Israel within the American Jewish community: "We recognize, of course, the danger that Israel's enemies may try to exploit such differences [over the principle of land for peace with secure borders], and so we say as clearly as possible: Let no one, friend or foe, mistake our differences with regard to particular policies as signifying any attrition whatsoever in our support for Israel's people and their right to a national life free of terrorism and war."[102]

How has this tension between basic American Jewish solidarity with Israel and the increasing feelings of misgiving about specific Israeli policies been manifested in American Jewish reactions to the turbulent events of recent months? There was widespread disappointment in the American Jewish community over Prime Minister Shamir's rejection of the compromise formula for tripartite talks leading to Palestinian elections that Secretary Baker had so arduously worked to achieve. From numerous conversations it is clear to me that those American Jews who follow Israeli internal affairs have come to share the Israeli public's close to universal feelings of dismay at the months of paralysis of the political process, frustration at the politicians' unwillingness to reform the current electoral system, and disgust over the unbelievably tawdry political bargaining that accompanied the unsuccessful efforts of Shimon Peres and the ultimately successful effort of Yitzhak Shamir to assemble a 61-seat majority in the Knesset.

The end of the Cold War and the triumph of freedom in many dictatorial parts of the world also have had their effect. After the leader of the apartheid regime of South Africa freed Nelson Mandela and agreed to negotiate with the African National Congress, which had long been officially branded as a "terrorist organization," American Jews were increasingly being asked by their liberal American Christian friends, "If De Klerk can speak to Mandela, why won't Shamir talk to Arafat?" (Presumably such comments have become less frequent since Arafat rushed to embrace Saddam Hussein after the Iraqi dictator invaded Kuwait.)

American Jewish leadership was outraged and flabbergasted when it was revealed, in the face of earlier denials, that the Government of Israel had secretly allocated $1.8 million to enable a Jewish religious zealot group to purchase St. John's Hospice in the Christian quarter of the Old City of Jerusalem adjacent to the Church of the Holy Sepulchre and to move in 150 adherents of the group at the precise moment when the world media had converged on Jerusalem to cover the rare congruence of Passover, Latin and Eastern Orthodox Easter, and Ramadan.

In a virtually unprecedented move, AIPAC informed the *New York Times* that it had strongly protested to the Government of Israel over this action, which AIPAC felt could seriously jeopardize continued U.S. financial support for Israel, especially the $400 million loan guarantee Israel was seeking to lower the cost of obtaining mortgages for the large number of new houses Israel would have to construct to shelter the ever growing influx of more than 100,000 Jews fleeing the Soviet Union. When the Presidents Conference met in emergency session to discuss what to do, the only question was whether to issue a public statement. Private expressions of concern and consternation had already been conveyed to Jerusalem by Seymour Reich and by the heads of many constituent organizations. Even those members who were most ardent supporters of the Likud and of the right of Jews to settle anywhere in the holy land, especially in Jerusalem, agreed that the Government of Israel had acted unwisely and imprudently in this matter.

This was also the consensus in the American Jewish community after Prime Minister Shamir had made his off-the-cuff remark to a Likud gathering that "big immigration requires Israel to be big as well."[103] When the administration in Washington criticized the statement and warned that American aid would continue to be restricted to use within pre-1967 Israel, Shamir tried to explain that he didn't necessarily mean a geographically large Israel but one large in spirit. But the damage was done.

Shamir's words galvanized into action the opposition that had already begun to brew in the Arab world. But potentially even more ominous, Shamir's words embarrassed the Soviet Union, which responded by delaying implementation of a draft agreement for direct flights to Israel, warning that it would have to reexamine its policy of free emigration unless Israel gave firm assurances that Soviet Jews were not settled in the occupied territories. Moreover, Shamir's words infuriated President Bush, who was viscerally opposed to new Israeli settlements in the territories, since he felt, rightly or wrongly, that they seriously impeded the prospects for Palestinian-Israeli peace. A majority of American Jewish leaders shared these sentiments. But even those American Jews who favored additional settlements in principle were critical of the prime minister for his public confrontational stance. They were also concerned that Shamir's words would not only endanger prospects for approval of Israel's request for the $400 million in housing loan guarantees but would also strengthen the hands of Chief of Staff John Sununu and other administration officials who wanted to subject all American aid to Israel to the same close scrutiny and line-by-line supervision given to other aid recipients to make sure that Israel could not, in the words of the *Post* editorial, pay "West Bank bills from another account." (The Bush administration approved the loan guarantees after Foreign Minister David Levy finally gave the assurances requested by the United States, but Levy's letter caused further controversy within Israel's right-wing Likud.)

But facing these recent developments that caused American Jews to express their displeasure with Israeli actions either privately to the Israeli Government or publicly, or both, there were other actions by the Bush administration, the Palestinians, the Arab states, and the United Nations that reinforced the perception of Israel as subjected to unfair criticism, and to threats to its vital interests. A statement by President Bush on March 3 opposing new settlements "in the West Bank or East Jerusalem," and other administration statements questioning Israel's sovereignty over the entire city, touched a raw nerve in the Jewish community. There was a concerted campaign by the Jewish leadership with strong grass-roots support that resulted in reassurances by the president and resolutions by both houses of Congress reaffirming a united Jerusalem as Israel's capital.

There was also outrage in the Jewish community when Cardinal John O'Connor of New York called the St. Johns Hospice incident "obscene" and raised unfounded questions about the Israeli Government's attitude to Christians in Israel. Similarly, while many American Jews had serious reservations about Prime Minister Shamir's settlement policy, they vigorously opposed Arab attempts to stop Soviet Jewish immigration to Israel.

American Jews also saw evidence of Israel's international isolation when only an American veto prevented the UN Security Council from voting 14 to 1 to send an investigative commission to Israel because of the violence that had followed the killing of seven Palestinians by a deranged Israeli. American Jews shared Foreign Minister Moshe Arens's anger at the double standard at the UN, which had not investigated a deranged Egyptian soldier's killing of Israeli tourists.[104]

This anger in the American Jewish community was multiplied many times over when the United States on October 12 supported a UN Security Council resolution especially condemning "the acts of violence committed by the Israeli security forces" which resulted in the killing of twenty-one Palestinians who had rioted on the Temple Mount, without equally forcefully condemning the Palestinians' stoning of thousands of Jewish Sukkot holiday worshippers at the Western Wall below, which had preceded and precipitated the Israeli action. The resolution also called on the UN secretary-general to send an investigative mission to Israel.[105] Ambassador Thomas Pickering, the American representative to the United Nations, was subjected to unusually sharp and universal criticism when he tried to explain the American position before a closed meeting of the Presidents Conference.

Finally, the bellicose statements of Iraqi President Saddam Hussein, who threatened to burn half of Israel with chemical weapons, and the attempted terrorist attack on Israeli civilians along the Tel Aviv beach resort area by the Palestine Liberation Front, a constituent group within the PLO, reinforced the feeling in the Jewish community that Israel was still surrounded by hostile elements.

In the face of clear threats to Israel's safety, American Jews remain quick to show their solidarity. After Arafat disclaimed any knowledge of or responsibility for the PLF's terrorist attack but refused categorically to condemn the attack or to take steps to expel PLF chief Abul Abbas from the PLO's executive committee, even the most dovish members of the American Jewish leadership voiced their outrage. Menachem Z. Rosensaft, one of the five Jewish leaders who had met with Arafat in Stockholm in December

1988, called his statement "woefully insufficient. It doesn't unambiguously renounce this latest terrorist attack against Israel, an attack I consider a violation of his statements to us that the P.L.O. has renounced terrorism." Rosensaft concluded that "under these circumstances I believe that the U.S. government should reassess, and probably abrogate, its dialogue with the PLO." Rita Hauser, who also took part in the Stockholm talks and had since been urging Israel to open discussions with the PLO, agreed that this was "a real test case. Arafat has to dissociate himself from this unequivocally and immediately."[106] American Jewish leaders welcomed the American decision in June to suspend dialogue with the PLO.

Disenchantment with the Palestinians and disgust for the PLO intensified among Jews and the general public in the United States in August 1990 after PLO Chairman Arafat appeared to back Saddam Hussein in his occupation of Kuwait and against the U.S.-led international coalition. Prospects for dialogue between Palestinians and American or Israeli Jews were further set back in January 1991 by reports of Palestinians in Jordan and in the West Bank and Gaza expressing delight that the Iraqi ruler had carried out his threats against Israel by repeatedly launching SCUD missiles to terrorize Israel's civilian population. The attacks also galvanized the American Jewish community into action, reawakened a sense of the Jewish people's vulnerability, and brought forth an outpouring of expressions of solidarity—in demonstrations, political action, financial contributions, and personal volunteering—that was reminiscent of the response to the earlier wartime crises of 1967 and 1973. It is too early to tell how lasting this effect will be and how the American Jewish community will divide when differences between Washington and Jerusalem again begin to erupt over resumption of the Arab-Israel peace process, and particularly on how to resolve the Palestinian grievances that led to the Intifada.

Notes

1. For an analysis and comparison of the Jewish and general American responses to specific questions on Middle East issues posed by the *Los Angeles Times*, see George E. Gruen, "The Not-So-Silent Partnership: Emerging Trends in American Jewish-Israeli Relationships," in *Israel after Begin*, ed. Gregory S. Mahler (Albany: State University of New York Press, 1990), 209–32.

2. A comparison of current attitudes with those of earlier years is contained in Steven M. Cohen, *Ties and Tensions: An Update, the 1989 Survey of American Jewish Attitudes Toward Israel and Israelis* (New York: American Jewish Committee, 1989) (hereafter cited as Cohen, NSAJ, with the year of the poll and the page of the report).

3. Steven M. Cohen, *Israel-Diaspora Relations: A Survey of American Jewish Leaders* (Tel Aviv: Israel-Diaspora Institute, Report No. 8, 1990). Of the sample of 1,310 American Jewish lay and professional organizational leaders and academics involved with Israel who were queried by mail, 780 filled out and returned the questionnaire.

4. Robert Scheer, "U.S. Jews for Peace Talks on Mideast," *Los Angeles Times*, April 12, 1988.

5. Some even threatened to cut back on their contributions to Israel. See Milton Goldin, "Politics and Philanthropy: The State of Jewish 'Giving'," *Congress Monthly* (September/October 1989), 8, and discussion in this chapter. See also Charles Hoffman, *The "Who Is A Jew" Controversy: Retrospect and Prospect* (New York: American Jewish Committee, January 1990); Robert O. Freedman, "Religion and Politics in the 1988 Israeli Election Campaign," *Middle East Journal* 43, no. 3 (Summer 1989): 406–22.

6. See note 1. First published as a monograph by the American Jewish Committee in September 1988. See also J.J. Goldberg, "For U.S. Jews, a Slightly Tarnished Golden Age," *Jewish Week*, January 5, 1990, 3, 33.

7. Cohen, *SAJL*, 41.

8. Ibid., 20–24.

9. Steven M. Cohen and Sid Groeneman, "American Jews and Israel: After a Year of Intifada," paper presented at the annual National Meeting of the American Association for Public Opinion Research in Lancaster, Pennsylvania, May 17–20, 1990 (mimeo), 3.

10. Wolf Blitzer, "U.S. Friends Are Still There, Despite the Criticism," *Jerusalem Post International Edition*, December 2, 1989, 1–2.

11. Interview by the author with Stanley Horowitz, December 14, 1989. Figures furnished by UJA headquarters in New York. Extraneous factors may have influenced the decline between 1987 and 1988. Impending changes in the tax law made it more advantageous to contribute in 1987. The stock market crash in November 1987 had a negative impact, most of which was apparently reflected in 1988 giving.

12. Oral communication from UJA national headquarters to the author on November 8, 1990.

13. United Jewish Appeal Campaign Hotline, October 26, 1990.

14. Goldin, "Politics and Philanthropy," 8–10.

15. Arthur Hertzberg, "The Illusion of Jewish Unity," *New York Review of Books*, June 16, 1988. Hertzberg contends that the percentage is likely to fall further if the current government led by Prime Minister Shamir

continues to be influenced by right-wing "hawks," since this will alienate many American Jewish supporters of Israel.

16. Personal conversation of the author with Rabbi Harold Kushner, New York, June 2, 1990.

17. Goldin, "Politics and Philanthropy," 8–10. For a fuller discussion of these issues, see Barry A. Kosmin, "The Dimensions of Contemporary American Jewish Philanthropy," paper delivered at the Conference on Jewish Philanthropy in Contemporary America, Center for Jewish Studies, Graduate School and University Center, CUNY, June 15–16, 1988. The papers of the conference were to be published by Roman and Littlefield in November 1990.

18. Joel Brinkley, "Soviet Jews Leave at a Record Pace, Many for Israel," *New York Times*, December 14, 1989. After initial plans to allocate only 25 percent of the Passage to Freedom funds to the Jewish Agency drew the ire of the Zionists, agreement was reached under which the UJA promised to allocate to the agency the "major portion" of $37.5 million in campaign proceeds earmarked for overseas needs (Jewish Telegraphic Agency dispatch from New York, April 18, 1989).

19. Goldin, "Politics and Philanthropy," 8.

20. Amos Elon, "Letter From Israel," *New Yorker*, February 13, 1989, 74–80.

21. Goldin, 8. See Hoffman, *The "Who Is A Jew" Controversy*.

22. New Israel Fund, *Annual Report*, November 1989, 4.

23. This view was expressed to the author by Rabbi Zelig Chinitz. See the paper prepared by Barry Kosmin, n. 17.

24. Cohen, *SAJL*, p. 45.

25. *Los Angeles Times* Poll conducted March 26–April 7, 1988, question 39.

26. Cohen, *SAJL*, p. 31.

27. Op-Ed article by Senator Robert Dole, *New York Times*, January 16, 1990; *Times* editorial, "Mr. Dole Milks a Miniature Cow," January 17, 1990. Senator Rudy Boschowitz (R-Minn.) responded to Dole in a letter to the editor, *New York Times*, January 29, 1990.

28. After reaching record numbers in 1985, American tourism to Israel, as well as to Europe, had suffered an even sharper decline in 1986 because of a wave of spectacular terrorist attacks against airliners and terminals in Europe. According to the Israel Ministry of Tourism, tourism from the U.S. reached a high of 380,000 in 1985, dropped sharply to 212,000 in 1986, picked up to 330,000 in 1987 and declined to 280,000 in 1988. The total for the first eleven months of 1989 was 240,700, with increases over 1988 figures in every month since April.

29. Israel Ministry of Tourism, North America, "Tourism to Israel Heading Toward a Record Year," press release, New York, May 29, 1990.

30. See for example, Uri Gordon, "Israel-Diaspora Relations at a Fateful Crossroads," *Forum* (New York: North American Jewish Forum/United Jewish Appeal) 2, no. 1 (Autumn 1989): 14–15, 18–19. Gordon is head of Immigration and Absorption for the Jewish Agency.

31. Cohen, NSAJ, 1988 poll, 9.

32. Ibid.

33. *Los Angeles Times*, 1988.

34. Cohen, *SAJL*, p. 27.

35. For texts of the agreement and discussion of the issues at the time, see *In Vigilant Brotherhood* [by George E. Gruen] (New York: American Jewish Committee, 1965), 53–58, 64–70. For reemergence of the issues in wake of the Pollard affair, see George E. Gruen, *Back To Basic Principles*, (Jerusalem: American Jewish Committee, 1987), and *The Not-So-Silent Partnership*.

36. Cohen, NSAJ, 1989 poll, 22.

37. Ibid.

38. Eytan Gilboa, "The Palestinian Uprising: Has It Turned American Public Opinion?" *Orbis* (Winter 1989): 24, table 1.

39. Cohen, NSAJ, 1989 poll, p. 27.

40. Ibid. See pp. 240–42 for a comparison with American non-Jewish opinion.

41. Steven M. Cohen, *Ties and Tensions: An Update*, 21, tables on 23.

42. Ibid.; see also 22–23 for related questions.

43. For some examples, see pp. 237–39, 251–54.

44. Goldberg, "For American Jews, It Was a Slightly Tarnished Age," p. 33.

45. The two conferences and other similar efforts at dialogue are discussed by Carolyn Toll Oppenheim, "Talking Peace: American Jews, Israeli Doves and Palestinians Push for a Political Settlement," *Present Tense* (September–October 1989): 32–38.

46. Andrew Silow Carroll, "Arens Warns U.S. Jewish Leaders Not to Fail Israel in Support," *Jewish Telegraphic Agency Daily News Bulletin*, March 17, 1989.

47. For text of letter see *New York Times*, April 7, 1989.

48. Advertisement printed in *Jewish Week*, April 29, 1989.

49. For text see *New York Times*, April 1, 1988.

50. Charlotte Holstein, a member of AJC's Board of Governors, has long been involved in an Arab-Jewish dialogue in Syracuse. She told the author that her own experience confirms the impression that many more Jews and Arab Americans are prepared to participate now than before the Intifada.

51. Oppenheim, "Talking Peace," 34.

52. Cohen, *Ties and Tensions*, 11–15, 21.

53. Mitchell Bard, "Israel: Some Surprising Polls," *Commentary* (Au-

gust 1989): 46. Bard presents a generally optimistic interpretation of recent opinion polls and denies that there is any evidence as yet of a decline in either general or Jewish support for Israel.

54. *New York Times*, March 6, 1988; text of letter, *New York Times*, March 7, 1988.

55. *New York Times*, March 7, 1989.

56. Ibid.

57. Both results were reported in a release, "The *New York Times*/CBS News Poll Foreign Policy Survey, May 9–11, 1989," question 12. There was no breakdown by religion in the American national sample of 1,073 respondents.

58. Ibid., question 11.

59. David Singer and Renae Cohen, *Israel and the Intifada: The Findings of the April 1989 Roper Poll* (New York: Institute of Human Relations, The American Jewish Committee, 1989), 4. The poll was conducted between April 15 and 22, 1989.

60. Alvin Richman, "The Polls: A Report," *Public Opinion Quarterly* (Fall 1989).

61. CBS News Poll/*New York Times*, press release, July 8, 1990, and William E. Schmidt, "Americans' Support for Israel: Solid, but Not the Rock It Was," *New York Times*, July 9, 1990.

62. "*Times*/CBS Foreign Policy Survey," question 10. As noted, the American poll results did not include a breakdown by religion. From other data it is clear that American Jews are closer to Israeli Jews than to American non-Jews in believing that Israel is not only interested in but eager to achieve peace.

63. Schmidt, "Americans' Support," and CBS News/*New York Times* Poll, press release, July 8, 1990. The question was somewhat ambiguous. While it asked about the "Palestinian minority in Israel" it presumably referred to the Palestinians in the Israeli-held territories rather than Palestinian Arabs who are Israeli citizens. In theory, even strong supporters of Israel's security concerns and opponents of a Palestinian state in the territories might favor a more sympathetic approach to the concerns of Israel's internal Arab minority.

64. Cohen, *SAJL*, 92.

65. Robert Scheer, "U.S. Jews for Peace Talks on Mideast," *Los Angeles Times*, April 12, 1988.

66. Gilboa, "The Palestinian Uprising," 31, table 6.

67. For texts of Arafat's statement in Geneva and Shultz's statement and news conference in Washington, see *New York Times*, December 15, 1988.

68. American Jewish Committee Press Release No. 88-960-218, December 15, 1989.

69. See Tamar Jacoby, "A Family Quarrel," *Newsweek*, April 3, 1989.

70. Mark J. Penn and Douglas E. Schoen, "American Attitudes toward the Middle East," *Public Opinion* (May/June 1988): 45.

71. "The Polls—A Report: American Attitudes toward Israeli-Palestinian Relations in the Wake of the Uprising," *Public Opinion Quarterly* (Fall 1989): 420. See Gilboa, "The Palestinian Uprising," 27–32.

72. Richman, "The Polls," 428, quoting from Marttila and Kiley/American Jewish Congress poll conducted April 18–24, 1988. However, in the same poll only 30 percent said the United States should recognize the PLO as "the official representative of the Palestinian people."

73. Ibid., 429, citing Media General/Associated Press poll conducted January 4–12, 1989. Yet in the same poll only 11 percent supported the PLO's claim to be the only group to represent the Palestinians, while 63 percent agreed that some other group, e.g., a joint delegation of Palestinians and Jordanians, could represent the Palestinians.

74. Cohen, *Ties and Tensions*, 28.

75. Cohen, SAJL, 89.

76. Singer and Cohen, *Israel and the Intifada*; NSAJ, 1989 poll.

77. Cohen, NSAJ, 1988 poll, 54.

78. Ibid., 27. The figures in the 1989 poll were 38, 30, and 31 percent, respectively.

79. Jacoby, "A Family Quarrel."

80. Robert Scheer, "U.S. Jews for Peace Talks on Mideast," *Los Angeles Times*, April 12, 1988, and Scheer, "Jews in U.S. Committed to Equality," *Los Angeles Times*, April 13, 1989.

81. Singer and Cohen, table 6. Gilboa found that the percentage of Americans who felt that Israel should talk to the PLO ranged from 27 percent to 63 percent in four different polls taken in early 1988. The highest figure was in an April *Chicago Tribune* poll. In that poll, however, an even larger majority insisted on the PLO's public recognition of Israel as a prior condition to talks (Gilboa, "The Palestinian Uprising," 32, table 7).

82. Gilboa, 28. See the Open Letter to Yasser Arafat by Menahem Rosensaft, *Newsweek*, December 11, 1989. Rosensaft, head of the Labor Zionist Alliance, had been one of the five American Jews who had gone to Stockholm the previous December to meet with Arafat and had been subjected to considerable criticism both within his own group and from the Conference of Presidents of Major American Jewish Organizations at the time. He now expressed his disappointment over Arafat's failure to deliver on his promises of coexistence with Israel, noting the continuation of attacks on Israeli civilians as well as the murder of Palestinians accused of "collaborating" with Israel.

83. Howard Rosenberg, "NJCRAC Narrowly Rejects Statement of Concern About the Territories," *JTA Bulletin*, February 22, 1989.

84. Robert Scheer, "U.S. Jews for Peace Talks on Mideast," *Los Angeles Times*, April 12, 1988, 14.
85. Ibid.
86. Cohen, 1989 NSAJ poll, 23.
87. *London Jewish Chronicle*, March 16, 1989.
88. On the Shamir plan, which was endorsed by the Israeli Government, and American Jewish reaction, see George E. Gruen, "Middle East Peace: A Progress Report," *AJC Journal* (Autumn 1989): 4–6.
89. *New York Times*, November 15, 1989.
90. Oral communication to the author from Hyman Bookbinder, one of the initiators of the letter, December 19, 1989.
91. Oppenheim, "Talking Peace," 35.
92. Ibid.
93. *New York Times*, April 27, 1988.
94. *New York Review of Books*, March 31, 1988.
95. For text of letter see *New York Times*, January 28, 1989.
96. Endorsers include Rabbis Max Vorspan, Marshall Meyer, Jacob Milgrom, Mordechai Liebling, and Balfour Brickner; entertainers Peter Yarrow and Ed Asner; writers Gloria Steinhem, Adrienne Rich, Anne Roiphe, Howard Fast, and Grace Paley; and Professors Robert O. Freedman, David Biale, Nathan Glazer, Stanley Hoffmann, and Sidney Morgenbesser. The American Advisory Board includes George McGovern, and most significantly, there is an Israeli Advisory Board including Moshe Amirav, city councilman in Jerusalem, Shlomo Elbaz of East for Peace, Chaim Shur, editor of *New Outlook*, Arie Jaffe of Mapam, and Victor Shemtov, a former Knesset Member.
97. Robert Peark, "U.S. Jews Organize to Urge Israel-PLO Talks," *New York Times*, July 23, 1989.
98. See, for example, Robert Spero, "Speaking for the Jews: Who Does the Conference of Presidents of Major American Jewish Organizations Really Represent?" *Present Tense* (January/February 1990): 15–27.
99. Oppenheim, "Talking Peace," 34.
100. Arye Naor, "Israel, Shunted to the Sidelines," *Jerusalem Post*, December 4, 1989.
101. Conversation by the author with Rabbi Schindler on December 7, 1989.
102. The *Washington Post* of November 17, 1989, headlined the story: "U.S. Jewish Officials Disagree with Shamir." The sentence reiterating basic support for Israel was relegated to the seventh paragraph. The *New York Times* headlined the story: "Warmth Does Not Mean Support, 41 American Jews Write Shamir." There was no reference to the sentence reiterating support for Israel. The *Times*'s article, by Thomas L. Friedman, concluded with a comment from Presidents' Conference Chairman

Seymour D. Reich calling the letter "mischievous" and declaring that it "does not reflect what I perceive to be the mood of the mainstream Jewish community, which is to give this Prime Minister his chance to wage peace his way."

103. Text as quoted in " 'Big Immigration . . . Big Israel'," a sharply critical editorial in the *Washington Post*, February 1, 1990.

104. "U.S. Vetoes U.N. Move" (United Nations, May 31), *New York Times*, June 1, 1990.

105. Text of Security Council resolution, *New York Times*, October 14, 1990.

106. Thomas L. Friedman, "Arafat Denies P.L.O. Tie to Raid but His Mild Stand Troubles U.S.," *New York Times*, June 1, 1990.

Part Three

The Impact of the Intifada on Israeli Politics and Society

Israeli Public Opinion and the Intifada

8

Asher Arian

Public opinion in Israel is characterized by high levels of knowledge and personal involvement regarding issues of security and by low levels of perceived influence.[1] This paradox points to the importance of the political leadership in forming both policy and public opinion. In a sense, this task is easier for the Israeli leadership, because the public is aware of the importance of the issue and is relatively well-informed. The public relies on the leadership and is aware of its own ineffectiveness. Having high levels of information but low levels of belief in their ability to influence policy, they keep their fingers on the pulse of the country (or on the on/off button of their remote-control television set), but the leadership's finger is on the trigger.

The public's reaction is often filtered by previous political leanings. An initiative by the right will always be harder for the left to oppose than the reverse situation, in which the left initiates and the right reacts. This is because of the central value of survival and the perceived relationship between that value and military preparedness and action. Because of the indecisive nature of political initiatives and the possibility that bargaining could lead to a weakening of military advantage, such proposals tend to be shied away from. The bombing of the Iraqi nuclear reactor under the

Begin government during the election campaign of 1981 left the Labor-Mapam alignment speechless at first and mildly supportive later. The 1982 incursion into Lebanon was preceded by warnings in closed session by the alignment leaders against the plans of the government headed by Begin and Sharon, but once the operation had started, these same leaders gave it, at least for the initial period, lukewarm public support. As Israeli political life is structured, it is hard to oppose military action; political initiatives are more easily questioned. In Nahum Barnea's phrasing, the Israeli left is experienced at shooting and then crying about it.

The public reflects these patterns. The instinct of supporting or rejecting a political initiative depending on its source is deeply ingrained in the Israeli collective psyche. However, an almost knee-jerk reflex of supporting "reasonable" military action is just as strong. Public opinion follows these underwater reefs and shoals in a remarkably predictable manner.

The Israeli population is alert, responsive, and malleable. Public opinion, although structured and sometimes organized, is not set in a firm and final manner. The fact that Israeli public opinion is formed primarily along political rather than class lines is enormously important, and this fact indicates the potential flexibility of public opinion if the proper conditions arise. It follows that the social institutions that might mediate in the process of forming the public's view are less important in Israel than is the role of political institutions, such as the party and the leader. The appeal of the party or a leadership group could possibly bring about change in the public stand regarding security and defense policy. This is more likely, it seems, than the possibility of class or group interests emerging to redefine public policy. While there is no necessary contradiction between the two, public opinion in Israel will likely follow a political route rather than a social one. This gives the political leaders enormous leverage. They can change policy, if they so decide, secure in the knowledge that they will be able to swing public opinion to their position if they properly present it; in short, if they lead. No less important, they can retain the status quo. They can make a case for that position as well.

Let me state clearly that there is no political message in what I write. While moderates and leftists might take heart, so too might hard-liners and rightists. The potential for change in Israeli public opinion has been identified, but we do not know the direction that change might take any more than we can predict whether or when it will take place. The important point is that it could go either way. For the first decades of Israeli history, with the dominance of the left-of-center party, Israeli public opinion supported a pragmatic policy of military strength and political flexibility. Since the 1967 war, policy—and public opinion—became intransigent regarding the territories (although Sinai was returned to the Egyptians during that period). In these years, a hard-line nationalist platform emerged with varying degrees of extremeness: Rabbi Meir Kahane was perhaps the most extreme, but the Tehiya party and some of the religious parties echoed some of his positions. The moderate overtures to the Arab states made by Shimon Peres during his 1984–86 premiership brought no clear results. Shamir and his election initiative followed the onset of the Intifada and the election results of 1988. The leadership was as polarized as was public opinion, but the major leaders worked together in a National Unity government.

But the system will probably not remain frozen, because public opinion can be changed. It is true that the 1980s have seen an almost even division in public opinion and in political power between the two major camps in Israeli politics. But that is an exception in Israeli history and in the experience of most nations. In the end, it is likely that *political* factors will bring about the shift in both policy and opinion.

THE Intifada has had far-reaching effects on Israeli politics and public opinion. Some of them are more obvious, others more subtle. This chapter will explore three features of this impact: first, the effects of the Intifada on Jewish public opinion as reported by respondents themselves; second, the influence of the Intifada on policy positions based on the responses of subjects who were interviewed at the outset of the Intifada and then reinterviewed about a year later; and third, the extent to which the Intifada drove the vote decision in the 1988 elections.

The emphasis of this chapter will be on Jewish opinion, but obviously Arab opinion has also been affected. The Intifada has had a major impact on them—both those who are citizens of Israel and those under its military rule. Israeli Arabs seemed to identify more fully than in the past with the nationalistic aspirations of the Palestinian cause;[2] but they also participated in the 1988 Israeli elections at higher rates than they had in recent elections, strengthening the analysis that sees them as active participants in Israeli democracy, aiming to further their individual and group preferences.[3] That they were divided among themselves explains the blurred effect their vote had on the election returns.

The Arabs of the territories, in turn, were galvanized by the Intifada into believing that they could play a major role in determining their own political future, while simultaneously giving the leaders of the PLO living outside Israel's jurisdiction a new political opportunity, just when it seemed that the organization had been eclipsed by its failures in achieving its goals.

FOR the Jews of Israel, the effect of the Intifada has been more subtle.[4] The uprising seemed to force the Israeli public and political leadership to think about the future of the territories in a more concrete and realistic manner than they had in the past. The Intifada spotlighted for the Israeli public anomalies that were evident, and even written about, but largely ignored. The implication of making no decision about the future of the territories and their inhabitants was brought home more powerfully than it had been in the previous twenty years. A low-level, protracted situation of constant violence forced Israelis to confront issues that many of them had conveniently pushed aside. This was brought to a head because much of the world's mass media treated Israel's policy of attempting to suppress the Intifada in a negative manner.

There is little doubt that the Intifada has had an impact on Israeli public opinion. Israelis said so quite clearly. In a survey[5] conducted in the weeks before the November 1, 1988, elections (and about ten months after the beginning of the Intifada), 55 percent admitted that their opinions regarding security and politics had changed as a result of the Intifada (see Appendix I). About one-fourth of the panel said that their opinions had moderated as a result of the Intifada, and an additional third said their opinions had hardened.[6]

Other indications of the Intifada's impact were clear in the answers: 59 percent thought that the national mood had become worse, and 41 percent reported that their own mood had soured. Only 4 percent thought that the Intifada improved the national mood and their own mood. Seventy-eight percent thought that the Intifada did not change their desire to live in Israel, but 13 percent said it strengthened this desire, and 9 percent said that it decreased it. About half the panel thought that the Intifada would have an impact on the elections which were about to take place; of those, two-thirds thought that the Intifada would work in the Likud's favor.

Using a slightly different measure but largely based on the same questions in Appendix I, only 8 percent reported that it had no effect on them or on the country.[7] For most people an effect was reported, and the pattern generated was an inverse-U pattern: 10 percent reported change on one item, 16 percent on two, 16 percent on three, 19 percent on four, 12 percent on five, 13 percent on six, 4 percent on seven questions, and 2 percent on all eight. Moreover, attitude change regarding the security policy issues was closely associated with change in vote intention (correlation of .46).[8] This is especially revealing because there was almost no correlation between attitude change regarding security issues and change in other related topics, such as personal mood, willingness to live in Israel, and level of political activity. Gender had a considerable impact on four of the topics (see table 1). Women's attitudes seemed to be more strenuously affected by the Intifada than were those of men. But they presented a complex mosaic. Women's orientation toward Arabs became much more negative, and they reported that their political attitudes hardened more than did the men.

Women's roles were crucial because their attitudes not only hardened, on the whole, but they were also more inclined to change their vote preference than were men; the overall net impact of their vote reconsideration was relatively more important for Labor and parties of the left than for the Likud and parties of the right. Half of the women reported that they were considering a shift of vote since the Intifada compared with a third of the men. A third of the women who considered change went in the direction of Labor and the left (16 percent of the 49 percent of the women who contemplated a shift), compared with 28 percent in this conciliatory direction for the men (10 percent of the 36 percent reporting a change). The men were more likely to think in terms of the Likud and parties to the right of it, with two-thirds of the men who shifted going in that direction, compared with 57 percent of the movable women. Women were more changeable in terms of political activity as well, being more likely than men both to increase and decrease their past patterns of activity.

REGARDING policy, the evidence shows that there were three simultaneous processes operating on Israeli public opinion: a generalized, short-term *hardening* of positions since the beginning of the Intifada; a steady and increasing *moderation* of Israeli public opinion on certain issues of security policy over the past few years; and a growing *polarization* of attitude and political power between the more conciliatory left and the more hard-line right.

Israeli public opinion has been and continues to be sensitive to political developments, both internal and external.[9] Israelis remained hawks on short-term issues, but increasingly they were conciliatory regarding long-term outcomes. A growing moderation has been evident regarding the future of the territories in survey results over the last number of years,[10] while the general finding of polls taken since the onset of the Intifada is that Jewish samples want it dealt with in a stern manner. National samples indicated that a growing percentage was willing to return territories, to consider an eventual Palestinian state, and to enter into eventual negotiations with the PLO, on condition that it recognized Israel and renounced terrorism.[11] Regarding the handling of the Intifada, however, 46 percent of the panel respondents opted for a harsher policy, while only 10 percent wanted softer measures. The respondents of the panel were asked a series of questions regarding policy issues (see Appendix II), among other things. Change took place, but it was neither monotonic nor uniform. The panel, on the whole (using a measure that will be presented in the next section), became more militant in the ten months that passed, but the change was a matter of degree, rather than a complete reversal. In fact, change occurred in both a more militant direction and in a more conciliatory direction, at the same time, within the panel.

When respondents' attitudes changed, it tended to be in the direction in which they were already leaning. This is evident when the perceived effect of the Intifada is compared with the answers of the respondents to policy questions. Those who said that the Intifada had a hardening effect on their attitudes were much more likely to have had hard-line views before the beginning of the uprising. The opposite was also true: Those who reported a softening of their views because of the Intifada were much more likely to have begun with dovish views. This is also seen with regard to political party preferences. Those who reported a 1987 vote intention for Labor and the left were much more likely to identify the parties that benefited from the developments as Labor and the left; those who said that they intended to vote for Likud and the right were much more inclined to see the Likud and the right as gaining from the Intifada. Moreover, most respondents who reported in 1988 that the Intifada influenced their vote choice in favor of the left and Labor had already been left and Labor supporters in 1987; the obverse is true for the right and the Likud.

Four of the nine questions in the policy scale occasioned change in a more dovish direction, while four others changed in a more hawkish direction. A ninth was indeterminate. Those that changed in a more dovish direction included the questions of agreeing with the principle of exchanging land for peace (question 1 in Appendix II), the eventual establishment of a Palestinian state (question 7), the assessment of the effect of the army's presence in the territories on its fighting ethic (question 5), and attitudes toward encouraging Arabs to leave the country (question 9).

Questions that generated a hawkish change concerned the forced choice the respondents were given between peace negotiations and increasing Israel's military power (question 2 in Appendix II) and whether security interests were more important than the rule of law when these two values were in conflict (question 4). These two questions displayed the highest rate of change among all policy questions. Change in a more hawkish direction also included the idea of an international peace conference (question 3) and negotiations with the PLO (question 6). It is likely that some opposed negotiations during ongoing violence, and not necessarily because they had come to far-reaching decisions about the Palestinian cause. This is probably an example of the panel members "rallying around the flag," especially because the two large parties steadfastly opposed negotiations with the PLO. An uncertain direction of change regarded the question of the civil rights of Arabs if the territories were annexed (question 8 in Appendix II).

Change on individual questions of the policy scale is reported in table 2. Two central policy issues—the future of the territories and the idea of a Palestinian state—generate the most stability. Two important points are to be made about the two crucial issues of establishing a Palestinian state and the issue of the territories: the degree of stability between the two interviews is higher than for any of the other questions, and the net change is in a dovish direction. These two patterns underscore the political importance of the shifts in public opinion during this period. Two other policy questions—encouraging the Arabs to leave the country and negotiations with the PLO—show low levels of stability between the two interviews. These issues were evidently heavily influenced by ongoing developments and by the election campaign.

The period of the Intifada brought a glimmer of potential and hope, and not only foreboding and gloom. For example, in the 1987 survey, 43 percent reported that they thought that the Arabs ultimately wanted to conquer Israel and to annihilate a good part of the Jewish people living there. A year later, the percentage giving that answer had dropped to 34 percent. Or, to use another example, 57 percent in 1987 said they thought that peace was possible between Israel and the Arab states; by 1988 that percentage among the panel respondents had risen to 64 percent. The emerging political situation was perceived as fluid. For instance, when asked about the chances of peace and war in the near future, more than 50 percent in both 1987 and 1988 rated the chances for peace and for war within the next few years as high or moderate.[12]

The answers to the nine policy questions, each weighted on a five-point scale, formed coherent scales in both 1987 and 1988.[13] The patterns of change are displayed in table 3 with the 1988 policy positions of the respondents displayed by their 1987 positions. The 1987 positions were divided into three groups of roughly equal size, and while the movement was complex, it tended to the hawkish end of the scale. The other movement that was significant was polarization—clearly seen by the depletion of the center. The middle position contracted by a fifth between the two time periods, from 34 percent to 27 percent. The hawk pole grew from a third to 41 percent, while the dove pole retained its third of the sample.

The largest categories were of those who did not change between the two questioning periods; in all, half the respondents were in the same category in both time periods. Change was fairly symmetrical, with about 5 percent of the total sample each switching from the extreme hawk to the extreme dove position, and from the extreme dove to the extreme hawk categories.

The mean score on the 1987 policy scale was 3.10, and for 1988 it was 3.20; using the t-test difference of means measure, this difference was statistically significant (see table 4). Several social categories were examined; in all of them there was a movement to the right. The hawkish direction of change was statistically significant among respondents from Asian and African backgrounds, the religious, those above thirty-five, and men. Those under thirty-five began more to the right than did the older group, but both groups shifted in that direction. So too with gender difference: Women and men both moved toward the hawkish pole, with the women starting more to the right. Those closer to the hawkish position had less room for movement than those who began more to the left and moved in a rightist direction. Levels of education followed the pattern to the hawk pole, but none of the differences was statistically significant. Despite considerable speculation to the contrary, army service in the territories showed no discernible impact on attitudes.[14]

ELEVEN months after the uprising began, on November 1, 1988, Israel held national elections. The results of these elections were not markedly different from the results of the previous elections held in 1984. Likud and Labor parties remained the two largest parties, and ultimately retained the National Unity government coalition, which had dominated the previous four years. In 1988, many smaller parties ran (twenty-seven in all, counting Likud and Labor), and more than half of them (fifteen in all) won representation in the Knesset. Most blocks of parties perpetuated their strength; the four orthodox religious parties gained seats. Much that was familiar in the past continued, but change was also evident.

The change between 1984 and 1988 was not great; neither was the change between political blocs reported by members of the panel. Vote intention by political bloc showed great stability,[15] with a total of 89 percent retaining their bloc-voting intention for the year between the interviews. Six percent of the sample shifted from the hawk camp to the dove side, while 5 percent changed in the opposite direction, with a net change of 1 percent in the dovish direction.

Attitude change, however, was considerable.[16] The only group for which no statistically significant change occurred was for those who responded in 1987 that they would vote for Labor were elections to be held at that time (see table 5). By 1988, those individuals had shifted slightly to the right, but not at a statistically significant level. The 1987 Likud voters switched to the right at an extensive rate.

The change among those who declared that they would vote for the Likud just before the 1988 elections was abundant. The Likud seems to have benefited from the general shift in public opinion in the direction of its stated policies. By extension, Labor was probably hurt by the flow of opinion away from its platform. Those who communicated their intention to vote Labor on the eve of the 1988 elections identified with the conciliatory ideas that Labor put forward. These voters generated the only instance in these analyses of statistically significant change in a dovish direction—from a score of 2.74 in 1987 to 2.50 in 1988. This underscores the impossible mission that Labor faced: to win a majority for its positions when all social categories were distancing themselves from those positions. It is little wonder that the election results appeared so glum for Labor.

Policy issues and party-performance evaluations centering on the Israeli-Arab conflict dimension were closely related to the vote in 1988.[17] In addition, policy preferences of voters and their evaluations of the parties' performance as shaped by the Palestinian uprising affected their vote decision, above and beyond their broader party identification and their reported vote intention before the Intifada began. By controlling for the earlier vote intention, it could be determined whether or not attitudes shaped by the Intifada had an impact on the 1988 vote and could be studied. The multivariate model estimated to predict the 1988 vote included long-term and short-term issue dimensions, vote intention as of December 1987, when the Intifada was just beginning, and a comparative measure of candidate evaluation, based on a ten-point thermometer scale rating Shamir and Peres, the Likud and Labor leaders.

The four policy variables used in the analysis affected the vote significantly beyond the vote intention in December 1987. Voters' policy positions on the territories, their position on whether government policy to keep order in the territories should be harsher or softer, and their evaluations of the performance of the two major parties all had an impact on the vote beyond the vote preference of the respondent from before the Intifada. The Intifada had an effect on the 1988 vote by changing part of the electorate's attitudes and/or by making those attitudes more relevant to the vote. The Likud and the right fared better on the performance evaluations and the short-term policy preferences; the mild movement on the long-term concerns favored the left and Labor. The net result of these complex processes was an election outcome not very different from the previous one.

An analysis of the relation between attitudes regarding the Intifada and the vote was also undertaken by Gad Barzilai.[18] He found that the public regarded the question of Israel's military response to the Intifada as crucial to the country's future and as having more influence on voting behavior than did other issues, including Israel's economic problems. When asked which issues most influenced their votes, 85 percent of the respondents answered the use of military force against the Intifada, the future of the territories, and Israel's national security policy toward the Arab states and the terrorist organizations. Fifty-five percent claimed that the first issue influenced them considerably; only 7 percent saw it as a marginal issue.

Barzilai reported that respondents' attitudes toward the Intifada tended to match other attitudes. "Thus, support for Israeli control over the territories, and especially for their annexation, was significantly associated with support for extensive use of military force against the Intifada ($r=0.33$) . . . Many people see the Intifada not as a popular uprising based on legitimate national rights, but as terrorism which should be quelled by military means."[19]

Moreover, he claimed that the more a voter favored the use of military force against the Intifada, the more likely he was to vote for the Likud or for parties to its right.

THERE is no doubt that the Intifada occasioned attitude change in Israel. But this change introduced confounding patterns of complex flux. Three strands of this change appear to be 1) a short-term *hardening* of positions; 2) a steady and increasing *moderation* of Israeli public opinion on certain issues of security policy; and 3) a growing *polarization* of attitude between the more conciliatory left and the more hard-line right.

The Intifada appears to have confronted Israelis with the implications of controlling the territories in an unprecedented manner. Individuals obviously process this confrontation in different ways. The overwhelming pattern seems clear: They do not agree to simply pull out or to annex; but neither are they willing to sit by passively. They want law and order more strongly than before, but they also tend more than before to accept the notion of a negotiated political solution. They realize that in the interest of security the rule of law may be weakened; they also think that the fighting ethic of the Israel Defense Force has been affected by the continuing uprising.

Israelis appear to have become more "realistic" as a result of the Intifada. At the same time, polarization was evident as the center shrank in size and political discourse became more shrill. This polarization grew as the activities of extreme groups (such as the Sikariim on the right and myriad Jewish groups on the left opposing Israel's policy in the territories) increased.

The apparent paradoxes found in the data can be at least partially explained by distinguishing between short-term and long-term issues and policies, on the one hand, and between political attitudes and core values, on the other. For example, immediate negotiations with the PLO lost support. This is an example of attitudes hardening regarding a position with short-term implications. Moreover, both Labor and Likud have consistently voiced opposition to negotiations with the PLO.

Two other instances of change in a hawkish direction on attitudes that seem to have short-term impact are the importance of security interests compared with the rule of law and positions toward an international peace conference. The percentage of panel respondents that sided with preferring security interests over the rule of law increased, as did the percentage of those opposed to a peace conference. Both of these had short-term implications and were part of the shifting political discourse.

In the opposite direction, we may cite returning the territories and the establishment of a Palestinian state. Support for returning most of the territories in a comprehensive peace arrangement grew, as did support for the eventual establishment of a Palestinian state. These were probably perceived as more long-term and probably reflected (for the people who shifted) a conclusion that seemed to them to flow from political developments.

In this complex and fluctuating situation, many forces can emerge. In the period of the Intifada, the intricate changes in attitude seemed to have strengthened the political power of the two biggest political parties, Likud and Labor, even if they did less well in the elections of 1988 than they did in the immediate past. The coalition that they formed strengthened both of them, and especially the Likud, a party that appeared to be emerging in the Israeli context as a party of the attitudinal center.[20] This center appears to have a wide degree of latitude in introducing tougher policies in the short run and also exploring far-reaching compromises for the long run. As the period is one of flux, so too is it one of fluidity and instability. Other ideas may gain support if the perception of threat grows and the hope for an acceptable settlement dwindles.

Notes

1. See A. Arian, I. Talmud, and T. Herman, *National Security and Public Opinion in Israel* (Boulder, Colo.: Westview Press, 1988).

2. In a survey done among Israeli Arabs and Jews by the Israel Institute for Applied Social Research, 97 percent of the Arab respondents agreed to a Palestinian state, 95 percent favored yielding territories, and 95 percent supported negotiating with the PLO. The corresponding figures for the Jewish sample were 20 percent, 44 percent, and 28 percent. The results for "all Israelis" were 33 percent, 52 percent, and 40 percent, respectively. See the articles by Elihu Katz, Majid Al-Haj, and Hanna Levinson in *Yediot Aharonot*, August 1989, and in the *Jerusalem Post*, by

Katz and Al-Haj, August 4, 25, 1989. See also the chapter by Elie Rekhees in this volume, "The Arabs in Israel and the Intifada."

3. Ian Lustick, "The Changing Political Role of Arabs in Israel," in *The Elections in Israel—1988*, ed. Asher Arian and Michal Shamir (Boulder, Colo.: Westview Press, forthcoming).

4. Lili Galili, "The Stone Has Not Hit Us," *Ha'aretz* (Tel Aviv), October 27, 1989, p. 6.

5. The data analyzed in this chapter are from two interviews with 416 respondents: The first was held between December 9, 1987 (the day on which the Arab uprising began) and January 4, 1988; the second was held in October 1988. Each respondent was interviewed twice; the original 1987/88 interview was part of a larger survey of 1,116 respondents, and 416 of these respondents were reinterviewed in the weeks before the November 1, 1988, elections. The fieldwork for the surveys was done by the Dahaf Research Institute. For details of the 1987/88 survey, see Asher Arian, "A People Apart: Coping with National Security Problems in Israel," *Journal of Conflict Resolution* (December 1989). Careful analyses indicated that the 1987 national sample was representative of the total Jewish adult population and that the 416 panel respondents were representative of both the population and the 1,116 respondents of the 1987 national sample in terms of policy distribution and demographic characteristics. The surveys were prepared and conducted by the National Security and Public Opinion Project of the Jaffee Center for Strategic Studies (JCSS) at Tel Aviv University, directed by the author. See the JCSS Memorandum no. 28, August 1989, by Asher Arian and Raphael Ventura for more information.

6. The attitude change dealt with here occurred in the period between December 1987 and November 1988. Later developments, such as the Arafat statements in Geneva regarding terror and Israel's right to exist, the American decision to conduct a dialogue with the PLO, and the Israeli government's plan for elections in the territories, may have had additional impact. Further research is under way.

7. Asher Arian, Michal Shamir, and Raphael Ventura, "Public Opinion and the Body Politic: Adjustment under Conditions of Stress," forthcoming.

8. Similar findings are reported in M.K. Jennings and R.G. Niemi, *Generations and Politics* (Princeton, N.J.: Princeton University Press, 1981).

9. See N. Keis, "The Influence of Public Policy on Public Opinion— Israel 1967–1974," in *State, Government and International Relations* (Hebrew) (September 1975), pp. 36–53; R.A. Stone, *Social Change in Israel: Attitudes and Events 1967–1979* (New York: Praeger, 1982); Y. Yishai, *Land or Peace: Whither Israel?* (Stanford, Calif.: Hoover Institution, 1987).

10. Surveys done by Modi'in Ezrahi between 1987 and 1989 show, for

example, that support for an autonomy arrangement rose from 8 percent in 1987, to 16 percent in 1988, to 25 percent in 1989. A territorial compromise with representatives of the Palestinians went from 9 percent to 8 percent to 14 percent during that same period. Similarly, support for annexing the territories dropped from 45 percent in 1987, to 42 percent in 1988, to 30 percent in 1989 (*Maariv*, February 17, 1989).

11. Hanoch Smith's time series, for example, reports the acceptability of negotiation with the PLO, if it officially recognizes Israel and ceases terrorist activity, moving from 43 percent in April 1987, through 53 percent in August 1988, to 58 percent in March 1989 (*New York Times*, April 2, 1989, pp. 1–2).

12. For comparative data, see J. R. Rabier, H. Riffault, and R. Inglehart, *Euro-Barometer 24* (Ann Arbor, Mich.: Inter-University Consortium for Political and Social Research, 1986).

13. The standardized alpha reliability coefficient for the 1987 policy construct was .72; for the 1988 battery it was .80. The higher coefficient in 1988 suggests that the different attitudes cluster together more strongly in 1988 than in 1987.

14. See Arian, Talmud, and Herman, *National Security and Public Opinion in Israel*, chapt. 6.

15. Respondents were divided into one of two categories: Labor and left; and Likud, right, and religious parties. The stability measure used was discussed in table 2.

16. Fifty-five percent of the 1988 television electioneering by the parties was reportedly devoted to the Intifada. See Gad Barzilai, "National Security Crises and Voting Behavior: The Intifada and the 1988 Israeli Elections," in *The Elections in Israel—1988*.

17. Michal Shamir and Asher Arian, "The Intifada and Israeli Voters: Policy Preferences and Performance Evaluations," ibid.

18. Barzilai, "National Security Crises and Voting Behavior."

19. Ibid.

20. Asher Arian, "Israel's National Unity Governments and Domestic Politics," ibid.

Table 1. Reported Effect of the Intifada by Gender
(percentages; N = 416)

	Women	Men	Total
Orientation to Arabs			
More positive	3	4	3
No change	50	65	58
More negative	47	31	39
Political attitudes changed by Intifada			
Yes, more conciliatory	25	22	23
No	39	52	46
Yes, less conciliatory	37	26	31
Vote inclination since Intifada			
More toward Labor camp	16	10	13
More toward Likud camp	28	24	26
More toward religious parties	5	2	4
No change	51	64	57
Political activity			
Increased	12	7	10
No change	81	90	85
Decreased	7	3	5

Table 2. Stability and Change, 1987–88

Question (Appendix II)	Total % stable	Stable hawk %	Stable dove %	Change to hawk	Change to dove	Net hawk[a] change
Palestinian state (7)	74	65	9	11	15	−4
Territories (1)	71	37	34	12	17	−5
International conference (3)	65	23	42	22	14	+8
Negotiations/ military (2)	64	14	50	24	13	+11
Civil rights (8)	61	33	28	24	16	+8
IDF (5)[b]	60	7	52	14	26	−12
PLO (6)[b]	49	22	18	29	22	+7
Arabs leave (9)	46	28	18	15	20	−5
Security/rule of law (4)[b]	42	16	21	42	16	+26

[a] The hard-line pole of the measure includes support for annexing the territories, giving priority to increasing military power rather than entering peace negotiations, not participating in an international conference for peace chaired by the superpowers, preferring security interests over the rule of law, assessing that ac-

tivities in the territories have a positive impact on the effectiveness of the army, opposing negotiations with the PLO, rejecting the establishment of a Palestinian state, denying civil rights to inhabitants of the territories, and encouraging Arabs to leave the country. (See Appendix II.)

[b] These variables include a middle category, which was not clearly hawk or dove. The "change to hawk" and "change to dove" categories include moves to and from this middle category.

Table 3. Change between 1987 and 1988

Policy 1988	Dove	Policy 1987 middle	Hawk[a]	Total
Dove	59.3	20.4	15.2	31.3%
Middle	23.0	32.4	26.1	27.2%
Hawk	17.8	47.2	58.7	41.4%
N (100%)	135	142	138	415[b]

[a] The hard-line pole of the measure includes support for annexing the territories, giving priority to increasing military power rather than entering peace negotiations, not participating in an international conference for peace chaired by the superpowers, preferring security interests over the rule of law, assessing that activities in the territories have a positive impact on the effectiveness of the army, opposing negotiations with the PLO, rejecting the establishment of a Palestinian state, denying civil rights to inhabitants of the territories, and encouraging Arabs to leave the country. (See Appendix II.)

[b] Apparent errors in addition are due to rounding.

Table 4. Change on Policy Score between 1987 and 1988, for Total Panel and by Place of Birth, Age, Gender, Religious Observance, and Service in the Territories

	1987 score	1988 score	N	t-value[a]
Total sample	3.10	3.20	415	−2.26**
Place of birth				
1. Israel born; father Asia-Africa-born	3.28	3.35	119	−0.87
2. Asia-Africa born	3.23	3.46	90	−2.77**
3. Self/father Israel-born	3.18	3.19	36	−0.06
4. Israel-born; father Europe-America-born	3.02	3.14	64	−1.01
5. Europe-America-born	2.81	2.82	103	−0.07

(Continued)

Table 4 (Continued)

	1987 score	1988 score	N	t-value[a]
Age				
Below 35	3.19	3.26	204	−1.04
35 and above	3.00	3.13	205	−2.33*
Gender				
Women	3.25	3.30	199	−0.85
Men	2.97	3.10	214	−2.21*
Religious observance				
Religious[b]	3.39	3.57	137	−2.34*
Traditional	3.15	3.19	177	−0.57
Secular	2.56	2.63	92	−0.71
Service in the territories				
Served since the Intifada began	3.18	3.18	37	0.02

[a] T-test values of the differences between means determined significance level: * $p < .05$; ** $p < .01$; *** $p < .001$.
[b] Includes two categories: those who reported that they observe the religious tradition fully (44 respondents) and those who report that they observe much of the tradition (93).

Table 5. Change between 1987 and 1988 by Vote

Vote	1987 score	1988 score	N	t-value[a]
Likud vote 1987	3.42	3.67	110	−2.78**
Labor vote 1987	2.73	2.79	111	−0.76
Likud vote 1988	3.34	3.73	137	−5.24***
Labor vote 1988	2.74	2.50	106	3.08**

[a] T-test values of the differences between means determined significance level: * $p < .05$; ** $p < .01$; *** $p < .001$.

Appendix I

%	Questions on the Intifada
	1. Has the Intifada changed or not changed your attitudes regarding the political and security situation?
46	My attitudes have not changed
23	My attitudes have changed—more prepared for compromise
31	My attitudes have changed—less prepared for compromise

Have the following things changed or not changed for you as a result of the Intifada?

%	
	2. Your general mood
4	Improved
55	No change
41	Become worse
	3. The national mood
4	Improved
37	No change
59	Become worse
	4. Your assessment of the upcoming election results
42	No change
37	The chances of the Likud camp have improved
19	The chances of the Labor camp have improved
2	The chances of the religious camp have improved
	5. Your political activity
10	Increased
85	No change
5	Decreased
	6. Your desire to live in Israel
13	Increased
78	No change
9	Decreased
	7. Your vote
57	No change
26	Decision to vote for the Likud camp has strengthened

%	Questions on the Intifada
13	Decision to vote for the Labor camp has strengthened
4	Decision to vote for a religious party has strengthened
	8. My orientation to Arabs is
3	More positive
58	No change
39	More negative

Appendix II

The Policy Scale

Frequency distributions		
1987 %	1988 %	Questions
		1. There are three long-range solutions for the territories held since the 1967 war. With which do you agree most? (Constructed from two questions, the first asking preference with a "leave as is" option, with a follow-up for those respondents, forcing a choice.)
33.5	38.0	A. In exchange for peace I would be willing to give up the territories as long as Israel's security interests were provided for.
10.9	10.3	B. Leave the situation as it is, but if Israel had to choose, I would be willing to give up territories if security was provided for
3.2	3.3	C. Leave the situation as it is, but no choice if Israel had to choose
26.4	23.5	D. Leave the situation as it is, but if Israel had to choose, I would choose to annex the territories.
25.7	25.0	E. Annex the territories.
		2. What is the main thing that Israel must do in order to prevent a war with the Arab countries?
72.7	61.9	A. Everything in her power to initiate peace negotiations
27.3	38.1	B. Increase her military power
		3. There is a suggestion to have an international peace conference with the big powers participating. To what extent do you support this suggestion?

(Continued)

Frequency distributions		
1987 %	1988 %	Questions
19.5	16.3	A. Definitely support
43.7	38.9	B. Support
22.4	23.4	C. Do not support
14.4	21.4	D. Definitely do not support

4. Recently there has been much talk about situations in which there is a contradiction between the principle of the rule of law and the security interests. On the following scale, "1" represents the opinion that states that when there is a conflict like that, security interests are to be given priority, while "7" represents the opinion that in that case the rule of law is always to be preferred. Where on this scale would you place yourself?

always prefer interests of security	1	2	3	4	5	6	7	always prefer rule of law
1987 (%)	13.8	14.3	18.7	26.8	10.3	8.6	7.4	
1988 (%)	20.3	27.4	20.8	14.4	8.3	4.9	3.9	

5. In the following scale, rung 1 represents the position that the Israel Defense Force's presence in Judea, Samaria and the Gaza Strip has a negative effect on the army's fighting ethic and the seventh rung is that the Israel Defense Force's presence in Judea, Samaria, and the Gaza Strip has a positive effect. Where would you rank yourself on the scale?

negative effect	1	2	3	4	5	6	7	positive effect
1987 (%)	9.0	10.7	10.0	33.1	11.2	13.6	12.4	
1988 (%)	11.1	14.0	13.5	36.0	9.9	9.4	6.2	

Frequency distributions		
1987 %	1988 %	Questions
		6. The way things are today, do you think that Israel should or should not be willing to conduct peace negotiations with the PLO? (Constructed from two questions, the first asking about negotiations, the follow-up for those respondents who opposed negotiations, probing opinion based on the conditions mentioned.)
36.8	31.7	A. Israel should be willing without preconditions
26.4	22.3	B. Israel should be willing if the PLO undergoes basic changes and announces that it recognizes the state of Israel and will completely give up acts of terror
36.8	46.0	C. Israel should not be willing under any conditions
		7. Do you think that Israel should agree or not agree to the establishment of a Palestinian state in Judea, Samaria and the Gaza Strip?
7.5	6.1	A. A Palestinian state should definitely be agreed to
12.1	18.5	B. A Palestinian state should be agreed to
26.7	29.0	C. A Palestinian state should not be agreed to
53.6	46.5	D. A Palestinian state should definitely not be agreed to
		8. If the territories are eventually annexed to the state of Israel, are you in favor of granting more civil rights to the Arab inhabitants than they have today, or decreasing them or leaving them as they are today?
21.8	15.0	A. Increase their civil rights, including giving them the right to vote in Knesset elections

(Continued)

Frequency distributions		
1987 %	1988 %	Questions
30.1	28.5	B. Increase their civil rights, but do not give them the right to vote in Knesset elections
26.7	41.0	C. Leave things as they are now
21.4	15.5	D. Decrease their civil rights
		9. Do you agree or disagree that Israel should encourage the Arabs to leave the country?
34.7	26.8	A. Certainly agree
32.8	37.2	B. Agree
25.4	26.1	C. Don't agree
7.1	9.9	D. Certainly don't agree

The Impact of the Intifada on the Likud Party in the Framework of Israeli Politics, 1987–1990

Nathan Yanai

The outbreak and gradual institutionalization of a massive and highly organized Palestinian Intifada came largely as a surprise to the Israeli defense and political establishment[1] and the public at large, creating in the process embarrassing military, legal, and moral dilemmas and tarnishing Israel's image. The Intifada generated political debate and party friction, manifestations of public dissatisfaction and media criticism, as well as opposing political pressures on the government and the army from the radical right and radical left; however, unlike earlier traumatic security crises containing an element of surprise, it did not create potent, consistent, or consensual mainstream political pressure for a significant change in government—either dismissal of leaders or radical change of policies. In the prewar crisis of 1967, public pressure brought about the formation of a government of National Unity and the appointment of Moshe Dayan as defense minister in place of Prime Minister Levy Eshkol. Similar pressure produced the Agranat Commission of Inquiry during the 1973 Yom Kippur war and brought about sweeping changes in the army command. Subsequently, in April 1974, it brought about the resignation of Prime Minister Golda Meir and Defense Minister Moshe Dayan.

The Intifada did not produce a strong and unified public perception of apparent villains or of inept leaders in the Israeli government and the army in terms of personal behavior and executive competence. Those who appeared as the villains from the perspective of the radical right (for example, General Amram Mizna, the former military commander of Judea and Samaria) appeared to be the heroes of the left, and vice versa. The political response to the Intifada converged with existing political differences and cleavages and did not create a new, well-defined and consensual message.

Moreover, most leaders in both major parties acted to defuse pressures on the government to introduce a radical change of strategy or dismissal of leaders, largely suppressing the Intifada as a major partisan issue throughout most of that period. Indeed, the events of the Intifada did not constitute the major issue in the 1988 elections, and the two major parties were equally responsible for this. The shadow of these events loomed large, however, in the background of the elections and created a major campaign debate, featuring retired generals, concerning the importance and relevancy of the West Bank and the Gaza strip to the security of Israel. The question of an international conference destabilized and threatened to topple the National Unity government during 1987 and 1988, following the initial secret agreement between King Hussein and Foreign Minister Shimon Peres in April 1987. However, it was relegated to a merely marginal campaign issue after the king's announcement, in July 1988, that he relinquished his residual claim to the West Bank and severed Jordan's legal links to it. Instead, the two major parties debated the question of withdrawal from the territories as an issue of national defense. The Likud maintained that Israel could not afford to terminate under any circumstances its control over the West Bank and the Gaza district, while Labor's campaign claimed that under proper security arrangements, Israel could withdraw from most of these territories without undermining its capacity to defend itself. The Likud felt obliged, late in the campaign, to present its plan for peace, resorting again to the Autonomy Plan. Labor continued to present its traditional position of territorial exchange for peace or "territorial compromise."

Six factors may have limited the role of the Intifada in the 1988 election campaign. (1) Political parties and political leaders, prior to the Intifada, were more preoccupied with issues relating to Israel's governing role and position in the West Bank and Gaza district rather than with Israel's capacity to maintain control over them and pacify their population. The latter task was considered to be the routine responsibility of the army and the defense establishment, which indeed had managed either to defuse or repress the sporadic and recurrent acts of civil disobedience and insurrection in the territories for twenty years. The "stick and carrot" policies (so described by an Israeli general, Shlomo Gazit, who was in charge of the Israeli administration in these territories)[2] seemed to have worked in the past, and thus some people could still have expected it to finally prove to be effective even in the case of the Intifada. (2) The realization that the Intifada was here to stay did not take hold at once, nor did the Intifada create a similar intense public reaction as did past security crises. It undermined public morale and had an impact on public opinion (Asher Arian found that Israelis became more "realistic" as a result of the Intifada), but it did not create an acute sense of crisis or large-scale protest and political mobilization.[3] (3) The hands of the two major Israeli parties were partially tied in relation to the Intifada, because the government had established, in fact, a bipartisan policy, tense and limited as it had been, concerning the handling of it. The National Unity government entrusted Defense Minister Yitzhak Rabin with an almost exclusive responsibility for this policy. (4) The full, potential electoral impact of the Intifada was far from being clear during the 1988 election campaign, and the established leaders of both parties, with few exceptions, feared the damaging impact of a radical image in the eyes of the voters. (5) The reluctance of most leaders of the Likud and the Labor alignment to open a full-fledged partisan debate concerning the responsibility for the emergence of the Intifada or the new dilemmas involving the use of force to control it. A similar, though lesser reluctance appeared earlier in the case of the war in Lebanon, which like the Intifada did not become a major campaign issue, in the 1984 elections.[4] It is noteworthy that whenever Ariel Sharon attacked Rabin's performance vis-à-vis the Intifada, the latter responded with a counter personal attack on Sharon's responsibility for the war in Lebanon. (6) The mainstream leaders of major Israeli parties in government shared a desire to minimize the overall impact of the Intifada at home and abroad, fortifying their reluctance to feature the Intifada at the center of their election campaigns.

The outcome of the 1988 elections did not convey any clear-cut message concerning the handling of the Intifada. The real winners, in terms of relative growth and coalition advantage, were the religious parties, which increased their total representation from twelve to eighteen members of the Knesset (MKs). These parties did not have any particular message on the issue of the Intifada. They have generally supported the established policies of the National Unity government in the areas of defense and foreign policy. The Labor alignment lost five seats—three of them due to the decision of Mapam, a former member of the alignment, to run independently. The overall strength of the Zionist left (together with the dovish centrist Shinui) declined by only one seat (from fifty to forty-nine MKs); however, the radical dovish parties increased their share in it—from six to ten MKs. The Likud lost only one seat—from forty-one to forty MKs—and the entire political right lost one seat—from forty-eight to forty-seven MKs. The more radical parties, however, increased their share of this bloc—from five (six, with Meir Kahane) to seven MKs. In sum, aside from the increase in the strength of the religious parties, the 1988 elections produced only minimal and inconsequential changes. The Likud was still able to form a narrow coalition, together with the religious parties and the parties of the radical right, but Yitzhak Shamir finally opted to reinstate the National Unity government, among other reasons because of the continuing Intifada and his desire to maintain the established bipartisanship in relation to it.

Until 1990, the Intifada did not produce a radical and sweeping change in Israeli politics—coalition government, leaders, and policies. It did make, however, such a change possible, as it had already left its imprint on both major Israeli parties, as well as on most other parties. At first, it looked as if the Intifada would have a more devastating impact on the Labor alignment; however, the Likud was finally the party that was more severely affected by it. The impact of the Intifada on the Likud, during the two years surveyed in this chapter may be identified in the areas of leadership and internal factional politics, ideology, and policy—in sum, the

Likud's competence as a governing party and its ability to share power in the National Unity government.

The Intifada clearly produced or deepened a schism within the Unity government between a mainstream position and a radical position in both major Israeli parties. The mainstream position accepted essentially a policy of containment toward the Intifada and was prepared to explore and exhaust possibilities for interparty cooperation within the National Unity government, given the conditions of near parity in parliamentary representation, the costs and risks of a narrow coalition government, and the national interest in an initial bipartisan move toward peaceful settlement. This approach finally produced the proposal for elections in the territories. Those taking the radical position in both parties lost patience with the slow moving, or deadlocked National Unity government and pressured their parties to resume a less inhibited interparty conflict. The radicals of both parties believed in the capacity of their party to sway the voters and gain a mandate to form a limited majority coalition government or to remain in power without an early election after the dismantling of the National Unity government. They were even prepared to go into opposition in order to articulate an undiluted partisan message and prepare for new, decisive elections.

Until 1990, the two mainstream positions were either able to reach a common ground in an arduous, difficult, and slow-moving process on several pressing issues of the peace process and the Intifada, or were finally deterred from turning them into a casus belli for the dismantling of the National Unity government. The Likud put up with Labor's initiatives concerning the withdrawal of the Israeli army from Lebanon (1985) and the settlement over Taba (1986). The Labor alignment unhappily acquiesced in the refusal of the Likud to consider the agreement between King Hussein and Foreign Minister Peres concerning the convening of an international peace conference; and Prime Minister Shamir finally accepted Rabin's proposal for elections in the territories. This proposal left, however, unresolved issues concerning the structure and participants in the negotiations over its implementation. These issues exposed the basic differences between Labor and the Likud and finally exhausted their capacity to continue to cooperate in a National Unity government.

Political Issues and Party Positions Concerning the Intifada

The divisions among and within Israeli parties concerning the Intifada related to three major issues:

First, the question of definition or legitimacy: Is the Intifada a legitimate struggle for freedom from occupation and for self-determination, just another form of war against Israel, or perhaps a combination of both?

Second, the question of Israel's strategy in the handling of the Intifada: Should it be one of containment and minimal pacification pending a political solution, or one of escalation and the expansion of the conflict in the hope of gaining a military victory and, thus, improving Israel's position in future negotiations? Another, more radical dichotomy on this issue was posed by the opposing extreme wings of Israel's party system—advocacy of voluntary capitulation to the demands of the leaders of the Intifada versus the advocacy of more repressive measures, including expulsion of those taking part in the Intifada.

Third, the question of political-diplomatic negotiations or the resumption of the peace process: With whom should Israel negotiate and on what? With only elected Palestinian leaders and officials from within the territories (with the exclusion of East Jerusalem), with a more diverse and less constrained Palestinian delegation, or directly with the PLO? Should Israel negotiate only the implementation of the election proposal or not be confined to it?

The mainstream positions of the Likud and the Labor alignment within the unity government were two among five identifiable partisan positions on the three major issues of the Intifada.

The first position is that of the radical anti-Zionist or a-Zionist political left, comprising the Communist party, the Progressive List for Peace, and the Arab Democratic List. (These parties won six Knesset seats in the 1988 elections.) This radical position defines the Intifada as entirely legitimate. It advocates the acceptance of the demands of the leadership of the Intifada and presses for negotiations with the PLO over the formation of a Palestinian state in the West Bank and Gaza.

The second position is that of the radical Zionist left, comprising Ratz and Mapam (together they won eight Knesset seats in the 1988 election), and a significant, though still minority position among the elected representatives of the Labor party. It has been supported openly by only one of eleven Labor ministers in Shamir's National Unity government (Ezer Weizman) and by about a third of the thirty-nine-member-strong Labor parliamentary faction. Potentially, however, it may entertain greater support among Labor leaders. Another party, the centrist Shinui (two MKs), has also been close to the position of the radical Zionist left on the issue of the Intifada.

The basic position of this group is that the Intifada is a legitimate struggle for self-determination; however, it does not condone its use of violence. This group claims that there is a readily available alternative to the use of force in combating the Intifada, in the form of negotiation with any designated Palestinian delegation, even the PLO, over the issue of an independent Palestinian state existing alongside Israel under stringent conditions and proper guarantees to Israel's security. This position is most sensitive to the issue of civil and human rights in the territories, especially during the Intifada.

The third partisan position—the established and majority position within the Labor party—may be defined as one of the two mainstream Israeli positions on the issue of the Intifada. The Labor mainstream position, however, is much more flexible and amenable to change than that of the Likud. This Labor position recognizes the Palestinians' aspirations for self-determination but not their exclusive right to determine its scope and form. It considers the Intifada as illegitimate and a threat to Israel's security and advocates essentially a strategy of containment, maintaining that in the final analysis there is only a political solution to the Intifada. On one hand, Israel cannot afford to lose this violent confrontation in order to save the option of a negotiated settlement; on the other hand, putting down the Intifada by the use of excessive force would not solve anything but further alienate the Palestinian population and isolate Israel in the world.

Peres and Rabin, the leaders of the Labor party, have rejected talks with the PLO, but they have refrained from criticizing the American administration for doing just that. They have certainly welcomed an extended Egyptian role concerning negotiations with a Palestinian delegation. The Labor alignment has traditionally accepted, perhaps even preferred, a gradual progression toward peace, which was manifested during Labor's regime in the separation of forces agreement (Sinai I) (1974), and the interim agreement (Sinai II) (1975) following the Yom Kippur war. This approach has produced the election proposal in the territories as a possible takeoff point for the resumption of the peace process. Beyond that, Labor maintained its basic position favoring the exchange of territories for peace. This general concept may still lend itself to diverse, even opposing alternatives: How much land for what kind of peace and with whom?

The internal radical-dovish challenge to the established policies of the Labor alignment, concerning the National Unity government and the Palestinians, was held in check. Two major reasons may have contributed to it.

One, this challenge was not fully adopted by a major contender for party leadership and was divorced of an immediate or full-fledged leadership struggle. It was supported by maverick leaders (Ezer Weizman and Arie [Lova] Eliav) or those who belonged to the younger generation of party leaders (among them, Uzi Baram, the former secretary general of the Labor party; Haim Ramon, the new chairman of its parliamentary faction; and Yossi Beilin, at the time the deputy minister of finance).

Two, the chairman of the Labor party, Shimon Peres, was partially, though not fully, sympathetic to the radical dovish message. At first, Peres supported a proposal to block Labor's entry into the new National Unity government following the 1988 election, but then reconsidered his stand and joined Rabin in supporting it. Rabin, in return, subsequently adopted a conditional attitude toward participation in the National Unity government, predicated on the Likud's consent, or mere acquiesence, to a more flexible and forthcoming approach to talks with Palestinian representatives on the issue of elections in the territories. If Rabin and Peres have represented together a mainstream position within the alignment, then

Peres has stretched this position toward the dovish left in his party, and Rabin has stretched it, at times, toward Prime Minister Shamir, in an effort to create a consensual basis for a bipartisan move toward the resumption of the peace process. Both, however, decided to bring down the National Unity government in March 1990 when Shamir rejected Labor's demand to accept U.S. Secretary of State James Baker's terms for negotiations with a Palestinian delegation for the implementation of the election proposal.

The emergence of a Likud mainstream position—the majority position in the leadership of the Likud headed by Shamir and Moshe Arens—made it possible to maintain a precarious and problematic form of bipartisan policy on the operative issues of the Intifada and prevent the breakdown of the National Unity government during the first two years of the ongoing conflict.

The Likud mainstream position emphatically rejected the legitimacy of the Intifada and viewed it in the context of the continued Palestinian struggle against Israel. It did recognize, however, the rights of the Palestinian inhabitants of the West Bank and Gaza to some measure of autonomy within the framework of the Camp David agreement. At first, both Shamir and Arens had reservations about the Camp David agreement and did not vote for its approval by the Knesset (1979). Nevertheless, upon gaining positions of responsibility in government, they made the concept of autonomy and the Camp David agreement the cornerstone of the official policy of their government.

Shamir has rejected Labor's assumption that there is only a political solution to the Intifada; nevertheless, he acquiesced in Rabin's basic strategy of containment, as inconsistent as it has been. Shamir, more than any previous prime minister in time of war and military conflict, has limited his input in the handling of the Intifada. The bipartisanship on this issue was essentially based on the acceptance of Rabin's leadership and policies rather than on an openly negotiated position of the two major parties.

The election proposal was finally acceptable to Shamir, Arens, and their young associates in the leadership of the Likud for a number of reasons. It prevented—albeit for a short time—a crisis with the American administration and provided a basis for a bipartisan policy concerning the resumption of the peace process, which temporarily removed the threat of Labor's defection and the dismantling of Shamir's National Unity government. Some of Shamir's young associates were also anxious to provide the Likud with a more pragmatic image. The major advantage, however, of the election proposal, from Shamir's point of view, was that it is in keeping with the autonomy plan, which enjoyed, as a concept, high legitimacy in the Likud due to Menachem Begin's past leadership and Zeev Jabotinsky's legacy.[5] The autonomy plan reflected the liberal ideological approach of Jabotinsky toward coexistence with minorities within the prospective Jewish state. At the Camp David conference, it seemed to reconcile the concept of Greater Israel with the historic opportunity to reach a peace agreement with Egypt. This agreement kept the door open, however, for the Israeli government to demand the annexation of Judea, Samaria, and Gaza, at the end of a period of autonomy. The Likud harbored the hope to one day convert the autonomy into an integral part of the State of Israel, rather than provide the basis for a Palestinian state.

The prospect of implementation of Camp David's Autonomy Plan raised immediate misgivings and serious apprehensions in Begin's government, and this contributed to the failure of the autonomy talks. The seeming advantage of the belated election plan, in this regard, was that it added a preliminary stage to a possible renewed negotiation over the implementation of the wider autonomy. As such, it could be viewed just as a modified repetition of past experience—the municipal elections twice held by the Israeli government in the territories (1972, 1976).[6] These elections (which may also be viewed as a stop-gap operation in the absence of a larger political solution) produced a PLO-backed leadership in most of the Arab cities of the West Bank and Gaza. This precedent, whether it was explicitly considered by Shamir and Arens or not, could have reassured these leaders that a similar or even more conclusive outcome of the election in the territories would not necessarily create a major embarrassment for their government; it may even provide the rationale for not according greater independence to the elected PLO leadership in the territories. Shamir accepted the elections proposal after much pondering and long vacillation. His residual misgivings, fortified by the strong internal opposition within the Likud, manifested itself in the tedious and ultimately unsuccessful talks with the leaders of the alignment, as well as discussions with the United States and Egypt concerning the structure and the participants in the negotiations on the implementation of the election proposal.

The fifth partisan position is that of the radical political right. This position is maintained by three small parties: Tehiya, Tzomet, and Moledet (altogether, seven MKs). The three leaders within the Likud who opposed elections in the territories (Ariel Sharon, David Levy, and Yitzhak Moda'i) could also have been placed, with some qualifications, in this group on the issues of legitimacy of the Intifada and the Israeli strategy toward it. Some of the supporters of these opposition leaders within the Likud even joined members of the three radical nationalist parties in forming an *Eretz Israel* lobby in the Knesset. Shamir castigated them, stating that the activities of this lobby were "superfluous and damaging."[7]

The radical right has defined the Intifada as just another form of war against Israel: an attempt to put an end, by civilian violence and a continued campaign of terror, to any Israeli presence in the territories. This group has advocated the employment of harsh military and legal measures to put down the Intifada, including the massive expulsion or transfer of all those who engage in it, and to destroy the political, social, and economic infrastructure of the Intifada in the territories. The radical right rejects any Israeli territorial concession in return for peace. Israel should offer, according to this view, not territories but peace in exchange for peace.

Sharon, Levy, and Moda'i posed in 1989 and early 1990 a joint challenge to the leadership of Shamir and Arens and acted in concert to tie their hands in the negotiations over the elections proposal. Their individual views, however, were not always identifiable or necessarily identical beyond a certain proximity to the positions of the radical right. Sharon has been the only one among the three leaders who has voiced coherent and consistent views on the Intifada over a long period of time. He was a constant critic of the government's handling of the Intifada, charging that Rabin has failed and therefore should give up his position as defense minister. A winning strategy against the Intifada, according to Sharon, must entail three basic elements: first, clear and open commitment to win the conflict rather than just to contain it; second, seizing the initiative, adopting nonroutine and unpredictable methods in order to prevent the leaders of the Intifada from determining alone the conditions and situations of this conflict; and third, acting against the political infrastructure and the front organizations of the PLO and the Intifada in the territories. Sharon has frequently referred to his own success as a military commander in 1971–72 in putting down the PLO activities in the Gaza Strip to support his contention that such a strategy is feasible and potentially successful.[8]

Sharon has been critical not only of governmental policies toward the Intifada but also of those concerning the condition and behavior of the other institutions of Israeli society. The main problem, according to Sharon, is creeping Jewish fatigue, the accessibility offered to the PLO's political campaign within Israeli society, and the lack of determination to wrestle with these problems.[9] Sharon strongly criticized the election proposal, arguing that it lacked sufficient assurances and might constitute the first step in an unrestricted progression toward a Palestinian state. His position on the political and diplomatic issues has been significantly different from that of the radical right. He is against annexation, though he is also against relinquishing military control of the West Bank and Gaza. Sharon has supported the Camp David Accords and the Autonomy Plan. He has tried for some time, however, to promote another agenda for the solution of the Israeli-Palestinian conflict. Jordan, according to Sharon, is already a Palestinian state for reasons of demography, geography, and history. The Palestinians should, therefore, satisfy their claim for national self-determination, as well as voting rights, in Jordan. He even went as far as to express his regrets that Israel had helped, though passively, to save King Hussein's regime in September 1970, by deterring Syria from interfering on behalf of the Palestinian uprising in Jordan.[10] Other leaders of the Likud share the claim that Jordan is a Palestinian state in order to undermine the Palestinians' claim for an independent state in the West Bank and Gaza Strip; however, they have not shared Sharon's support for a change of regime in Jordan.

Sharon's overall plan or perspective is far from being coherent or consistent. He planned and led the Israeli military campaign against the PLO "ex-territorial" in Lebanon, even advocated the liquidation of its commanders; yet, he was apparently prepared to accept in 1970 a PLO state in Jordan in even greater proximity to the centers of the State of Israel. The war in Lebanon produced, according to Sharon, one major positive advantage: "It did away with an independent PLO kingdom of terror in Lebanon. . . . Terror has now an address—The Arab States."[11] Some may argue that this logic can also be applied to a Palestinian state, but Sharon did not go as far as to embrace it. Sharon is vehemently opposed to any negotiations with the PLO, let alone any on their demand for an independent state in the West Bank and Gaza.

The complexity of Sharon's approach is due, in part, to the fact that he is addressing the issues of the current political agenda (elections, autonomy, Intifada), while entertaining the hope and promoting the perspective of an alternative one. This duality makes him a radical leader; however, one who is amenable to change.

There is no independent position of the religious parties on the issues of the Intifada. The National Religious Party (five MKs) is divided. The majority has been close to the Likud mainstream position, while a strong minority is closer to the position of the radical right. Shas (six MKs) is closer to the Likud on the first two issues of the Intifada (legitimacy and strategy) but has become increasingly closer to the Labor alignment on the issues of political settlement. Its spiritual leader, the former Sephardi chief rabbi, Ovadia Yoseph, stated his readiness to exchange territories for peace and pressured Prime Minister Shamir to accept the Baker terms for negotiations with a Palestinian delegation. He even instructed members of the Shas faction in the Knesset not to participate in the no-confidence vote (March 1990), thereby bringing down the government for not accepting this demand. Agudat Israel (five MKs) and Degel Hatorah (two MKs) have been closer to Labor on all issues of the Intifada. Agudat Israel became the first religious party to change its coalition orientation, and most of its parliamentary delegation was prepared to join a Labor-led narrow coalition.

Struggle for Leadership: Factional Politics

As the largest faction, Herut has always nominated the leader first of the Gahal (bloc of Herut and Liberal parties) (1965-73) and then of the Likud (since 1973). Menachem Begin was repeatedly selected to the post without a nominating race in his party or the wider electoral bloc led by it. Upon Begin's abrupt resignation from his post as prime minister in August 1983, Shamir became the obvious choice of Herut ministers to succeed him, with the sole exception of Levy. Shamir was considered to be a member of the veteran generation of the movement—the commanders of the anti-British underground—despite the fact that he had belonged to the more extreme Stern Group, rather than to the Irgun underground, the commanders of which founded the Herut party. Shamir joined active party leadership only in 1970, five years after retirement from active duty in the Israeli Mosad. He served consecutively as chairman of the Party Executive (1975), speaker of the Knesset (1977), and foreign minister (1980), before being chosen as prime minister.

As in the case of Mapai (following the retirement of Prime Minister Ben-Gurion in 1963), Herut preferred a unifying and nonassertive veteran party leader who enjoyed the trust of party ministers and most party activists and who represented the prospect of continuity without crisis at a time of a painful and embarrassing leadership succession in Herut and the Likud. The previous heir apparent, Ezer Weizman, resigned from Begin's government in 1980, renouncing its policies toward the peace process, and actually left the party. The desertion of a maverick leader and the sudden retirement of an ailing, charismatic leader, who had exhausted his capacity for leadership, or even for continued involvement in public life, accelerated the search for a party leader who could successfully manage and minimize the crisis of succession. Levy, however, refused to go along with the choice of Shamir and introduced the nominating contest as a permanent feature in the post-Begin era of the Herut party and the Likud. Levy became the most powerful and skillful leader to emerge within the new and largest group of Likud voters—the Jewish immigrants from Arab and Moslem states. He rose first to a position of leadership within the Herut faction in the Histadrut (the General Federation of Labor) and later moved his leadership bid to the Knesset (1969) and the government.

In 1981, Levy was nominated to the number two slot on the Likud list of candidates to the Knesset and was appointed as deputy prime minister. He refused to let his party forget this decision, notwithstanding the fact that it was designed to enhance the Likud's electoral appeal rather than constituting at the time, a compelling indication of a possible line of succession. Shamir, however, failed to unify his party in subsequent years and had to face and win successive nominating races against Levy and Sharon. The Intifada contributed to an early resumption of the ongoing personal leadership struggle in the Likud and added another dimension to it—an issue of policy and a clash between a mainstream and a radical position on the issues of the Intifada. This clash altered to some extent the structure of factional politics in the Likud.

Since the 1978 split in Herut (which gave birth to the nationalist Tehiyah party in protest over the Camp David agreement), the major political factions within the parties of the Likud constituted, in fact, an organized following of a single leader—such as Levy and Sharon in Herut or Moda'i in the Liberal party—or the organized following of a group of leaders—such as Shamir and Arens in Herut. These personality-oriented factions have gained a certain degree of legitimacy and some measure of organizational success during the nominating races in the parties of the Likud. They were, however, considerably less legitimate and much less successful in maintaining a viable and cohesive organization between elections. Levy has been effectively isolated in the national leadership of his party and the Likud primarily because he persistently claimed the right to be recognized and rewarded as a factional leader and to be considered as a contender, even an heir apparent, to the leader of the party. The Intifada brought back at least a semblance of the policy-oriented opposition faction in the Likud against a two-fold background—the crisis of the existing personality-oriented factions and the emergence of a new political agenda. The new policy-oriented opposition faction within the Likud also came into being as a temporary alliance among three leaders; however, the given rationale for the formation of the new organization and the claim for its legitimacy were markedly different.

The three leaders of that opposition faction, Sharon, Levy, and Moda'i, have increasingly found themselves outside the new centers of partisan power and governmental policymaking that emerged around Prime Minister Shamir and Foreign Minister Arens. It was particularly apparent in the 1988 election campaign of the Likud, which prominently featured Shamir and his loyal young associates

(Dan Meridor, Ehud Olmert, Binyamin Netanyahu, Moshe Katzev) over the protests of Levy, Sharon, and Moda'i. The same trend was also apparent during the complex coalition negotiations following the elections. Sharon and Levy took an active part in these negotiations; however, they acted most of the time as self-appointed free agents, and in opposite directions, rather than as trusted spokesmen of the leadership of the party. The new opposition faction constituted, therefore, a defensive alliance of these leaders as much as a policy-oriented faction. The major purpose of this alliance was to obtain at least veto power over Prime Minister Shamir's political and partisan initiatives, and if successful, to take over the leadership of the party and create a new political agenda for the government. These leaders followed the old rule of politics: If you are not a party to an agreement, try to block it; if you are not part of the pack, try to dissolve it. Indeed, each one of these three opposition leaders had reasons of his own to cooperate in the new factional venture. Sharon found in it a vehicle to reassert his candidacy for leadership in the area of national defense, after the war in Lebanon, which led to his enforced resignation from the Ministry of Defense (following the recommendation of the Kahan Commission of Inquiry, investigating possible Israeli involvement in the Christian Phalangist massacre in the Palestinian refugee camps of Sabra and Shatilla in Lebanon), which at least partially discredited him as a national leader. Sharon never fully recovered from this political reversal. He later charged that he was "abandoned in the political battlefield." Furthermore, he was frustrated by being excluded from the inner policymaking circle. Sharon complained that Shamir refused even to bring his proposals for a new strategy to fight terrorism to the deliberations of the government. Against this background Sharon developed his challenge to Shamir's leadership, which was joined by Levy and Moda'i. Sharon's challenge had another target: the National Unity government. After the 1988 elections, Sharon campaigned against the renewal of this government and was instrumental in reaching a tentative agreement with the religious parties for the formation of a narrow coalition under Prime Minister Shamir. The latter, however, backed down at the last moment, to the dismay of the religious parties, who expected Shamir to deliver the long list of promises and concessions made to them.

Levy, who unlike Sharon came out for the continuation of the National Unity government after the elections, later joined Sharon's challenge to Shamir's leadership. This surprising move could be viewed as an attempt to gain credibility for his frustrated and faltering bid for leadership which, until then, was based primarily on the assertion of personal leadership, an implicit ethnic appeal, and most of all, the manipulation of organizational and political power within the party. Paradoxically, Levy had to radicalize his stand and challenge the majority leadership of the party in an effort to gain a new access to it or even be considered as a unifying and consensual leader in the future.

Modai of the Liberal party was appointed to the Shamir-led National Unity government in December 1988 after being forced out of the government by Prime Minister Peres in 1986 with Shamir's tacit consent. Moreover, he was rejected by Shamir as a candidate for a major ministry in the new Unity government. Moda'i's past concerns were certainly matched by a new concern for his political future: seeking access to the new, emerging factional politics within the Likud as a united and integrated party, following the formal merger of his Liberal party with the Herut party in 1989. Indeed, the failure of the opposition alliance to achieve its goal prompted Moda'i (in February 1990) to try to reassert the independence of the Liberal party within or outside the Likud. This move enjoyed the support of five Likud MKs who asked to be recognized as an independent faction in the Knesset.

Shamir tried at first to avoid a showdown with the three opposition leaders by bowing to their pressure to place limits on the proposal for elections in the West Bank and the Gaza Strip. He accepted and incorporated their specific demands in his speech before the central committee of the Likud on July 5, 1989. This party body approved in its resolution the continuation of the peace process according to the Camp David agreements and the peace initiative of the government. To this supportive language, however, it added the following limits: (1) the Arab inhabitants of East Jerusalem will not participate in the elections; (2) the terror (Intifada) will stop before the commencement of negotiations; (3) Jewish settlement in Judea and Samaria will continue; (4) there will be no foreign sovereignty, and there will be no Palestinian state in any part of the Land of Israel; (5) there will be no negotiations with the PLO. Facing Labor's uproar over his capitulation, Shamir moved to regain some of his freedom of action by stating the obvious, that the government, rather than the party, remains sovereign in making binding decisions for the state.

Shamir's strategy to defuse rather than confront the challenge of the opposition faction, despite his reported majority in the Likud's Central Committee, did not prove to be successful. The three opposition leaders kept their alliance and continued to press their challenge. Sharon, who had maintained the position of chairman of the Likud Central Committee, made an effective use of this post to force Shamir into another confrontation on February 12, 1990. Shamir refused this time to accept any further concessions and asked for a vote of confidence in the Central Committee. The belated showdown did not produce an orderly vote and legitimate decision, but rather a competitive and disorderly hand vote called by Shamir and Sharon simultaneously without a conclusive count. This bizarre confrontation raised procedural charges and counter-charges and failed to put the challenge to rest. Nevertheless, the fact that Sharon chose to read his letter of resignation from the government at the outset of this meeting was taken both as a sign of admission that he lacked sufficient votes to defeat Shamir, as well as a possible indication that he might have expected to be fired from the government. Shamir was empowered to do that according to Israeli law and was apparently moving closer to such a decision at the time.

Sharon's resignation was followed by a wider political crisis, which put an end to the National Unity government. The Labor party issued a public ultimatum to Shamir to accept the "Baker terms" by March 7, or else it would leave the National Unity government. Shamir found himself facing conflicting pressures, which not only threatened his position of leadership but also questioned the capability of the Likud party to govern. Upon the fall of the government by a no-confidence vote in the Knesset, on March 15, 1990, the ad hoc internal opposition alliance lost its relevancy and unity. Concerned that he might be blamed for the loss of power, and struggling to block the efforts of the Labor alignment to form a narrow coalition government, Sharon rushed, in a complete turnabout, to express his support for Shamir as the leader of the Likud. Levy tried to advance his own candidacy as a possible new head of a Likud-led coalition, given the rift among Agudat Israel, Shas, and Shamir. And, Moda'i exploited the new political crisis to gain recognition for his splinter group of the Liberal party as an independent faction in the Knesset and later to secure appointment to the post of finance minister in Shamir's June 1990 narrow coalition government in which Levy was appointed foreign minister and Sharon minister of housing.

The Ideological Dimension

Two years of the Intifada posed a new challenge to both the traditional ideology of annexation, espoused by the nationalist political right, as well as to an ideology of coexistence in a binational state, which could have been embraced at some time in the future by segments of the Israeli radical left. Meron Benvenisti's perception of the irreversible linkage between Israel and the West Bank and the Gaza Strip could have provided a possible rationale for it.[12]

The position of Herut, Gahal, and the Likud have already undergone several subtle changes on the issue of annexation, even prior to the onset of the Intifada.[13] The formation of Gahal, the precursor of the Likud, had already forced Herut to accept a less-firm commitment to the concept of Greater Israel. Gahal ceased to apply this concept to both banks of the Jordan River and certainly did not relate to it as a concrete political goal. The sudden occupation of the West Bank and Gaza in the 1967 war made the concept of Greater Israel initially more acceptable and more legitimate even among a sizable and important group of Labor intellectuals and kibbutz leaders, primarily of HaKibbutz HaMeuhad.[14] The renewed interest in Greater Israel was manifested, however, in the campaign to settle parts of the West Bank and Gaza more than by potent partisan pressure for outright legal annexation, with the exception of Jerusalem.

Gahal's platform for the 1969 elections called for the imposition of Israel's sovereignty and law over the "liberated territories." Nevertheless, Gahal stayed on after the election in a Labor-led National

Unity government that rejected annexation. It decided to move back to the opposition under Begin's insistence only when the government accepted U.S. Secretary of State William Rogers's peace initiative which made it possible to reach a cease-fire agreement in the long and costly war of attrition over the Suez Canal in 1970.

The concept and strategy of settlement, which at first was selective in its goals and restrictive in its application, still provided a consensual framework for the policies of the National Unity government (1967–70) under the leadership of the Labor alignment, as well as a basis for the unity of the Labor party itself, torn between doves and hawks on this issue. The formation of the Likud in 1973, which added two small parties and a third political group to Gahal, caused another change in the attitude toward annexation. The 1977 Likud platform used a formula that since then has become the major credo of the Likud on this issue: to prevent the transfer of Judea, Samaria, and Gaza to foreign rule and sovereignty. The platform still maintains that "between the sea and the Jordan River there will be only Israeli sovereignty." However, it does not spell out how this will come into being, nor does it contain a demand for the annexation of these territories.

A less restrictive and more far-reaching policy of settlement was adopted by the Likud government (1977–84), without, however, resorting to annexation.[15] The settlement campaign, which was embedded in the prestate concept of pioneering, nurtured by the Labor and kibbutz movements, offered the Likud and the National Religious party (NRP) a vision of gradual progression toward annexation. It also provided an ideological and political rationale for avoiding or postponing annexation, which threatened Israel with internal and external crises. When the leaders of the Likud did speak on annexation, however, they generally related to it in liberal terms based on the concept of equal citizens' rights, which was found in Jabotinsky's concept of autonomy. The de facto avoidance or deferment of annexation and the initial hope to effect sweeping demographic changes in the pacified territories (adding Jews, encouraging Arabs to leave) exempted the leaders of the Likud from the need to grapple with the prospect of a large Arab minority, close to a parity in strength with the Jewish population in a greater State of Israel.

When the Likud came to power, it twice made important, though qualified, commitments against annexation. Forming his first government, Prime Minister–designate Begin gave a written personal pledge to Moshe Dayan not to annex as long as there were negotiations over the issue of the territories. This personal and informal commitment, which was not even entirely clear in its formulation, did not constitute a concession and was part of the understanding that Begin's government should engage in efforts to achieve peace. The written reassurance concerning the issue of annexation paved the way for Dayan's decision to defect from the Labor party and join the Likud government. The failure to obtain such a commitment earlier, because of Begin's illness and hospitalization, stopped Dayan from joining the Likud list of candidates in the 1977 elections. Dayan had been a foe of annexation, even that of the Golan Heights in 1981; however, he also objected to the return of the West Bank and Gaza to foreign sovereignty, thereby turning the Israelis into "strangers—by his definition—within their own historic homeland."[16] The minimal policy concerning the issue of sovereignty in the West Bank and Gaza enabled the Likud government to negotiate peace with Egypt. In fact, it also provided the basis for a consensual position within the Likud itself on this issue.

In the Camp David conference in 1978, Begin presented the Autonomy Plan for the Arab inhabitants of the West Bank and the Gaza Strip. In the final agreement, Begin and the Israeli government actually gave up Israel's right for unilateral annexation at the end of the autonomy period. This particular concession (unlike the agreement to evacuate the settlements in Sinai) provoked only scant criticism except for the radical minority, which split the Herut party in protest over the Camp David Accords. The reason for it may have been the fact that full legal annexation was not on the concrete political agenda of the Likud even prior to the Camp David conference. Moreover, the Camp David agreement was in keeping with the commitment not to accept foreign rule in the territories. It was interpreted, even celebrated, by the leaders of the Likud in government as a contractual barrier for the emergence of a Palestinian state or for any other solution without Israel's consent. Moreover, Begin and the leaders of the Likud believed that by making concessions to Egypt they had acquired a freer hand in the West

Bank and Gaza. The Likud government also maintained that Israel had the right to claim sovereignty in the negotiations over a final political structure at the end of the prescribed period of autonomy. All Israeli governments since Camp David have restated their subscription to this agreement, despite the early cessation of the talks to implement the autonomy plan and the refusal of Egypt to renew them. Labor has been prepared to bypass and go beyond this agreement. The Likud, under Shamir, was prepared to adopt a different procedure (the proposal for elections in the territories) but clung to the Camp David Accords as the overall framework for progression toward the settlement of the issue of these territories.

The Intifada reflected the failure of pacification in the territories and certainly questioned Israel's capacity to maintain occupation by force for very long. Moreover, the Intifada made the prospect of total integration, which is the logical and legal outcome of annexation, much less attractive, if not entirely unacceptable, even to the hawkish constituency of the Likud. The mass demonstrations in Ashkelon and other incidents directed against Arab workers from the territories provided extreme indications of this new public mood. The emerging fear of integration and the concern over the violence of the Intifada (which has been reinforced by the specter of prolonged and inconclusive civil war in Lebanon) came at a period when the early hope for large immigration, following the 1967 war, was succeeded by growing concern over the demographic issue: the changing demographic trends in favor of the Arab population in Israel proper and in Greater Israel (Israel and the West Bank and Gaza Strip). The low birth rate among Jews in Israel, the dwindling immigration (until December 1989, when Soviet Jews began to arrive in large numbers), and the increased emigration from Israel turned the prospect of annexation, on democratic liberal terms, into a haunting and threatening challenge to the Jewish dominance in Israel.[17]

The emergence of the demographic issue in Israeli politics against the background of the Intifada actually left the Likud in an ideological quandary or limbo. The smaller and more extreme parties of the nationalist right were the first to respond to it by seeking new legitimacy to the old historic concept of transfer of minorities, put forward by the British government in the 1930s in the search for a partition solution to the Arab-Jewish conflict over Palestine.

The leadership of the Likud in government has not followed the more extreme radical right in embracing the "transfer" solution in response to both the Arab demographic threat and the Intifada. It was thus left (beyond the Autonomy Plan, which failed to materialize) with only a curtailed policy objective—to prevent the return or "surrender" of any part of the West Bank and Gaza Strip to "foreign control and sovereignty"—and without much confidence in the desirability of annexation under adverse demographic conditions. The leadership of the Likud was actually trying to buy time and keep the door open for Jewish settlement and possible future annexation under more favorable conditions without being clear or concrete about it. This ideological quandary may lead to a more radical nationalist position, especially if the Likud is out of the government and divorced of executive responsibility and compelling consideration of foreign (especially American) opposition to annexation. It may, however, still lead to a more pragmatic approach to a slow-moving gradual peace process, as was manifested by Shamir's acceptance of the election proposal in the territories.

It is hard to assess what will be the full impact of what appeared to be, at the end of 1989, the beginning of a mass Jewish immigration from the Soviet Union to Israel. On the one hand, it may offer new vitality to the policy of Jewish settlement in the West Bank and Gaza and strengthen resistance to territorial concessions. Shamir already said in an unguarded statement, which he was immediately forced to qualify, that "great Aliya requires a big Israel." On the other hand, the mass Russian immigration may offer the rationale and impetus for a change of national priorities. A historical analogy, which has only limited application in the case of the Likud, may underscore the latter possibility. In 1957, Ben-Gurion rejected any notion of remaining in the Gaza Strip. He wrote that following the Sinai campaign, Israel faced a choice: the absorption of hundreds of thousands of Jews arriving in Israel or undertaking the burden of hundreds of thousands of Arab refugees against their will in the Gaza Strip.[18] Subsequently, following the Six-Day War, Ben-Gurion was perhaps the least interested among mainstream Israeli leaders in any appreciable territorial gains, other than the unification of Jerusalem.

The Capacity to Govern

Seeking to establish a dominance in government, upon gaining power in 1977,[19] or subsequently struggling to maintain or even to share power, the Likud has constantly faced an uneasy dilemma: whether to pursue its own political agenda or adopt a widely shared one; whether to assume a consensual or divisive approach, a pragmatic or a programmatic one.

A consensual approach is not necessarily antithetical to adversary politics. It is an effort to remain within a wide national consensus on basic issues or act vigorously to establish a new one. In the latter case, it is the purpose and the outcome of the policy or the political initiative that counts: Is it designed to respond to the demands and beliefs of only one part of the society at the expense of the rest, or to provide a possible basis for national compromise and/or consensual acceptance? A consensual approach leads to coalition politics—sharing responsibilities inside and outside the government; to pragmatic politics—selecting policies designed to avoid or manage crises and reduce conflict; and to responsive politics—screening and aggregating sectorial demands placed on the government.

Mapai under Ben-Gurion was successful in creating the basis for a new national consensus concerning the authority of the state (the Altalena affair), severing the old political ties of army units (dismantling the Palmach), establishing a state system of elementary education and a system of a labor exchange, as well as adopting a pragmatic foreign policy with an early orientation to the democratic free world, and even readiness to sign a reparations agreement with the Federal Republic of Germany. Ben-Gurion recognized the need for national compromise concerning the economic structure of Israel and concerning the relationship between state and religion; however, he tested the applications of the latter through hard political bargaining and intermittent crises. Working with a coalition government, he strove to change its rules and modes of behavior in order to make it more responsible, cohesive, and disciplined. He pressed for the adoption of the constituency system of elections instead of the proportional system, which promotes partisan fragmentation, in order to make the coalition form of government optional rather than mandatory.

Upon his election as prime minister, Menachem Begin, the leader of the Likud, made an effort to pursue consensual politics on several major issues. Unlike Ben-Gurion, he accepted the coalition government as a positive and fully legitimate form of government within an acceptable system of elections—proportional representation. This system has been supported by most of the smaller parties, especially the religious ones, his allies in government. Begin promoted a proreligion stand, which he hoped to turn into a new national consensus. (Indeed, it came close to becoming one, though only much later, in 1988–90, because of the decision of the Labor party to win over the religious parties in order to be able to form a coalition government.) Begin invited Moshe Dayan, the maverick Labor leader with an international reputation, to serve as foreign minister, accepting his terms for the appointment. He also acted to induce a new reformist party, the centrist Democratic Movement for Change (DMC), to join the coalition government, despite his success in forming a government without it. Dayan and the DMC served as legitimators for Begin's government both at home and abroad. Begin's understanding of the need for such support reflected his decision not to give up the other part of the society, which remained antagonistic to his rule, and not to impose a new radical agenda upon it. In foreign policy, Dayan's secret diplomatic initiatives and the subsequent visit of President Anwar Sadat to Jerusalem gave Begin the opportunity to tackle first a potentially consensual issue—settlement with Egypt.

Begin's approach during the Camp David conference was not only consensual in content (actually outflanking the Labor party from the left) but also in form. In a manipulative and symbolic gesture, he conditioned the final acceptance of the Camp David agreement on a ratifying vote in the Knesset. Begin clearly deviated from a consensual approach on the issue of settlement in Judea, Samaria, and Gaza. Nevertheless, he did accept an unprecedented demand for a coalition party, made by the DMC, to be permitted to challenge from the outside, in the Knesset Security and Foreign Relations Committee, the decisions of the government concerning the construction of new settlements. Jewish settlements symbolized for Begin and the Likud the continued commitment to the concept of a Greater Israel, in the absence of a viable policy of annexation. They provided a positive rationale for not having one. It should be noted that the strategy of settlement was at first launched by a Labor-led National Unity government following the 1967 war. A Labor government also made the controversial decision to build the Jewish city of Kiryat Arba adjacent to the Arab city of Hebron, and a Labor government was the first to capitulate to the expansionist drive of Gush Emunim, in the case of Kadum.

Begin changed his approach in 1980–81, balancing his initial tendency toward consensual policies with a clear readiness to undertake divisive initiatives. The change became apparent in the autonomy talks with Egypt, the war in Lebanon, and the annexation of the Golan Heights. Begin, who was criticized for making risky concessions in the Camp David autonomy agreement, capitulated in 1979 to the demands of the NRP concerning both the opening positions of the Israeli government in the autonomy talks, as well as the composition of its negotiating team. Dayan resigned from the government in March 1980, in protest over this concession, feeling that he no longer enjoyed the trust of Begin and his coalition associates as the Israeli negotiator on this issue. He also concluded that President Sadat would be reluctant to reach a second agreement with Israel concerning the Palestinians without their participation or at least the inclusion of another Arab state in this round of negotiations. Begin certainly felt politically relieved not having to negotiate the implementation of the Autonomy Plan so close to the Camp David agreement.

Begin's decision to invade Lebanon in order to destroy the PLO's militarized enclave in its southern section exhibited elements of both a divisive and a consensual approach. The planned invasion was conceived within the framework of the retaliatory policy traditionally acceptable to both parties in Israel. Begin even consulted the leaders of the Labor party and received their conditional support for a limited military operation in Lebanon (not to reach beyond forty kilometers inside that country). Another consensual element in Begin's approach was apparent at a later date in his decision to finally respond to public pressure and form a commission of inquiry to examine whether there was an Israeli involvement in the Christian Phalangist massacre in the Palestinian refugee camps of Sabra and Shatilla. Subsequently, Begin accepted the recommendation of this commission and removed Sharon from his post as minister of defense, though he allowed him to remain a member of his government.

Begin gradually lent his support to a wider and more ambitious military campaign in Lebanon, but he seemed to have lost control over the development of this war, which escalated and failed to achieve its larger goals beyond the enforced exit of the PLO from Beirut and the destruction of its bases in southern Lebanon.[20] The growing opposition to the war in Lebanon, coupled with internal friction in his government, eroded the efficacy and stability of Begin's government, exhausted his own capacity for leadership, and eventually prompted his resignation from the government and exit from public life.

Yitzhak Shamir succeeded Begin as prime minister in October 1983. He did not offer forceful and innovative leadership to the government, nor was he successful in extricating it from an almost continuous state of crisis. The Likud coalition government continued to engage in a holding operation in Lebanon without developing any new political or diplomatic agenda. Increased internal disunity finally resulted in an early election to the Knesset in 1984.

Shamir actually lost the 1984 elections. The Likud was relegated to the position of the second largest party in the Knesset (Labor, forty-four seats; the Likud, forty-one seats). Both Labor and Likud were unable to form a coalition government and Shamir was immediately receptive to the initiative of forming a National Unity government, which averted the threat of a constitutional crisis. The National Unity government was based on parity in representation and rotation in the office of prime minister between the two major parties. This difficult structure threatened to institutionalize a continuing deadlock in government, which did not immediately materialize, certainly not in the first two years of the National Unity government under Prime Minister Peres. Shamir was, in part, responsible for this outcome. Waiting for his turn to assume the position of prime minister, he prevented the emergence of irreconcilable conflict between the two power-sharing parties in government.[21] Shamir either disallowed or gave up the opportunity to adopt a blocking decision of the Likud on critical issues in government and actually accepted the leadership of Prime Minister Peres and Defense Minister Rabin in resolving the issue of withdrawal from Lebanon. As prime minister, Shamir became at times more assertive, especially in objecting to the Peres-Hussein agreement concerning the convening of an international peace conference. He did not, however, move in any resolute fashion to challenge Peres's interpretation of his prerogatives as foreign minister and as the leader of one-half of the National Unity government to explore his own diplomatic initiatives. Shamir thus acquiesced in a new visible condition of shared power and conflicting partisan positions within the National Unity government.

Peres was determined to head the National Unity government (1984–86) as a regular coalition government, even attempting to fire two ministers of the Likud (Sharon and Moda'i) in disregard of the explicit restrictions placed on him by the coalition agreement. Shamir, by comparison, adopted a different style as prime minister, taking constant cognizance of the bipartisan structure of the National Unity government.

The two major parties that found themselves locked into a unity government, as a result of the 1984 coalition impasse, sought a decisive outcome in the 1988 election. Shamir, more than Peres, however, left the door open for the resumption of the National Unity government. After scoring only a hairline victory in the elections (Likud, forty; Labor, thirty-nine seats), Shamir won the postelection race to form a narrow coalition government. Having apparently secured such a possibility, Shamir changed course and concluded an agreement with the Labor alignment to reinstate the National Unity government (without, however, rotation of the office of the prime minister), at the cost of alienating the religious parties (his prospective partners in a narrow coalition), which later contributed to the fall of his government in March 1990. Shamir made this decision, despite protests from Ariel Sharon and some other leaders of the Likud, because he feared to be forced to adopt the divisive, programmatic and crisis-bound agenda of both the ultra-Orthodox religious parties and the parties of the radical right.

Beyond their divisive impact on the Israeli society, the religious parties threatened at that time to create a crisis in the relationship with American Jewry on the issue of "who is a Jew?" The parties of the radical right threatened to create a crisis in Israel's relationship with the American administration and to force Shamir to block the passage for any renewal of the peace process, at a period of continued violent conflict—the Intifada—which enhanced the need and the pressure for peace negotiations.

Renewed cooperation with the Labor alignment enabled Shamir to maintain the bipartisan policies on the issue of the Intifada and, no less important to him, to guarantee the continued service of Rabin as defense minister, who enjoyed vast public support and who apparently was more acceptable to him, at that juncture, than any other potential candidate for this office from his own party, the Likud, especially Sharon.

The reestablishment of the National Unity government in December 1988 also created a framework for a more pragmatic search for slow and gradual steps toward a political settlement, within a tense and prolonged dialogue with Labor and the American administration. Shamir's low key and anemic search for consensual and pragmatic policies concerning the election proposal and the wider peace process reflected his conservative approach and leadership style, as well as the growing and conflicting pressures of both the radical opposition within the Likud and the leaders of the Labor party in government. Shamir constantly sought ways to reduce conflict on all his political fronts but found himself sinking deeper into it because of his failure to effectively reorder his political goals. He failed to develop assertive leadership, that is, to win the conflicts or resolve them through conclusive agreement. He engaged instead in an effort either to continue to buy time and exhaust his rivals through mini-agreements, or to inch toward the resolution of the conflict without taking any decisive action, unless he felt he could afford to take it with impunity or was forced to do so.

After accepting the demands of the radical opposition within the Likud to place limits on the election proposal (in an attempt to arrest the party conflict), he hesitantly continued to search for an understanding with Peres and Rabin over the conditions for negotiations with the Palestinians over its implementation. Claiming later to win another showdown with the opposition ministers, Shamir did not opt either for a decisive contest with this opposition group or for an agreement with Peres and Rabin. The ultimatum of the Labor party to accept the Baker terms placed Shamir in an impossible situation. Aside from his basic reluctance to accept the terms for negotiations, Shamir could not afford to lose face and capitulate under an open ultimatum of a rival party. Suspecting for a long time that Peres was seeking opportunities to form an alternative government by winning over the religious parties, Shamir undertook a defensive but equally humiliating move. He fired Peres from the government, a move designed to keep the Labor alignment out of the interim government, in case it fell in a no-confidence Knesset vote. The firing of Peres ruled out a compromise, forced the Labor alignment to conclude its political initiative, and thus contributed to the fall of Shamir's government.

Shamir's conservative and largely passive style of leadership helped him to survive many crises; by the same token, it also prevented him from preempting crises or conclusively resolving them. Finding himself under conflicting pressures, in the midst of a continuous crisis, Shamir exhausted his options to keep the National Unity government in office. He finally failed to meet the sense of urgency not only of the Labor alignment, but also of the conservative, ultra-Orthodox Shas party. The fall of the National Unity government in March 1990 proved again that only a pragmatic approach, or what appears to be such an approach, may provide the basis for consensual politics and in the long run maintain the capacity to govern. The intermediary forces—the religious parties—turned, surprisingly, into a balancing, legitimating force that may pass judgment on the pragmatic and potentially consensual nature of government decisions in the areas of defense and foreign policy. The positive attitude of Shas (which created a problem with its pro-Likud constituency) and Agudat Israel toward the "Baker terms" served as an indication that the Likud's negative position toward these terms no longer appeared pragmatic and consensual, although Shas was later to join Shamir's narrow government in June 1990 and Agudat Israel was to follow suit several months later.

Notes

1. See Ze'ev Schiff and Ehud Ya'ari, *Intifada: The Palestinian Uprising—Israel's Third Front* (New York: Simon & Schuster, 1990), pp. 17–51; see also Don Peretz, *Intifada: The Palestinian Uprising* (Boulder, Colo.: Westview Press, 1989), pp. 1–38.

2. Shlomo Gazit, *The Stick and the Carrot: The Israeli Administration in Judea and Samaria* (Tel Aviv: Zmora-Bitan, 1985) (Hebrew).

3. Asher Arian and Raphael Venture, *Public Opinion in Israel and the Intifada: Changes in Security Attitudes 1987–88* (Tel Aviv: Jaffee Center for Strategic Studies, Memorandum no. 28, August 1989); Michael Shamir and Asher Arian, "The Intifada and Israeli Voters: Policy Preferences and Performance Evaluation," in *The Elections in Israel—1988*, ed. A. Arian and M. Shamir (Boulder, Colo.: Westview Press, forthcoming).

4. Nathan Yanai and Shlomo Aronson, "The 1984 Elections: A Test for the Israeli Political System," (Jerusalem: Medina, Mimshal Viyahasim Benleumiyyim 25, 1986), pp. 61–62 (Hebrew).

5. Yaacov Shavit, *Jabotinsky and the Revisionist Movement 1925–1948* (London: Case, 1988), pp. 258–64. *Ze'ev Jabotinsky—The Man and His Teachings*, ed. Joseph Nedava (Tel Aviv: The Defense Ministry Publishing House, 1980), pp. 242–51 (Hebrew).

6. M. Benvenisti, D. Rubinstein, and Z. Abu-Ziad, *West Bank Handbook* (Jerusalem: Jerusalem Post, 1986), pp. 72–73. Emile Sahliyeh, *In Search of Leadership: West Bank Politics since 1967* (Washington, 1988), pp. 36–86.

7. *Haaretz* (Tel Aviv) October 11, 1989.

8. Ariel Sharon and David Chanoff, *Warrior: The Autobiography of Ariel Sharon* (New York: Simon and Schuster, 1989).

9. Ariel Sharon, speech at the Dayan Public Forum, *Bama* (Tel Aviv), June 11, 1987 (unedited proceedings of this meeting), pp. 39–41.

10. Sharon and Chanoff, *Warrior*, pp. 244–47; Sharon's speech at the Dayan Public Forum, p. 49.

11. Sharon's speech at the Dayan Public Forum, p. 65.

12. Meron Benvenisti, *The West Bank Data Project: A Survey of Israel's Policies* (Washington: American Enterprise Institute, 1984), pp. 68–69; see also Joel Brinkley, "Hard Facts Defeat Israeli Researcher," *New York Times*, October 22, 1989.

13. Efraim Inbar and Giora Goldberg, "Is Israel's Political Elite Becoming More Hawkish?" *International Journal* 45, 3 (1990): 631–60.

14. Moshe Shamir, *Nathan Alterman: The Poet as a Leader* (Tel Aviv: Dvir, 1981) (Hebrew).

15. On the Likud in government, see Yaacov Shavit, "Ideology, World View, and National Policy: The Case of the Likud Goverment," *Jerusalem Journal of International Relations* 9, (1987): 101–16; Efraim Torgovnik,

"The Likud 1977–81: The Consolidation of Power," in *Israel in the Begin Era*, ed. Robert O. Freedman (New York: Praeger, 1982), pp. 7–27; David Pollock, "Likud in Power: Divided We Stand," ibid., pp. 56–75; Amos Perlmuter, *The Life and Times of Menachem Begin* (New York: Doubleday, 1987), pp. 301–96; and Ilan Peleg, *Begin's Foreign Policy 1977–1983* (New York: Greenwood, 1987), pp. 95–142.

16. Nathan Yanai, "Moshe Dayan on the Palestinian Problem: His Proposal for Unilateral Implementation of the Camp David Autonomy Plan (1980–1981)," in *The Middle East and North Africa: Essays in Honor of J.C. Hurewitz*, ed. Reeva S. Simon (New York: Middle East Institute of Columbia University, 1990), pp. 158–81.

17. See, for example, Arnon Sofer, "Demography and the Shaping of Israel's Borders," *Contemporary Jewry* 10, no. 2 (1985): 92–105.

18. David Ben-Gurion, *Netsah Israel* (Tel Aviv: Ayanot, 1963), p. 280 (Hebrew).

19. On the Likud's road to power, see Benjamin Akzin, "The Likud," in *The Elections in Israel, 1977*, ed. A. Arian (Jerusalem: Academic Press, 1980), pp. 39–56; Giora Goldberg, "The Struggle for Legitimacy: Herut's Road from Opposition to Power," in *Conflict and Consensus in Jewish Political Life*, ed. Stuart A. Cohen and Eliezar Don Yehiya (Jerusalem: Bar Ilan University Press, 1986), pp. 146–69; Jonathan Shapira, *Chosen to Command* (Tel Aviv: Am-Oved, 1989), pp. 162–80 (Hebrew).

20. Shlomo Aronson, "Israel's Leaders, Domestic Order and Foreign Policy, June 1981–June 1983," *Jerusalem Journal of International Relations*, 6 (1984): 1–29.

21. Nathan Yanai, "Unity Government: The Second Phase," *Jerusalem Letter* (Jerusalem Center for Public Affairs, 1986).

The Labor Party and the Intifada

10

Myron J. Aronoff

After having dominated the political system for nearly five decades, in 1977 the Labor party was forced into the opposition for the first time since the birth of the State of Israel in 1948. During the seven-year period that it led the coalition government, the Likud failed to establish either its political or its ideological dominance. The end of the dominant party system was accompanied by the renewal of political polarization, as competition between the two major parties intensified during the 1981 election, and the protest demonstrations against the controversial war in Lebanon.

The national election in 1984 resulted in a virtual tie between Labor and Likud, with neither able to form a politically acceptable, stable narrow coalition with the minor parties. Therefore, they formed a coalition government with each other. The 1984 National Unity government, in which the leaders of the two parties rotated in the premiership and the foreign ministry, enabled Israel to withdraw its army from most of Lebanon following the debacle of the Orwellian named war ("Peace for Galilee"), which the Likud-led government had waged. It also promoted significant steps toward economic reform.

As long as prospects for peace appeared to be remote and there did not appear to be an acceptable partner willing to negotiate with Israel over the fate of the Palestinians and the status of the territories occupied by Israel as a result of the 1967 war, the Israeli government functioned relatively well. However, when Shimon Peres succeeded in negotiating an agreement with King Hussein of Jordan that involved a symbolic ceremonial international peace conference as prerequisite for opening negotiations between Israel and a Jordanian/Palestinian delegation, Yitzhak Shamir went all out to mobilize the defeat of this initiative. This signaled the end of the honeymoon between Shamir and Peres and opened the campaign for the 1988 election. It was in this atmosphere of partial political paralysis that Israel confronted the beginning of the Intifada.

On December 8, 1987, an Israeli truck collided with two vans carrying Palestinian workers in the Gaza Strip, killing four Palestinians and injuring seven. Rumors spread that this was a deliberate reprisal for the murder of an Israeli businessman in Gaza two days previously. As the rumor spread, crowds of Palestinian protestors, mostly youths, threw stones and Molotov cocktails at Israeli vehicles. The first victim of the Intifada was killed the next day by the Israel Defense Forces who were attempting to break up a demonstration. Roadblocks and burning tires were added to the stones and Molotov cocktails as the protests spread from the Gaza Strip to the West Bank.

On December 15, accompanied by much publicity, Ariel (Arik) Sharon moved into his apartment in the Moslem Quarter of Jerusalem's walled Old City. Commercial strikes closed stores in East Jerusalem, Ramallah, Nablus, and throughout the West Bank. On January 3, 1988, nine Palestinians were deported for their role in what the government was then calling the "disturbances." On January 19, Defense Minister Yitzhak Rabin announced a new policy of using might, power, and beatings rather than live ammunition to quell the disturbances. Until then nineteen Palestinians had died since the outbreak of the uprising. On January 23, 1988, Abd al-Wahab Darwasha announced at a large demonstration of Israeli Arabs that he was resigning from the Labor party and establishing an independent Knesset faction in protest against Rabin's policy of beatings.

During February, U.S. envoy Richard Murphy met separately with Prime Minister Shamir, who expressed reservations about new U.S. peace initiatives, and with Foreign Minister Peres, who welcomed them. Peres continued to push for an international peace conference, and Shamir, threatening to force early elections, blocked an inner cabinet vote on a U.S. initiative presented by Secretary of State George Shultz. Peace Now sponsored a rally of 50,000 demonstrators in support of the Shultz initiative, and Chief of Staff Dan Shomron called on the government to reach an accord with Arab leaders in order to end the uprising. In April, PLO leader Khalil al-Wazir (Abu Jihad) was gunned down in his home in Tunis, reportedly by an Israeli hit team. On April 21, 1988, Israel celebrated its fortieth year of independence.

On May 6, 1988 *Ma'ariv* reported a survey indicating that support for the Likud had risen from 33 percent in January to 39 percent, while support for Labor declined from 46 percent to 38 percent during the same period. Later that month, in unprecedented democratic internal elections, the Labor party selected its Knesset list, which was composed of many fresh new faces of younger candidates. There were also large numbers of candidates from Middle Eastern backgrounds as well as dovish candidates.[1]

King Hussein surrendered claims of Jordanian sovereignty over the West Bank and called on the PLO to take responsibility for it on July 31, 1988. On August 4, as part of his severing ties with the West Bank, he announced the termination and forced retirement of 21,000 civil servants. Since Peres and the Labor party had emphasized the Jordanian option as their preferred scenario for solving the Palestinian problem for twenty-one years, this decision dramatically undercut the credibility of Peres and Labor.

At first, when Avraham Tamir, director-general of the Foreign Ministry, stated that the PLO was the national organization of the Palestinians (on September 1, 1988), it looked as if the Labor party was signaling a major shift in its position. However, rather than declaring even conditional willingness to negotiate with the PLO under specific circumstances, Labor announced somewhat vaguely that, if elected in November, it would terminate Israeli rule over 1.5 million Palestinians. Four days later, Salah Khalaf announced that the PLO was ready to recognize Israel, if Israel recognized the PLO and recognized the right to Palestinian self-determination. Foreign Minister Peres claimed he would negotiate with any Palestinian who recognized Israel's right to exist and renounced terrorism regardless of his biography.[2]

A poll published in the *Los Angeles Times* on October 14, 1988, indicated that among a representative sample of Israelis, 60 percent were willing to trade some land for peace, 46 percent favored trading all of the territories for peace, and yet 71 percent were convinced that the PLO did not want peace. The Intifada dominated public attention throughout the year and dominated the November 1988 election, focusing attention on questions of peace, security, and relations with the Palestinians.[3]

I argued in my recent book (which was in print prior to the election) that one of the political ramifications of the Palestinian uprising was to strengthen the shift to the right toward more nationalistic positions. I also suggested that, "with the doves becoming more dovish and the hawks more hawkish, people who had previously managed to avoid taking a position are being forced to do so. The population is becoming more polarized and the situation is moving in the direction that characterized the 1981 election campaign and the period of protest against the war in Lebanon."[4] Don Peretz and Sammy Smooha, analyzing the results of Israel's twelfth Knesset election (November 1, 1988), concur that the Intifada polarized the electorate and that "both ends of the political spectrum were radicalized."[5]

Labor received thirty-nine Knesset seats in 1988, having absorbed Ezer Weizman's Yahad party (which received three seats in 1984). It had received forty-four in 1984 when it was part of an electoral alignment with Mapam. Mapam received three seats in 1988. The new Arab Democratic party headed by Darwasha, who had been elected on the Labor list in 1984, received one seat in 1988. The Citizen's Rights and Peace Movement (Ratz) received five seats in 1988, two more than it received in 1984, but the same number it had after Yossi Sarid and Mordecai Wirshubsky defected from Labor and Shinui (Change), respectively, to join Ratz during the Eleventh Knesset. The renamed Center-Shinui received two Knesset seats in 1988, down one from 1984 before Wirshubsky's defection. Therefore, although Labor declined in strength, its dovish potential coalition partners gained what it lost, and the total for the camp remained exactly the same (fifty Knesset seats).

Whereas the Likud lost one seat, going from forty-one in 1984 to forty in 1988, this loss was absorbed by its potential partners to its right. Similarly, Tehiya declined from five to three seats, but Rafael Eitan, who had been elected on the Tehiya ticket in 1984, picked up two seats in 1988 for his revived Tzomet movement. Meir Kahane's Kach, which received one seat in 1984, was barred from running in 1988, but the new Moledet (a slightly more polite version of Kach) received two seats in 1988. Therefore, the combined camp remained with forty-seven Knesset seats in 1988, as it had in 1984.

The surprisingly strong showing of the non-Zionist ultra-Orthodox Shas (six Knesset members), Agudat Israel (five members of the Knesset), and Degel HaTorah (two MKs) had little to do with the Intifada.[6] Forty-two days of protracted negotiations with the aforementioned religious parties, with the National Religious Party (five MKs), and with the three ultranationalist parties convinced Shamir that a new unity government with Labor was the lesser evil among the available options. Having unsuccessfully attempted to entice religious parties into a narrow coalition government led by Labor, Peres, supported by Rabin, persuaded his colleagues, who were deeply divided on this issue, to join a new coalition with the Likud under much less favorable terms than previously. Led by Moshe Baram, who resigned his position as party secretary-general in protest against joining the new unity government, at least fifteen of Labor's thirty-nine MKs argued that the party should remain in the opposition to protect the party's identity and to strengthen Israeli parliamentary democracy.[7] Peres and Rabin successfully persuaded the majority to join the coalition in order to save the country from an ultranationalist government.

The greatest single consequence of the formation of the new unity government has been the perpetuation of the stalemate on the most pressing issue facing the nation. On the day after President Chaim Herzog called upon Shamir to form a new government, the Palestine National Council (PNC) proclaimed a Palestinian state, with Jerusalem as its capital. At the historic meeting in Algiers on November 15, 1988, the PNC accepted United Nations Resolution 242 and vaguely called for peaceful coexistence in a durable and lasting peace. Following Yasser Arafat's clarification of his speech in a United Nations meeting in Geneva, the United States announced that it would engage in a political dialogue with the PLO. There is little doubt that the leadership of the Intifada played a major role in influencing the PNC to moderate its position.

Meanwhile, Peres was still pushing for his international peace conference and pretending that King Hussein had not been serious about washing his hands of the West Bank. Shamir reiterated his rejection of both an international peace conference and talking with the PLO. An Israeli intelligence report was leaked, which suggested the need to talk with the PLO in order to end the Intifada. On April 6, 1989, Prime Minister Shamir proposed elections in the territories to choose leaders to negotiate with Israel on the terms of self-government. The plan had been worked out with Defense Minister Rabin, which prevented Peres from presenting the plan on which he had reportedly been working.[8]

Peres had taken the Finance Ministry in order to save the kibbutz movement and Chevrat Ovdim of the Histadrut from bankruptcy, which is why these institutions had pressured assiduously for Labor to join the unity government in the first place. He felt compelled to safeguard these last bastions of Labor support, but the price was significant. Not only was he no longer in a major foreign policy position, but he was also saddled with responsibility for Israel's deteriorating economic situation.[9] On April 19, 1989, a poll of Israeli Jews was published, indicating that Defense Minister Rabin was the most popular cabinet member. On May 14, 1989, the Israeli cabinet endorsed the Shamir/Rabin election proposal in a twenty to six vote.

The PLO had made further gestures of moderating their position. On May 2, 1989, Arafat called the PLO charter statements on Israel null and void. On June 18, Muhammed Milhelm stated that the PLO would accept Israel's election proposals so long as the elections would be conducted with superpower guarantees. But on June 26, 1989, Shamir told the Knesset Foreign Affairs and Defense Committee that the election proposal was more important for public relations than for practical purposes.

Rather than face a test of power in the Likud Central Committee with Sharon, David Levy, and Yitzhak Moda'i, Shamir bowed to their demands that he pledge that the Likud would never return territories to foreign sovereignty, that Palestinians in East Jerusalem would not be allowed to participate in the elections in the territories, and that the elections would not be held until the uprising ended. Whereas Shamir personally agreed with these conditions, it was embarrassing to have to make them public and thereby to risk alienating American support and also risk losing Labor's participation in the government.[10]

In fact, U.S. officials criticized these new strict conditions. Secretary of State Baker stated that the United States might support an international conference if Israel made its election plan impossible for the Palestinians to accept. Labor threatened to withdraw from the government. However, on July 23, 1989, after tense negotiations, the cabinet reaffirmed the original election proposal without mention of the Likud hard-line conditions, thereby averting the collapse of the unity government.

Three days later the PLO issued its own conditions for approving elections in the territories. Residents of East Jerusalem must be allowed to participate, freedom of speech and immunity from prosecution must be insured, the army must be withdrawn from population centers on election day, the Israeli government must accept the principle of land for peace, and the United States and Egypt would provide monitors for the election.

The Labor party Central Committee met in August and adopted a compromise solution, which would enable Arabs of East Jerusalem who are Jordanian citizens to participate in the elections, but not in East Jerusalem. Although this compromise satisfied the contending factions within the party, it was not acceptable to the Likud.[11] During this period a group of Labor Knesset members established a "Centrist Forum" to repair what they viewed as the false dovish image given by an influential minority within its ranks. Mordechai (Motta) Gur, who announced his ambition to become prime minister when he joined the party upon retirement as the chief of the general staff of the Israel Defense Forces (IDF), is one of the leading spokesmen of the forum. The lead editorial in the September 4, 1989, *Jerusalem Post* concluded: "Labour's message to the voters, in its essence, is that Israel's survival as a democratic Jewish state is incompatible with the permanent retention of all the occupied territories. If that 'leftist' message is muffled, let alone erased, out of 'electoral' considerations, Labour will no longer be an actor in Israeli politics but, at best, a spectator watching it from a supposedly good seat in the center."

Deliberate delaying tactics by Prime Minister Shamir created considerable doubts in Labor about the viability of the election proposal, and there was talk of examining alternatives to it.[12] Peres engaged in open disputes with Shamir, which many observers viewed as connected with the former's fighting to retain leadership of the party in light of the rising popularity of Rabin.[13] President Hosni Mubarak of Egypt called Shamir's bluff by proposing a ten-point plan to break the deadlock in the stalled peace process. Both Peres and Rabin, who was sent to Cairo to represent the government in talks with Mubarak, responded favorably to the Egyptian president's initiative. A disgruntled Likud politician was reported as having said, "it's more like the ten plagues, only the Labor party treats it like the ten commandments."[14]

The tension between Labor and the Likud over the Mubarak proposals are reflected in the banner headlines of the *Jerusalem Post International Edition* during the period: "Cabinet rift over Mubarak plan averted, Likud and Labour leaders agree to put off response," (September 23, 1989); and "Shamir ready to go to polls, Unity cabinet may break up over Egypt plan," (September 30, 1989). The latter lead article reported threats by Shamir to go to elections rather than compromise his initiative and consensus among Labor ministers that they should leave the government if the Likud dealt a death blow to the Mubarak proposals. The prime minister's office charged Labor with "disloyalty" to the government's own proposals.

The September 30 article speculated that a split in the government would likely lead to a challenge to Peres' leadership of the party by Rabin, whose popularity was steadily rising. Rabin has been called Labor's "teflon man." It was thought that he would be drafted to lead the party if it had to face elections at the time.[15] Several polls conducted during the year indicated that Rabin was the most popular minister in the cabinet. Even some doves in Labor turned to Rabin as representing the best hope of dislodging Labor from the unity government and leading Labor to electoral victory. Some argue that Rabin could use his "hawkishness" to Labor's political advantage.[16]

Peres was therefore reluctant to hold new elections, since he risked losing his position and the polls were not optimistic about Labor's chances. He assiduously courted the religious parties in the hope of forming a narrow coalition with them. Failing this, he backed down from the coalition crisis as he had done in July when Rabin had pressed to remain in the government. In a lengthy interview published prior to his visit to the United States, Peres discussed his view of the peace process. The key tone was captured by the headline "The Americans are the critical link." He stated: "A new opportunity has now been created. And much depends on the Americans."[17] In an analysis entitled "Why Bush is in no hurry to take the plunge," Wolf Blitzer correctly predicted, "the administration has no real stomach for undertaking the tough kind of decisions, the dogged hard work, and the political risks necessary to achieve progress."[18]

Frustrated in his attempt to get the United States to "save Israel from itself," Peres showed his irritation with his American allies in an interview published in *Ha'aretz*. One observer commented that the interview "was marked by a tone of petulance, which clearly reflects the Labor leader's frustration at his inability either to influence official policy or to extricate his party from a government in which it seems doomed to play second fiddle."[19] Peres courted the religious parties more fervently, hoping to establish a coalition with them. Labor's threats to leave the government lost credibility. Shamir claimed that he would welcome new elections and reminded Labor that the coalition agreement stipulated that if one of the partners bolted the government, both parties must join in submitting a bill for early elections. Peres hoped that when Shamir returned from his trip to the United States (conveniently after the Histadrut election on November 13), he would be able to prove to the religious parties that the diplomatic initiative had been killed by Shamir.[20]

Secretary of State James Baker's proposed five-point framework proposal for achieving Israeli-Palestinian talks, which was designed to initiate a dialogue, became the next stumbling block over which

Labor, the Likud, the PLO, and Washington argued. A letter from Foreign Minister Moshe Arens accepting Baker's proposals "in principle," but with "minor" reservations that essentially amounted to their rejection, was seen by the Americans as a ploy.[21] In spite of increased pressure from Washington, Arye Naor suggested that "those who are waiting for heavy American pressure, as if we were still in 1956, 'to save Israel from itself' will probably be disappointed . . . Scaling down and disengagement, as indicated by Baker, are much more likely."[22]

Since the United States appeared to be disinclined to force the Israeli government to do what the Labor ministers wanted it to do, Labor was once again forced to face its perennial dilemma—to stay in or get out of the coalition. Only seven of the thirty-nine Labor MKs complied with the request by Shimon Peres that they support the government in a no-confidence motion. The others abstained.[23] Yossi Sarid challenged his former colleagues in Labor: "Be honest with yourselves, withdraw from this government and tell the public what you know to be the truth—that there can be no peace without the PLO and without a withdrawal from the territories. Believe it or not, if you do you may even have a chance of winning." Dan Petreanu quotes the Labor faction's leader, Haim Ramon, as saying, "If our ministers thought it was electorally attractive they would immediately announce that they favor negotiations with the PLO."[24] Having been maneuvered by Shamir into squabbling over marginal details, Labor feared breaking up the government or facing the voters after having done so for what might appear to be trivial issues.

A major factor that prevented Agudat Yisrael from leaving the government at the time (although they did so—at least temporarily—later), according to one MK, was: "They [Labor] just can't be trusted to bolt the government. Rabin constantly indicates he doesn't want a narrow government—and he certainly doesn't want Peres to be prime minister . . . Peres can't deliver the party by himself. This being the case, we have to look out for our own interests as best we can."[25]

On November 5, 1989, the "forum of four" (Prime Minister Shamir, Foreign Minister Arens, Finance Minister Peres, and Defense Minister Rabin) arrived at a compromise formula in which the government accepted Secretary Baker's five-point plan for Israeli-Palestinian dialogue but sought assurances from the United States that Israel would not be obliged to talk with the PLO. The Likud wanted Israel's agreement to be *subject to* the assurances, while Labor felt the United States would not agree to such a conditional acceptance. The decision exacerbated tension between the Shamir-Arens camp and the hard-line ministers led by Sharon, who threatened to convene the Likud Central Committee to oppose the decision. Shamir attacked his opponents, warning this could lead to the break up of the coalition. He warned that "Labor might conceivably be able to form a narrow government which," he charged, "would begin negotiations with the PLO."[26]

When Labor had previously threatened to leave the government, Shamir taunted them, knowing that they feared to face new elections. However, this was before Agudat Yisrael withdrew from the coalition to force the Likud to honor prior commitments, including freezing legislative efforts for electoral reform and a civil rights law. Peres claimed that there was now a Knesset majority favoring territorial compromise, citing Halachic rulings of the spiritual leaders of Shas and Degel HaTorah. He claimed that Labor's increased coordination with the Orthodox parties could lead to a "coalition for peace."[27] Shamir was beginning to take seriously the possibility that Labor's wooing of the religious right might pay off.

Labor had hoped the U.S. government would pressure Prime Minister Shamir to soften his qualified acceptance of Baker's five points, which Shamir called euphemistically "assumptions." However, Shamir was fortunate to arrive in Washington while Egypt and the PLO were still officially undecided about the Baker proposals. Predictions in the media of an imminent collision between the Bush administration and Shamir did not materialize.[28]

In the meantime, the ultra-Orthodox parties, enraged by a Knesset vote in favor of a human rights bill and progress in preparing legislation for electoral reform, threatened to break their alliance with the Likud.[29]

The Likud had steadily encroached on traditional strongholds of Labor control. For example, in the local elections in March 1989 the

Likud captured Beersheba, Holon, Ashdod, and other municipalities that Labor had previously controlled. For the first time in history, the Likud succeeded in getting one of its mayors elected to the chairmanship of the Local Authorities Center, a voluntary association of all the mayors and local authority chairpersons in the country. Maxim Levy, the mayor of Ramle and brother of Deputy Prime Minister David Levy, was elected to the office on June 20, 1989.

Given this trend and the tendency of the public to hold Finance Minister Peres and secretary general of the Histadrut, Yisrael Kessar, responsible for Israel's economic recession and its unemployment, the party faced the Histadrut election with some trepidation.[30] Therefore, Labor's morale received a much needed boost with the results of the Histadrut election. Labor won 55 percent, to the Likud's 27 percent. Mapam received 9 percent, and a Jewish-Arab list and the Citizens' Rights and Peace Movement, 4 percent each. Labor and Mapam ran on the joint Ma'arach list in 1985 and received 66 percent to the Likud's 22 percent. "The Labor Party's joy . . . was not so much because of the victory, but because of the absence of defeat."[31] The results were strongly influenced by deals made by Secretary General Kessar with the religious parties. This is another indication of a political rapprochement between Labor and the religious parties.

Conclusions

The most significant consequence of the Intifada is that it convinced almost everyone that the status quo was no longer a viable solution. For example, a June 1989 survey conducted by the Israel Institute of Applied Social Research indicated that "only 13 percent of the population (16 percent of the Jews, 4 percent of the Arabs) consider the status quo a solution."[32] "Israel's occupation was once dubbed benign. Today, with some 12,000 Palestinians under detention without trial, it would seem to merit a somewhat different epithet."[33] The very notion of a "benign occupation" has begun to be perceived for what it is—an oxymoron.[34] Amos Oz said of the Intifada, "What was will never be again, and what will be, is not what was."[35] The Palestinian uprising has successfully challenged many assumptions that had been previously taken for granted by many, if not most, Israelis and many Palestinians as well. Among other things, it renewed or redrew the Green Line, which had disappeared from many Israeli maps and minds.

Asher Arian reports a hardening of attitudes on issues that had short-term implications, but on areas of policy that have more long-term importance, such as territorial compromise, more dovish views have gained slightly.[36] The short-term effect gave the Likud a slight edge over Labor in the 1988 election. The long-term effect could work to Labor's advantage under certain circumstances. One of the conditions is that it clearly articulate a plausible scenario for peace that is an alternative to the Likud's policy of perpetuation of the occupation.[37]

Two additional ramifications of the Intifada had a direct impact on Labor. First, the uprising influenced King Hussein to abdicate official responsibility for the West Bank, putting an end Labor's two-decade-long policy of relying on the Jordan option. Second, the Intifada forced the PLO to moderate its stance, moving it toward a compromise political solution. Lacking political courage, the leadership of Labor continues to follow public opinion polls rather than lead the nation; it has failed to adapt to the new realities. Instead, through participation in the government, it has provided what *Tikkun* editor Michael Lerner has described as a "fig leaf" for Shamir's policies.

Perennial rivalry between Peres and Rabin, internal divisions such as those between doves and hawks, economic interests of the kibbutz movement and the Histadrut, and other factors led Labor to enter the government. Some of these same factors have thus far prevented it from leaving the coalition. (Labor was finally to leave the National Unity government in March 1990, but Peres proved incapable of winning over the religious parties to form a narrow Labor-led government.)

The new "Centrist Forum" is pushing Labor to emulate the Likud, partly in reaction to the dovish forces in the party, partly as an electoral ploy, and, for Motta Gur, as a personal vehicle to carry him to the premiership. There is a growing movement to support Rabin's return to the helm of the party. Even a leading dove like

Ezer Weizman has switched support to Rabin to exploit the defense minister's electoral appeal. This has provided a serious constraint on Peres, who perceives that if Labor must face the electorate, he is not likely to head the ticket.

Peres has followed a policy of wooing the religious parties. He appears to have counted on the Americans to either pressure Shamir into accepting terms agreeable to Labor but not to the Likud to advance the peace process. In the absence of successfully pressuring Shamir, Peres seemed to hope that the failure to do so would precipitate a crisis with Israel that would provide a legitimate pretext for Labor to leave the government. Ideally, for Peres, such a crisis would provide a sufficient excuse to allow Labor to violate the coalition agreement it signed with the Likud to support new elections. Failing this, it would at least provide Labor with a legitimate excuse to bring down the government and give it an issue to use against the Likud in an election campaign.

Unfortunately for Peres, the American administration has been reluctant to play the role for which it has been cast in his scenario. Thus far Shamir has been a much more skillful player and has succeeded in maneuvering and balancing Labor off against his Likud rivals, while keeping American pressures to a tolerable level. Whereas it is seriously doubtful that Begin ever intended to fully implement the Autonomy Plan to which he agreed at Camp David, it is obvious that Shamir has no intention of implementing this plan, which he opposed from the outset. There is no question of the seriousness of his refusal to negotiate with the PLO (even through surrogates) or to contemplate territorial compromise. He brilliantly aborted initiatives and stalled the process of a possible Israeli-Palestinian dialogue, which could potentially lead to a political compromise. Tragically, the window of opportunity, which was opened, appears to be closing.

There is no military means of ending the Palestinian uprising without undermining the ethical foundation on which Israeli democracy is based. Ironically, the Intifada, which began without PLO initiative or direction, has proven that Israel cannot achieve a political resolution of the conflict without negotiating with the PLO. Therefore, the charade of haggling over whether surrogates must be restricted to those who presently reside in the territories or may include expellees is absurd. By playing Shamir's game Labor becomes a party to the tragic consequences, if this results in aborting the initiative.

If Labor ever hopes to regain the confidence of a sufficient proportion of the Israeli public to once again lead the nation, it must risk the possibility of electoral defeat. It must articulate a vision to the nation that explains the opportunities created by the new realities. It must convince the nation that these opportunities make the risks that must be taken worthwhile. What is required is nothing short of a new paradigm to give meaning to the new realities. It must articulate policies that realistically relate to these new conditions, even if they violate what had previously been taboo, such as negotiating with the PLO. It cannot do this by emulating the Likud. The original will always be more convincing and authentic than a cheap copy.

Notes

1. Myron J. Aronoff, "Better Late than Never: Democratization in the Israeli Labor Party," *Israel in the Post-Begin Era*, ed. Gregory Mahler (Albany: State University of New York Press, 1990). Labor has the largest number of Knesset members of Middle Eastern background (fourteen), compared with twelve for the Likud.

2. *New York Times*, September 25, 1988.

3. Don Peretz and Sammy Smooha, "Israel's Twelfth Knesset Election: An All-Loser Game," *Middle East Journal* 43, no. 3 (Summer 1989). The authors cite an August 1988 poll in the Continuing Survey of the Institute of Applied Social Research and the Smart Family Communications Institute of the Hebrew University of Jerusalem, which indicated that 60 percent of the respondents indicated issues of peace and security and 11 percent chose the territories as the most important issue of the election campaign.

4. Myron J. Aronoff, *Israeli Visions and Divisions: Cultural Change and Political Conflict* (New Brunswick, N.J.: Transaction Press, 1989), p. 153. Dan Horowitz and Moshe Lissak, *Trouble in Utopia: The Overburdened Polity of Israel* (Albany: State University of New York Press, 1989), also discuss the process of polarization in Israel but not the role of the Intifada in this process. Mordecai Bar-On, "Israeli Reactions to the Palestin-

ian Uprising," *Journal of Palestine Studies* 17, no. 4 (Summer 1988): 42, mentions a similar radicalization to the right and to the left as a reaction to the uprising.

5. Peretz and Smooha, "Israel's Twelfth Knesset Election," p. 392.

6. For analyses of the role of the religious parties in the election, see Robert O. Freedman, "Religion, Politics, and the Israeli Elections of 1988," *Middle East Journal* 43, no. 3 (Summer 1989): 406–22; and Avishai Margalit, "Israel: The Rise of the Ultra-Orthodox," *New York Review of Books*, November 9, 1989, pp. 38–44.

7. See Peretz and Smooha, "Israel's Twelfth Knesset Election," pp. 400–401. For an analysis of the position of Labor members of the Knesset on Israel/Palestine and on socioeconomic issues, see Haim Baram, "The Decline of the Labor Party," *Tikkun* 4, no. 5 (September/October 1989): 55–58. Baram divides the Labor MKs into doves (seven), two-staters (nine), and pragmatic expansionists (twenty-one) with one undecided on the Israel/Palestine issue. The opponents to joining the new unity government came from the two-staters, who believe the Israeli government should negotiate directly with the PLO, and from among the doves who accept the inevitability of serious territorial concessions.

8. See for example, Allan E. Shapiro, "A Paradoxical Optimism," *Jerusalem Post International Edition*, July 8, 1989.

9. See, for example, Shlomo Maoz and Avi Temkin, "The Devaluation of Peres," ibid., pp. 1, 4.

10. See the chapter by Nathan Yanai in this volume, "The Impact of the Intifada on the Likud Party in the Framework of Israeli Politics, 1987–1990."

11. Allan E. Shapiro, "The Key Issue in the Peace Plan," *Jerusalem Post International Edition*, August 19, 1989.

12. Dan Petreanu and Michal Yudelman, "Doubts in Labour Party over Peace Initiative," ibid., September 9, 1989.

13. Michal Yudelman, "Strains Appear in Government," ibid., September 7, 1989, pp. 1–2.

14. Peretz Kidron, "The Thunderbolt from Cairo," *Middle East International* (hereafter *MEI*), September 22, 1989, p. 3.

15. Dan Petreanu, "Labour's Man Who Can Do No Wrong," *Jerusalem Post International Edition*, September 30, 1989, p. 3.

16. Ezer Weizman, Labor's leading dove in the cabinet, is reported to have switched his support from Peres to Rabin after Rabin came out firmly in support of the Mubarak proposals. See Peretz Kidron, "Israel's Leaders Pulling in Different Directions," *MEI*, October 6, 1989, p. 3, subtitled "Weizman's Bombshell."

17. Menachem Shalev and Jeff Black, "Spotlight: The Americans Are

the Critical Link," *Jerusalem Post International Edition*, September 23, 1989, p. 7.

18. Wolf Blitzer, "Why Bush Is in No Hurry to Take the Plunge," ibid., September 23, 1989, p. 3.

19. Peretz Kidron, "If the PLO Is In, Israel Is Out," *MEI*, October 20, 1989, p. 9.

20. Dan Petreanu, "Labour's Threat: Is It Real This Time?" *Jerusalem Post International Edition*, October 21, 1989, p. 2.

21. See Wolf Blitzer and Menachem Shalev, "Peace Process: U.S. Steps up the Pressure," ibid., October 28, 1989, pp. 1-2; and Wolf Blitzer, "U.S.'s Not-so-subtle Pressure on Israel," ibid., November 4, 1989, pp. 1-2.

22. Arye Naor, "U.S. Edges to the Sideline?" ibid., November 4, 1989, p. 8.

23. Dan Petreanu, "Labour's Dilemma," ibid., November 4, 1989, p. 3.

24. Ibid.

25. Ibid.

26. *Jerusalem Post* staff, "Israel Accepts Baker's Five Points; Shamir Facing Rift with Rebel Likud Ministers—PLO May Block Israel-Palestinian Talks," ibid., November 11, 1989, p. 1.

27. Dan Petreanu, "Agudat Yisrael Leaves Government; Shamir Confident He Can Overcome Rebel Likud Ministers Challenge—Coalition Strains as Labor Woos Religious Parties," ibid., November 18, 1989, p. 3.

28. Wolf Blitzer and Menachem Shalev, "Shamir Skirts the Brink," ibid., November 25, 1989, pp. 1-2.

29. Asher Wallfish and Dan Petreanu, "New Threat to National Unity Coalition—Ultra Parties Enraged by Human Rights Bill," ibid., November 25, 1989, p. 3.

30. Ehud Katz, "Hobson's Choice: Labor at a Crossroads," *Israel Scene*, August 1989, pp. 3-4.

31. Dan Petreanu and Jeff Black, "Labour Buoyed by Histadrut Poll," *Jerusalem Post International Edition*, November 25, 1989, p. 3.

32. "Polls Apart on Policy for the Territories," ibid., September 2, 1989.

33. Editorial, "Law of Occupation," *Jerusalem Post*, November 16, 1989, reprinted in *Jerusalem Post International Edition*, November 25, 1989.

34. Eyal Ben-Ari, "Masks and Soldiering: The Israeli Army and the Palestinian Uprising," *Cultural Anthropology* 4, no. 4 (November 1989): 372-89.

35. " 'What was will never be again, and what will be is not what was', says Amos Oz," cited in report by Robert Rosenberg, *Jerusalem Post*, February 19, 1988, p. 4.

36. Data cited from a Jaffee Center for Strategic Studies memorandum, by Asher Arian and Raphael Ventura, entitled *Public Opinion in Israel*

and the Intifada: Changes in Security Attitudes, 1987–1988, printed in "Polls Apart on Policy for the Territories," September 2, 1989. See the chapter by Asher Arian in this volume, "Israeli Public Opinion and the Intifada."

37. Baram, "The Decline of the Labor Party," p. 58.

The Arabs in Israel and the Intifada

11

Elie Rekhess

The academic community in Israel has been divided in recent years over the question of whether the Arab minority in Israel has been undergoing a process of Israelization or Palestinization. The controversy has been significantly sharpened since the eruption of the Intifada. One school has argued that the uprising in the West Bank and Gaza had little effect on the national orientation of the Israeli Arabs, whose main concern remained focused on civil equality rather than on "national Palestinian issues."[1] The opposing opinion contended that the Intifada constituted a landmark in the continued strengthening of the Palestinian component in the Arab minority's national identity.[2] In light of the ongoing argument, this chapter seeks to examine the influence of the Intifada on the national orientation of the Israeli Arabs. It surveys their emotional reaction and their direct involvement in the struggle; it further discusses the modes of identification, reviews attitudes of major political organizations and finally analyzes the cumulative effects of the uprising not only from the narrow angle of developments which took place since December 1987, but also from the broader perspective of sociopolitical processes of change.

Modes of Identification

The Intifada gave an added impetus to the growth of solidarity and fellow-feeling between the Israeli Arabs and the inhabitants of the West Bank and Gaza.[3] A new sense of sharing a common fate sprang up. Arabs in Israel shared with the Palestinians of the territories their pride over the very outbreak of the uprising and over its successes, their pain over the killed and the wounded, their fury at Israel's "iron fist" policy, and the great upsurge of national sentiment. A closer look allows one to discern the feelings of restored honor and high regard for the "stone-throwing kids" who overcame the legendary "invincibility" of the Israeli army. The extensive television coverage allowed them to follow closely the unfolding of the Intifada. Much like many Arabs elsewhere, most Israeli Arabs admired the sheer tenacity of the uprising, which left the Israeli security forces with no effective reply to the mass demonstrations, the roadblocks, the burning tires, and incendiary bombs. Against this, the measures taken to put the uprising down, the heavy casualties, the occasional cases of brutality on the part of the Israeli soldiers, the scenes of humiliation, the arrests and expulsions gave rise to pain and sorrow among Israeli Arabs and made them feel that they shared the suffering of the West Bank and Gaza populations. In the words of Tariq Abd al-Hayy, chairman of the Tira village local council: "If a man dies in [the West Bank town of] Tulkarm, [the Israeli Arab village of] Tira too is in mourning."[4]

Solidarity demonstrations and strikes became more frequent. On December 21, 1987, less than two weeks after the beginning of the uprising, Israeli Arab leaders called for a general strike of the Arab sector in Israel: "Nobody can stop the Arabs who are Israeli citizens from expressing their identification with their brothers in the territories," said Ibrahim Nimr Husayn, chairman of the National Committee of Chairmen of Arab Local Authorities and one of the organizers of the strike.[5] The response was almost complete and, unlike in the past, the strike was observed not only in the Arab localities in the Galilee and the Triangle area (in central Israel) but also among the Arab sectors of the mixed towns. At noon, a minute of silence marked the Israeli Arabs' mourning for those killed in the territories.[6] Although the initiators had called the strike "Peace Day," it turned into a day of disorder and violence, which culminated in the blocking of the Wadi Ara (Nahal Iron) highway. Subsequently, the pattern of general strike, as a means to express solidarity with the uprising, was frequently repeated.

The blocking of the Wadi Ara highway, a major road linking the coastal plain and the Jezre'el Valley, indicated a clear attempt to transfer to within the Green Line the means of struggle characteristic of the Intifada. Such attempts were to multiply in months to come. First, the number of "nationalist-subversive" acts (as defined by government officials) increased considerably. These included the scrawling of hostile graffiti, the display of Palestine Liberation Organization (PLO) flags, the public chanting of the PLO anthem, and the circulation of inflammatory leaflets.[7] Second, there was a noted rise in the scope of damage inflicted upon property owned by Israeli Jews: setting fire to vehicles, smashing car windshields, destroying agricultural produce, and arson. Third, the intensity of disturbances and disruption of public order had also increased: erection of roadblocks, setting tires on fire, and stone throwing. Finally, there was a sharp escalation in terrorism. According to government sources, in 1987 there were 60 terror-related acts of sabotage carried out in Israel. In 1989, the number of such acts rose to 208. These incidents included 170 petrol-bomb attacks on Israeli traffic; 20 bombings; and 18 attempts of knife stabbing, hand-grenade throwing, and gun shooting.[8] Senior officials in the ministry of Arab minorities assessed that 70 to 80 percent of these cases were to be attributed to Israeli Arabs.[9] In addition, security forces had uncovered in 1988 fifteen terror networks clandestinely established by Fatah and other PLO organizations. In 1987, only two such cells were revealed.[10]

The growing solidarity between the Israeli Arabs and the Palestinians of the territories was simultaneously expressed in the form of a spontaneous, countrywide movement of humanitarian aid. The many casualties resulting from the clashes in the West Bank and the Gaza Strip, and the hardships suffered in places subjected to repeated curfews or declared "closed areas," led Israeli Arabs to organize shipments of food, blankets, and medical supplies. In many villages "Popular Committees for the Support of the Intifada" (*lijan shabiyya limusanadat al-intifada*) were set up. Sums reaching several tens of thousands of Israeli shekels were collected in a brief span of time. Hundreds of trucks reportedly made trips to the West Bank and Gaza (assisted there by United Nations Relief and Works Agency [UNRWA] staff).[11] In other instances, the initiative came from the territories. The Red Crescent organization, for example, appealed in February 1988 to the National Committee of Chairmen of Arab Local Authorities to send first-aid equipment and medicines. Within two days, 27,000 shekels worth of medical supplies was dispatched.[12]

The Effect on Political Parties and Ideological Trends

The tide of nationalist feeling in the territories has markedly influenced the political attitudes and ideological worldview of the Arab Israelis. Day after day, they were exposed to the symbols of the Palestinian uprising: the Palestinian flag, PLO slogans, the V signs, the traditional headdress. The closing of ranks in the territories behind the PLO led many Israeli Arabs to identify with the aims of the Intifada and, as a result, the nationalist-Palestinian component in their self-view came to the fore more forcefully than ever before. No political trend among Israeli Arabs remained unaffected. The Intifada became a central plank in the ideological platform of virtually all Arab political movements active within the Green Line.

The "Sons of the Village"

Ultranationalist organizations, such as the "Sons of the Village," were strongly inspired by the national awakening of the West Bank–Gaza Palestinians. These groups were now further encouraged to believe in the maximalist approach, calling for the ultimate establishment of a secular democratic Palestinian state over all of British mandatory Palestine.[13] Members of this radical grouping attributed utmost importance to the consolidation of national unity among the dispersed factions of the Palestinian people. Past emphasis on the binding cohesion between the sons of al-Jalil (the Galilee, in Israel) and the sons of al-Khalil (Hebron, in the West Bank) acquired, since December 1987, a much more significant meaning. As the Intifada unfolded, the identification of the ultranationalists with the fate of the West Bankers and Gazans deepened. Spokesmen for the trend heatedly argued that any attempt to separate the two Palestinian communities was bound to fail, because "the struggle of our Palestinian masses within the Green Line" was an integral part of the more general Palestinian effort.[14] Furthermore, according to the extreme radicals, the Arab minority had been given an active task: to generate change from within the Jewish state. "We, inside the Green Line, are the largest Palestinian concentration which can pressurize the Israeli rulers and hit the Israeli economy and the Zionist thought directly . . . in a manner which would assist accomplishing the targets of the Intifada," explained Raja Ighbariyya, member of the Regional Committee of the "Sons of the Village."[15] In addition to harsh verbal protests, the nationalists also acted aggressively. Militant members were presumably responsible for acts of a violent nature, striving to escalate the struggle and calling upon the Israeli Arabs to adopt an activist approach and an open confrontation with the authorities.[16] Israeli government quarters hinted that the nationalists were acting on instructions from like-minded counterparts in the territories.[17]

When the level of the radicals' involvement in subversive activity reached a critical point, the security forces responded by resorting to preventive steps, mostly administrative detentions. Yet these countermeasures did not deter the "Sons of the Village" from continually calling for action. *Al-Raya*, the group's weekly organ, often accused the Arabs of Israel of falling into "a crisis of impotence," in comparison to the territories, and of failing to "fulfill their potential."[18] Similarly, the group condemned the more established political parties for having dedicated time and effort to the twelfth Knesset election campaign, which the radicals boycotted, instead of diverting all their energies toward the promotion of the Intifada. Most of the reproach was directed to the Israeli Communist party (ICP, also known by its Hebrew acronym Rakah) and the Progressive List for Peace (PLP).

The Israeli Communist Party

The ICP, acting consistently with its past record, made every effort to demonstrate its identification with the uprising and to serve as its mouthpiece in Israel. As soon as the Intifada started, the party tabled a no-confidence motion in the Knesset, blaming the government for events in the territories.[19] Further parliamentary action followed on a regular basis. The party press gave extensive coverage to developments in the West Bank and Gaza. Party statements spoke of the "most barbaric acts" committed in the occupied territories, and party leaflets described Israeli repressive measures as "war crimes."[20] Affiliated groups (such as the League for Human and Citizen Rights and the National Association of Students) were active in attempts to get detainees released and to prevent expulsions. The ICP faction in the Histadrut protested regularly against the arrest of trade union leaders in the territories. ICP Knesset members visited prisons and detention centers in the territories.[21]

Of special concern to the ICP were the Communists in the West Bank and Gaza. The ICP profited from the Palestine National Council (PNC) decision of 1987 to grant Palestinian Communists official representation in the PLO's leading bodies. Every gesture of support for Communists in the territories now became a pro-PLO gesture as well.[22] As in the past, the party took up the cause of Communist detainees[23] and made room for Communist statements from the territories in the party press.[24]

In its election campaign, the ICP made great play of the Intifada, referring to it as "the great fateful turning point after 1948."[25] The official election platform spoke of the "new hopes" the uprising had given rise to, and of the opportunity it offered "to realize the aspirations of both peoples [the Israeli and the Palestinian] to live in peace and security."[26]

The ideological identification with the West Bank and Gaza and the emphasis on Palestinian loyalty illuminated a coherent feature in the ICP's policies. Much more problematic was its stand toward the question of actual engagement in the struggle. From the outset, Rakah rejected the demand of the nationalists to transfer the means of struggle from the territories into Israel. Rather, it opted for pursuing legitimate channels of action within the boundaries of the law. Accordingly, it hastened to initiate in mid-December 1987 the general strike, labeled as "Peace Day." Israeli officials claimed that the decision to organize the strike was received following consultation with the PLO.[27]

Yet as the scope of the struggle in the territories widened, the party began to succumb to growing internal and external pressures. The spreading anxiety within its inner ranks was well illustrated in the way the ICP manipulated its policy regarding the display of Palestinian-PLO flags, a phenomenon which, as I have indicated earlier, became increasingly popular after the Intifada began. Initially, the party opposed the hoisting of PLO flags in Arab villages of the Galilee and the Triangle. "Lifting the Palestinian flag," explained the Jewish secretary-general of the party, Meir Vilner, "was an honorable act in the territories, but when displayed in Israel it was as if we say: the territory of Israel should also be included in the Palestinian state."[28] Vilner's view was shared by leading Arab figures in the party such as politburo member Zahi Karkabi of Haifa.[29]

Less determined and more ambivalent on the flag issue was Tawfiq Ziyyad, the Communist mayor of Nazareth, known for his hard-line and occasional nationalist approach. On the one hand, Ziyyad staunchly opposed attempts to burn down Israeli flags. "We are citizens of the State of Israel," he said. "This state has a flag; this flag is officially the flag of the citizens of the state." He then immediately added: "As for the Palestinian flag it is the flag of our nation; there is no dispute about it."[30] Ziyyad's "tilting" statement was designed to accommodate to both the Israeli sense of affiliation of the Arab minority and its Palestinian sense of belonging. It reflected the unique characteristics of the ICP, being a biethnic, binational "super"-orthodox Communist organization, governed by a small minority of Jewish leaders, yet based upon a predominantly Arab membership and body of voters. It illustrated how the party was compelled to maneuver between contradictory constraints: the need to attract the Arab minority's support by emphasizing loyalty to the national Palestinian cause; the need to respond to Arab internal pressure calling for a more radical policy; an obligation not to indulge in unlawful hostile activity; pressure by more moderate Jewish party circles that rejected radical tendencies; the need to preserve the binding framework of a Jewish-Arab consensus;

and finally, the strict, uncompromising commitment to the political and ideological *diktat* of Moscow.[31]

In April 1988, the minister of the interior did, in fact, order the closure for a week of *al-Ittihad*, the party's Arabic-language organ, in which Ziyyad's statement regarding the Palestinian flag was published. The government's countermeasure did not seem to impress an opposition group, which began to operate within party ranks in the course of the year. The group came out against what was regarded as the "quietist," hesitant way in which the veteran party leaders handled the question of the Intifada. In May 1989, a nucleus of "reform-seeking members" published a sharply worded manifesto, condemning the "corrupt and stagnated" leadership. "No doubt that the courageous Intifada of the Arab Palestinian people disclosed the inability of the local present leadership [of the ICP] to mobilize the political and moral support and aid for the legitimate struggle [of the uprising]," the statement said.[32] *Al-Kashshaf*, the group's organ, published in Haifa, declared its commitment to purge the party and establish a new leadership, which would carry "the burden of the mass struggle," thus expressing its identification with the Intifada in a much more profound and sincere manner. In practical terms, *al-Kashshaf* called for a dramatic reversal of past party policies. Rather than boycotting the action-oriented "Sons of the Village," the paper suggested the ICP should cooperate with them as well as with the "conscientious elements" of the PLP.[33]

The Progressive List for Peace

The political and ideological world of the PLP has been similarly filled with the actions of the Intifada since late 1987. Its Arabic organ, *al-Watan*, reported Intifada events in great detail. The serialized proclamations of the Unified National Leadership of the Uprising were reprinted in full on the front page whenever they appeared. Party leaders and journalists commented at length on the uprising and its implications.[34] PLP Knesset members competed with their ICP counterparts in making frequent visits to the territories.[35] The second party conference in August 1988 was made the occasion for underlining the PLP's concern with events there. It opened with a minute's silence in memory of the "martyrs [*shu-*

hada] of the Intifada" and with greetings to the "children of the stones . . . [who] had vowed to fight the occupation army" and who had turned "their blood into rivers of freedom" and "their bodies into bridges for the return ['awda—the return of the refugees to their former towns and villages]." Among the messages read at the conference were greetings from the leaders of the West Bank pro-PLO youth organization al-Shabiba and from the brother of Fahd Qawasima, the late mayor of Hebron, and from Izz al-Din Arayan, the "senior" detainee at the Ansar-Three detention camp.[36] The conference resolutions underlined the success of the uprising and called on Israeli Arabs to prove their solidarity with the men and women of the Intifada. This motif was repeated in the PLP's election platform. One of its slogans spoke of the bond "with the Intifada of our people on Palestinian soil"; another said that a vote for the PLP was a vote of "support for our Palestinian people . . . [and] the courageous Intifada."[37]

During the election campaign, the PLP made a special effort to emphasize the movement's commitment not only to verbal declaration but, more importantly, to deeds as well. The party's Central Committee endorsed, therefore, the following resolution: to encourage visits by party members to the "cities, villages and refugee camps" (of the West Bank and Gaza), in expression of solidarity and support; to organize routine blood donations; to lead popular marches toward "siege foci" in the territories; to have families from within (fi al-dakhil) adopt fellow families from the West Bank and Gaza; and to establish teams of attorneys in defense of Intifada detainees.[38] In practical terms, however, the PLP contribution remained minimal. In fact, the movement found itself entangled by the same constraints that forced its major adversary, the ICP, to refrain from direct involvement in the Intifada. Just as the Communists voted against the transformation of violent means of struggle from the territories to Israel, so did the Progressives, in compliance with the need to act within the law.

This rather passive approach drew criticism, as happened with the Communist party, and PLP leaders were compelled to reply. Knesset member Muhammad Miari, the PLP's Knesset representative, responded apologetically, by relating to the particular, differentiating circumstances underlying the minority status of the Arabs in Israel. The Israeli Arabs, he explained, were not merely voicing "solidarity" with the fate of the West Bankers and Gazans, their sentiments could not be simply compared to the sense of identification of, for example, the people of Sweden. For us, Miari clarified, it was much more; it became a question of "welding" the ranks. Yet, he defensively argued, the distinctive situation of the Arabs living in a Jewish state imposed limitations and dictated restricted patterns of response. The consideration behind the Israeli Arabs' decision to avoid unlawful action, Miari further contended, was similar in nature to that of Palestinians in the territories who have opted against the use of live ammunition.[39] He was thus repeating a traditional slogan often raised by the Arab Communists in Israel, to whom "adventurism was not revolutionism."

The Labor Party and the Democratic Arab Party

The Intifada had similarly affected the Arab members of the Labor party. It constituted a major, although not singular, cause for internal division, leading to a split in ranks and the establishment of the new Democratic Arab party, headed by Abd al-Wahhab Darwasha. Held shoulder high by enthusiastic supporters, the former Labor member of the Knesset proclaimed at a Nazareth rally in January 1988 that he could no longer belong to the same party as Defense Minister Yitzhak Rabin, whom he called a "murderer." "I could no longer tolerate Yitzhak Rabin's 'iron fist' in the territories," he explained later.[40] Before leaving Labor, Darwasha said that he had tried to work for a better understanding in the occupied territories. He made an effort to mediate between Rabin and a group of thirteen personalities from the territories, including Elias Freij, Hanna Siniora, Ziad Abu Ziad, Bassam Shaka, and Fayez Abu Rahme. He proposed that Rabin release Faysal al-Husayni and Radwan Abu Ayyash from administrative detention by way of a goodwill gesture toward the group of thirteen. He was turned down by Rabin's staff—a rebuff that seemed to have confirmed to him his resolution to disown the Labor party.[41]

Having established himself independently, Darwasha dedicated his efforts to the promotion of a dual goal: the achievement of civil equality for the Israeli Arabs and the attainment of a solution to the Palestinian problem. On the latter sphere, much of his activities were related to the Intifada. In April 1988 Darwasha's party held its first convention. Speakers for the newly founded organization repeatedly mentioned "our people's uprising," reiterating that they themselves were "the people of Palestine."[42] When the first party congress was convened in the summer of 1988, the delegates were addressed by Radwan Abu Ayyash, who brought greetings from the "land of the Intifada."[43] In the Knesset, Darwasha consistently raised the question of the territories. He militantly denounced the army's policies and the measures imposed to quell the uprising. "A democracy which kills 500 Palestinians a year," he accused, "[a democracy] which kills children and women, a democracy which wounds 50 thousand souls in a year—this is no democracy."[44]

No longer restrained by what he had regarded as hesitant Labor policy, Darwasha now openly advocated direct negotiations with the PLO. The unequivocal support for a PLO-led Palestinian state became a cornerstone of his political outlook. He sought personal involvement in the peace process, and in a possible Israeli-Palestinian dialogue, and therefore cultivated contacts with West Bank/Gaza leaders, and through them, with the external PLO and Arab leadership.[45] It seemed as if Darwasha was attempting to establish himself as a go-between figure, acceptable to both the Israeli and the Palestinian side.

Darwasha's departure from Labor led many of the party's Arab activists to reassess their positions. True, speakers for the "moderate camp" continued to emphasize their loyalty to the state and commitment to the principles of integration and Jewish-Arab coexistence, but at the same time, new motifs, relegated to the sidelines in past years, were now being strongly asserted. Among the newly stressed themes were support for Palestinian statehood (to include Israeli presence on the Jordan River) and insistence on emphasizing the Palestinian component of national identity. Leading moderate personalities alluded more often to their "unlimited emotional identification" with the Intifada,[46] yet remained vehemently opposed to any attempt on the part of Israeli Arabs to participate actively in the uprising. It should be noted that the moderate camp, as well as a broad spectrum of Arab public opinion, had dissociated itself from the acts of sabotage perpetuated in Israel.

With the approach of elections to the twelfth Knesset, Labor's campaign in the Arab sector played down the role of Rabin and underlined that of Shimon Peres as a leader seeking a just peace with the Arab world.[47] The pivotal figure in Labor's campaign among the Arab community was Ezer Weizman. His liberal and dovish attitudes were given great play, at times to the point of counterproductivity among Jewish voters.

The Islamic Movement

Since the Intifada began, fundamentalist Islam established itself as one of the central forces on the Israeli Arabs' political map. This new, vigorous trend registered an outstanding achievement when, in February 1989, it won a decisive victory in the municipal elections. Forty-five Islamic representatives were elected as councillors to fourteen Arab localities, gaining nearly 10 percent of the vote. Members of the movement also won the mayoralty of four villages and one Arab town (Umm al-Fahm). These stunning results indicated a significant breakthrough for Islam in Israel. In the previous local elections in 1983, there were only six Islamic activists elected, from four localities.

Moslem fundamentalism has steadily gained power among Israeli Arabs since the late 1970s. Among the major factors that nourished the advance of Islam were the post-1967 exposure to the intensive religious life of the West Bank and Gaza, access to the Moslem holy sites of Jerusalem and Hebron, and the growing interest of the West Bank religious establishment in the Moslems of Israel.[48] In the West Bank and Gaza, it was Islamic radicalism that generated much of the Intifada. It is, therefore, of special interest to examine the interrelation between the two fundamentalist movements, in Israel and the territories, as they drew together under the impact of the uprising.

The Islamic trend in Israel interpreted the events in the territories in a purely religious context. *Al-Sirat*, the movement's monthly organ, had continuously highlighted the Islamic nature (as it saw it) of the uprising, terming it an "Islamic Revolution" (*thawra Islamiyya*).[49] Accordingly, Israel's "iron-fist" policy was presented as a dual strategy designed to deprive the Palestinians of human rights, on the one hand, and to eradicate Islam and its holy sites, on the other. The chronicles of the Intifada were widely covered in the Israeli Islamic press. Leading Islamists, among them Sheikh Ahmed Yasin, head of HAMAS (Arabic acronym for Harakat al-Muqawama al-Islamiyya, the Islamic Resistance Movement), and Abd al-Aziz Rantisi, were frequently interviewed, and the serialized leaflets of the movement were fully reproduced in the Israeli press. *Al-Sirat* dedicated special sections to the life story of the Moslem *shuhada*, members of HAMAS, and the Islamic Jihad, killed by Israeli soldiers. Members of the Israeli movement paid condolence visits to the families of the dead in the West Bank and Gaza.[50]

The impressive success of the West Bank–Gaza fundamentalists had undoubtedly inspired their counterparts in Israel and had contributed to their triumphant victory in the February 1989 municipal elections. Islamic personalities in Israel viewed the leadership role that HAMAS had assumed in the territories as a heavenly sign, marking the reestablishment of God's guidance upon the *umma* (the community of believers). The striking achievements of Palestinian Islamic militancy proved, so they argued, that there existed a cohesive interrelation between faith and pious conduct, on the one hand, and worldly political prosperity, on the other. The direction of historical evolution was thus restored to its right, appropriate course of development.

The Intifada was, therefore, seen by the Israeli fundamentalists as "God-supported" (*Muayyada min Allah*).[51] The cumulative effect from the religious point of view was summarized by the newly elected Islamic mayors and heads of local councils during a visit to the United States in late 1989. "The Intifada," they explained, "had made [the 1948 Palestinians, i.e., the Arabs of Israel] be aware again of the truth regarding the importance of the mosque and its historic mission. . . . [it] nourished and strengthened the ties between Haifa [in Israel] and Gaza, between Hebron and Galilee. . . . it had revived the core of faith, it narrowed the distance between

Allah and the people, it had reinstated the [spirit of] confidence and the feeling of potence and value; it had revived the hope; it had spread conviction among the 1948 Palestinians."[52]

The mounting sense of self-assurance was not transformed, however, into violent deeds. On the question of direct involvement in the Intifada, the Israeli Islamic movement adopted the same stance followed by the Communists and the Progressives. Sheikh Abdallah Nimr Darwish, the uncontested leader of the trend, made the distinction clear: "identification—yes; violence—no."[53] Instead, he urged his disciples to raise money and collect food for the West Bankers and the Gazans. Indeed, the movement was successful in organizing aid shipments to the territories.

The essence of the ties between the Israeli fundamentalists and their militant counterparts in the West Bank and Gaza remained, nevertheless, to a large extent, blurred and obscured. *Filastin al-Muslima*, an Islamic journal published in England and known to represent the views of HAMAS, laconically stated that "the Islamic movement inside the Zionist entity [i.e., Israel] is a natural extended-line of the Palestinian and world Islamic movements."[54] Some Israeli observers contended that there existed a measure of coordination between fundamentalist activists on both sides of the Green Line.[55] Ziad Abu Amr, after thoroughly researching the resurgence of Islam in the West Bank and Gaza, alluded to a possible secretive nature of relations binding the two groupings. When he specifically asked Sheikh Yasin about such linkage, the leader of HAMAS declined to elaborate. Yasin's only comment was that "Islam makes it obligatory to maintain relations of understanding and cooperation with the Islamists inside and outside Palestine."[56] In Israel, Sheikh Darwish vehemently denied all reports on institutionalized linkages with HAMAS or the Islamic Jihad.[57]

The Israeli Arabs in Palestinian Perspective

The political initiative adopted by the PLO in late 1988 had considerably enhanced the process of Palestinization within the Israeli Arab community. Palestinian independence and the proclamation of statehood, announced during the nineteenth session of the PNC convention in Algiers, were enthusiastically received by wide sectors of the Israeli Arab population. The sense of satisfaction was due in part to the emphasis laid in the PNC resolutions with regard to the growing national role of the "1948 Palestinians" as an integral part of the Arab Palestinian people. The Algiers resolutions had also reasserted the PLO's status as the sole representative of the Palestinians, wherever they were, including those living "inside" (*fi al-dakhil*), that is, in Israel proper.[58]

The Algiers statement corresponded with the PLO's overall policy toward the Israeli Arabs. Since the early 1970s, the PLO demonstrated stronger interest in, and concern for, the Arabs in Israel as well as a desire to incorporate them into the general Palestinian struggle. Consequently, the organization developed the "three circles" concept, integrating the 1948 Palestinians, those from the West Bank and Gaza and the Palestinians in the Diaspora. In the 1980s, PLO officials made strenuous efforts to narrow the gap dividing the three orbits of Palestinian affiliation, with a special emphasis on consolidating national solidarity between the Arabs in Israel and in the territories.

The profound identification with the fate of the West Bankers and Gazans and the marked support for Palestinian national objectives, as professed by the Israeli Arabs since the Intifada began, were, therefore, warmly welcomed by the PLO leadership. Senior PLO officials, among them Jamal Surani, a member of the organization's Executive Committee, made a point to clarify that "the uprising [was] the political resurgence of the Palestinian people shared by all [Palestinians] whether the 1948 Arabs or [the] 1967 [Palestinians of the occupied territories] or those outside the boundaries [of Palestine]." "The participation of the 1948 Arabs [in the general struggle] was not new but continuous," Surani further asserted.[59] This view was shared by the Unified National Leadership of the Uprising, which, in a leaflet published in March 1989, for example, congratulated the Israeli Arabs on the commemoration of "Land Day" and called upon them to "intensify the efforts in support of the Intifada."[60]

Salim Tamari, a prominent scholar of Bir Zeit University, similarly praised the contribution of Israeli Arabs. The firm reaction of the Arab minority, he asserted, served as "a signal to the Israelis that if they continue along this road [of oppression] then they will have to deal not only with the Arabs of the territories, but with their Arabs as well."[61] Other political quarters in the West Bank, however, were less impressed with the Israeli Arabs' performance, arguing that they remained far from exhausting their potential. Ghassan Bishara, for example, in an article published in the East Jerusalem *al-Fajr* in late 1989, critically deplored what he regarded as indifference and "very little concern for what [was] happening in the West Bank and Gaza." The Arabs of Galilee, he maintained, seemed "to live a life of their own, detached from what their government [was] doing [in the territories] . . . go[ing] about their daily business quite undisturbed."[62] Bishara's observations echoed similar criticism voiced by the more radical wings within the Arab sector itself, as we have seen.

Of special relevance to the Arab minority was the PLO's revival of UN General Assembly Resolution 181, popularly known as the 1947 Partition Plan. This resolution was adopted as the juridical basis for the declaration of Palestinian statehood in the November 1988 PNC convention. While no operative strategy to implement the resolution was proposed in Algiers, the mere suggestion that the PLO was seriously considering the option of a partitioned Palestine, according to the 1947 plan, had far-reaching repercussions for the Israeli Arabs. The original U.N. plan spoke of an Arab state in which vast parts of the Galilee and the Triangle were to be included. By the late 1980s, these regions, under Israeli rule since 1948, came to be densely populated by Arab citizens. In the case of the Galilee, the Arabs constituted the majority. In all likelihood, renewed discussion of the 1947 Partition Plan led certain political factions within the Arab community to reexamine favorably the notions of autonomy and, possibly, irredentism.[63]

The option of separating the Galilee and the Triangle from the State of Israel was not altogether new. It was widely discussed in the late 1940s and during the 1950s. In 1952, the ICP (then called MAKI, after its Hebrew acronym) endorsed a resolution calling upon Israel to recognize the right of the Arab Palestinian people for self-determination "till secession." Arab radicals within party ranks went even further in their demand for an autonomous party infrastructure to be established in the Galilee, corresponding to the 1947 lines of division.⁶⁴ At the time, the Israeli leadership was considerably concerned. Yigal Alon, who later became Israel's minister of foreign affairs, called "political struggle by raising demands for regional autonomy and . . . the mass return of refugees" one of five security threats that, he believed, the Arab minority posed to the State of Israel.⁶⁵

In the 1960s and 1970s, the notion of separation continued to be ambiguously alluded to by Arab members of the ICP, often representing more radical nationalist tendencies. Reference was often made to the traditional Soviet concept, according to which Israel was established on a territory much larger than originally allotted by the UN.⁶⁶ On May 1, 1976, Knesset member Tawfiq Ziyyad declared that if full equality was unattainable, the Israeli Arabs "will advertise announcements in the marketplace and in the press [in order] to search for another state that would accept them *with their lands*" (emphasis added). When accused of hinting at the possible detachment of the Galilee from the rest of Israel, Ziyyad demurred.⁶⁷ The ICP's official leadership similarly tried to minimize the significance of any utterance suggesting irredentism, while restating the party's formal commitment to UN Resolution 242 and the June 4, 1967, borders.

Senior Israeli government officials held a different view. In 1983, Binyamin Gur-Aryeh, who then served as the prime minister's adviser on Arab affairs, claimed that the ICP spoke in a double-tongued language: While in public it supported the establishment of a Palestinian state alongside Israel, within the party's inner circles, especially among the Arabs, there were groups discussing the 1947 Partition Plan borders.⁶⁸ The ICP staunchly rebutted Gur-Aryeh's interpretation. Four years later, another prominent official in charge of Arab affairs raised similar speculations. Brig. Gen. (ret.) Amos Gilboa, then the senior assistant to the minister in charge of the minorities, stated that within the Arab community there was a "clear orientation toward separatism from the Israeli state system."⁶⁹ It is interesting to note that after a relatively lengthy period in which the ICP made no reference to the 1952 resolution regarding "secession," the formula reemerged in several party publications in the late 1980s.⁷⁰

Conclusions

The discussion hitherto focused on the immediate reaction of the Israeli Arabs to the Intifada. Surveyed were emotional expressions, professed political viewpoints, and various actions. Yet the effects of the Intifada should be contextualized within broader historical perspectives. Hence, an attempt will be made to illustrate how the uprising served as a powerful catalyst that intensified and accelerated existing processes of political and socioeconomic change.

One of the central outcomes of the Intifada is the consolidation of a growing sense of solidarity between the Arabs of Israel and the residents of the territories. In a closely related development, the national awakening of the West Bank and Gaza had sharpened the Israeli Arabs' dilemma of identity, subsequently resulting in a marked strengthening of Palestinian assertiveness. The formula defining the Arab population as "Palestinian in nationality and Israeli in citizenship" became more widely popular.[71] Overall, the process of Palestinization had been significantly enhanced. The major breakthroughs in the political arena, namely the PLO 1988 initiative, led a considerable portion of the Israeli Arabs to reformulate their views regarding the national problem.

In this respect, the effect of the events in the late 1980s was strikingly similar to that which came about in the mid-1970s, following the 1973 October War. The analogous reaction revealed a repetitive pattern of political conduct. In both cases, the political outlook of the Arabs in Israel was acutely shaken, and the balance between the Palestinian and Israeli components in their national identity was severely disrupted. In 1988, as well as in 1973, they shared the feeling of restored pride and self-esteem with the rest of the Arab world. Being closely integrated into Israeli society, they were able to witness in the mid-1970s, just as in the late 1980s, signs of internal Israeli weakness and increasing demoralization, while increasingly identifying themselves with the reasserted "power-image" of the Arab side.

The advanced prestige of the PLO in the international and inter-Arab arenas following the 1973 war, the Rabat conference of November 1974, Arafat's speech at the UN that year, and the acceptance of the PLO as an observer at the UN, all served to promote the stature of the organization in the eyes of Israel's Arab minority. Open sympathy for the PLO and identification with its political goals spread considerably.[72] Similar, almost identical, developments took place as a result of the Intifada. International sympathy with the Palestinians and with their stand against the Israeli security forces augmented the Israeli Arabs' own self-respect as well as their solidarity with their kinsmen across the Green Line. By the late 1980s, all ideological trends in the Arab sector came to be united in common support for the establishment of a PLO-led independent Palestinian state in the West Bank and Gaza. Traditional differences dividing Communists from Progressives and radicals from moderates had virtually disappeared. A new, solid consensus of Palestinian consciousness in Israel was thus firmly established.

One may assume that a solution that will secure Palestinian statehood in the occupied territories, alongside Israel, will satisfy the national aspirations of the majority of Israeli Arabs.[73] Yet this assessment should be modified and linked to another central development caused by the Intifada: the revival of the 1947 Partition Plan and the renewed discussion of irredentism. It seems that very few Israeli Arabs seriously believe in the feasibility of implementing the 1947 plan at this stage. The vast majority rejects the notion of separatism or the possibility of moving into the projected Palestinian state. Nevertheless, present cautions voiced by Israeli government officials and the lessons of past years should serve as a warning regarding possible shifts in the future.

The Intifada undoubtedly contributed to the substantive increase in the involvement of Israeli Arabs in terror-related acts of violence. These actions reflect an additional facet of the encroaching process of Palestinization. The fact that these acts "pale in comparison to the tens of thousands of such acts perpetrated inside the occupied territories"[74] does not reduce the seriousness of the trend. Active participation of the Arab minority in sabotage activity, however, is not a new phenomenon, and one may observe a certain "cyclic pattern," which seems to characterize its periodic recurrence. The first massive wave of recruitment to the militant Palestinian organizations took place after the 1967 war and was followed by a similar tendency evident after October 1973. The involvement in sabotage activity after 1967 and 1973, as in 1988, was a manifestation of culminating national sentiments, diverted to violent channels, as a result of dramatic events in the Arab-Israeli conflict.

In another development relating to the Intifada, and reflecting the process of Palestinization, public figures in the Arab sector began to demonstrate growing eagerness to be involved directly and personally in promoting the peace process. Attempts to establish contact with PLO personalities are no longer restricted to the more established Arab Knesset members such as Darwasha and Miari. In late December 1989, the Israel Security Service revealed that Ahmad Tibi, an Arab physician and an independent political activist from the village of Taiba, played a central role in arranging an alleged meeting between an Israeli cabinet minister, Ezer Weizman, and high-ranking PLO officials. In preparation for the meeting, Tibi had met with the PLO leadership, traveling extensively to various Arab capitals. The Security Service disclosure seemed to have damaged Tibi's image as a devoted national figure. In a demonstrative "rehabilitative" move, Abu Iyyad, Yasser Arafat's deputy, came out in Tibi's defense, labeling him a "loyal Palestinian nationalist."[75] This recent episode, marginal as it may seem, forcibly illustrates the change in the self-perception of the Israeli Arabs. In the past they were viewed as a "bridge to the rest of the Arab world." Today they reject the metaphor, because bridges are "stepped on." Instead, they prefer to be seen as links in a chain, central to any resolution of the Palestinian problem.

Concurrently, the ramifications of the Intifada should be examined from the perspective of domestic politics and socioeconomic change. The uprising erupted at a time when the political system of the Arab sector in Israel has been undergoing profound transformation. The process began in the late 1960s with the gradual disappearance of the Labor-affiliated "Arab satellite lists," which represented a moderate line. The Communist-led "national camp" subsequently filled the vacuum created by the diminishing presence of the Labor party and its Arab dependents. The magnitude of the change was well illustrated in the 1977 Knesset elections, when the ICP won approximately 50 percent of the Arab vote.

The ICP's hegemony over the Arab sector, however, was short-lived. Since the late 1970s, its leadership position had been eroded by the rise of new national and nationalist forces. The establishment of the PLP and its determination to operate within the parliamentary arena tangibly threatened the Communist monopoly. The PLP's advantage over the ICP was accentuated, as it offered a pro-Palestinian nationalist platform, minus the Marxist dogma. In addition, the Communist party became crucially weakened as a result of internal divisions: ideological controversies with regard to the party's stand on the Palestinian question; the consolidation of inner opposition criticizing the stagnation of the veteran leadership; intergenerational strife; and mounting condemnation of "factionalism" and "bossism."

Since the mid-1980s, all secular political forces in the Arab sector came to be commonly challenged by the rise of a new threatening power, that of fundamentalist Islam. The success of the Islamists echoed frustration over the failure of the Communists and the Progressives to achieve any substantial gains regarding equality and civil rights. It also reflected, inter alia, disappointment with the manifest inability of these circles to bring about change on the national front.

The Intifada, then, began at a stage in which the political order of the Israeli Arabs was being reshaped. In the local competition over power, the question of who was more strongly committed to the Palestinian cause and the Intifada came to be an indication of prestige and influence. But the origins of the rivalry, as has been demonstrated, were rooted in past developments and in a structural crisis totally unrelated to the uprising in the territories. The Intifada assumed the role of a catalyst. It served as a central, yet not singular, agent affecting the process of an overall political change.

To illustrate: The source of dispute between the Communists and the "Sons of the Village" regarding the transformation of the Intifada's means of struggle into the Green Line was anchored in the past controversy of the 1970s over the question of how to commemorate Land Day—militantly or peacefully. The circles condemning the ICP for its "Intifada passivity" came from within the party's ranks as well. Yet their opposition was predominantly generated by the long-standing crisis in the party's inner circles. The ICP's internal cohesion was simultaneously shaken by the repercussions of an entirely different and far-removed development, namely *glasnost* and the liberalization in the USSR, the limited renewal of Soviet-Israeli relations, the fall of the Berlin Wall, and the partial collapse of the communist system. The party's policies regarding the Intifada served as an additional stimulating factor, accelerating the spread of agitation and discontent.

Similarly, the Intifada provided Knesset member Darwasha with an appropriate time to announce his breach with the Labor party, yet it was definitely not the sole consideration behind his decision to form a new political organization. In an analogous way, the Intifada played a tremendously important role in the promotion of fundamentalist Islam, yet the roots of Islamic resurgence in Israel are to be found in an earlier period.

The multidimensional nature of the process of change was well demonstrated by the results of the elections to the twelfth Knesset held in July 1988. In contrast to the expectations of numerous observers, there was no dramatic turnabout in the patterns of the vote of the Arab sector. Nonetheless, the aggregate vote for the parties campaigning on a nationalist platform (ICP, PLP, and the Democratic Arab party) increased by some 10 percent, while that for Zionist parties dropped by the same margin. Almost certainly, the Intifada accounts for this shift. It shows that, although the process of "Palestinization" is indeed at work, it moves gradually and by small steps. Furthermore, the election results tell us that Palestinian loyalty is not the only consideration presently shaping the worldview and conduct of Israeli Arabs. The old social loyalties, for instance, have not been altogether replaced by the new authority of party leaders. Heads of families and clans still influence the voting pattern of their kinsmen to some extent. Moreover, the process of "Israelization" has not been suspended.[76] The very self-assurance with which Israeli Arabs have taken up protest action over the Intifada is also a sign of their rootedness in Israeli society and politics and their adaptation to patterns of action acceptable there.

The Israeli Arabs' reaction to the Intifada has had an unmistakable nationalist coloration but has also, with equal vigor, expressed their frustration over the lack of equality and the socioeconomic gap between Jews and Arabs in Israel. Commenting on the possibility that the situation might change in the future, Knesset member

Muhammad Miari warned in April 1988 that if the Israeli Arabs continued to be denied equal rights in all spheres, they might join in the uprising.[77] His statement confirms that the upsurge of nationalist views and sentiments draws from two distinct but interrelated roots—events on the Palestinian scene and the sense of being discriminated against in Israel. Miari thus illustrates a pivotal fact in the Israeli Arab political outlook: the blurring of the line dividing the struggle for civic rights in Israel from the national struggle of the Palestinians.

Notes

1. See statements by Yossef Ginat and Majid al-Hajj, *Davar* (Tel Aviv), January 21, 1988.
2. For example, Eliezer Tsafrir and Amos Gilboa in *Yediot Aharonot* (Tel Aviv), December 10, 1989, and *Maariv* (Tel Aviv), December 15, 1989.
3. The following paragraph is partly based on my article "Israeli Arabs and the Arabs of the West Bank and Gaza Strip: Political Affinity and National Solidarity," *Asian and African Studies* 23, nos. 2–3 (November 1989): 119–54.
4. Cited in *Al-Hamakom* (Kfar Saba, Israel), February 12, 1988.
5. *Zu Haderech* (Tel Aviv), December 23, 1988.
6. See comments by Rafiq Halabi, cited in *Newsday* (USA), February 24, 1988.
7. For example, the following slogans are depicted in Taiba: "Intifada—till the last drop of blood," "God is with you, heroes of the Intifada." See *Haaretz* (Tel Aviv), September 9, 1988. For reports on the display of PLO flags and the distribution of leaflets, see *Maariv*, September 15 and November 2, 1988; and *Yediot Aharonot*, November 14, 1988.
8. *Jerusalem Post*, March 28, 1989; *Yediot Aharonot*, June 23, 1989.
9. Alexander Bligh, interviewed by Aitan Goelman, "The Intifada and Israel's Arab Citizens," in *Background Analysis* (New York: American Jewish Committee, December 1989).
10. For details on the Samir Sarsawi's network, responsible for a hand-grenade attack carried out in Haifa, see *al-Sinara* (Nazareth, Israel), December 9, 1988. For similar cells uncovered in Taiba, Jatt, and Nazareth, see *Yediot Aharonot*, April 13, 1989, November 3, 1989.
11. *Hadashot* (Tel Aviv), March 7, 1988.
12. *Haaretz*, February 21, 1988; Ran Kislev, "The Quandary of Double Loyalty," ibid., March 18, 1988; and Rekhess, "Israeli Arabs," 50.
13. On the ultraradicals, see Elie Rekhess, "The Arab Nationalist Chal-

lenge to the Israeli Communist Party (1970–1985)," *Studies in Comparative Communism* 22, no. 4 (Winter 1989): 337–50.

14. *Al-Raya* (Nazareth, Israel), September 9, 1988.

15. Ibid.

16. The "Sons of the Village" weekly, *al-Raya*, frequently elaborated on these points. See, for instance, an article by Awad Abd al-Fattah, "The Role and Attitude of the Inside (*fi al-dakhil*) Palestinian Masses with Respect to the Intifada," *al-Raya*, August 18, 1988, and a similar article by Sulayman Abu Irshid, *al-Raya*, August 26, 1988.

17. See report by Yoram Hamizrahi, *Yediot Aharonot*, July 11, 1988.

18. *Al-Raya*, August 18, 1988.

19. *Zu Haderech*, December 16, 1987.

20. Ibid., February 3, 1988.

21. For example, Knesset members Tawfiq Tubi's and Tawfiq Ziyyad's visit at the Junayd prison in Nablus and their meeting with six out of twenty-five people about to be expelled (*Zu Haderech*, August 31, 1988).

22. See, for instance, a joint statement by the ICP and the Jordanian and the Palestinian Communist parties late in 1987 in *Zu Haderech*, November 25, 1988. On the earlier roots of the relationship between the ICP and the Palestinian Communists, see Rekhess, "Israeli Arabs," p. 52.

23. It tried, for example, to prevent the expulsion of Taysir Aruri, a physics lecturer at Bir Zeit University and a prominent activist of the Palestinian Communist Party (a member of its Ramallah regional committee) (*Zu Haderech*, September 15, 1988).

24. It reprinted, for example, the text of the speech made by Abd al-Rahman Abdallah, a member of the Palestinian Communist Party's Central Committee, to the Central Council of the PLO, in August 1988 (ibid., August 24, 1988).

25. Ibid., February 17, 1988; Salim Jubran, ibid., December 14, 1988.

26. Ibid., August 24, 1988; Rekhess, "Israeli Arabs," p. 152.

27. Amos Gilboa, cited in *Haaretz*, January 8, 1988.

28. *Zu Haderech*, April 13, 1988.

29. Cited in *Haaretz*, February 21, 1988.

30. *Al-Ittihad* (Haifa), March 6, 1988; *Zu Haderech*, March 30, 1988. On a similar incident involving a Palestinian flag, see Rekhess, "Israeli Arabs," pp. 140–41.

31. On the major constraints shaping the ICP's policies, see Elie Rekhess, "Jews and Arabs in the Israeli Communist Party," in *Ethnicity, Pluralism and the State in the Middle East*, ed. Milton Esman and Itamar Rabinovich (Ithaca: Cornell University Press, 1988), p. 134.

32. Cited by Afif Salim, *Venus* (Nazareth), June 14, 1989.

33. Ibid.

34. For instance, Kamil al-Dahir, "The Intifada Has Begun to Attain its

Objectives," *al-Watan* (Nazareth), March 18, 1988; "The Blessed Intifada," ibid., August 12, 1988; Badr Yunis, "The Intifada and the Support of the Palestinians," ibid., September 23, 1988; Hasan Zubi, "The Palestinian Teacher under the Shadow of the Intifada," ibid., March 24, 1988.

35. Miari succeeded in entering Qalqiliyya at a time when it had been declared a closed area (ibid., September 16, 1988).

36. Ibid., August 12, 26, 1988.

37. Ibid., September 23, 1988; also an election advertisement in *al-Sinara*, September 16, 1988.

38. *Al-Watan*, August 26, 1988.

39. Speech at a conference on "The Intifada and the Operations of Occupation in Occupied Palestine," held by the PLP in Nazareth in summer 1989. Among the Palestinian delegates were Faysal Husayni; Khalid al-Kadra, deputy head of the Gaza Strip Bar Association; and Zakariyya al-Agha, head of the medical association in Gaza (*Al-Watan*, June 30, 1988). Also compare the interview with Miari published in *al-Usbu al-Arabi* (Beirut), cited by *al-Watan*, April 21, 1989. For a similar, rather apologetic, description of the "special circumstances" characterizing the Israeli Arabs, see the following statement by Mariam Mari of Acre: "Don't forget that we are Israeli citizens and that we are judged by that. We cannot be up front. We have to play the game very carefully. . . . we are trying to walk in the rain without getting wet" (*Israeli Democracy* [Summer 1989]: 16).

40. Interviewed by *Koteret Rashit* (Tel Aviv), January 27, 1988.

41. Ibid., *Hadashot*, April 7, 1988; *Haaretz*, July 24, 1988. Also compare with Yitzhak Reiter, "The Democratic Arab Party and Its Place in the Israeli Arabs' Orientation," in *The Arab Sector in Israel and the Results of the Elections to the Knesset, 1988*, ed. Jacob Landau, Jerusalem Institute Studies 35 (Jerusalem, 1989): 63–84 (Hebrew).

42. *Al-Sinara*, April 15, 1988.

43. *Haaretz*, July 24, 1988.

44. Speech in the Knesset, February 13, 1989, distributed by MK Darwasha.

45. See Darwasha's meeting with Arafat and with the foreign minister of Egypt in Summer 1989, *al-Diyar* (Nazareth), August 5, 1989, and *al-Hayat* (London), April 18, 1989.

46. See, for example, Umar Masaliha, *Davar*, February 2, 1989, and *Al-Hamakom*, April 7, 1989.

47. Mapam used similar slogans, e.g., "No to Rabin's Stick" or "The Voice is Shamir's—the Stick is Rabin's," *al-Mirsad*, August 25, September 15, 1988.

48. On the influence of the territories on the resurgence of Islam in Israel, see Rekhess, "Israeli Arabs", 134–35. On the Islamic movement in

Israel, see Thomas Meier, "Muslim Youth in Israel," *Hamizrah Hehadash* 32, nos. 125–28 (1989): 10–20 (Hebrew).

49. *Al-Sirat* (Umm al-Fahm, Israel), 10, vol. 2 (February 1988): 19, 22.

50. See, e.g., report of the death of the *Shahid* (martyr) Muhammad Khalid al-Shrim, member of HAMAS (ibid., March 24, 1989).

51. *Al-Sirat*, 10, vol. 2 (February 1988): 19, 22.

52. *Filastin al-Muslima* (Manchester), 7, nos. 5–6 (January 1990).

53. Interviewed by *Al-Hamishmar*, June 13, 1988.

54. *Filastin al-Muslima* (January 1990).

55. Ran Kislev, *Haaretz*, March 5, 1989.

56. Ziyyad Abu Amr, *Al-Haraka al-Islamiyya fi al-Daffa al-Gharbiyya waqita Ghazza* (Akka: Dar al-Aswar, 1989): 42 (Arabic).

57. Interviewed by *Davar*, March 17, 1989.

58. See Asher Susser, "From the Intifada to Algiers," *Davar*, December 9, 1988.

59. *Al-Ukaz* (Saudi Arabia), April 4, 1989.

60. *Haaretz* and *Maariv*, March 28, 1989.

61. Salim Tamari, "What the Uprising Means," *Middle East Report* 152 (May–June 1988): 27.

62. *Al-Fajr* (English), September 4, 1989.

63. Susser, "From the Intifada to Algiers."

64. For a detailed discussion of the issue, see my article "On the Question of Relations between Jews and Arabs in MAKI," *Medina Umimshal* 27 (Winter 1988): 71–73 (Hebrew).

65. Yigal Alon, *Masakh Shel Chol* (Tel Aviv: Hakibutz Hameuchad, 1969), pp. 322–23 (Hebrew).

66. See, e.g., Samih Ghanadri, *Al-Jamahir al-Arabiyya fi Israil-Banorama al-Idtihad wa-l-Tamayyuz al-Qawmiyin* (Al-Nasira: Dar 30 Adhar, 1987), p. 12 (Arabic).

67. Recorded by the author. See *Maariv*, May 16, 1976, and *Haaretz*, June 10, 1976.

68. Interview, *Haaretz*, April 29, 1983; *Al-Hamishmar*, May 6, 1983; the ICP response, *al-Ittihad*, May 3, 1983.

69. In a report prepared in September 1987, cited by *Haaretz*, March 14, 1988.

70. For example, *Zu Haderech*, January 6, 1988.

71. See Mariam Mari, ibid., p. 15.

72. Rekhess, "Israeli Arabs," p. 132.

73. Among the supporters of this view is Aharon Layyish, "The Israeli Arabs in a Crisis of Identity," *Hamizrah Hehadash* 32, nos. 125–28 (1989): 8.

74. Goelman interview (n. 9). See Yossef Goell, "Israel's Arabs and the Intifada," *Jerusalem Post*, March 3, 1989; and Yossef Goell, "Israel's Arabs," *New Republic*, October 23, 1989.

75. Cited by Avinoam Bar Yossef, *Maariv*, January 14, 1990.

76. For an in-depth discussion of the process of Israelization, see the works of Sammy Smooha, including his latest book, *Arabs and Jews in Israel* (Boulder, Colo.: Westview Press, 1989).

77. *Al-Hamishmar*, May 22, 1988.

Economic Consequences of the Intifada in Israel and the Administered Territories

12

Howard Rosen

The Intifada has had various effects on the landscape of the Middle East. Most public attention has been on the periodic riots and Israeli efforts at suppressing the disturbances. There has been little attention paid to the economic consequences of the Intifada, in part because they are more difficult to measure. The Intifada has placed real economic costs on both Israelis and Palestinians, and these costs lend another dimension to discussions concerning any settlement in the region.

Estimates of the economic costs of the Intifada to the Israeli economy since December 1987 are about $1 billion.[1] These costs are concentrated in certain sectors in the economies of Israel and the West Bank and Gaza.[2] During its first two years, the Intifada has probably cost the Israeli economy 2–2.5 percent of its Gross Domestic Product (GDP).[3]

The economic consequences of the Intifada have been unevenly distributed among the various parties. Within the Israeli economy, the costs have been concentrated in construction, agriculture, and tourism. These broader effects have been overshadowed by a longer-term adjustment to stabilization efforts in the Israeli economy. Most of the economic effect of the Intifada was felt at the outset in 1988. In contrast, the economic consequences of the disturbances on the

Note: Reprinted with permission of the Institute for International Economics, Washington, D.C.

economies of the West Bank and Gaza appear to be increasing as the Intifada continues.

One of the greatest handicaps in estimating the economic costs of the Intifada is the lack of quality statistics measuring economic activity in the West Bank and Gaza. Even before the disturbances began it was difficult to locate comparable economic data for Israel and the administered territories. This problem has been further exacerbated by the Intifada. Due to the Palestinian boycott of Israel and security concerns, few economic data on Palestinian activities since December 1987 are available. This lack has made it particularly difficult to estimate accurately the actual costs of the Intifada and to check various assertions by Israeli and Palestinian leaders and the press.

In order to appreciate fully the economic consequences of the Intifada, they must be seen in the context of recent economic developments in Israel and the administered territories. In this chapter I summarize these developments as well as discuss the economic aspects of the Intifada more specifically. I discuss developments in the Israeli economy during the 1980s and look at recent economic developments in the West Bank and Gaza. Then I discuss the direct economic consequences of the Intifada on five major areas of the Israeli economy—construction, agriculture, tourism, government expenditures, and the labor market—and present the direct effects of the Intifada on the economies of the West Bank and Gaza. I then draw some conclusions concerning the economic consequences of the Intifada.

Recent Developments in the Israeli Economy

The transition of the Israeli economy from near collapse to stabilization has dominated much of the 1980s. From the outset of the decade the Israeli economy was characterized by low growth and high inflation. It grew slowly, about 2 percent annually between 1979 and 1982, continuing the trend of a decline in growth rates from close to 10 percent between 1953 and 1973 to approximately 3.5 percent between 1973 and 1979. Inflation, averaging 123 percent between 1979 and 1982, relative to 7 percent between 1953 and 1973 and 45 percent between 1973 and 1979, was already beginning a trajectory that would take it to historic highs. Israel's chronic budget deficit and current account deficit also continued to grow during the early part of the 1980s.[4]

During the first few years of the 1980s, the Israeli government was ineffective in reversing these economic developments. The budget deficit continued to grow, primarily due to an erosion of the tax base which in turn was a result of accelerating inflation. Devaluations aimed at protecting the country's hard currency reserves served only to push inflation higher. By July 1985 the monthly inflation rate approached 30 percent, citizens were losing confidence in the government's ability to control the economy, and it was unclear if the country's reserves could meet its international financial obligations.

A state of economic emergency was called, and the government implemented a comprehensive stabilization program in July 1985. The program included strict controls on prices and wages, a significant one-time devaluation of the currency followed by pegging the shekel to the value of the U.S. dollar, and a package of new taxes and levies and government cutbacks aimed at reducing the government's budget deficit. In support of the program, the United States made a special emergency grant of $1.5 billion over two years to stem the hemorrhage in the balance of payments and assist in restoring credibility to the shekel. As a result of these measures, the government posted a budget surplus, inflation fell to below 20 percent annually, and the current account was in surplus for the two years of U.S. supplemental aid.

By 1987 there was evidence that the stabilization efforts were successful. Personal consumption was up, leading imports to rise. Strong export sales also contributed to the economy's well-being. Inflation stood at approximately 20 percent and unemployment was approximately 6 percent. Economic activity grew by over 5 percent in 1987, the strongest growth rate since 1973. By most indicators, 1987 was a good year for the Israeli economy.

Strong economic performance in 1987 helped shield the Israeli economy from some of the consequences of the Intifada. On the other hand, given its unique status, comparing economic activity during the Intifada with that prior to the outbreak of the disturbances in 1987 results in overstating the impact of Intifada on the Israeli economy. In addition, longer-run effects of structural changes in the economy, resulting from the stabilization efforts, have also made it difficult to isolate any actual economic downturn that may have occurred due to the Intifada. (See graph 1.)

Recent Economic Developments in the West Bank and Gaza

Economic developments in the administered territories paralleled those in Israel during much of the 1980s until the outbreak of the Intifada in December 1987. Economic growth in the West Bank and Gaza averaged 6 percent annually in the late 1970s. West Bank GDP fell to approximately 3 percent during the first half of the 1980s and the Gaza GDP to approximately 2 percent annually. (See graphs 2 and 3.) Over the same period the population of the administered territories rose from less than a million people in 1967 to approximately 1.5 million people in 1987.

During the twenty years of Israeli rule, the West Bank and Gazan economies have become increasingly dependent on Israel. Forty-six percent of Palestinian exports went to Israel and 38 percent went to Jordan in 1970. By 1987 Israel was the dominant market for West Bank and Gaza exports, constituting 79 percent of their total exports. The Jordanian market had fallen to only 20 percent (see graph 4).

Less dramatically, the Israeli share of West Bank and Gaza imports rose from 84 percent in 1970 to 91 percent by 1987. Imports from Jordan fell from 4 percent to less than 1 percent of total imports from the administered territories. (See graph 5). This concentration in Israeli goods coincided with a fall in the import ratio from 73 percent to 57 percent of the combined GDP of the West Bank and Gaza over the same period.

Increasing economic dependence on Israel is also evident in the West Bank and Gaza labor market. Twelve percent of the Palestinian labor force worked within the pre-1967 borders of Israel in 1970. The number of Palestinians working in Israel increased steadily over the twenty-year period, reaching 40 percent of the total Palestinian work force in 1987. Almost half of these workers were employed in the construction sector. (See table 1 and graph 6.)

The flow of lower-wage Palestinian workers into Israel serves many purposes. First, employment opportunities in Israel ease some of the internal pressure due to the growing labor force in the West Bank and Gaza. Wages earned from work in Israel are greater than those for the same work in the territories. Lower-wage Palestinian workers help reduce costs in highly labor-intensive sectors of the Israeli economy, such as agriculture and construction. On average, Palestinians tend to earn approximately one-third of an Israeli's wages. This differential is smaller in sectors employing a higher proportion of low-skilled workers. For example, Palestinian wages in construction, where almost half of the Palestinians working in Israel are employed, are closer to 40 percent of average Israeli wages in the same sector.[5]

Economic Consequences of the Intifada on the Israeli Economy

As stated earlier, most of the economic consequences of the Intifada on the Israeli economy have been concentrated in agriculture, construction, and tourism. In order to present a more comprehensive accounting of the additional costs incurred due to the outbreak of the disturbances, one must also include some discussion of the Intifada's effect on Israeli security expenditures. Given Israel's history of chronic budget deficits, and the importance of these deficits to recent economic developments, this area cannot be overlooked.

It is impossible to isolate clearly the Intifada's economic impact even in specific sectors of the economy. By the end of 1987, when the disturbances began, the economy had already begun to lose a lot of its momentum from its strong performance earlier in the year. It now appears that the initial costs of the uprising and the Israeli response may have cost the Israeli economy approximately 1.5 percent of GDP growth in 1988, which it might have experienced in the absence of the Intifada.[6] As the economy adjusted to changes brought about by the Intifada, these costs and their effect on Israeli growth have declined. I now identify the sectors in which most of these costs were concentrated and place them in the context of other recent developments in these sectors.

Agriculture

For Israeli agriculture, 1988 was not a good year. To begin with, the sector continued to feel aftershocks from the near collapse and continued financial woes of many Kibbutzim and Moshavim over the preceding few years. Many of these operations remained constrained by their outstanding debts and had little cash on hand to make the necessary improvements in equipment. Adverse weather conditions during the crucial planting season also had a negative effect on agricultural output in 1988. Finally, a 9 percent drop in agricultural employment between 1987 and 1988 was due in large part to a decline in Palestinian employment. In 1987 Palestinians accounted for 45 percent of paid employees in agriculture.[7]

The Intifada presented Israeli farmers with several problems. First, they had to secure their fields and equipment from vandalism and fires. Second, assuming that their crops were not destroyed by weather or fire, they had to find workers to pick their produce. Unannounced and erratic work stoppages gave farmers little time to find alternative means to pick produce before it spoiled. Finally, once the product was picked and marketed, there was a reduction in the share of output exported, due in part to international conditions, which in turn reduced the farmers' income from exports.

Graphs 7 and 8 present two examples of recent downward trends in agriculture. Citrus production following the outbreak of the Intifada dropped rather significantly during critical months in 1988 and 1989. Vegetable production in 1988 and 1989, while lower than its 1987 level, does not appear to have experienced the same magnitude of decline.

Construction

The data in graphs 9 and 10 suggest that the construction sector has been in long-run decline since 1975. It is due in part to general growth and investment conditions over the period, as well as the inability of the Israeli financial market to support this sector properly. There is some evidence of an upward reversal in this trend, probably associated with the stabilization of the economy since 1986 and coinciding with capital market reforms recently put in place.

Another trend in this sector has been the increasing dependence on Palestinian workers from the West Bank and Gaza. (See graph 11). While the inflow of a cheaper and more flexible work force from the territories has helped ease the downward trend in construction, the dependence on Palestinian workers was questioned at the outset of the Intifada.[8] Before the uprising, approximately 40,000–50,000 Palestinians, 70 percent from Gaza, were working in the Israeli construction sector.[9]

In the first few months of 1988, when absenteeism was reported at almost 50 percent of the Palestinian work force, it was unclear how the construction sector would adjust.[10] By raising the total number of both Israeli and Palestinian workers, builders and contractors were able to overcome the effects of sporadic work stoppages. As a result the Palestinian share of labor input into the Israeli construction industry remained constant between 1986 and 1988. Total output rose, although only slightly, over the same period.[11]

The average number of days worked by all construction employees fell to 17.3 days per month in the first quarter of 1988, down from an average of 18.6 days per month during 1987. By the end of 1988 this number rose to 19.2 workdays per month, so that the monthly average for the entire year was only 3 percent below that for 1987. The average number of days worked by all construction employees in 1989 returned to its 1987 level.[12] Increases in productivity and the number of Israeli workers may explain this adjustment. (See graph 12.)

As in the agriculture sector, the effects of the Intifada on construction must be seen within the context of over a decade of decline. It appears that work shortages and shifting from Palestinian to Israeli workers may have contributed to slowing down the recovery that this sector began experiencing in 1987. On the other hand, some economists argue that there is excess capacity in the sector and it is possible actually to raise output at the same time that there is a drop in employment. Most important, the slowdown in the general economy had an adverse effect on the demand for new buildings.

Tourism

Tourism appears to be the one sector in which the effects of the Intifada are relatively unambiguous and pronounced. Tourism is important to Israel for many reasons. First and foremost, Israel depends on it as its most important source of hard currency income, which is crucial in helping Israel offset its international financial obligations, like interest on outstanding foreign debts. Beyond balancing its service account, Israel must also attract foreign currency to help finance its dependence on imported raw materials and capital goods. Income from tourism has been increasing in importance relative to Israel's international income from all service transactions. This trend stopped between 1987 and 1988, as foreign currency income from tourism fell from 28 percent to 26 percent of total services income.[13]

This is not the first time that Israel has experienced a slowdown in tourism (see graph 13). Tourist arrivals in Israel fell sharply between 1981 and 1982, primarily because of the Lebanon war, and again in 1986, following several terrorist attacks on tourists in Europe and the Mediterranean region. In 1987 tourism reached its historical peak, approximately 1.4 million people. This upswing may have been due to postponed visits scheduled in 1986, international economic conditions, and Israel's strong economic recovery since 1986.

A significant drop in tourists entering Israel occurred between February and May 1988 (graph 14). This decline was particularly worrisome in the eyes of the Israeli government, as it occurred precisely as the government was preparing to celebrate the country's fortieth anniversary. The government had hoped that a gala celebration would help attract tourists and hard currency, as well as help stimulate the economy. These dreams were not realized, and the Intifada seems to have been the primary cause.

The significant decline in tourism occurred in the second quarter of 1988. The seasonally adjusted number of tourist arrivals between April and June of 1988 was 20 percent below that of the previous year. The number of tourists remained low throughout the remainder of the year but began picking up in the middle of 1989.

It is inaccurate to compare the decline in tourism in 1988 to the historical peak achieved during the previous year. When viewed in the context of the overall trend in tourism since 1975, the decline in 1988 is not as pronounced. Tourist arrivals in 1988 were only 6 percent below the fourteen-year trend, while the number of tourist arrivals in 1987 was 14 percent above the historical trend. Total foreign currency revenue from tourism remained virtually unchanged in current dollar terms between 1987 and 1988 at approximately $1.35 billion, almost 40 percent greater than the revenue from tourists in 1986 (see graph 15).

Approximately 60 percent of tourists to Israel come from the United States, West Germany, France, and the United Kingdom. Contrary to 1986, when almost 95 percent of the decline resulted from fewer U.S. tourists to Israel, the decline in tourism following the outbreak of the Intifada was more evenly distributed. The number of tourists from the United States and Germany fell by the average decline in tourists from all locations (15 percent). Tourism from France declined more than the average (21 percent), and those from the United Kingdom declined less than the average decline in the total number of tourists (6 percent). Tourism from other than these four countries fell by 16 percent between 1987 and 1988. (See graph 16.)

Hotel occupancy rates also fell between 1987 and 1988, although this development cannot be entirely associated with the disturbances in the West Bank and Gaza. The number of beds in tourist hotels has shown a steady increase in recent years—up 14 percent since 1980. At the same time, the occupancy rate has remained below 55 percent of available beds, except for the peak year of 1987 when it rose to 59.1 percent.

This growth in the number of available beds made the decline in occupancy rates between 1987 and 1988 more pronounced. Although the rate in 1988 was significantly lower than in 1987 (52.6 percent to 59.1 percent of available beds), it was above the rate in 1986 (50.6 percent) and only slightly lower than 1985 (53.9 percent). The financial condition of many hotels before the outbreak of the disturbance lends additional evidence to suggest that there may be an oversupply of hotels and beds, given the number of tourists visiting Israel over the last few years.

Direct Government Expenditures

Following the military pullout from Lebanon and the implementation of economic stabilization efforts in 1985, there was a slowdown in the growth of total Israeli military expenditures, and even declines in some areas. This trend has been affected by the outbreak of disturbances in the administered territories.

In early 1989 the government announced that the military spent $225 million in 1988 in responding to the disturbances in the West Bank and Gaza and estimated that it would need $125 million above its original military budget for 1989.[14] This increase in military expenditures includes an additional $100 million in salaries and compensation, in large part to cover the additional costs of increasing reserve duty. This 8 percent real growth in compensation was offset by a 17 percent decline in military imports, which was due in part to an uneven schedule of shipments, the canceling of the Lavi project, and a reduction of military activity on Israel's northern border. In spite of the Intifada, total military expenditures may have actually declined in real terms between 1987 and 1988.[15]

The Labor Market

Probably the most significant direct effect that the Intifada has had on the Israeli economy has been experienced in the labor market. Prior to the outbreak of the disturbances, the number of Palestinians from the West Bank and Gaza working in Israel had been steadily increasing, reaching approximately 110,000 in 1987. This inflow of predominantly low-skilled and low-wage workers had enabled the economy to continue growing, albeit moderately, in spite of rising domestic labor costs.

During the first half of 1988, when the number of hours Palestinians worked in Israel fell by approximately one-third, Israeli unemployment remained relatively unchanged and real wages continued to rise.[16] These trends suggest that Israelis did not immediately begin replacing Palestinian workers from the administered territories with the onset of the boycott. By the beginning of 1989, after the bulk of the economic slowdown due to the Intifada had been experienced, the unemployment rate began to rise rapidly, approaching 10 percent of the workforce. It is therefore difficult to draw any strong connection between the outbreak of the Intifada and the significant increase in the Israeli unemployment rate.

There are reports that individual business concerns have brought foreign workers into Israel to perform jobs held by Palestinian workers prior to the outbreak of the Intifada. Since there is no official government approval of such action, it is difficult to get accurate statistics concerning the number of temporary workers and in which industries they are employed. There are estimates that as many as 15,000 workers have been brought from places like Portugal and Turkey.[17] These workers are predominantly employed in labor-intensive industries, including textiles and footwear. There is also evidence that firms have been recruiting craft workers from abroad for such activities as book publishing. The government does not seem to be alarmed by this new kind of addition to the labor force, and it may be harder to stop than it was to begin. This development raises many questions, especially given the current high unemployment rate and the difficulty the economy has been having in integrating new Soviet immigrants.

The one area in which the effects of the Intifada have been widely felt throughout the economy has been the increase in mandatory reserve duty. With the outbreak of the Intifada, the military went on special alert, and the average number of days for which individuals were called for reserve duty doubled to approximately fifty. In addition to holidays and vacations, an employer could count on an Israeli worker only for three-fourths of the year. In general, the magnitude of the impact of mandatory reserve duty on the Israeli economy continues to be debated. Whatever effect there is, any increase due to the doubling of reserve service must also be attributed to the Intifada.

The Economic Consequences of the Intifada on the West Bank and Gaza

It is more difficult to measure the actual economic effects of the uprising in the administered territories, largely because of the economy's informal nature and the lack of statistics measuring economic activity in the territories. Much of the following material is based on eyewitness accounts and press reports.

Several economic actions were central to the Intifada's initial design. On general strike days all commercial activity in the West Bank and Gaza was closed, and Palestinians refused to show up for work in Israel. The Israeli army initially responded by trying to force Palestinians to open their shops, in the hope that normal economic activity would restore stability to the areas. This policy was not effective and was soon stopped.

There are no statistics on commercial activity within the West Bank and Gaza. Given their sizes and importance, Israeli exports to the territories, which in 1987 accounted for 60 percent of their GDP, can be used as a proxy to measure the effect of commercial strikes in the territories. Israeli exports to the West Bank and Gaza fell by 30 percent, or $278 million between 1987 and 1988, and there appeared to be little recovery in 1989. This decline in sales is a result of a drop in Palestinian income and their boycott of Israeli products.

Initially there were reports that Palestinians in the West Bank and Gaza were being financially supported by the PLO and other organizations outside of Israel, although the sums reported seemed modest.[18] In an effort to restrict outside financing of the Intifada, the Israeli government reduced the amount of money per trip that individuals could bring into the West Bank from Jordan from 2,000 Jordanian dinars to only 400 dinars, or approximately $650 at current exchange rates.[19] The real effect of these controls has been greater since the value of the Jordanian dinar has fallen by about 50 percent over the last two years. Prior to the outbreak of the Intifada, over one-fourth of the income of West Bank originated in Jordan or from Palestinians working in Israel. The reduction in the number of Palestinians working in Israel and the tighter limits on foreign currency brought in from Jordan, as well as the fall in the dinar's value, together placed severe pressure on the West Bank's economy. As a result, the business community placed demands on the Intifada's organizers, and by mid-1988 commercial strikes were shortened and Palestinians were permitted to open their shops for several hours each day.

On July 31, 1988, Jordan's King Hussein announced that Jordan was canceling a $1.3 billion development plan which was under way for the West Bank and that Jordan would cease payments to 20,000 civil servants, health care employees, and teachers in the West Bank. Until this announcement Jordan contributed $60 million annually for West Bank administration and economic development. Most analysts suggested that King Hussein took these actions in order to give the PLO more control in the West Bank, but these steps also served to increase economic pressure on the population in the territories.[20]

As the Intifada continues, the economic consequences for the Palestinians have intensified. Realizing this, the local leadership has begun relaxing various aspects of the economic boycott. Strikes have become more sporadic, and Palestinians have returned to work in Israel. Changes in Israel's policies have tended to keep economic pressure on the Palestinians in the territories. The introduction of ID cards, reduced border crossings, and military-imposed curfews has made it harder for Palestinians to travel to Israel for work.

At the outset of the Intifada, the Palestinian leadership tried to capitalize on sympathetic press and world opinion. Some of these efforts did not bear fruit, and one actually worked against the Palestinians. In May 1988, as the Palestinian leadership was widening its actions beyond civil unrest to the political arena, the Arab-American Anti-Defamation League brought to the U.S. Trade Representative (USTR) a complaint about Israel's human rights policies in the territories.

Under recent revisions in U.S. trade law, any country found to be in violation of basic worker rights, among them the right of workers to organize, could lose preferential treatment in selling its goods in the United States.[21] The league's complaint claimed that Israel denied Palestinians the right to organize, as well as other workers' rights. The leadership hoped that the political climate in the United States prior to the 1988 presidential election would help their case. In addition, the complaint was filed at the same time the United States and Israel were involved in serious negotiations over violations to the U.S.-Israel Free Trade Agreement.[22]

After months of investigations and several public hearings, the

USTR found that Israel was not in violation of workers' rights within Israel's pre-1967 borders. Furthermore, the USTR announced that since the official political status of the West Bank and Gaza was still undetermined according to U.S. policy, and since the trade preference program is for countries only, goods from the territories could not be afforded preferential treatment under the program. The Palestinian petition resulted in jeopardizing the trade preferences that it was receiving as part of exports from Israel.

In Europe, the Palestinians were more successful in delaying several motions concerning Israeli trade before the European Community's Parliament. In exchange for final passage of these motions, the Israelis agreed to allow direct exports from the West Bank and Gaza to Europe. Under these new guidelines, products from the West Bank and Gaza would no longer face internal competition in Israel for a share of Israel's export markets and would compete directly with Israeli products in the European market. The Palestinians thus appeared to be more effective in their efforts in Europe than they were in the United States.

It appears that the bulk of the economic burden of the Intifada is shifting onto the economies of the West Bank and Gaza. While the Israelis are attempting to tighten economic constraints on the Palestinians by, among other actions, imposing curfews and limiting the transfer of funds from outside the territories, the Palestinian leadership has been taking action against people not abiding by their self-imposed economic boycott. Jordanian reductions in its economic involvement in the West Bank and Gaza come at the same time that the Jordanian dinar has been falling, reflecting instability in the Jordanian economy. The net effect is that the Intifada has paid a toll on the economies of the West Bank and Gaza. Furthermore, it has provided an opportunity to test the vitality of these economies and their ability to withstand internal and external pressures.

Economic developments in the West Bank and Gaza during most of the 1980s has helped overstate some of the immediate changes brought about by the Intifada. In addition, difficulties in attracting capital, creating local jobs, and supporting local production have made it more difficult for the economies of the West Bank and Gaza to adjust adequately to the economic consequences of the disturbances and economic boycotts in a timely manner. This notion is summed up in a recent article in *Middle East International*:

> As the Palestinian uprising approaches its second anniversary, it is becoming increasingly clear that it can no longer be sustained by its sophisticated political organization and popular commitment alone. Rather, if the rebellion is to remain an institutionalized way of life until it succeeds in forcing a breakthrough in the diplomatic stalemate, it will have to provide a viable economic framework for survival as well. This means not only the continued infusion of Arab funds clandestinely funneled by the PLO to assist those who have made visible sacrifices, but more importantly, the achievement of economic and financial stability to protect the population of the occupied territories from a further erosion of their rapidly disintegrating livelihoods and to prevent the unpredictable fruits of economic desperation from ripening.[23]

Conclusions

Several conclusions arise from this review of the economic consequences of the Intifada. The initial effect on the Israeli economy was rather considerable, given the recent path of Israeli growth rates. As the Intifada continued, the magnitude of its effect has seemed to fall. One estimate places the cumulative cost of the Intifada on the Israeli economy in 1988–89 at approximately $1 billion or 2–2.5 percent of Israel's annual GDP. Due to the lack of dependable statistics, it is difficult to make a similar calculation of the Intifada's effect on the West Bank and Gazan economies.

The economic burden on the Israeli economy has been concentrated in agriculture, construction, tourism, and military expenditures. These costs have been declining as the individual sectors have adjusted and made the necessary substitutions. This additional burden comes as the Israeli economy continues to feel the aftershocks from the stabilization efforts put in place in 1985. The result is that the economy has slipped into its most severe economic downturn since 1967. Evidence suggests that the economy was beginning to pull out of this downturn at the end of 1989.

The consequences of the Intifada on the economies of the West Bank and Gaza are more widespread and more significant. Their inability to adjust and support their own economic boycott points to weaknesses in their economies. The future economic status of the West Bank and Gaza has not been given the attention it requires, and in fact its current structure may serve to undermine any efforts at political autonomy. This area demands more research, and significant economic development must take place before any viable political solution can succeed.

Notes

1. Bank Hapoalim, "The Potential Impact of the Uprising in the Territories on the Israeli Economy" (Economics Department memo, January 1990).
2. I realize that certain terms have taken on political significance in describing the territories, which include the West Bank of the Jordan River and the Gaza Strip. The use of these various terms in this chapter does not in any way represent my opinion concerning these territories or their future status.
3. The Bank Hapoalim study suggests that the effect of the Intifada on the Israeli economy was estimated at 1.5 percent of GDP in 1988 and another 0.5–1 percent of GDP in 1989.
4. Data presented are taken from various publications of the Central Bureau of Statistics, Jerusalem.
5. Dan Zakai, "Economic Development in Judea-Samaria and the Gaza District 1985–1986," Bank of Israel Research Department (Jerusalem, Israel, December 1988), table 21.
6. Bank of Israel, *Annual Report 1988* (Jerusalem, Israel, May 1989), p. 153.
7. Central Bureau of Statistics, *Statistical Abstract of Israel 1989* (Jerusalem, Israel, 1989), table XIII/9.
8. *New York Times*, May 18, 1989.
9. *Statistical Abstract of Israel 1989*, table XXVII/25.
10. *New York Times*, May 18, 1989.
11. *Statistical Abstract of Israel 1989*, table XVI/5.
12. Central Bureau of Statistics, *Monthly Bulletin of Statistics*, Jerusalem, Israel, various issues.

13. Central Bureau of Statistics, *Monthly Bulletin of Statistics Supplement* (Jerusalem, Israel), 41, no. 5, May 1990.

14. *New York Times*, February 13, 1989.

15. *Monthly Bulletin of Statistics Supplement* (May 1990), p. 233.

16. *Monthly Bulletin of Statistics*, various issues, and unpublished data from the Central Bureau of Statistics.

17. Although this number may seem small, it constitutes 1 percent of the total Israeli work force, including workers from the West Bank and Gaza.

18. An article in the *New York Times* reported that the PLO promised $50 million to help support the local economy in the West Bank and Gaza. These funds supposedly came from Kuwait and Saudi Arabia (*New York Times*, June 26, 1988).

19. *New York Times*, May 15, 1988.

20. *Washington Post*, August 12, 1988.

21. The Generalized System of Preferences (GSP) affords developing country exports duty-free entry into the United States, subject to certain product and country limits. The worker-rights conditions to receiving GSP were included in the Trade Act of 1984, as amended.

22. Howard Rosen, "The U.S.-Israel Free Trade Area Agreement: How Well Is It Working and What Have We Learned?" in *Free Trade Areas and U.S. Trade Policy*, ed. Jeffrey J. Schott (Washington, D.C.: Institute for International Economics, 1989).

23. Muin Rabbani, "Occupied Palestine: An Economy in Crisis," *Middle East International* 359 (September 22, 1989).

Table 1. Workers from the West Bank and Gaza Employed in Israel

	1970	1972	1975	1979–80	1984–85	1986–87	1988
Number of employed from the territories (in thousands)	22.8	57.9	73.0	81.8	92.8	103.3	109.4
Labor input from territories as percentage of total domestic business sector labor input	2.6	6.0	7.8	8.4	9.8	10.6	8.3
Construction	11.7	19.4	28.6	30.8	39.8	46.0	38.2
Agriculture	5.0	12.3	11.4	12.1	17.0	19.7	17.5
Labor input from territories as percentage of wage earners in							
Agriculture	15.5	31.4	34.8	37.2	38.6	43.9	43.3
Industry	1.0	3.4	4.6	5.6	5.8	6.3	4.6

Source: Bank of Israel, Annual Report 1988 (Jerusalem).

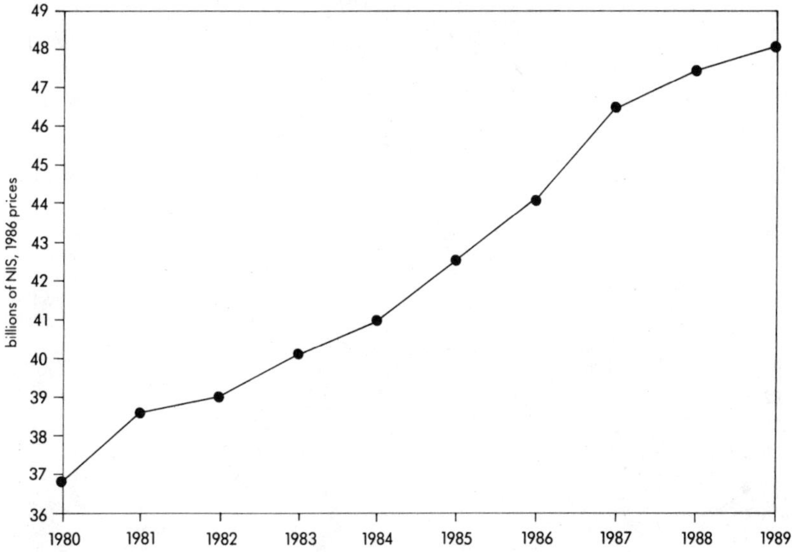

Graph 1. Israel's Gross Domestic Product, 1980–89. Source: Israel Central Bureau of Statistics, Monthly Bulletin of Statistics.

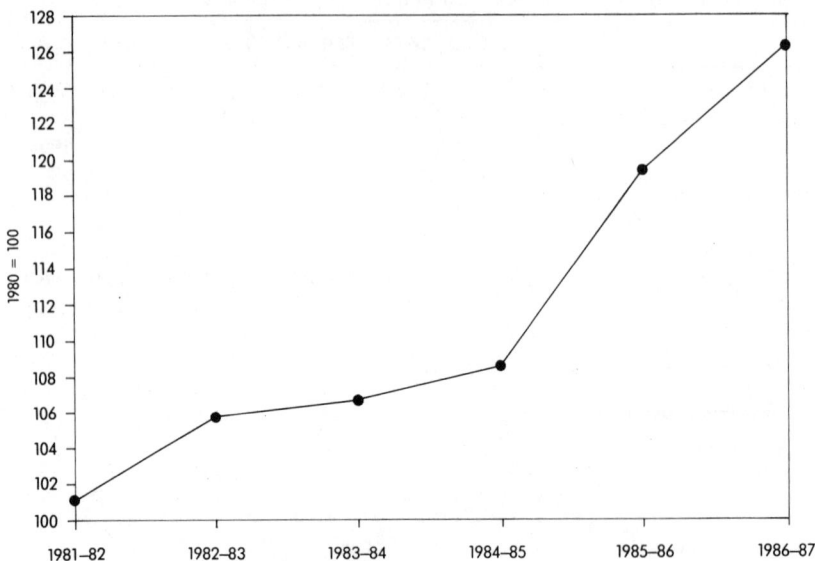

Graph 2. Index of West Bank GDP Growth (two-year moving average), 1981–87. Source: Israel Central Bureau of Statistics, Statistical Abstract of Israel.

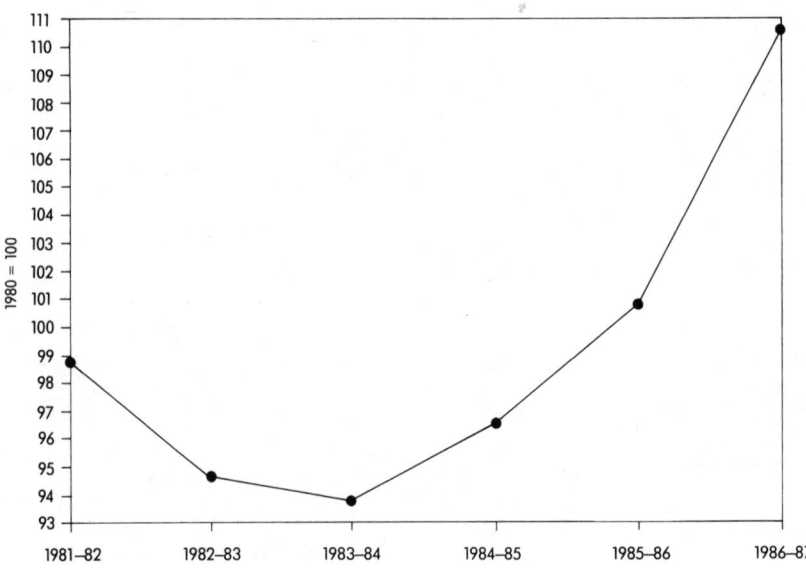

Graph 3. Index of Gaza GDP Growth (two-year moving average), 1981–87. Source: Israel Central Bureau of Statistics, Statistical Abstract of Israel.

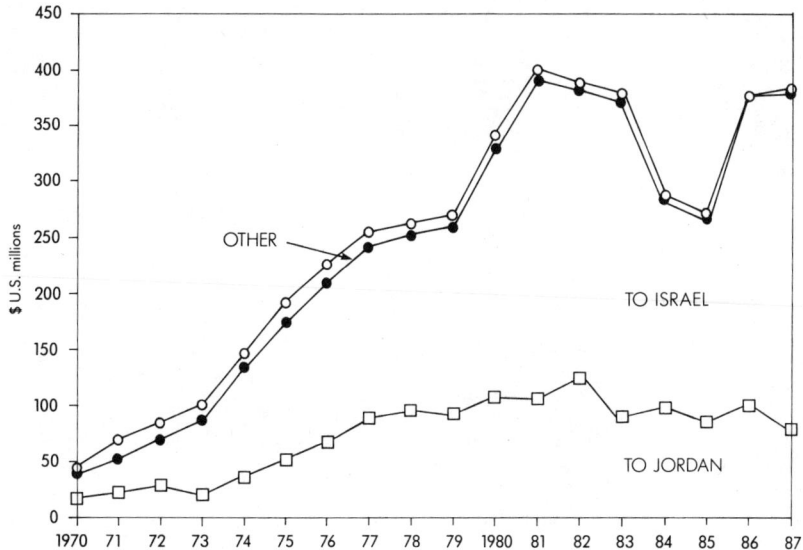

Graph 4. West Bank and Gazan Exports, 1970–87. Source: Israel Central Bureau of Statistics, Statistical Abstract of Israel, 1989.

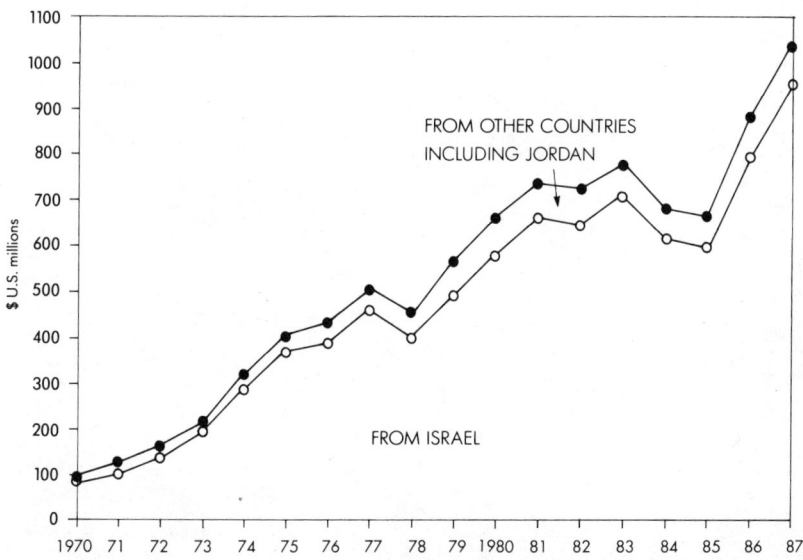

Graph 5. West Bank and Gazan Imports, 1970–87. Source: Israel Central Bureau of Statistics, Statistical Abstract of Israel, 1989.

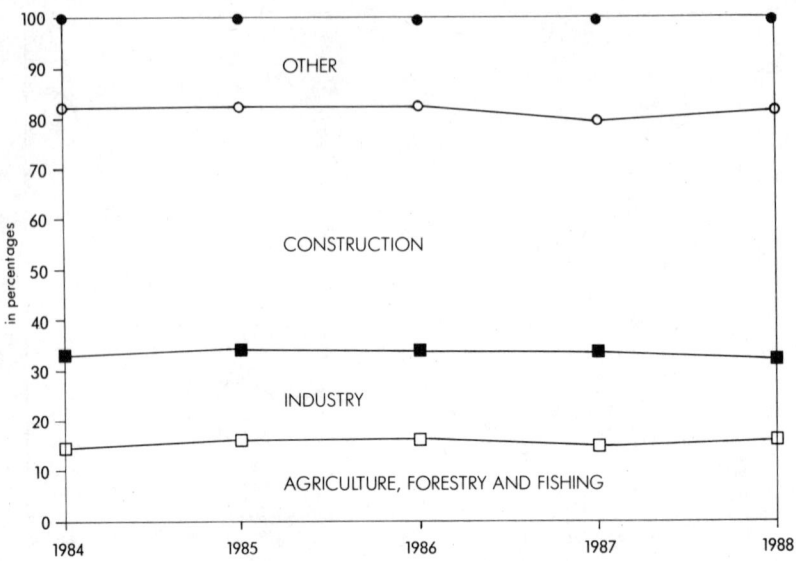

Graph 6. Palestinians from the West Bank and Gaza Employed in Israel by Selected Economic Branches. Source: Israel Central Bureau of Statistics, Statistical Abstract of Israel, 1989.

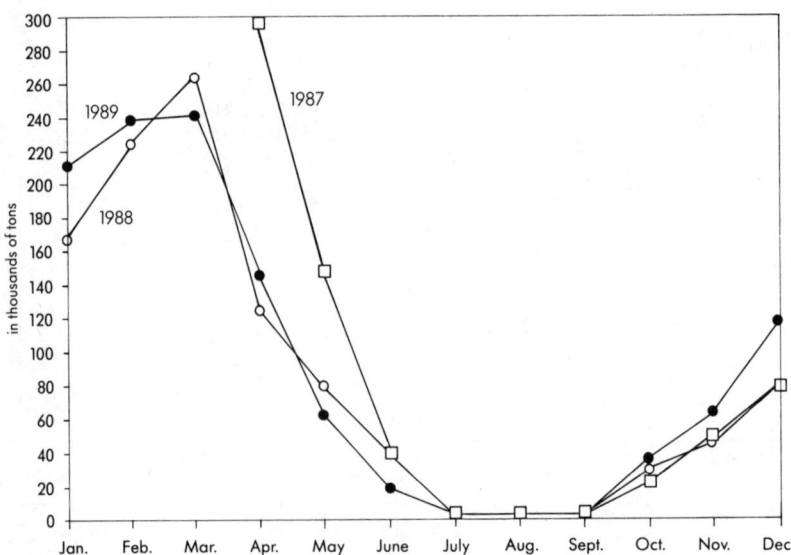

Graph 7. Production of Citrus Crops. Source: Israel Central Bureau of Statistics, Monthly Bulletin of Statistics.

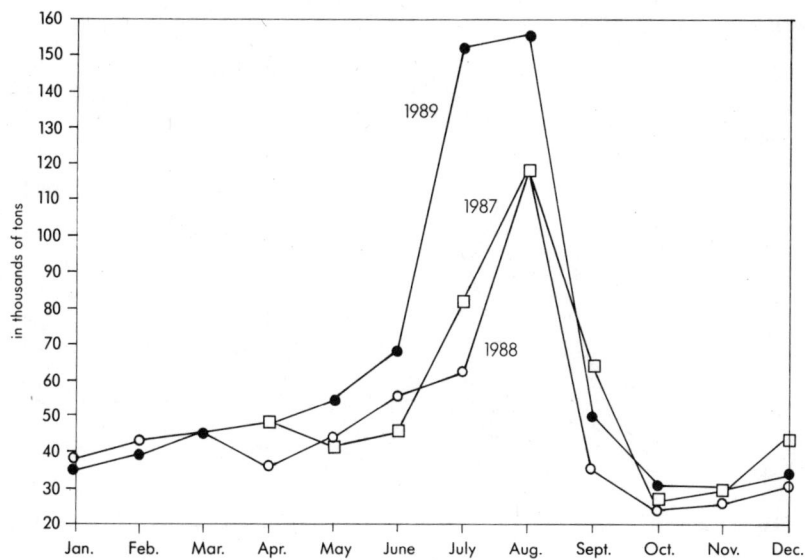

Graph 8. Production of Vegetable Crops. Source: Israel Central Bureau of Statistics, Monthly Bulletin of Statistics.

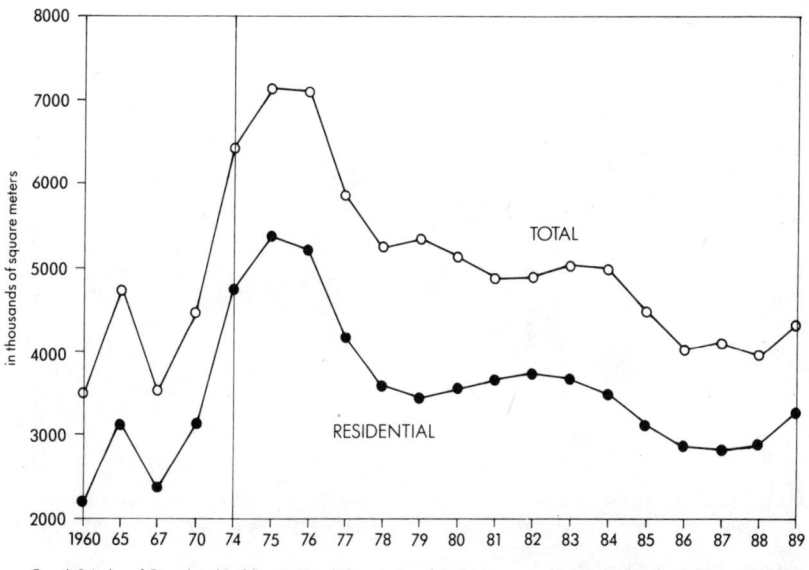

Graph 9. Index of Completed Buildings in Israel. Source: Israel Central Bureau of Statistics, Monthly Bulletin of Statistics.

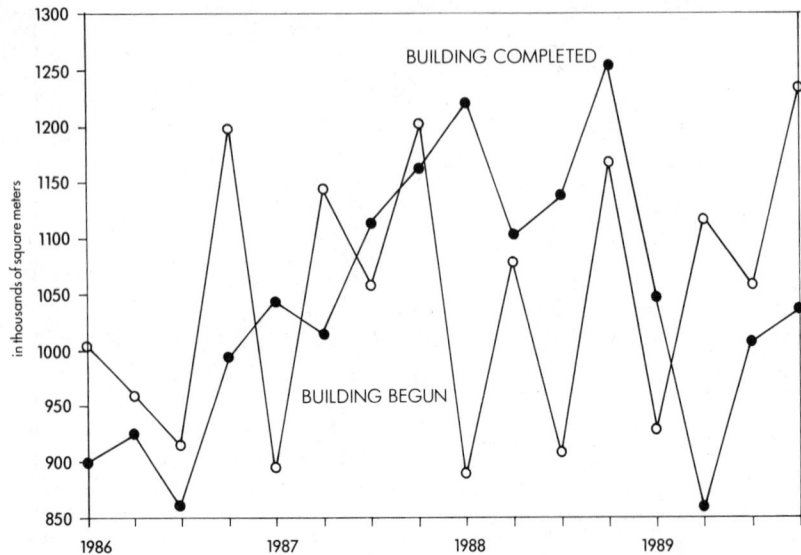

Graph 10. Indicators of Israeli Construction Sector. Source: Israel Central Bureau of Statistics, Monthly Bulletin of Statistics.

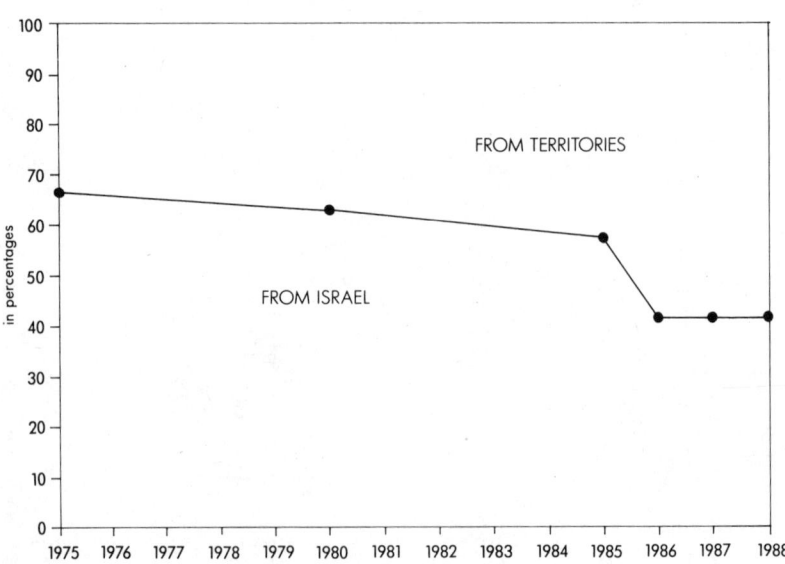

Graph 11. Composition of Employment in Construction. Source: Israel Central Bureau of Statistics, Statistical Abstract of Israel 1989.

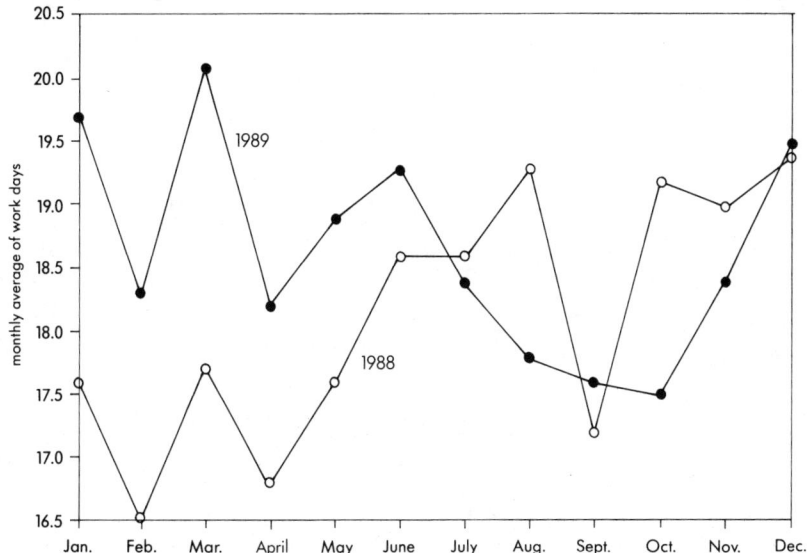

Graph 12. Labor Input in Construction Sector. Source: Israel Central Bulletin of Statistics, Monthly Bulletin of Statistics.

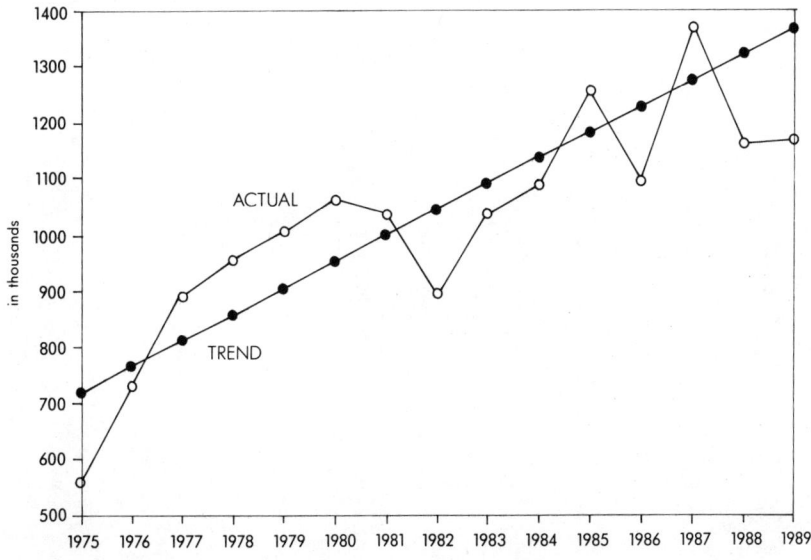

Graph 13. Tourist Arrivals in Israel, 1975–89. Source: Israel Central Bureau of Statistics, Statistical Abstract of Israel, 1989.

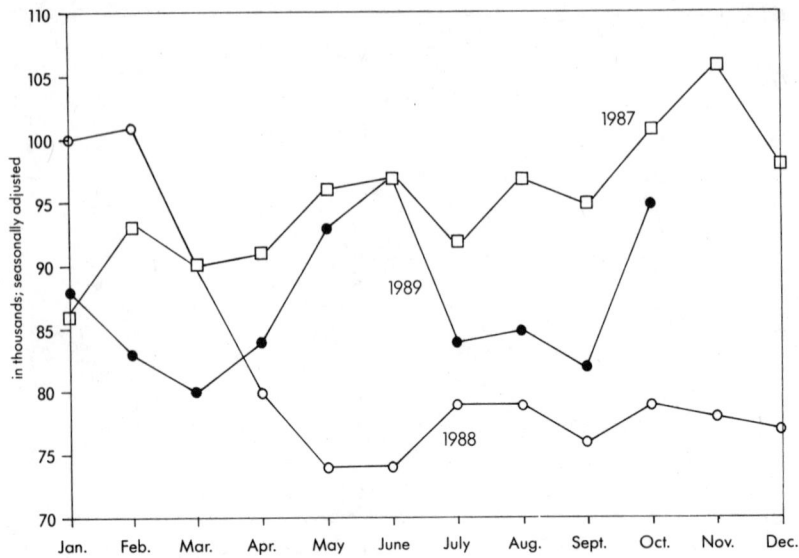

Graph 14. Tourist Arrivals in Israel. Source: Israel Central of Statistics, Tourism and Hotel Services Statistics Quarterly.

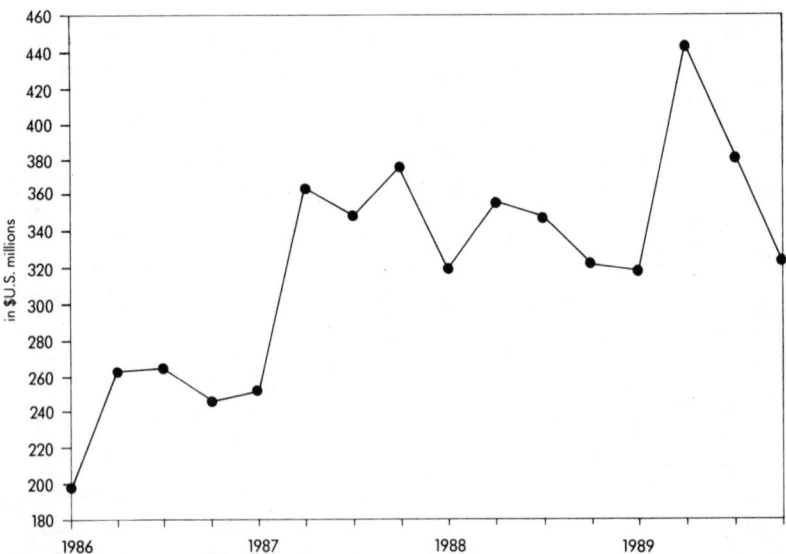

Graph 15. Revenue from Tourism (balance of payments basis), 1986–89. Source: Israel Central Bureau of Statistics, Monthly Bulletin of Statistics.

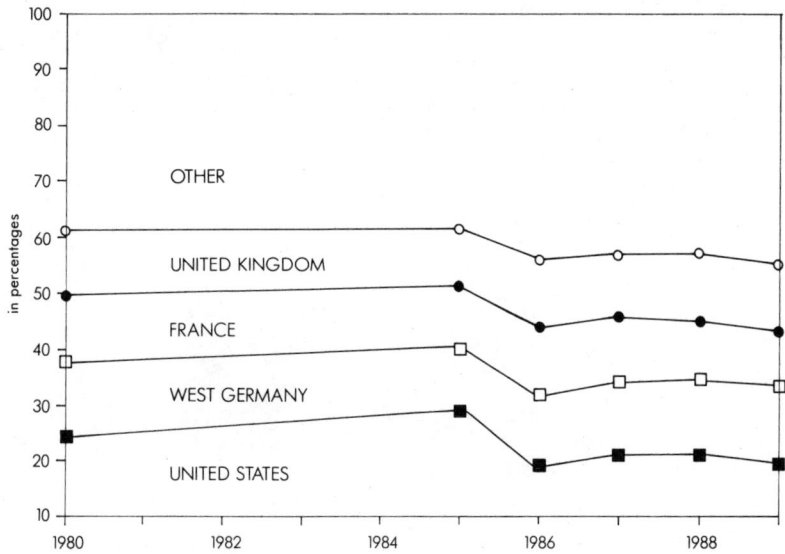

Graph 16. Composition of Tourism to Israel by Country of Origin. Source: Israel Central Bureau of Statistics, Statistical Abstract of Israel 1989.

About the Authors

Asher Arian is distinguished professor of political science, City University of New York, and former professor of political science at Tel Aviv University. Among his numerous publications are *National Security and Public Opinion in Israel* and *Politics in Israel: The Second Generation*, which has just been published in a new edition.

Myron Aronoff is chairman of the Department of Political Science at Rutgers University. Among his many publications on Israeli politics are *Power and Ritual in the Israeli Labor Party* and *Israel Visions and Divisions: Cultural Change and Political Influence.*

Helena Cobban is a research associate at George Mason University and the author of *The Palestine Liberation Organization.* For many years she served as a correspondent for the *Christian Science Monitor* in the Middle East.

Robert O. Freedman is Peggy Meyerhoff Pearlstone Professor of Political Science and dean of the Graduate School of Baltimore Hebrew University. Among his numerous publications are *Soviet Policy toward the Middle East since 1970*, now in its third edition, and *Moscow and the Middle East: Soviet Policy since the Invasion of Afghanistan.*

Gregory Gause is professor of political science at the Middle East Institute of Columbia University and assistant director of Columbia's Middle East Institute. Among his many publications is the forthcoming book *Saudi-Yemeni Relations: Domestic Structures and Foreign Influence.*

George Gruen is director of the Israel and Middle East Affairs Division of the American Jewish Committee. Among his many publications is *The Palestinians in Perspective: Implications for Mideast Peace and U.S. Policy.*

Bard O'Neill is director of Middle East Studies and director of Studies of Insurgency and Revolution at the National War College. He is author of a number of books, including *Armed Struggle in Palestine* and *Insurgency in the Modern World.*

David Pollock is Near East research analyst for the United States Information Agency and a former visiting lecturer in government at Harvard University. Among his publications are *The Politics of Pressure: American Arms and Israeli Policy since the Six-Day War* and *The Iranian Revolution: Implications for the Middle East.*

Elie Rekhess is a senior research associate of the Moshe Dayan Center for Middle East Studies at Tel Aviv University. Among his numerous publications on the Middle East is the forthcoming book *Between Communism and Arab Nationalism: The Israeli Communist Party and the Arab Minority in Israel.*

Howard Rosen is an associate of the Institute for International Economics in Washington, D.C. He has served as an economist of the Research Department of the Bank of Israel and as an International Economist in the Bureau of International Labor Affairs of the U.S. Department of Labor. Among his publications is *The U.S.-Israel Free Trade Area Agreement: How Well Is It Working and What Have We Learned?*

Kenneth Stein is director of the Middle East Studies program of the Carter Center of Emory University and professor of history at Emory University. Among his many publications are *The Blood of Abraham*, cowritten with former President Jimmy Carter, and *The Land Question in Palestine, 1917–1939*.

Nathan Yanai is a visiting Fulbright Professor at Gratz College from Haifa University, where he served as chairman of the Department of Israel Studies. Among his many publications are *Party Leadership in Israel* and *Political Crises in Israel in the Begin Era*.

Index

Abbas, Abul, 258
Abd al-Hayy, Tariq, 344
Abdallah, Abd al-Rahman, 366n.24
Abdallah ibn-Husein, 25, 26, 197, 201
Abd al-Majid, Ismat, 211
Abd Raboo, Yasser, 98, 156
Abu Amr, Ziad, 37, 57, 58, 89, 356
Abu Ayyash, Radwan, 89, 352, 353
Abu Iyad. See Khalaf, Salah
Abu Jihad. See al-Wazir, Khalil
Abu Musa, 14, 67n.17, 206, 208, 209
Abu Nidal, 13, 50
Abu Rahme, Fayez, 85–86, 352
Abu Sharif, Bassam, 90
Abu Za'im, 198, 203
Abu Ziad, Ziad, 91, 352
Aeroflot, 167, 172
Afghanistan, Soviet Union and, 137, 138, 142, 158
African National Congress, 255
Afro-Asian Peoples Solidarity Organization, 140, 141
al-Agha, Zakariyya, 367n.39
Agranat Commission of Inquiry, 293
Agriculture, Intifada and Israeli, 375
Agromir, 166
Agudat Israel, 305, 311, 322, 329, 334, 335
Ahmed Jibril, 14

AIPAC. See American Israel Public Affairs Committee
AJC. See American Jewish Committee
Algeria, 208; as PLO inspiration, 40, 41, 65n.7
Algiers conference, 28
Alignment. See Labor party, Israeli
Allen, Woody, 252
Alon, Yigal, 359
Al-Quds Palestinian Arab Radio, 72
Altalena affair, 316
Amal, 206
American Council for Palestine Affairs, 233
American Friends of Peace Now, 233
American Israel Public Affairs Committee (AIPAC), 120, 252–53, 256
American Jewish Committee (AJC), 221, 243
American Jewish Joint Distribution Committee, 224
American Jews, xviii–xix, 115, 131, 189n.161; and American Arabs, 262n.50; and American Jewish causes, 225; Arafat's meeting with, 234, 235, 259, 264n.82; Conservative, 226; criticism of Israel by, xi–xii, 248–57, 265n.102; dialogue with Palestinians,

American Jews (continued)
233–37, 253; financial support of Israel by, 224–27, 260nn.5, 11, 15; and intermarriage, 226; and Intifada, 220–66; and Israel, 220–83; and Israeli-Lebanon war, 220, 223, 233; Israeli religious parties and, 321; and Israel/PLO dialogue, 247–48; and occupied territories, 245–47, 189n.161; politics of, 223; Reform, 226, 254; unaffiliated, 228; and U.S./PLO dialogue, 242–45
Amirav, Moshe, 265n.96
Amman Summit, 19, 29
Angola, Soviet Union and, 137, 139
Ansar-Three detention camp, 351
Anti-Zionism, Israeli, 298
Aoun, Michel, 208
Arab-American Anti-Defamation League, 382
Arab Democratic party, 298, 328
Arab Higher Committee, 15, 16, 21, 28
Arab League: and Egypt, 192–93, 210; and Intifada, 192–96
Arab Liberation Front, 75
Arab Republic of Egypt. See Egypt
Arabs, xi–xii, xvii–xviii; Intifada and non-Palestinian, 46, 191–219; Israeli (see Israeli Arabs); of occupied territories (see Palestinian Arabs); Palestinian (see Palestinian Arabs); U.S., 262n.50. See also Arab League; Egypt; Iraq; Israeli Arabs; Jordan; Kuwait; Lebanon; Libya; Palestine; Palestinian Arabs; Saudi Arabia; Syria; United Arab Emirates
Arad, Moshe, 146
Arafat, Yasser, 25, 44, 53, 188n.150, 192–97, 203–9; Abu Musa vs., 67n.17; American Jews' meeting with, 234, 235, 259, 264n.82; Arab challenge to, 13–14; and Assad, 146, 149, 205–6; and cashiered civil servants, 217n.32; charisma of, 99; early career of, 77; and East Jerusalem intellectuals, 87; FRC vs., 50; Gorbachev and, xvii, 140, 143, 145, 177; and King Hussein, 141, 178, 197, 198–99, 203–4, 212; King Hussein, Mubarak, and, 212; and Husseini contrasted, 26; and "internationalization" of Palestinian question, 13; and Islamic Jihad, 100; Israel recognized by, xviii, 26, 30, 61, 80, 90, 116, 136, 235, 242, 247, 248, 282n.6; and Jordan, 203; in Moscow, 143–45; Moslem fundamentalists vs., 100; and Mubarak, 212, 213, 219n.72; Palestinian Arab critics of, 12; and PLF violence, 258; as "president" of Palestine, 208; and Saddam Hussein, 255; and Shevardnadze, 160; and Shultz, 243; Syria vs., 58, 100, 193, 205–10, 214; terrorism renounced by, xi, 30, 90, 116, 136, 235, 242, 247, 248, 282n.6; at UN, 117, 156, 245, 329–30, 360; U.S. visa denied to, 117. See also Fatah; Palestine Liberation Organization
Arayan, Izz al-Din, 351
Arens, Moshe, xx, 173, 174, 307; American Jews chastized by, 234; and Baker initiative, 334; and Camp David Accords, 301; and Shamir, 301, 302, 335; and Shevardnadze, 157–58, 160, 167, 172, 177; on Soviet TV, 167; and UN "double standards," 258
Arian, Asher, xiii, xix–xx, 295, 337
Armenia, earthquake in, xvii, 157, 164, 177, 180
Aronoff, Myron J., xiii, xxi
Aruri, Taysir, 366n.23
Ashdod, voting patterns in, 336
Ashkelon, demonstrations in, 314
Asner, Ed, 265n.96
al-Assad, Hafiz, xviii, 76, 136, 139, 177, 215; and Arafat, 146, 149, 205–6; and Gorbachev, 149, 159; and Shevardnadze, 159–60
Atallah, Atallah, 198, 203
'Awda, 351
Awqaf, 202

Baker, James, 118, 120, 121, 125, 128, 174, 213–14, 250; peace initiative of, 124, 255, 301, 305, 322, 333–35; and Shamir proposals, 331
Balfour Declaration, 17
Baram, Haim, 340n.7
Baram, Moshe, 329
Baram, Uzi, 300
Bard, Mitchell, 237, 262n.53
Barnea, Nahum, 270

Barzilai, Gad, 279
al-Baz, 'Usama, 212
Beersheba, 60, 336
Begin, Menachem, xx, 239, 270, 302, 305–6, 312, 313; and Camp David Accords, 338; political philosophy of, 317–19; resignation of, 53
Begun, Yosef, 183n.27
Beilin, Yossi, 300
Bein, Yochanan, 156
Beirut: PLO expelled from, 319; PLO in, 52; siege of, 52; U.S. losses in, 237
Beit Sahour, intellectuals of, 92
Ben-Aharon, Yossi, 80, 147, 163
Ben-Gurion, David, 231, 306, 315–17
Benvenisti, Meron, 55, 67n.21, 311
Berlin, Isaiah, 250
Biale, David, 265n.96
Bir Zeit, 103n.8
Bir Zeit University, 87
Bishara, Ghassan, 358
"Black September," 197
Blaustein, Jacob, 231
Blitzer, Wolf, 333
Bludan Congress, 28
B'nai B'rith International, 251
Bombings, 344, 345
Bookbinder, Hyman, 239
Boschowitz, Rudy, xix, 238
Boycotts: as Intifada tactic, xxii, 5, 60, 73, 83, 88, 371, 379, 381; by U.S., xvi
Brezhnev, Leonid, 138, 139
Brezhnev Plan, 14
Brickner, Balfour, 236, 265n.96
Britain: conciliatory efforts of, 26; Jews of, 250; Palestine mandated by, 17; Palestinian Arab uprising against, xiii–xiv, 3–36 (see also Arab Higher Committee; Husseini, Hajj al-Amin; Palestinian Arabs)
Bronfman, Edgar, 146
Brotherhood. See Moslem Brotherhood
Brutents, Karen, 151
Brynen, Rex, 31
Buil-Buil, Polad, 165
Bush, George, xi, 113, 118–19, 223, 333; on East Jerusalem, 257; and Gorbachev, 169–71, 230; and King Hussein, 204; and Israel, 243; and Mubarak, 212, 213; and occupied territories, 246; and Shamir, 240, 257, 335; and Shamir election plan, xvi, 250; and Soviet Union, 169; on West Bank, 257

CAMERA. See Committee for Accuracy in Middle East Reporting in America
Camp David Accords, 14, 15, 114, 211, 309, 313–14; Herut opposition to, 307; Jordan and, 115; Knesset approval of, 317; Shamir and, 239, 301, 338; Sharon and, 304; Syria and, 115. See also Begin, Menachem; Sadat, Anwar
Camp David conference, 313
Caplan, Neil, 31
Casablanca, Arab summit in, xviii, 28, 29
Center-Shinui, 328. See also Shinui
Chamberlain, Neville, 32n.5
Change (party). See Shinui
Chemical weapons, Saddam Hussein and, 258
Chess, Israeli-Soviet, 175, 189–90n.174
Chevrat Ovdim, 330
Children: "exchange" of Israeli/Soviet, 175; in Intifada, 17. See also Students; Youth groups
China. See People's Republic of China
Chinitz, Zelig, 261n.23
Chomsky, Noam, 233, 252
Christians: Jerusalem, 256; Lebanese (see Maronites; Phalangists; Christian); West Bank, 77, 79
Church of the Holy Sepulchre, 256
Citizen's Rights and Peace Movement. See Ratz
Civil Administration, 104n.9
Cobban, Helena, xii, xv–xvi
Cohen, Steven M., 221, 222, 224, 227, 230, 232, 236, 241, 245, 246, 247, 248
Cold War, end of, 255
Collaborators, Palestinian Arab, 8, 24–25, 57–58, 130, 264n.82; PLO and, 25
Committee for Accuracy in Middle East Reporting in America (CAMERA), 235
Communications, 68n.28, 71–75, 86–87; of Islamic extremists, 59–60; UNLU, 56–57; UNLU/PLO, 58–59
Communism, collapse of world, 364. See also Soviet Union
Communist Party of the Soviet Union (CPSU), 139

Communists. *See* Israeli Communist party; Palestine Communist party
Conference of Presidents of Major American Jewish Organizations, 250, 264n.82
"Countermobilization," Intifada as, 54, 67n.19
CPSU. *See* Communist Party of the Soviet Union
Cuba, as PLO inspiration, 40, 41–42, 65n.7
Curfews, 62, 84, 345, 382, 383; in East Jerusalem, 85
Currency, devaluation of Israeli, 372
Czechoslovakia: and PLO, 176; on proposed Israeli ouster from UN General Assembly, 168

Dahaf Research Institute, 282n.5
Darwasha, Abd al-Wahab, 326, 328, 352–53, 362, 364
Darwish, Abdallah Nimr, 356
Dayan, Moshe, 293, 317; defection from Labor party by, 313, 318
Dayan, Yael, 246
Degel HaTorah, 305, 329, 335
De Klerk, F. W., 255
Democratic Arab party, 352–54, 364. *See also* Darwasha, Abd al-Wahab
DFLP. *See* Democratic Front for the Liberation of Palestine
Democratic Movement for Change (DMC), 317
Deportations, xvi, 9, 30, 62, 86, 94–96, 116, 326, 344
Detention centers, 348, 351
Detention without trial, 62, 85, 336
Democratic Front for the Liberation of Palestine (DFLP), xv, 75, 98, 99; in 1989 Jordan elections, 204; labor unions of, 82; in Moscow, 151; and UN resolution 153, 242
Diaspora: Jewish, 9; Palestinian, 75, 357
DMC. *See* Democratic Movement for Change
Dole, Robert, 125, 228–29
Druze, 47
Dubynin, Yuri, 147
Dukakis, Michael, 223
Dzingickadze, Vaza, 165

East Bank, 197, 204; ethnic makeup of, 216n.16; Palestinians of, 198, 199–203, 205, 216n.16
East Germany: and PLO, 176; on proposed Israeli ouster from UN General Assembly, 168
East Jerusalem, 3, 124; Arab intellectuals of, 84–91, 92; curfews in, 85; Israeli administration of, 19; Israeli annexation of, 85; Palestinians of, 84–91, 92, 213, 309, 331; Soviet Jews as settlers in, 127; strikes in, 326; trade unionism in, 81–82
Egypt, xviii; and Arab League, 192–93, 210; Gaza Strip Arabs deported to, 94; Israel and, 3, 111, 121, 131, 132–33, 156, 160, 181, 210, 212–14, 302, 313, 317, 318 (*see also* Egypt, peace between Israel and); and Israeli-Arab negotiations, 123–24; and Jordan, 211; 1967 defeat of, 38; non-Egyptian Arabs vs., 51; and Palestinian problem, 19, 154–55, 191, 192, 210–14, 215; peace between Israel and, 3, 51, 238; PLO and, 27–28, 210–14; and PNC, 211; and proposed territorial elections, 331; religious extremism in, 69n.40; and Soviet Union, 160–62, 168; and Syria, 149, 208; and U.S., 210, 212–14. *See also* Camp David Accords; Mubarak, Hosni; Nasser, Gamal; Sadat, Anwar; Sinai
Eitan, Rafael, 329
El Al, into Soviet Union, 164, 167, 172
Elbaz, Shlomo, 265n.96
Eliav, Arie Lova, 300
Ellenoff, Theodore, 243
Elscint, 166
Emigration. *See* Soviet Union, emigration to Israel from
Eretz Yisrael. *See* Israel; Jordan; Palestine
Eshkol, Levy, 293
Estiani, Valery, 165
Estonia, 188n.128; and Israel, 165, 166
Ezrahi, Modi'in, 282n.10

Al-Fajr, 85, 233
Fast, Howard, 265n.96
Fatah, xv, 27, 56, 75, 98–99, 195; emergence of, 38, 77; FRC/PFLP-GC vs., 50; goals of, 40; internal problems of,

66–67n.17, 206; and Islamic Jihad, 60; labor-union activities of, 82; in Moscow, 151; PFLP vs., 58; PLO dominated by, 98; Syrian faction of, 14; Syrian support for, 38; violent nature of, 41. See also Arafat, Yasser; Khalaf, Salah; Unified National Leaderhsip of the Uprising; al-Wazir, Khalil
Fatah–the Revolution Council (FRC), 50
Fatwas, 22–23
Fedayeen, 39n.; foreign influences on, 40, 41, 65n.7; politics of, 65n.5
Fellaheen, Palestinian, 12, 17, 18, 21
Fez Plan, 14
Filastin al-Muslima, 356
Foxman, Abraham H., 239
FRC. See Fatah–the Revolution Council
Freedman, Robert O., xiii, xvii, 265n.96
Freij, Elias, 352
Friedan, Betty, 250
Friedman, Thomas L., 265n.102
Front of Steadfastness and Confrontation, 51
Fuller, Graham, 70, 91

Gahal, 305; and annexation of territories, 311–12
Galilee, 347; Arabs of, 358; effects of partition on, 358, 359; PLO flags in, 349; strikes in, 344
Gause, F. Gregory, III, xiii, xvii–xviii
Gaza Strip, xi, 84, 144; annexation of, 311–14; Ben-Gurion position on, 315–16; Bush on, 212, 243; Communists of, 348; construction workers from, 376; deportations from, 94; economy of, xxii, 31, 370–71, 373–74, 380–85; Egyptian control of, 38; elections proposed in, 121, 128; exports/imports of, 373; as "inherently Israeli," 311; Islamic Jihad in, 78; Islamic millennialism in, 76–77; Israeli administration of, 19; Israeli occupation of, 302, 311; and Israeli security, 294; Jewish settlement of, 317; Jordanian-paid public employees of, 202, 217n.32; Likud position on, 51, 312; "magnetic cards" battle in, 74; Moslem Brotherhood in, 77, 78; population of, 42, 66n.12; poverty in, 15; refugee camps of, 23; religious life of, 354; Russian immigrants to, 173; Sharon in, 304; violence in, 326; youth movement in, 53–55. See also Palestinian Arabs
Gazit, Shlomo, 295
Geivandov, Konstantin, 152
Gemayel, Amin, 53
Gemayel, Bashir, 52, 53
General Federation of Trade Unions Based in Nablus, 81–82
Generalized System of Preferences (GSP), 386n.21
Gerasimov, Genady, 141, 162, 185nn.62, 65
Germany. See East Germany; West Germany
Gesher, 91
Ghandi, Mohandus, 67n.19
al-Ghusayn, Jawid, 195, 216n.12
Gilboa, Amos, 359
Gilboa, Eytan, 231, 242
Glasnost, 137, 151; and ICP, 364; and Israeli relations, 166–67
Glazer, Nathan, 265n.96
Golan Heights, 144; annexation of, 313, 318; Syrian designs on, 50
Goldberg, J. J., 233
Goldin, Milton, 225, 226
Golitsyn, Alexander, 171
Gorbachev, Mikhail, xi, xvii, 136–45, 147–50, 155, 156, 161, 163, 178, 180, 189n.153; and Arafat, 177; and Assad, 149, 159; and Bush, 169–71, 230; and Peres, 168, 175; rabbinical blessing for, 164, 179; and Soviet tourists to Israel, 183n.28. See also Glasnost; Perestroika
Gordon, Uri, 172, 262n.30
Great Britain. See Britain
Green, Jerrold, 54, 67n.19
Greenberg, Blu, 233
Green Line, 337, 345
Groeneman, Sid, 224
Grosz, Karoly, 146
Gruen, George E., xiii, xix
GSP. See Generalized System of Preferences
Guerrilla warfare, 39, 39n., 40, 41, 43, 63, 66n.9; Israeli response to, 49
Gulf war. See Iran-Iraq war
Gur, Mordechai, 331, 337
Gur-Aryeh, Binyamin, 359

Gurfeld, Edward, 189n.174
Gush Emunim, 318

Ha'aretz, 48
Habash, George, 58
Habib, Philip, 141
Habimah Theatre, 165, 175
HaKibbutz HaMeuhad, 311
HAMAS, 24, 73, 79–81, 100; creation of, xv, 23, 79; Israeli encouragement of, 68n.36; and Israeli Islamic movement, 355–56; and UNLU contrasted, 79–80; UNLU/PLO and, 59–60; See also Yasin, Ahmed
al-Hamid Sa'ih, Sheik Abd, 203
Hammer, Zvulun, 175
Hamula, significance of, 18
Harakat al-Muqawama al-Islamiyya. See HAMAS
al-Hasan, Khalid, 29
Hashemite Kingdom of Jordan. See Jordan
al-Hassan, Khaled, 97
Hauser, Rita, 235, 236, 259
Hawatmeh, Naef, 141
Hebron, 318, 347, 354
Hecht, Chic, 239
Hertzberg, Arthur, 225, 260n.15
Herut, 305, 306; and annexation of territories, 311, 313; and Camp David accords, 307, 313; merger of Liberal party and, 309; split in, 307. See also Arens, Moshe; Begin, Menachem; Levy, David; Shamir, Yitzhak; Sharon, Ariel; Weizman, Ezer
Herzog, Chaim, 127, 329
Hezbollah, 52, 54
Hijacking, Soviet Union to Israel, xvii, 156, 177, 180
Histadrut, 306, 330, 337; ICP in, 348
Hoffman, Abbie, 250
Hoffman, Stanley, 265n.96
Holocaust, 164, 234, 236
Holon, voting patterns in, 336
Holstein, Charlotte, 262n.50
Holy Land. See Palestine
Horowitz, Stanley B., 224
Hungary, Israel and, 146, 167
Husayn, Ibrahim Nimr, 344
al-Husayni, Faysal, 352, 367n.39

Hussein, Saddam, 230; anti-Israel threats by, 258; and Arafat, 255
Hussein, King, xviii, xx, 112, 151, 152, 214–15, 216n.16, 304, 330, 337, 382; at Amman summit, 193; and Arafat, 141, 178, 197, 198–99, 203–4, 212; and Bush, 204; Mubarak, Arafat, and, 212; Palestinian Arab loyalty to, 45; and Peres, 199, 294, 297, 320, 326; and Shamir peace plan, 203; and Shultz Plan, 115; in U.S., 204; and West Bank, 100, 102. See also Jordan; "Jordanian option"
Husseini, Faisal, xv, 85, 88, 89, 90, 91, 95, 97
al-Husseini, Hajj Amin, 12, 13–16, 23, 24, 25, 26
Husseini, Jemal, 32n.4
al-Husseini, Musa Kazem Pasha, 13
Husseini family, 11

Iatematov, Genghis, 167
Ibn Saud, Abdul-Aziz, 25
ICP. See Israeli Communist party
IDF. See Israel Defense Force
Ighbariyya, Raja, 347
Immigration of Jews into Palestine, 26. See also Soviet Union, emigration to Israel from; White Paper (1939)
India, and Tamil separatism, 68n.40
Inflation, in Israel, 371–72
International Monetary Fund, Jordan and, 204
Intifada: Arab vs. Arab within, 25; components of, 12; economic aspects of, xxi–xxii, 6, 370–87; and "insurgency," 67n.19; international media and, 272; international sympathy/support for, xiv–xv, 60, 61–62, 361, 382; Israeli radical right vs., 303; leadership of, 17, 25; and 1936–39 Palestinian Arab uprising contrasted, 3–36; outbreak of, xi, 16, 54, 56, 110, 112, 326, 373; political makeup of, 20, 25, 27. See also Democratic Front for the Liberation of Palestine; East Jerusalem; Fatah; Gaza Strip; HAMAS; Islamic Jihad; Israel; Moslem Brotherhood; Palestinian Arabs; Popular Democratic Front for the Liberation of Palestine; Popular Front for the Liberation of Palestine; Palestine Liberation

Organization; *Sumud*; Unified National Leadership of the Uprising; West Bank
Iran, 210; Arabs vs., 111; fear of Soviets by, 142
"Irangate," 111
Iran-Iraq war, xii, 19, 192; end of, 195, 196, 208; financing of, 195; and oil, 195, 196
Iraq: financial support of PLO by, 194, 195, 196; Israeli bombing of nuclear reactor in, 269; Kuwait invaded by, 219n.78, 230, 255; and Palestinian Arabs, 19, 133; vs. PLO, 100; poison gas used by, 184n.52; and Syria, 149, 184n.52, 208; and war with Iran (see Iran-Iraq war). *See also* Arab Liberation Front; Hussein, Saddam
Irgun, 306
"Iron Fist" policy, 95
Islam: fundamentalist, 6, 354–56, 363; militant, xiv, 5, 6, 11, 22–24, 210; and terriorism, 247. *See also* HAMAS; Islamic Jihad; Moslem Brotherhood; Shi'ites
Islamic Conference (1931), 13
Islamic Jihad, xv, 23–24, 76, 78–79, 355; and Arafat, 100; depredations of, 78; Fatah and, 60; and Israeli Islamic movement, 356; and UNLU, 78; UNLU/PLO and, 59–60
Islamic Resistance Movement. *See* HAMAS; Moslem Brotherhood
Israel, xi–xii; American public image of, 224, 228, 235, 240–42, 249, 262n.53, 263n.62; attacks on settlers of, 15–16; Christians of, 256, 257; and economic aspects of Intifada, 370–87; economy of, 371–80, 384–85; emigration from, 314; fundamentalist Islam in, 354–56; 1988 elections in, 271, 272, 277–81, 283n.16; Palestinian Arab citizens of, 263n.63; and "Palestinianism," 93; and PLO, 47–50, 52–54, 274, 275–76, 280, 281n.2, 283n.11, 298, 299, 304, 310, 327, 330–35, 338, 339, 340n.7; and proposed PLO dialogue, 264n.81; public opinion within, 269–92; measures of security forces of, 49, 61, 62–63; Soviet Jews as students in, 165; and Soviet republics, 165, 188n.129; Soviet WWII casualties memorialized in, 175. *See also* Arens, Moshe; Balfour Declaration; Begin, Menachem; Ben-Gurion, David; Dayan, Moshe; Galilee; Haifa; Hebron; Israeli Arabs; Israeli Jews; Jerusalem; Judea; Knesset; Labor party, Israeli; Likud; National Unity government; Palestine; Peres, Shimon; Rabin, Yitzhak; Samaria; Shamir, Yitzhak; Sharon, Ariel; Tel Aviv; Weizman, Ezer; Zionism; Zionists
Israel Defense Force (IDF): brutality of, 344; effect of Intifada on, 280; internal criticism of, 63; vs. Lebanon, 51–52, 54; PFLP-GC action against, 76; tactics of, 344
Israeli Arabs, xxi; civil equality for, 343, 353, 365; and ICP, 362–63; and Intifada, 326, 343–69; vs. Israeli Jews, 345; and Moslem fundamentalism, 254–56, 363; and PLO, 345, 346, 349, 356–57, 358, 360–62; and PLP, 363; and terrorism, xxi, 345, 361; ultranationalist, 346–47; and UNLU, 357; violence of, 345. *See also* "Sons of the Village"
Israeli Communist party (ICP), xxi, 82, 298; and Arab self-determination, 358, 359; internal problems of, 363; and Intifada, 347–50; and Israeli Arabs, 362–63; and 1988 elections, 364; and PLO, 348–49; and "Sons of the Village," 350; and Soviet Union, 350
Israeli Council for Peace and Security, 251
Israeli Jews: anti-Arab violence by, 48–49; birth rate of, 314; Conservative, 227; ethnic background of, 277; and Intifada, 272–81; Orthodox, 222, 277; Reform, 227; ultra-Orthodox, 321 (see also Agudat Israel; Degel HaTorah; Shas)
Istiqlal, 13
al-Ittihad, 350
Ivanov-Golitsyn, Alexander, 145
Iyyad, Abu, 362

Jabotinsky, Zeev, 302, 312
Jackson-Vanik amendment, 174, 179
Jaffe, Arie, 265n.96
Jaffee Center for Strategic Studies (JCSS), 282n.5
al-Jalil. *See* Galilee

Jerusalem, 11; Christian quarter of, 256; Georgian art fair in, 165; as Moslem holy site, 354; Moslem quarter of, 326; Old City of, 256; as proposed Palestinian Arab capital, 329; sovereignty over, 257; world spotlight on, 256. *See also* East Jerusalem
Jewish Agency, 227
Jewish-Arab list, 336
Jewish Community Federation of San Francisco, 221
Jewish Peace Lobby, 252–53
Jewish Women's Leadership Consultation on Israel, 233
Jews. *See* American Jews; Diaspora, Jewish; Israel; Israeli Jews; Soviet Union, Jews of; Zionists
Jews Opposed to the Occupation, 252
Jihad, 23, 157. *See also* Islamic Jihad
Jordan, 9; and Camp David accords, 115; civil war in, 44; economic problems of, 381, 383; and Egypt, 211; fedayeen expelled from, 44, 47; and Intifada, 7, 191, 192, 197–205, 214–15; and Israel, 205; Israeli reprisals against, xiv; mufti and, 25; and 1936–39 Palestinian uprising, 7; 1967 defeat of, 38; 1989 parliamentary elections in, 30; 1989 riots in, 197, 200, 204; and Palestine, 46; Palestinian Arabs of, 4, 59; as Palestinian homeland, 304; and PFLP, 45, 58, 198, 204; and PLO, xviii, 99–100, 191, 193–205, 217n.30 (*see also* "Black September"); religious extremism in, 69n.40; and Shultz Plan, 142; and Soviet Union, 151; and Syria, 198, 206; trade between occupied territories and, 373; West Bank members of parliament of, 198; and West Bank Palestinians, 42–43; West Bank renounced by, 26, 115–16, 151, 152, 180, 192, 197, 200, 215, 294, 330, 337. *See also* East Bank; King Hussein; "Jordanian option"; Transjordan; West Bank
"Jordanian option," xvi, xx, xxi, 19, 118, 128, 201, 203, 327, 337
Jordanian-PLO Accord, 14
Judaism, taught in Soviet Union, xvii
Judea: Israeli hopes for, 302; Jewish settlement in, 309, 317; Likud position on, 312
Junayd prison, 366n.21

Kach, 235, 329
Kaddafi, Muamer, 139, 150
Kaddumi, Faruq, 194
al-Kadra, Khalid, 367n.39
Kadum, 318
Kahan Commission of Inquiry, 308
Kahane, Meir, 235, 271, 296, 329
Karkabi, Zahi, 349
Al-Kashshaf, 350
Katzev, Moshe, 308
Katz-Oz, Avraham, 166
Kelly, John, 87, 122, 123, 134n.1, 171
Kessar, Yisrael, 336
Khaddam, Abd al-Halim, 186n.88
Khalaf, Salah, 27, 36n., 92, 169, 194, 203, 207, 327
al-Khalil. *See* Hebron
Khomeini, Rudollah, 67n.19, 77
Khrushchev, Nikita, 137
Kibbutz movement, 312, 330, 337
Kiryat Arba, 318
Kisseleva, Marina, 166
Klibi, Chedli, 185n.57
Knesset, xxi; Arab members of, 326, 366n.21; and Camp David accords, 301; Columbia University peace conference attended by members of, 234; Darwasha in, 353; *Eretz Israel* lobby in, 303; ICP members of, 348; 1988 elections to, 277–81, 294–96, 300, 320, 328–29, 364; PLP members of, 350; radical doves of, 296; religious parties' clout in, 296; Shkolnik visit to, 175; Zionist left in, 296
Kol Israel, Soviet jamming of, 158
Komsomol, 145
Kook, Simha, 184n.48
Kuneitra (Syria), 159
Kushner, Harold S., 225
Kuwait: Iraqi invasion of, 219n.78, 230, 255; Palestinian Arab support from, 386n.18; PLO support from, 195

Labor, Intifada and Israeli, 379–80. *See also* Trade unions
Labor party, Israeli, xii, xxi, 312; accommodationism of, 51; Arab members of, 352, 353, 362; in ascendency, 53, 325; current dilemma of, 339; Darwasha resignation from, 326; and Egypt, 300; hawk/dove dissent within, xxi; and In-

tifada, 295, 296, 299–302, 310, 325–42; and "Jordanian option," xx; and Mapam, 270, 336; members of Middle Eastern background in, 339n.1; and 1988 elections, 296; and occupied territories, 232, 294; and religious parties, 317, 336; socioeconomic patterns of, 340n.70; support for, 327; voting patterns re, 273–74, 275, 277–81. *See also* Peres, Shimon; Rabin, Yitzhak; Weizman, Ezer

Labor Zionist Alliance, 264n.82
Lautenberg, Frank, 238
Lavi project, 379
Law of Return, 226
League for Human and Citizen Rights, 348
League of Nations, and Palestine mandate, 17
Lebanon, 29; agreement between Israel and, 237; civil war in, 51, 314; Israeli invasion of, xviii, 13, 51–52, 270, 295, 318–19, 325; Israeli MIAs in, 175; Israeli reprisals against, xiv; Israeli withdrawal from, 111, 297, 320, 379; PLO in, 47, 51–53, 83, 97, 318 (*see also* Beirut, PLO in); Sharon in, 304–5; Syrian influence in, 52, 53; Syria/PLO competition in, 76; U.S. and, 110–11; war in, xii, 295, 325, 328. *See also* Aoun, Michel; Beirut; Druze; Gemayel, Bashir; Hezbollah; Maronites; Phalangists, Christian; Shi'ites
Lerner, Michael, 233, 250, 337
Levies and taxes, Israeli, 372
Levin, Aryeh, 161, 166, 173
Levin, Carl, xix, 238
Levy, David, xx, 257, 303, 330; background of, 306–7; politicking of, 311; vs. Shamir, 306, 308–9
Levy, Maxim, 336
Liberal party, Israeli, 305, 307, 311; Herut merged with, 309. *See also* Moda'i, Yitzhak
Libya: financial aid to PLO by, 195; Soviet armament of, 138, 163, 177
Liebling, Mordechai, 265n.96
Lijan shabiyya limusanadat al-intifada, 346
Likud, xiv, xix–xx, 219n.78, 257, 325, 329–38; ascension of, 223; and annexation of territories, 311, 312, 313–14; conflict within, xii, 305–11, 321; counterinsurgency measures of, 49; formation of, 312; hard line of, 50–51, 62; Intifada and, 293–324; and Labor party, 238; members of Middle Eastern background in, 339n.1; and Mubarak proposals, 332; and 1988 elections, 296, 307; and Samaria, 312; settlement program of, 55; support for, 327; and "the territories," 232; voting patterns re, 273–74, 275, 277–81. *See also* Arens, Moshe; Begin, Menachem; Levy, David; Modai, Yitzhak; Shamir, Yitzhak; Sharon, Ariel
Likud–Herut USA, 235
Local Authorities Center (Israel), 336
Los Angeles Times, 1988 poll by, 221

Ma'arach list, 336
McGovern, George, 265n.96
Maddy-Weitzman, Bruce, 31
MAKI. *See* Israeli Communist party
Mandela, Nelson, 255
Mann, Theodore, 248
Mao Tse-tung, 41, 44
Mapai, 306, 316
Mapam, xx, 328; and Intifada, 299; Labor party and, 270, 336; and 1988 elections, 296; slogans of, 367n.47; Soviet Union visited by members of, 145
Mari, Mariam, 367n.39
Maronites, 44, 52. *See also* Phalangists, Christian
Martirosov, Georgy, 164
al-Masri, Tahir, 202
Media, international, 22, 27
Medvenko, Leonid, 151
Meir, Golda, 293
Merchants' committees, 83
Meridor, Dan, 308
Metzenbaum, Howard, 238
Meyer, Marshall, 265n.96
Miari, Muhammad, 351–52, 362, 365, 367n.35
Milgrom, Jacob, 265n.96
Milhelm, Muhammed, 330
Milson, Menahem, 70
Mishal, Saul, 57, 67n.25
Mitterand, François, 163
Mizna, Amram, 294

Moda'i, Yitzhak, xx, 303, 307, 330; Peres vs., 309, 320; politicking of, 311; vs. Shamir, 308, 309
Moledet, 303, 329
Molotov cocktails, xv, 54, 60, 89, 326
Morgenbesser, Sidney, 265n.96
Moscow: Israeli films in, 165; Israeli Philharmonic in, 164
Moscow Business, 166
Moslem Brotherhood, xv, 7, 23, 59, 76–79. See also HAMAS
Moslems. See Islam
Mubarak, Hosni, xviii, 27, 160, 161, 210–14, 332; Arafat and, 212, 213, 219n.72; Arafat, King Hussein, and, 212; Bush and, 212, 213; and Palestinian problem, 168, 204; proposals of, 340; and Rabin, 219n.72; and Shamir, 211, 212; and Shultz, 212; and Shultz Plan, 142
Mufti. See al-Husseini, Hajj Amin
Murphy, Richard, 114, 115, 141, 146, 326–27
Musa al-Maragha, Sa'id. See Abu Musa

Nablus: strikes in, 326; union activity in, 81–82
Nakhleh, Emile, 31
Naor, Arye, 253–54, 334
Nasser, Gamal, 46, 215
National Association of Students (Israel), 348
National Committee of Chairmen of Arab Local Authorities, 344, 346
National Guidance Council (NGC), 44, 93
National Jewish Community Relations Advisory Council (NJCRAC), 189n.161, 248–49
National Religious Party (NRP), 305, 312, 318, 329
National Survey of American Jews (NSAJ), 221
National Unity government, xi, 111, 125, 169, 271, 277, 293, 294, 297, 300–302, 319–22, 325, 329, 337; establishment of, 319; Labor domination of, 319–20; Likud domination of, xx, 177, 309; 1990 collapse of, xii, xxi, 219n.78, 310, 322; Rabin's role in, 295, 300; reestablishment of, 321; religious parties and, 296; and settlement of occupied territories, 318; Sharon vs., 308. See also Arens, Moshe; Labor party, Israeli; Likud; Moda'i, Yitzhak; Peres, Shimon; Rabin, Yitzhak; Shamir, Yitzhak; Sharon, Ariel; Weizman, Ezer
NATO, Soviet Union and, 137
Natta, Alessandro, 143
Netanyahu, Binyamin, 244, 308
New Israel Fund, 227
New Outlook, 233
Newspapers, Palestinian, 55
NGC. See National Guidance Council
Nishma, 251–52
NJCRAC. See National Jewish Community Relations Advisory Council
Not-So-Silent Partnership, The (Gruen), 222
Novick, Nimrod, 147
NRP. See National Religious Party
NSAJ. See National Survey of American Jews
Nuclear reactor, Iraqi, 269
Nuri al-Said, 25
Nuseibeh, Sari, 71, 72, 89, 90

Obeid, Sheikh, 164
O'Connor, John, 257
October War, 360
Oil, 10; and Iran-Iraq war, 195, 196
Olmert, Ehud, 166, 308
Oman, 51
O'Neill, Bard E., xii, xiv–xv
"Operation Exodus," 224
Operation Litani, 51
Oppenheim, Carolyn Toll, 236
Ottoman Empire, Palestine as part of, 18
Oz, Amos, 336

PACs, pro-Israeli, 224, 226
Palestine: British mandate of, 4; Jewish immigration to, 5–8; Jordanian goals re, 46; Legislative Council proposed for, 14; militant Islamic view of, 59; proposed partitioning of, 10, 15, 24, 29, 315, 358, 361 (see also Peel Commission); physical nature of, 43; Syrian goals re, 46
Palestine Communist party (PCP), xv, 56,

Index   411

75, 93, 98, 99, 366n.23; strength of, in territories, 81–82
Palestine Liberation Army (PLA), 38
Palestine Liberation Front (PLF), 50, 75, 258
Palestine Liberation Organization (PLO), xi, xv–xix, xxi, 26–31, 78, 86, 233, 264n.73, 272; attack on Israeli bus by, 60; in Beirut, 52, 319; and collaborators, 25; Communist China support for, 46; Democratic Arab party and, 353; and Egypt, 27–28, 210–14; electoral victories of, 45; emergence of, 38; Fatah dominance of, 98; financial support of Intifada by, 381, 384, 386n.18; headdress of, 346; and ICP, 348–49; international sympathy/support for, 44, 46–47, 63; and Intifada, 23, 37, 56–64, 70–106; Iraq vs., 100; Israel and, 47–50, 52–54, 274, 275–76, 280, 281n.2, 283n.11, 298, 299, 304, 310, 327, 330–35, 338, 339, 340n.7; Israeli Arabs and, 345, 346, 349, 356–57, 358, 360–62; and Israeli ceasefire, 51; Israel recognized by, xviii, 26, 30, 61, 80, 90, 116, 136, 235, 242, 247, 248, 282n.6; and Jordan, xviii, 99–100, 191, 193–205, 217n.30 (see also "Black September"); in Lebanon, 47, 51–53, 83, 97, 318 (see also Beirut, PLO in); maverick Arab groups vs., 50; organizational structure of, 44; pan-Arab support for, 61; "peace initiatives" of, 26; PFLP vs., 50; popularity of, 16; religious extremists vs., 59–60, 64; Saudi Arabia's support for, 29, 194, 195, 196, 216n.12, 386n.18; Shamir and, xvi, 102, 338; Sharon vs., 304; and Shultz Plan, 142; Soviet Union and, 46, 136–37, 141, 143, 145, 151–55, 158, 160, 162, 173, 175–76, 180–81, 188n.150; and Syria, 47, 50, 53, 76, 149, 205–10; and territorial elections, 331; terrorism of, 40, 65n.6, 183n.25, 185n.62; terrorism renounced by, xi, 30, 90, 116, 136, 235, 242, 247, 248, 282n.6; and UNLU, 57–60; and UN Resolution 181, 152–53; UN status of, 171–72, 181, 360; U.S. boycott of, xvi; U.S. public image of, 241, 244–45; and Weizman meeting, 362. See also Arafat, Yasser; Khalaf, Salah; Palestine Liberation Front
Palestine National Council (PNC), 99, 141, 194, 329; Egypt and, 211; and Palestinian Communists, 348; and Palestinian National Charter, 39; and two-state solution, 26, 90, 117, 151, 153, 329, 356–57
Palestine National Fund, 195, 204
Palestine National Salvation Front, 14, 27, 208
Palestinian Arab Executive, 13
Palestinian Arabs: civil rights of, 276; collaborators among, 8, 24–25, 57–58, 130, 264n.82; Communists among, 348 (see also Palestine Communist Party); deportation of, xvi, 9, 30, 62, 86, 94–96, 116, 326, 344; destruction of homes of, 62; dialogue with American Jews by, 233–37, 253; dissension among, 8; evictions of, 15–16; goals of, 39–40; international support for, 10–11, 13; and Iraq, 19, 133; in Israel, 60; Israeli Arab support for, 344–65; Israeli citizens among, 263n.63, 272; Israeli Jews' perception of, 276; intellectuals among, 84–93; with Jewish employers, 60, 84, 373–74, 379–80, 382; of Jordan, 4, 59; merchant class of, 18; nationalism of, 3–36; mistreatment of, 62, 254, 326; organizational structure of, 43–45; 1936–39 uprising of, xiii–xiv, 3–36; 1968–73 uprising of, xiv; and Palestinian Arab Israeli citizens contrasted, 263n.63; pan-Arab support for, 6–7; popular support for, 45–57; pre-Intifada resistance of, 3–54; religious extremism among (see HAMAS; Islamic Jihad); restrictions on businesses of, 55; rioting by, 229; Saudi Arabia and, 19; social clubs of, 55; social distinctions among, 18, 19–20, 25; Soviet Union and, 136–90; "statehood" for, 196–97, 207, 212, 275, 276, 281, 281n.2, 329, 356, 358; strategy of, 40–42; Syria and, 19, 133; and Transjordan, 19; U.S. sympathy for, 240–42; violence against, 254, 258. See also Arafat, Yasser; Fatah; Fedayeen; Husseini, Faisal; Husseini, al-Hajj Amin; Palestine Liberation Organization; Popular Democratic Front for the

Palestinian Arabs (continued)
  Liberation of Palestine; Popular Front for the Liberation of Palestine; Popular Front for the Liberation of Palestine–General Command; Siniora, Hanna; Unified National Leadership of the Uprising
"Palestinianism," 93
Palestinian National Charter, 39, 65n.5
Palestinian National Front, 93
Palestinian Popular Struggle Front, 75
Paley, Grace, 265n.96
Palmach, dismantling of, 316
"Passage to Freedom," 226, 261n.18
Pasternak, Boris, 138
Pazner, Avi, 170
PCP. See Palestine Communist party
PDFLP. See Popular Democratic Front for the Liberation of Palestine
"Peace for Galilee." See Lebanon, war in
Peace Now, 327
Peel Commission, 15
Pelletreau, Robert, 156
People's Republic of China: as PLO inspiration, 40, 65n.7; PLO support from, 46; Syrian missile-shopping in, 150
Peres, Shimon, 53, 112, 125, 149, 162, 166, 319, 330, 334; and Arab states, 271; and Dubynin, 147; and Gorbachev, 168, 175; in Hungary, 146; and King Hussein, 199, 294, 297, 320, 326; and "Jordanian option," 327; and Labor party Arabs, 354; vs. Moda'i, 309, 320; and 1988 elections, 279; political wheeling-dealing of, 255; Rabin and, xxi, 329, 332, 337, 338; and radical doves, 300–301; religious parties courted by, 333, 338; Shamir and, 127, 322, 332; vs. Sharon, 320; and Shultz, 238; and Shultz Plan, 142; and U.S. peace initiatives, 327; Weizman and, 340n.16. See also Labor party, Israeli; National Unity government
Perestroika, 137, 166
Peretz, Don, 328
Petreanu, Dan, 334
Petrovsky, Vladimir, 172, 189n.155
PFLP. See Popular Front for the Liberation of Palestine
PFLP–GC. See Popular Front for the Liberation of Palestine–General Command
Phalangists, Christian, 52, 308, 319
Pickering, Thomas, 258
PLA. See Palestine Liberation Army
PLF. See Palestine Liberation Front
PLO. See Palestine Liberation Organization
PLP. See Progressive List for Peace
PNC. See Palestine National Council
Pogroms, Russian, 225
Poison gas, 150, 184n.52
Poland: and PLO, 176; Solidarity movement in, 67n.19
Pollard, Jonathan Jay, xviii, 223
Pollock David, xiii, xvi
Popular Democratic Front for the Liberation of Palestine (PDFLP), 42, 45, 56. See also Unified National Leadership of the Uprising
Popular Front for the Liberation of Palestine (PFLP), xv, 42, 56, 75, 79, 98, 101, 141; and Jordan, 45, 58, 198, 204; labor unions of, 82; vs. PLO, 50; and UN Resolution 242, 153. See also Habash, George; Unified National Leadership of the Uprising
Popular Front for the Liberation of Palestine–General Command (PFLP–GC), 14, 36, 41, 208; influence in occupied territories of, 75–76; maverick operations of, 50. See also Ahmed Jibril
Popular Struggle Front, 50
Prisons, 348, 366n.21. See also Detention centers
Progressive List for Peace (PLP), xxi, 298, 347; and Intifada, 350–52; and Israeli Arabs, 363; and 1988 elections, 364
Pugachova, Alla, 145

Qadi, office of, 202
Qalqiliyya, 367n.35
al-Qasim, Marwan, 201, 203
al-Qassam, Izz al-Din, 22–23
Qawasima, Fahd, 351
al-Qiyada al Muwahhada. See Unified National Leadership of the Uprising
Quandt, William, 119, 128
Quayle, Dan, 171
Quqa, Khalil, 59

Raab, Earl, 251
Rabin, Yitzhak, 94, 162, 301, 320, 330–35, 354; Darwasha vs., 352; hard line of, 254, 326; and Mubarak, 219n.72; in National Unity government, 295, 300; and Peres, xxi, 329, 332, 337, 338; popularity of, 321, 330, 332, 337–38; Shamir and, 322; Sharon vs., 303; and Soviet arming of Syria, 184n.51; Weizman and, 340n.16
Rakah. See Israeli Communist party
Ramallah, strikes in, 326
Ramon, Haim, 300, 334
Rantisi, Abd al-Aziz, 355
Ratz, xx, 299, 328, 336
Al-Raya, 347
Reagan, Ronald, xi, xvi, 113, 118, 147, 148; and Israel, 243; and occupied territories, 246; peace initiatives of, 237; and PLO dialogue, 212; social program cutbacks under, 226
Reagan Plan, 14
Recession, in Israel, 336
Red Crescent, 346
Red Cross, Intifada appeals to, 87
Refugee camps: East Bank, 216n.16; of Gaza Strip, 42, 351; in Jordan, 44, 45; in Lebanon, 44, 45, 206, 207; West Bank, 42, 351. See also Sabra; Shatilla
Reich, Seymour D., 251, 256, 266n.102
Rejection Front, 101
Rekhess, Elie, xiii, xxi
Reza Pahlavi, Mohammad, 77
Rich, Adrienne, 265n.96
Richman, Alvin, 240, 244
Rida, Rashid, 22
al-Rifai, Zayad, 198
Ritz, Ester Leah, 253
Rogers, William, 129, 312
Roiphe, Anne, 265n.96
Rosen, Howard, xiii, xxi–xxii
Rosensaft, Menachem Z., 258–59, 264n.82
Ross, Dennis, 119
Rudman, Warren, 238
Russia. See Soviet Union

Sabotage, xxi, 345, 354, 361
Sabra, massacre at, 52, 308, 319
Sadat, Anwar, 207, 317, 318
Saint James Palace conference, 26

Saint John's Hospice, Jerusalem, 256, 257
Saiqa, 75, 208
SAJL. See Survey of American Jewish Leaders
Sakharov, Andrei, 137–38
Samaria: Israeli hopes for, 302; Jewish settlement of, 309, 317; Likud position on, 312
Sarid, Yossi, 328, 334
Sartawi, Issam, 50
Saudi Arabia: and Palestinian Arabs, 19; PLO financial support from, 29, 194–96, 216n.12, 386n.18; Soviets feared by, 142
Sayigh, Yezid, 56, 58
Scheer, Robert, 221
Schiff, Ze'ev, 95
Schindler, Alexander, 254
Segal, Jerome, 252
al-Shabiba, 351
Shah of Iran. See Reza Pahlavi, Mohammad
Shaka, Bassa, 352
Shamir, Yitzhak, xx–xxi, 147, 213, 226, 228, 229, 248, 296, 334; and Arens, 301, 302, 335; and Baker peace initiative, 255, 301, 335; and "big Israel," 173, 178, 256–57, 315; Bronfman and, 146; and Bush, 240, 257, 335; and Camp David accords, 239, 301, 338; career of, 306; election proposals of, 80, 102, 121–22, 125, 162–63, 167, 177, 181, 203, 240, 250, 271, 301–2, 315, 330–33; on Gorbachev, 149; hard line of, 234, 259, 260n.15, 330; international support for, 249–50; and Likud turmoil, 309–11; Moda'i vs. 308, 309; and Mubarak, 211, 212; and 1988 elections, 279; and Peres, 127, 322, 332; vs. Peres/Hussein agreement, 326; and PLO, xvi, 102, 338; political fall of, 127; political strategies of, 255, 319–22, 329; and Rabin, 322; and Russian immigration, 126, 169; and settlement of occupied territories, 258; and Sharon, 308, 310, 311; and Shevardnadze, 177, 184n.46; and Shultz, 238; and Shultz Plan, 142; and Soviet Union, 167, 170; and Tarifi, 92; in U.S., 177, 235, 237–38, 240, 250, 254, 333, 335; U.S. Jewish pressure on, xix, 233; and

Shamir, Yitzhak (continued)
  U.S. peace initiatives, 112, 326–27; vs. Weizman, 175. See also Likud; National Unity government
Shari'ah, 59
Sharon, Ariel, xx, 188n.128, 270, 307, 330, 335; and Camp David accords, 304; dismissed as defense minister, 52, 308, 319; and Intifada, 303–5; in Jerusalem's Moslem Quarter, 326; and Lebanese war, 295, 304–5; vs. National Unity government, 308; Peres vs., 320; vs. PLO, 304; vs. Rabin, 303; resignation of, 126, 310; and Shamir, 308, 310, 311
Shas, 305, 311, 322, 329, 335
Shatilla, massacre at, 52, 308, 319
Shekel, devaluation of, 372
Shemtov, Victor, 265n.96
Shevardnadze, Edward, 141, 142, 143, 146, 149, 179, 180; and Arafat, 160; and Arens, 157–58, 160, 167, 172, 177; and Assad, 159–60; in Cairo, 160–62; and Khaddam, 186n.88; on Mubarak, 168; and Shamir, 177, 184n.46; and Shamir plan, 163; and Soviet émigrés, 157; in Syria, 158–60; and Weizman, 175
Shi'ites, 44, 52, 237
Shinui, xx, 296, 299, 328
Shkolnik, Leonid, 175
Shomron, Dan, 327
Shuhada, 350–51
Shultz, George, xvi, 85, 118, 141, 147, 242; in Amman, 198, 199; and Arafat, 243; as "friend of Israel," 243; in Israel, 87, 92, 112, 114, 115, 238; in Moscow, 146; Mubarak and, 212; peace initiative of, 15, 29, 113, 114–16, 142, 150, 237, 246, 248, 327; and Peres, 238; senatorial letter to, 238, 240; and Shamir, 238
Shultz Plan. See Shultz, George, peace initiative of
Shur, Chaim, 265n.96
Sikariim, 280
Sinai, 51; Israeli evacuation of, 239, 271, 313
Sinai I and II, 300
Siniora, Hanna, xv, 85–87, 88, 89, 92, 352
Al-Sirat, 354, 355
Sit-ins, 87
Six-Day War, 230, 315
Smith, Hanoch, 283n.11

Smooha, Sammy, 328
Solidarity (Poland), 67n.19
"Sons of the Village," xxi, 346–47, 350, 363
Soviet Academy of Sciences, Weizman and, 175
Soviet Union: anti-Semitism in, 172, 180; and Arab-Israeli problem, 136–90; and arms control, 137; and Cambodia, 137; and cultural exchanges, 165; and Egypt, 160–62, 168; emigration to Israel from, xvii, 125–27, 129, 136, 147, 149, 165, 169, 172–74, 176, 177, 178, 219, 222–23, 224, 226, 256–57, 258, 261n.18, 314, 315 (see also "Operation Exodus"; "Passage to Freedom"; Tourists, Soviet Jews as Israeli); and Ethiopia, 139; exchange of consular delegations with Israel by, 140; glasnost in, 145; and Hungary, 146; and ICP, 350; and Intifada, xi, xvii, 136, 139, 150–53, 176–79, 180–81; and Israel, 136–49, 153, 156–58, 160–81, 256–57, 364; Israeli agrotechnical assistance to, 179; Israeli diplomatic delegation to, 149; Israeli teachers in, xvii, 165; Jews of, 145, 164–65 (see also Soviet Union, emigration to Israel from); and Jordan, 151; liberalization in, 364; Moslems of, 140; Palestinian Arabs and, 136–90; and PLO, 46, 136–37, 141, 143, 145, 151–55, 158, 160, 162, 173, 175–76, 180–81, 188n.150; pogroms threatened in, 225; and proposed Israel ouster from UN General Assembly, 168; Shamir and, 167, 170; and Syria, 149–50, 158–60, 177, 180, 184nn.51, 54; and U.S., 111, 137, 140, 141–43, 163, 169–72, 189n.154. See also Armenia; Estonia; Glasnost; Gorbachev, Mikhail; Moscow; Perestroika; Shevardnadze, Edward
Specter, Arlen, 239
Sri Lanka, 63, 68n.40
Stein, Kenneth W., xii, xiii–xiv
Stein, Martin, 226
Steinhem, Gloria, 265n.96
Stern Group, 306
Stevenson amendment, 179
Stonings, by Israeli Arabs, xv, 54, 60, 89, 258, 326, 344, 345, 351
Strategic Defense Initiative, 137

Strikes, xxii, 9, 15–16, 24, 57–58, 60, 79–80, 326, 381, 382; commercial, 73, 103n.8; hunger, 87; Israeli Arab sympathy, 344–45, 349. See also Sit-ins
Students, 12, 17, 55–56, 87; in 1936–39 uprising, 21
Student unions, 82, 83
Suez Canal, 312
Sumud, 19
Sununu, John, 257
Surani, Jamal, 357
Survey of American Jewish Leaders (SAJL), 221
Syria, xviii, 188n.150; vs. Arafat, 58, 100, 193, 205–10, 214; and Camp David accords, 115; and Chinese missilery, 150; defeat of in 1967, 38; Egypt and, 149, 208; Fatah support by, 38; and Intifada, 191, 192, 205–10, 214, 215; and Iraq, 149, 184n.52, 208; vs. Israeli Lebanon invasion, 52; and Jordan, 198, 206; and Lebanon, 52, 53, 76; and new Palestinian state, 196; and Palestine, 46; and Palestinian Arab accommodation of Israel, 28; and Palestinian Arabs, 19, 133; and PLO, 47, 50, 53, 76, 149, 205–10; religious extremism in, 69n.40; Shevardnadze in, 158–60; and Shultz Plan, 142; and Soviet Union, 149–50, 158–60, 177, 180, 184nn.51, 54. See also Assad, al-Hafiz; Golan Heights; Saiqa

Taba, 297
Talas, Mustapha, 184n.50
Tamari, Salim, 357
Tamil-Nadu, 68n.40
Tamils, 68n.40
Tamir, Avraham, 327
Tarasov, Genadi, 147, 158, 173, 174
Tarifi, Jamil, 92
Tartus (Syria), Soviet navy in, 150
Taxes, Israeli, 372
Tehiya, 271, 303, 329; birth of, 307
Tel Aviv: Arabs attacked in, 48; violence near, 229, 258
Temple Mount, violence on, 258
Terrorism: against airliners/terminals, 261n.28; Arafat's renunciation of, xi, 30, 90, 116, 136, 235, 242, 247, 248, 282n.6; Gorbachev's view of, 138–39; by Israeli Arabs, xxi, 345, 361; Israeli citizens' attitudes toward, 279; in occupied territories, 39, 39n., 48, 49, 247; PLO, 40, 65n.6, 183n.25, 185n.62; "rejectionist," 50; on Tel Aviv beachfront, 258; transnational, 49–50
Tibi, Ahmad, 362
Tourism: Europe to Israel, 378; Intifada and Israeli, xii, xxii, 370, 377–78; Israeli to Soviet Union, 164; Lebanon war and Israeli, 377; Soviets and Israeli, xvii; terrorism and, 261n.28, 377; U.S. to Europe, 261n.28; U.S., to Israel, 229–30, 261n.28, 378
Tourists: murder of Israeli, 258; Soviet Jews as Israeli, 145, 175, 183n.28
Trade, Soviet-Israeli, 175, 177–78, 179
Trade unions: as element in Intifada, 12, 55, 81–82; in 1936–39 uprising, 21; PFLP, 82
Transjordan, 19. See also Abdallah ibn-Hussein
Trans-Siberian Railway, crash on, 164, 180
Triangle, the: effects of partition on, 358; PLO flags in, 349; strikes in, 344
Tripoli (Lebanon), Arafat driven from, 206
Tubi, Tawfiq, 366n.21
Tunisia, Arafat retreat to, 53, 56
Turkey: Israel laborers from, 380. See also Ottoman Empire
Tzomet, 303, 329

UAHC. See Union of American Hebrew Congregations
UJA. See United Jewish Appeal
Ukrainian Soviet Socialist Republic, 188n.129
Ulamas, 22–23
Umm al-Fahm, xxi, 354
Unemployment: Israeli, 336, 372, 379–80; among Palestinians, xiv, 5
Unified Command. See Unified National Leadership of the Uprising
Unified National Leadership of the Uprising (UNLU), xv, 21, 31, 56–60, 72–76, 81, 84, 91, 198, 350; founding of, 72; and HAMAS contrasted, 79–80; and Islamic Jihad, 78; and Israeli Arabs, 357; makeup of, 75, 98; PLO and, 57–60; power of, 93; religious front vs., 59–60,

Unified National Leadership of the Uprising (continued) 64; Shamir plan rejected by, 212. See also Democratic Front for the Liberation of Palestine; Fatah; Jordan, West Bank renounced by; Palestine Communist Party; Popular Front for the Liberation of Palestine
Union of American Hebrew Congregations (UAHC), 254
Unions. See Trade unions
United Arab Emirates, financial aid to PLO from, 195
United Jewish Appeal (UJA), 222, 224, 225, 226–27; "Passage to Freedom" campaign of, 261n.18; Shamir before, 251
United Kingdom. See Britain
United Nations: Arafat before, 117, 156, 245, 329–30, 360; depoliticization of, 189n.155; double standard of, 258; Israel condemned by, 140, 258; lobbied by Arafat, 13; and Palestinian question, 14, 90, 144, 152–53; PLO status in, 171–72, 181, 360; proposed ouster of Israel from General Assembly of, 178; relief agencies of, 346; and Zionism/racism equation, 169, 171–72, 178, 189n.155
United Nations Relief and Works Agency (UNRWA), 346
United States: and aid to Israel, 126, 127, 133, 150, 195, 227–30, 256, 257, 372; Arafat/PLO and, 14; Egypt and, xviii, 210, 212–14; and Intifada, xi, xvi, 109–35; Israel and, 27, 145 (see also U.S., and aid to Israel); Jews of (see American Jews); and Lebanon, 110–11; 1987 stock market crash in, 260n.11; and Palestinian question, 29–30; and PLO, xvi, xix, 14, 16, 26, 87, 90, 102, 116–17, 120–21, 124, 128, 145, 155–56, 162, 180–81, 189n.154, 235, 242–45, 259, 264n.72, 282n.6, 330; PLO public image in, 241, 244–45; pre-Intifada policies of, 110–13; and proposed territorial elections, 331; Soviet Jews as immigrants to, 165, 167, 169, 172, 178; and Soviet Union, 111, 137, 140, 141–43, 163, 169–72, 189n.154; and UN condemnation of Israel, 258. See also American Jews; Baker, James; Bush, George; Dole, Robert; Reagan, Ronald; Shultz, George
United States Interreligious Committee for Peace in the Middle East, 234
Universities, Palestinian, 55
UNLU, See Unified National Leadership of the Uprising
UNRWA. See United Nations Relief and Works Agency
USSR. See Soviet Union
U.S. Trade Representative, (USTR), 382–83

Venice Declaration, 14
Vietnam, as PLO inspiration, 40, 41, 65n.7, 89
Village Leagues, 93–94
Vilner, Meir, 349
Vocational schools, Palestinian, 55
Voice of Palestine, 72–73
Vorontsov, Yuli, 170, 173, 181
Vorspan, Max, 265n.96

Wadi Ara highway, blockading of, 345
al-Watan, 350
Water, Israeli restrictions on Arab use of, 55
al-Wazir, Khalil, 72, 77, 82–83, 101, 198; assassination of, 145–46, 206–7, 327
Weizman, Ezer, 166, 299, 300, 306, 328, 338; as Labor party force among Arabs, 354; and Peres, 340n.16; PLO meeting with, 362; and Rabin, 340n.16; Shamir vs., 175; Shevardnadze and, 175; WWII record of, 190n.177
Weizmann, Chaim, 32n.5
West Bank, xi, 15, 17, 84, 144; annexation of, 311–14; Bush calls for Israeli withdrawal from, 212; business restrictions in, 55; charitable organizations of, 83; Christian population of, 77; communism in, 81, 348; construction workers from, 376; economy of, xxii, 31, 370–71, 373–74, 380–85; elections proposed in, 121, 128, 174 (see also Shamir, Yitzhak, election proposals of); ethnic makeup of, 42; exports/imports of, 373; as "inherently Israeli," 311; Islamic millennialism in, 77; Israeli administration of, 19; Israeli conciliatory efforts in, xiv; and Israeli security, 294; Jordan-paid civil servants of, 202, 217n.32, 327, 382;

labor unions of, 81–82; land seizures in, 55; Likud position on, 51; religious life of, 354; renounced by Jordan, 26, 115–16, 151, 152, 180, 192, 197, 200, 215, 294, 330, 337; represented in Jordan's parliament, 198; Russian immigrants to, 173; school closings in, 80; schools of, 74; Shultz on, 243; strikes in, 79–80, 326; water restrictions in, 55; women's groups of, 81; youth movement in, 53–55. See also Palestinian Arabs

West Bank Data Project, 55

Western Wall, violence at, 258

West Germany, and Israeli reparations, 316

WFTU. See World Federation of Trade Unions

White Paper (1939), 15, 26

Wirshubsky, Mordecai, 328

Women: Israeli, 273–74, 277; in 1936–39 uprising, 21; of occupied territories, 12, 17, 81, 82, 83

World Congress of Jewish Studies, Soviet scholars at, 165

World Federation of Trade Unions (WFTU), 140

Yahad, 328
Yanai, Nathan, xiii, xx–xxi
Yarrow, Peter, 265n.96
Yasin, Ahmed, xv, 79, 80–81, 100, 355, 356
Al-Yawm al-Sabi', 89
Yom Kippur War, 293, 300; American Jewish financial support of, 225
Yoseph, Ovadia, 305
Young, Ronald, 234
Young Men's Muslim Associations, 21
Youth groups, 57, 83. See also Students

Zionism: alleged cooperation with Nazism, 190n.177; as "racism," 169, 171–72, 178, 189n.155; as Soviet bugbear, 139
Zionists: Hashemite courting of, 7; Palestinian Arabs vs., 5–36, 39–42; "Revisionist," 9
Ziyyad, Tawfiq, 349, 350, 359, 366n.21
Zotov, Alexander, 146

/956.94054I61>C1/